ADVENTURING IN ALASKA

by *Peggy Wayburn*

illustrations by Jody Horst

SIERRA CLUB BOOKS   San Francisco

The Sierra Club, founded in 1892 by John Muir, has devoted itself to the study and protection of the earth's scenic and ecological resources—mountains, wetlands, woodlands, wild shores and rivers, deserts and plains. The publishing program of the Sierra Club offers books to the public as a nonprofit educational service in the hope that they may enlarge the public's understanding of the Club's basic concerns. The point of view expressed in each book, however, does not necessarily represent that of the Club. The Sierra Club has some fifty chapters coast to coast, in Canada, Hawaii, and Alaska. For information about how you may participate in its programs to preserve wilderness and the quality of life, please address inquiries to Sierra Club, 530 Bush Street, San Francisco, CA 94108.

Grateful acknowledgment is made to the following for permission to publish copyrighted material: Dave Bohn, Louise MacLeod, Charles W. Hartman, Neil Davis, Richard Nelson, Richard Cooley, and Jack Calvin.

Library of Congress Cataloging in Publication Data

Wayburn, Peggy.
    Adventuring in Alaska.

    Bibliography: p. 302
    Includes index.
    1. Alaska—Description and travel—1981—Guide-books. 2. Outdoor recreation—Alaska—Guide-books.
    I. Title
    F902.3.W33   917.98′045   81-18222
    ISBN 0-87156-299-5 (pbk.)   AACR2
Cover design by Howard Jacobsen
Book design by Joan Rhine
Illustrations by Jody Horst
Maps by Joan Rhine
Printed in the United States of America

10 9 8 7 6 5 4

To my husband, Edgar Wayburn, for his vision, dedication and effective leadership: he inspired and informed the recent great national effort to preserve Alaska's unspoiled wilderness. And to our grandchildren and the countless other people whose lives will be the richer because that effort, in large part, succeeded.

CONTENTS

Acknowledgments

It has been my great good fortune over the years to come to know many Alaskans. Their hospitality has nurtured me, their knowledge informed me, and their friendship warms my heart. A number of them have, directly or indirectly, had to do with this book. Among them are Jack and Mary Kaye Hession, Sharron and Cliff Lobaugh, Peg, Nancy, Anna and Jules Tileston, Bob and Judy Weeden, Mike and Marilyn Miller, Jan Wrentmore, Joel Bennett, Jack Calvin, Don Schmiege, Bob Belous, Jay and Bella Hammond, Bruce and Gail Gilbert, Bob Howe, Skip Wallen, Carmen and Orvel Holum, Will Troyer, Larry Edwards, Roy Barnes, Sally Gibert, Clem and Diana Tillion, Jim Barnett, Clare Fejes, Darlene Billings, Bob Palmer, Roger Lang, Jim King, Cal Lensink, Burt Silcock, Sterling Bolima, Jerry and Jan Brookman, K. J. Metcalf, Paul Lowe, Richard Nelson, Mark and David Hickok, Charles Evans, Dave Spencer, Sandy and Monda Sagalkin, Lin Sonnenberg, Averill Thayer, Doris Hugo, John Adams, Carol Kasza, Keith Schreiner, Ginny Wood, Celia Hunter, Lucy and Harold Sparck, Dave Hardy, David Finkelstein, Neil Davis, Dick Hensel, John Sackett, Riley Morrey, and Douglas Anderson, who is Alaskan by virtue of his anthropological studies in the state. To them all goes my appreciation. In particular, I am grateful to Rich Gordon of Juneau whose knowledge of Alaska is encyclopedic: he read my entire manuscript and contributed invaluable corrections and suggestions.

I am also grateful for the cooperation of the staffs of the National Park Service, U.S. Fish & Wildlife Service, U.S. Forest Service, the University of Alaska, the Bureau of Land Management, Knik Kanoer and Kayakers Association, and the Arctic Environmental Information and Data Center.

My husband, Edgar Wayburn, has borne with me lovingly throughout the trials and tribulations of creating, editing and correcting the manuscript for the book. Betty Schallenberger generously lent me her home for uninterrupted work. Margaret Berson was of immense help in typing and retyping the manuscript. Without the support of Mary Watson, my friend of nearly thirty years, the work that went into the book would not have been possible. And without the interest, generosity, and flying expertise of Jim Roush, I could never have learned to know and love Alaska as I do.

With the assistance I have had in preparing this book, there should be few errors. I am, however, responsible for any which might occur in my text.

Part I

THE GREAT LAND

INTRODUCTION

Alaska is many things. It is nearly a continent in size—a land so vast that to see it all would take more than a year of viewing one million acres every day. It is a land of few people; were Manhattan Island populated to the same density, it would have only sixteen residents. And it is a place of fascinating extremes: its topography includes the lowest ocean trough as well as the highest mountain on North America; between these two points there are 45,000 vertical feet. Its arctic winter is one long night, and its summer one long day; temperatures can zoom to 100 degrees and skid to minus 80; frozen tundras can receive as little as two inches of rain a year, while lush Southeast forests may get over 300. Alaska is also a place of superlatives: its mountains dwarf the Alps; its fjords surpass Norway's; its large free-roaming animals rival East Africa's; its glaciers are outnumbered only by Greenland's and Antarctica's; its avian and marine life are unmatched anywhere; its first pipeline is the most costly private construction project in history—the list goes on and on. While Alaska is a treasure house of natural resources as well, and presently the site of profound changes, it is still a land of wilderness, with miles of untracked terrain, hundreds of unclimbed mountains, and countless lakes and rivers as bright and pure as liquid jewels. Varied, unique, challenging, unspoiled—Alaska is, in sum, one of the greatest places left on earth to adventure.

It is manifestly impossible for a single small volume to deal fully with the scope and diversity of Alaska, and *Adventuring in Alaska* does not attempt to do so. (Every section of this book could probably be expanded into a volume of its own, and many have been, as the Bibliography suggests.) Instead, this book provides pertinent information and know-how for you who want to adventure in Alaska with both understanding and enjoyment. Be you traditional tourist, footloose traveler, rugged outdoors-person, hiker, biker, river-runner, student, senior—or even an armchair adventurer—you will find facts, details, and background material that will add to your knowledge and appreciation of one of this world's most beautiful areas.

What is the climate really like in Alaska? How can you take a bicycle to Alaska—free? On which wild river could you spend an entire summer and still come back for more? What places should you *not* visit, and why? What is "the bush," "a cheechako," "the Sag"? How can you minimize your impact on Alaska's fragile wilderness? What should you wear? When is the best time to visit the Arctic or Southeast? Why did Congress pass an Alaska Lands Act—

at such a late date, 113 years after the United States acquired Alaska—declaring who should have what land, and how will this affect your travels in Alaska? What is the proper way to visit a Native village? Are the mosquitoes in Alaska really as bad as everyone says? You will find the answer to these and many, many more questions in the following pages.

These pages reflect my personal experiences in Alaska during twenty-one visits there, which add up in time to more than two years out of the last fifteen. *Adventuring in Alaska* also represents a great deal of research conducted both inside and outside Alaska. To organize and present the material I have gathered on this large and complex subject, I have necessarily had to make a number of choices, many of them arbitrary. In making these choices, I have generally followed three guidelines. First, I have heeded my curiosity and attempted to answer many of the questions for the reader that arose in my own mind as I traveled in Alaska. Second, I have looked for and described opportunities for travelers in the parts of Alaska that are the most accessible, and the least expensive, to visit. Third, I have discussed only those more inaccessible areas that have been identified by the Congress or the state of Alaska as having exceptional scenic, wildlife, historical, and/or recreational values; thus the off-the-beaten-track traveler in Alaska can turn to the federal and state agencies that administer these areas for additional information and help.

The book is organized to provide ready reference to the information it contains. The first section gives general, overall, and background facts and figures about Alaska; this will be useful to anyone interested in Alaska as well as to those who contemplate traveling there. The next three sections of the book—II, III, and IV—present more in-depth and detailed information about three major regions of Alaska: the Southeast, the Southcentral and Southwest, and the Interior and Arctic. My division of Alaska into these three general areas is one of my arbitrary choices; it was influenced not only by major physiographic features of Alaska but also by the fact that journeys into Alaska routinely start in one of the state's three principal cities—Juneau, Anchorage, or Fairbanks. Each city serves, then, as a natural gateway to one of the regions I have described as well as a destination of its own. A fifth section of the book provides a bibliography and index.

The material in *Adventuring in Alaska* is presented in more or less short essays that discuss both subjects and places. Although these essays deal with specifics—and can be referred to separately—virtually all of them also contain general information about Alaska. It is therefore my suggestion that the book be read as a whole before it is used more specifically for its parts. That way you will have a better overall picture of Alaska before you decide how you will adventure there.

Throughout the text of the book, I have had to emphasize the fact that the topical information presented is "as of this writing." This is because Alaska, as noted, has been and continues to be changing so rapidly. Major and far-reaching changes occur almost daily in such important arenas as land use, and little, mundane things like telephone numbers and addresses seem to be in a state of perpetual flux too. For example, friends of mine in Juneau have lived in the same house for more than twenty years; during this period their address has officially been changed five times. Thus, my apologies and disclaimers in advance if the book gives you an obsolete phone number or so.

It is manifestly impossible to list all of the services available to tourists in Alaska. (Other publications are devoted to this; see Bibliography.) I have, however, included as many references as possible to various facilities, using my own experience and the recommendations of knowledgable Alaskans as a basis for selection. This does not imply an endorsement by either myself or the publisher of the book, but it will give the reader some options. My apologies to the many excellent operations which have been inadvertently omitted. I welcome suggestions and corrections; write me care of the publisher.

As I began writing this book, I wondered if, by introducing prospective travelers to the beauties and wonders of many of Alaska's wild and vulnerable places, the book would contribute to overvisiting of these places and so impair their special values. I decided that just the opposite should be the case. Along with the rest of Alaska, these wild places are now identified and officially classified for particular uses that include, and indeed emphasize, wilderness recreation; they will inevitably be visited by an increasing number of people whether or not new books are written about them. How these wilderness travelers—and Alaska's land administrators—treat these precious wild places is what will determine their ultimate fate. Therefore, along with being a guide to adventuring in Alaska, this book is intended to be a guide to understanding, appreciating, and ultimately protecting Alaska's superb wilderness and the life and the life-style it supports.

SIZE

Think of immensity: of lakes that stretch out like inland seas, of mountains that fill up half the sky. Consider distance: the faint shimmer of mountains a hundred miles away across the tundra or a wild river so long it takes a month to run. Then let your mind dwell on space—uncluttered, infinite, pristine. This small exercise gives just the barest hint of Alaska's scale. The size of Alaska, in fact, has been a challenge to convey since the first explorer found the place. Explorer-geologist Alfred Hulse Brooks could only come up with a continent as an adequate measure of comparison. John Muir, rarely at a loss for words, found the magnitude of Alaska's scenery "hopelessly beyond description." Perhaps the Aleuts did best when they simply chose the name, "a Great Country."

Consider the figures: Alaska's land area is 586,000 square miles, or a little over 375,000,000 acres. Its tidal shoreline is close to 45,000 miles. Its span from north to south is about 1,400 miles, and from east to west, it is nearly 2,400 miles, embracing four time zones.

These dimensions make Alaska a record holder on several counts. World-wide, it is one of the biggest peninsulas on the planet. Nationwide, it is the largest by far of the 50 United States, or—as Alaskans like to put it—their state is not only first in size, but if it were divided in half, Texas would still rank third. Alaska has more coastline than all other states put together. Its landmass equals one fifth that of the 48 conterminous states—actually totaling more land than the 21 smaller states (measured in ascending order of size).

For one last mental yardstick, try this: to cover the entire terrain of Alaska, a surveyor would have to measure six square miles every day for more than 267 years. (This helps account for the fact that Alaska was largely unsurveyed and unmapped until the advent of aerial photography.)

Alaska's size offers any adventurer both challenges and hard choices. If you are a mountaineer, for instance, you'll find some of the world's greatest moun-tains in Alaska, and many of them are unclimbed. But you will also have to accept the fact that you'll never live long enough to climb them all. The same thing goes for Alaska's beautiful wild rivers, if you're a river-runner. And if

The Nabesna Glacier, one of Wrangell Mountains' largest. Source: National Park Service.

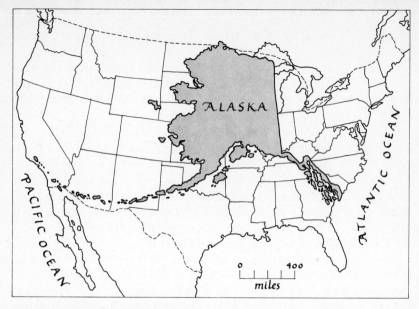

ALASKA AND THE LOWER 48

you like backpacking, unless you're a Paul Bunyan, don't count on covering all the wilderness of this state.

If you want to travel just to see and enjoy Alaska, you might find it useful—because of the size of the place—to consider it as you would Europe. If you have only a couple of weeks to visit, you may elect to take a general overview, traveling perhaps on an organized air tour and foregoing the more intimate experiences. Or you may decide, instead, to spend your time exploring a particular part of the state more in depth, getting to know the country and the people there a little better.

Whichever way you choose to travel in Alaska, expect to be awed by the scope, the space, and the sense of limitless horizons.

LOCATION AND NEIGHBORS

Close to one third of Alaska's land area falls inside the Arctic Circle, and its northernmost tip, Point Barrow, is very near 72 degrees north latitude—less than 1,300 miles from the North Pole. Thus Alaska gives the United States a firm, important presence in the Arctic.

From north to south, Alaska spans over twenty degrees of latitude; its southern-most tip, Amtignak Island in the Aleutians, juts south of 52 degrees north latitude—lining it up closely with Portsmouth, England. Eastward, Alaska stretches to Camp Point on the Canadian border at 130 degrees west longitude.

DISTANCES IN ALASKA

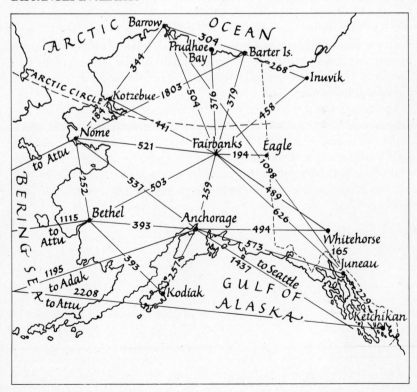

To the west, it sweeps across the planet so far into the Aleutian chain that it crosses the 180th meridian, the boundary between the east and west longitudes. This means that Cape Wrangell on Attu Island, near 172 degrees east longitude, is more than halfway around the world from the prime meridian in Greenwich, England. It is therefore the easternmost point of the United States and, indeed, of the North American continent.

Anchorage, the population center of Alaska, is situated approximately on 61 degrees north latitude and 150 degrees west longitude—a strategic location on the great circle route. This puts it about midway between New York and Tokyo by direct air flight.

On its eastern side, Alaska borders Canada for 1,538 miles. This boundary was set by agreement between Russia and Great Britain in 1825, close to half a century before the United States acquired Alaska. Alaska's other near neighbor is Russia, which is separated from the Seward Peninsula by the shallow waters of the Bering Strait. The distance between the two countries—and two continents—is less than 55 miles. (Road-builders and road-building engineers dream of linking Russia to the United States by highway.)

The approximately 1,000 mile water boundary between Russia and the United States was established by the United States–Russia Convention of 1867, and it runs along the 169 degrees west longitude between the Seward Peninsula and Siberia. This border falls between the two Diomede Islands so that Big Diomede belongs to Russia and Little Diomede to the United States. In recent years, all commerce between these two small islands—whether by summer sea, winter ice, or air—has been forbidden. The Eskimos of the two Diomedes spring from common roots and are closely related, yet cannot legally visit one another.

To accommodate the boundary drawn between Alaska and Russia, the International Date Line had to be manipulated considerably. It was first bent to the east to pass through the Bering Strait, then to the west to give most of the Aleutian chain to the United States. On a clear day, you can see Siberia while flying from Kotzebue to Nome—looking west, of course, into tomorrow. And the people on the two Diomede Islands live one day but less than five miles apart.

GEOLOGY

Geology is something like science fiction. It deals only in part with proven facts; it sets forth scenarios that may or may not turn out to be true; and it benefits greatly from innovative thinking.

Of course, a major difference between the two fields is that geology is largely concerned with the past, while science fiction projects into the future. It might seem that looking backward would be easier than looking forward, but this is not the case for geologists; the time frame they deal with is mind boggling—4.5 billion years, the estimated age of our planet. Furthermore, expanding the catalog of geological facts is extremely difficult; the evidence is diverse, fragmented, widespread (indeed, global), and often hard to decipher and interpret. Geology is, in fact, full of fascinating mysteries and challenges, and perhaps nowhere on earth are they presented in a more vivid way than Alaska.

Aniakchak Crater, now quiescent; one of the 47 active volcanoes in the Aleutian Range. Source: National Park Service.

Consider the geological scene in our 49th state. To begin with, the terrain is incredibly varied. It ranges vertically from the offshore Aleutian Trench that plunges 25,000 feet below the sea to the highest mountain on the North American continent, 20,300-foot Mount McKinley; this is a distance of close to nine miles. Horizontally, there are 586,000 square miles to take into account. Three impressive mountain systems demarcate this landmass. The Coast Range outlines the southern arcuate sweep of Alaska and includes the Saint Elias and Chugach-Kenai-Kodiak mountains; it dips below the sea southwest of Kodiak. The Alaska-Aleutian Range is separated from the Coast Range—which it roughly follows in its curving sweep—by a discontinuous trough that is partially filled by the Wrangell and Talkeetna mountains. To the east the Alaska Range peters out in the immense plateaus of Yukon and British Columbia; to the southwest, the active volcanoes of the Aleutian Range comprise part of the Pacific's "ring of fire." The Brooks Range more or less delineates the Arctic Circle and lies to the north of it. In between the Alaska-Aleutian and the Brooks ranges is the Interior of Alaska, an immense plateau that undulates into lower mountains in places and contains great river valleys. To the north of the Brooks Range is the Arctic Slope, a wide apron of land that tilts very gently to slip beneath the Arctic Ocean.

To put Alaska's vast terrain into perspective, it helps to look at its relationship to the rest of the North American continent. The Coast Range is analogous to the Olympic and Klamath ranges, the Alaska-Aleutian Range to the Cascades and the Sierra Nevada. The trough between these two ranges corresponds roughly to the Puget-Willamette lowlands and California's central valley. Alaska's immense Interior corresponds geographically to the Great Basin. The Brooks Range is the geographical northern arm of the Rockies, although it was upthrust at another time (see section on Interior), and the Arctic Slope is analagous to the Great Plains.

The extraordinary landmass that makes up Alaska is relatively new when looked at in terms of geologic time. Its most ancient rocks are mica-schists that date back to only 600 million years, plus or minus a few million years, and its youngest rocks are mere decades old. Forming part of the edge of a continent, this is a very uneasy piece of the earth's crust; over half of the state is seismically active, with some regions being wracked by earthquakes frequently, while others are often showered with volcanic debris. Ten percent of the world's earthquakes occur in Alaska. The town of Valdez on Prince William Sound averages something like a major earthquake—one that measures five or more points on the Richter scale—a year. Along with this, Alaska is one of the few places on the planet where active glaciation is occurring on a grand scale, and it is possible to observe conditions resembling those that prevailed during Pleistocene times. Much of the unglaciated land in Alaska is also being worked over and profoundly shaped by the processes of permafrost and active freezing and thawing. All of this adds up to the fact that in Alaska it is possible to observe, at first hand, an unusually broad spectrum of earth forces in action.

This is a great time in the history of geology. The new theory of plate tectonics—which has been characterized as being as significant to the earth sciences as the atomic theory is to chemistry or evolution is to biology—has revolutionized geologists' thinking. Many fresh ideas are presently being examined and tested, and many interesting new aspects of the plate tectonic theory are being explored as well.

According to this theory, the earth can be thought of as something like an egg with a cracked shell. The yolk would correspond to the earth's molten core, the white to its somewhat gelatinous mantle, and the shell to the earth's crust. This crust, as it happens, is fractured into a dozen or so large fragments that have been called tectonic plates; these plates rest on and are being moved over the mantle continuously. They may collide, jam, grind along one another and, in places, ride over one another like pieces of pack ice. The latter happens frequently when the plates forming the floors of the Pacific and Atlantic oceans encounter the continental landmasses that border them. (Continents, incidentally, are much less dense than the earth's mantle and, perhaps to mix metaphors, can be likened to whipped cream floating on jello, or so says one geologist.) Where the collision occurs, the ocean floors are thrust under—or subducted beneath—the continental landmass. Accompanying this often violent tectonic action, there may be massive earthquakes, mountain building, volcanism, and movements along faults of related land areas.

All of this seems to explain very well what is happening in parts of Alaska. Indeed, a description of Alaska's present topography and tectonic activity can read like a textbook illustrating the theory of plate tectonics. Along the southern margin of Alaska, the Pacific plate is being subducted—in a generally northwestern direction—under the North American plate. The Aleutian Trench marks the large area where the ocean floor is plunging beneath the land. There has been and continues to be immense mountain building around this tectonically active region. Volcanism and jolting earthquakes accompany this massive collision of plates, and strong pressure and pulling on the adjacent landmass causes extensive motion along fault lines.

One major fault can be easily defined in Alaska's Southeast. With the help of earlier glacial action, this fault has split the earth open and allowed the ocean to intrude to form the Lynn Canal and Chatham Strait. Known as the Farewell Fault at its eastern end and the Denali at its western end, this fault extends north and westward and can be observed in several places from the air. According to at least one school of geologists, it does not stop until it reaches Bristol Bay; thus it generally marks the great curve of upthrust land that has resulted from the collision of the Pacific and North American plates.

For many years, the Brooks Range was considered to be a continuation of the Rocky Mountains. Now geologists explain its formation differently: the Range is explained as being a heaping up of the earth's crust formed when a wedge of the continent broke free from its position as part of Canada and rotated gradually to the west and south. As this wedge swung farther and

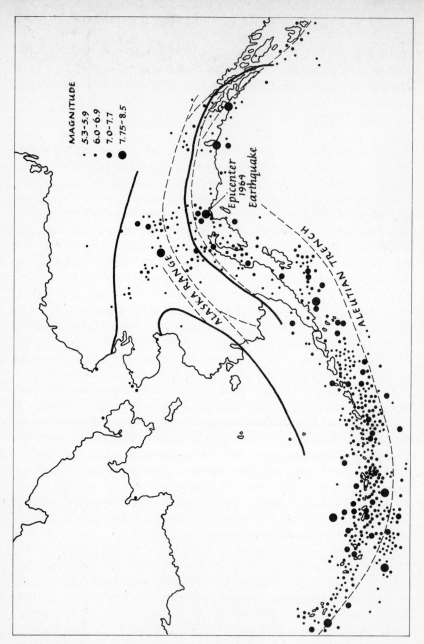

EARTHQUAKES IN ALASKA

farther on its pivotal point, this theory goes, it shoved the land up higher and higher.

Other traditional geological concepts are also giving way to new theories and conjectures in Alaska. One idea is noteworthy for its somewhat bizarre character. It was believed for a long time that if the ages of rock formations and their geological makeup could be deciphered, the rocks could provide a generally good chronology of the particular part of the earth in which they were located. This theory, however, assumed that continents were stable and left no room for the anomalous rocks that kept showing up here and there in formations all over the earth—and quite frequently in parts of Alaska. Some geologists now believe that these anomalous formations are, in fact, bits and pieces of other parts of the earth that have been detached from their mother continents and rafted along on moving ocean plates until they collided with another continent and formed a new and grand sort of mosaic. Pursuing this new theory, University of Alaska geologists have identified nine different disparate formations in the Alaska Range between Mount Deborah and Farewell, a distance of about 150 miles; they believe these formations originated in other and distant parts of the earth. They have also identified another fifty or so alien fragments in other parts of the Alaska Range. Some of these, it is believed, originated in the same place, and it now remains to fit them together, like pieces of a huge jigsaw puzzle, to explain where they came from and how they got to be where they were found. There are also two identified segments of Southeast—Wrangellia and Stikinia—whose origins are believed to be exotic.

Some old ideas and data remain valid and continue to be accepted—for example, the fact that most of what is now Alaska has at one time or another been under the sea (as has most of the earth), or the fact that the climate of what is now Alaska once widely supported broadleaf trees and conifers. (At least one species, *Pinus monticola*, grew simultaneously in Siberia.) Other data, however, must now be questioned, and some concepts must be discarded and new ones evolved. While the age of rocks may be readily established and verified, and the stuff they are made of can be identified, just how they got where they are is no longer explained so glibly as it was just a short time ago. A leading Alaskan geologist recently told me that no period earlier than the Quaternary in Alaska could presently be explained in a definitive way that would be universally accepted; there are just too many new and unanswered questions. However, from the beginning of the Quaternary period to the present, Alaska's landmass has remained generally in place. The geological record appears to be relatively clear, and it is fascinating.

Sometime between one and a half and two million years ago, the earth's climate began to undergo a series of extreme changes, swinging from warm to cold and back again. During the ensuing millennia, there were four periods of heavy glaciation interspersed with periods of warming. This glaciation did much to shape the Alaskan landscape that you can see today, for about 50 percent of the state's area, it is believed, was buried under ice at one time or another. The glaciation that persists today—largely in the Southeast—may give a clue to what other periods of snow and ice were like, but the present ice sheets are positively meager compared to the grand, 4,000-foot-thick slabs of ice and snow that once weighted down large areas of Alaska.

GLACIATION IN ALASKA

Glaciers soften the harsh edges of new rocks. They round off low hills as they move over them. When glaciers melt, they leave behind potholes and lakes and great deposits of glacial debris that form ridges, eskers, and hill-like moraines. Glaciers also spawn great rivers. They carry rocks great distances before they drop them. They quarry valleys into rounded U shapes, and the dust from their till is swept up by the wind and deposited as fine soil or loess over vast regions of the landscape. All these phenomena can be observed in different parts of Alaska.

The monumental sheets of ice that built up at times in Alaska had other interesting side effects. They formed immense and nearly impenetrable walls that cut Alaska off from the rest of the continent in places. They also stopped short of Alaska's Interior; being more or less ice free, the Interior became a refugium—or place of refuge—for many different plants and animals which were unable to disperse or travel freely during those frigid times. (The Interior may also have been a refugium for people during the past 25,000 years. See History.) Migratory birds, however, were able to fly above the vast frozen land and to use the Interior as they had through the millennia; they continue to do so today. Earth scientists and biologists sometimes refer to this refugium as being part of an area they have named "Beringia."

When the earth's waters were locked into ice the sea level dropped everywhere. At times of maximum cold, it was at least 300 feet lower than it is today—and probably more. During these bleak glacial periods, what is now the northern part of the Bering Sea did not exist; instead, the Bering Land Bridge linked Alaska to Siberia. This was no mere narrow strip of land, however, as the word *bridge* suggests. It was a stretch of land from 900 and 1,000 miles wide that actually joined the two continents. (Although now submerged again, this land still joins North America to Eurasia as far as tectonic plates go. The boundaries of the North American plate are actually in Siberia.) The bridge was ice free and provided access for wandering animals and, later, it is believed, for the first people to enter the New World. This region made up the rest of the area now referred to as Beringia, and it, too, acted as a vast refugium for many kinds of living things.

Takahula Lake, Gates of the Arctic National Park and Preserve. Source: National Park Service.

It is worth noting that during warmer periods when Beringia was inundated (as it is today), there was exchange through its waters between the Pacific and Atlantic oceans.

The permafrost that presently and persistently grips so much of Alaska is believed by some geologists to be a relict of those earlier, cold Pleistocene times. Its effects are many (see section on Permafrost), and it has resulted not only in fascinating land patterns but in thousands of thaw lakes and puddles. (Alaska has a total of more than three million lakes.) The more straightforward processes of freezing and thawing affect the earth's surface as well.

As you travel through Alaska, you will have the chance to observe—just as the geologists do—how the marvelous forces of the earth have shaped this landscape in the past and are actively continuing to shape it today. Alaskans in many parts of the state have learned to live with these irresistible earth forces, but the potential for radical change and even for disastrous geological events is always with them. This is, of course, one of the things that makes Alaska not only a paradise for curious geologists but also a very exciting place to live and to visit.

CLIMATE

That Alaska is a land of extraordinary contrasts is nowhere better illustrated than in the wide—and even wild—extremes of its weather. Alaska has places with the highest precipitation of any of the 49 continental states and places with nearly the lowest. The difference between the precipitation in two such places can amount to over 300 inches. Thus at McCleod Bay on Montague Island in Prince William Sound, the precipitation has been as high as 332 inches in one year. Less than 1,000 miles away at Point Barrow it has added up to as little as 1.61 inches in a similar time span. Snowfall in Alaska is also record setting and extraordinarily variable. In the Southeastern mountains, the overall snowfall ranks among the highest in the world. An average of ten feet of snow per month in the higher elevations is common enough, and 225 inches of snow—almost twenty feet—was once measured as falling in a single month at Thompson's Pass near Valdez. North America's greatest recorded snowfall in one season was chalked up on the Wolverine Glacier in the Kenai mountains in the winter of 1976–77, when 356 inches of snow piled up and stayed. Yet on the North Slope only three or four inches of snow may fall in an entire winter. (This snow may confound a visitor by appearing to be totally airborne, kept aloft by sixty-mile-per-hour winds.)

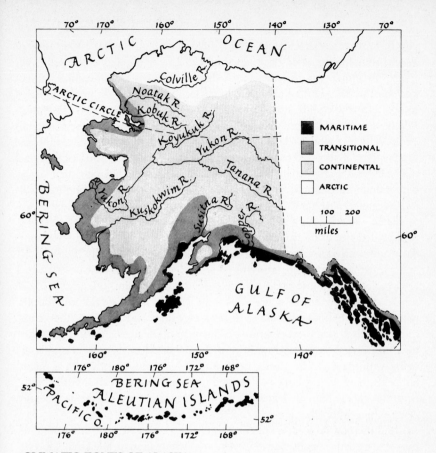

CLIMATIC ZONES OF ALASKA

Alaskan temperatures can gyrate as wildly between record highs and record lows, and they do—often in the same spot. In the Interior, a winter reading of minus 50 to 60 degrees Fahrenheit hardly raises eyebrows (although it may frost eyelashes), and in Fairbanks, the smog routinely freezes. Summer readings of 80 to 85 degrees in the same location are common. At Fort Yukon, not far from the Canadian border, a minus 78-degree reading was racked up (or down) one midwinter, and a plus 100-degree temperature was recorded late one June—giving the place a temperature range of 178 degrees. Interesting to try dressing for life in a climate like that!

All of this emphasizes the fact that while it can be very cold in winter, Alaska is not a land of perpetual ice and snow as the ancient myth goes. It can and obviously does get very hot in many areas in summer. After all, in about one third of the state, the sun remains above the horizon for 24 hours a day for more than two straight months. Actually, over 97 percent of the Alaskan land thaws under the summer sun and stays snow free.

Alaska's overall climate can be broadly classified into zones. These can cue you in to what to expect generally in different parts of the state. One zoning system uses the presence or absence of a marine influence as the principal index. By employing this measure, Alaska's southeast, southcentral coasts, and most of the Aleutian chain are in a Maritime Zone, with heavy rainfall, frequent fog and clouds, strong winds, and moderate temperatures. The Alaska Peninsula and the lowlands along Alaska's western coasts are in a Transitional Zone with less cloudiness and rainfall, strong winds, and a mean annual temperature of about 25 to 35 degrees Fahrenheit. The area north of the crest of the Brooks Range is in the Arctic Zone, with light but persistent foggy clouds and precipitation, strong winds, and a mean annual temperature of 10 to 20 degrees Fahrenheit. (Note the presence of strong winds in all three zones of Alaska—making for a potentially severe chill factor.) The rest of Alaska— the vast reaches of the Interior—are in a Continental Zone, with enormous daily and yearly temperature variations, little rainfall, generally light winds, and a mean annual temperature of 15 to 25 degrees Fahrenheit.

Using another, more traditional, weather zoning system, the great body of Alaska can simply be considered Subarctic; that is, it has at least one month with a mean temperature of 32 degrees or colder and no more than four months with a mean temperature greater than 50 degrees. According to this measure, only a fairly narrow strip of the Arctic Slope is then classified as being within the Arctic Zone, or having at least one month with a mean temperature of 32 degrees or colder and no months with mean monthly temperatures greater than 50 degrees. The Southeast then falls into the Temperate Zone, along with other areas of the 48 contiguous states.

I find the best indications of Alaska's climate—and the most interesting to use—the presence or absence of forests, and, where present, the kind of forests that grow. For example, the lush Southeastern forests of spruce and hemlock are clear indicators of a moderate climate, relatively warm winters, pleasantly cool summers, and lots of rain. The boreal forests of the Interior—or the taiga community (*taiga* is a Russian word that came from a Turkish word meaning "rocky high places")—on the other hand, are sparse in places and comprised of hardy trees and plants, white spruce and stunted black spruce, willows, birch, balsam poplar (cottonwoods), and aspen. These more marginal forests bespeak much harsher climatic conditions, long periods of cold, and a mean annual temperature below freezing. The tundra communities (*tundra* is a Finnish word that means "barren land") of the west and the north of Alaska are virtually without trees except for a few dwarf spruce and birch. These tundras tell of consistently cool to cold weather, of frequent cloudiness, and of harsh compelling winds that sweep across the low-growing grasses and lichens and forbid the growth of forests.

Wherever you travel in Alaska, you will find miniclimates. These can vary enormously within a fairly circumscribed area, too. For instance, you can expect to bake in the heat of Interior Alaska for at least a few days during July, but if you fly only a hundred or so miles from Fairbanks into the Brooks Range, you may find snow powdering the lower foothills.

The most important thing about Alaska's climate to keep in mind is how rapidly it can change. In every part of the state, from the temperate regions of the Southeast to the frigid reaches of the North Slope, you can expect the weather to deteriorate or to improve dramatically in just a matter of minutes. Clouds can clot a flawless blue sky as you watch, and rain can pour down almost before you can rig a shelter. The thermometer can drop ten or twenty degrees in an hour, and fog can well up to blot out the daylight or white out a mountaintop. Fierce winds can suddenly roar in—winds strong enough to whip up high waves on inland lakes or set the spindrift scudding off ocean coasts, blow a raft upstream or skid a small aircraft across the ground.

Camping on a lake in southwest Alaska, I once had a tent wrenched from my hands by the wind one cloudy July morning. The wind bore down with the speed, force, and sound of a racing locomotive and the tent took off. Tumbling and touching the ground now and then like a big blue balloon it finally soared skyward in an updraft, skimmed over some treetops and disappeared completely from sight. Fortunately, our party retrieved it, unscathed, a good quarter of a mile away.

Remember, however, that bad weather can change just as rapidly into good. Winds can silence, rains can let up, fog can vanish before delighted eyes, and the sun can return while a glorious blue day embraces you, all in a matter of minutes.

When you visit Alaska, rely less on official weather predictions than you would elsewhere. Meteorologists work under handicaps that are compounded by the normal capriciousness of the local climates. Be ready to seize the blue days—or portions of them—that come your way and enjoy them thoroughly. Alaskans all over have learned to do just this. At the same time, be prepared to sit out foul weather and have adequate shelter in which to do so. This book will help you select the right equipment. With proper gear, rain or cold alone should not ground you; but winds, fog, or a heavy storm can. Should you encounter such bad weather, a paperback will help, but good company is immeasurably better—another reason to plan an Alaskan trip with someone whose company you enjoy.

PERMAFROST

A unique feature of Alaska's terrain is the phenomenon known as permafrost. Permafrost is defined as any part of the ground—rock, soil, or sand—that has remained frozen for more than two years. Permafrost requires a "frost climate," an average annual temperature generally below freezing, to form and persist. The weather over most of Alaska is ideal for it, and permafrost underlies more than 80 percent of the state. North of the Arctic Circle and in extensive regions of the Interior, permafrost is continuous. Farther south and in the west, it occurs sporadically—on the northern slopes of hills, for example, but not on the southern. Only in the warmer parts of Alaska, particularly along the Pacific Coast, is there no permafrost. Much of Alaska's extensive permafrost has probably been around not just for two years or even for two hundred but for many millennia; it is a relict of the great Ice Ages.

Permafrost has some interesting characteristics and side effects. The lens of frozen ground may lie a few inches or a few feet below the surface, and it can vary in thickness from a few inches to hundreds of feet. Around Tok, in the Interior, the permafrost is 100 feet thick; around Bethel, in the southwest, it is 600. On the Arctic Slope it is up to 2000 feet thick, a condition that posed problems for the oil drillers near Prudhoe Bay and even more problems for the builders of the oil pipeline.

An essential part of permafrost is the integral "active layer" that forms its upper, insulating skin. This active layer thaws in the summer while the ground beneath it, being protected, remains frozen, a condition required for its perpetuation. The skin of permafrost can be composed of debris—for example, rocks that have been shattered by the freezing process—or it can be a tundra or forest community of one kind or another. On the Arctic Slope, for instance, the permafrost wears a velvety green cloak of tundra that is embroidered with wildflowers in the summer. In the Interior, a thick layer of living and dead mosses often carpets the frozen ground. In areas of greater rainfall, on the other hand, permafrost can be covered by peat or other moss communities, or its active layer can be a soggy meadow with big clumps of coarse grasses, or tussocks (bad news for hikers).

Without the active layer of ground protecting it, the upper stratum of permafrost is exposed to the summer sun. It then melts and collapses upon itself, forming a declivity that becomes an icy puddle—or thermokarst. As Arctic erosion proceeds, the puddle—being alternately frozen and thawed—may grow into a pond or lake. In regions of extreme cold, where the active layer can be cracked and torn by weathering, this process occurs as part of the

PERMAFROST IN ALASKA

natural evolution of the frozen landscape. Thus you will find hundreds of thousands of ponds and lakes dotting the North Slope tundra. Erosion is often initiated by other means today, however: when you see twin canals cutting across the same Arctic tundra, you can be sure that heavy equipment has passed this way—and it might have been many decades ago, so long does it take this fragile land to heal itself.

In many parts of Alaska, spectacular ground patterns are associated with permafrost. Frost circles and immense networks of polygons are fractured into the Arctic tundras. On slopes where the frozen land thaws in summer and creeps downhill, solifluction lobes scallop the hillsides. Pingos, or large ice blisters, like hundred-foot-high frozen volcanoes, relieve the flatness of the Arctic landscape.

Because it is frozen solid, permafrost functions as bedrock in the Arctic. This causes heavy runoff of surface water and makes the construction of standard reservoirs or the use of conventional water and sewage systems impossible. Not only do water pipes and septic tanks freeze in permafrost, but the act of installing them opens up the active layer, and the permafrost starts to erode. To locate any kind of structure, in fact—whether railroad ties, roads, piers or bridges, an office building, or even a small house—in or on permafrost is a major challenge to a builder or engineer. Digging a cellar for a house and putting in a furnace, for instance, can cause the house to collapse. Putting a house on blocks on the frozen ground can still cause the permafrost to sink and heave, which means buckled floors, leaning walls, and doors that won't close. Standard road building also invites disasters—such as huge thermokarsts that swallow up sections of pavement. Unwary farmers clearing frozen ground have been known to have their tractors swallowed up, too.

As building increases in Alaska, engineers are experimenting with a variety of techniques to cope with permafrost conditions. If you see large slabs of styrofoam going under a building, this is an attempt to provide for long-lasting insulation. Look for freezer systems incorporated into foundations in the Arctic—not a new idea but one now being tried more widely. Notice the use of steel beams that are sunk deep into the frozen ground, for example, as pipeline supports. Time will tell how these innovations hold up.

When you run an Arctic river, you may have a chance to see permafrost at work firsthand. Along the cut-back banks where the frozen ground is exposed, the earth erodes easily, leaving the topsoil layer draped over like a torn curtain and the trees and plants rooted in it canted at crazy angles. On Interior rivers like the Charley, you can see the icy lenses of permafrost exposed in the open banks.

LIGHT

In Alaska, the sun is never directly overhead. Furthermore, there are long months of complete darkness or dim twilight during the winter in many parts of the state. Despite these phenomena, Alaska receives more light overall (sunlight and twilight together) during a year than do territories in the lower latitudes. Fairbanks, for example, located at 65 degrees north latitude, receives light of one sort or another for more than 62 percent of the year. In the tropics, the light is stronger, but the periods of sunlight and twilight add up to only a little more than 53 percent of the year. There are two reasons for this seemingly odd discrepancy. First, in the northern latitudes, the sun moves across the sky at an angle low to the horizon, which means it takes longer to rise and to set, and consequently there are longer periods of twilight. Second, refraction—the atmospheric bending of the sun's rays—which occurs only slightly at the equator, becomes more pronounced the farther north you travel, and this causes the sun's rays to remain visible even after the sun itself has dipped below the horizon. The energy delivered to the ground by the sun's

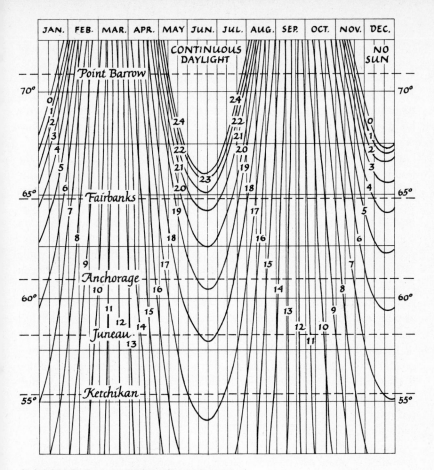

| JAN. | FEB. | MAR. | APR. | MAY | JUN. | JUL. | AUG. | SEP. | OCT. | NOV. | DEC. |

CONTINUOUS
DAYLIGHT

NO
SUN

Point Barrow

70°   70°

0
1
2
3
4
5
6   0
7   Fairbanks   1
65°   2 65°
8   3
                                                                       4
9   5
Anchorage   6
10   7
60°   8 60°
11   9
12
14   Juneau   10
13   11

Ketchikan
55°   55°

SUNLIGHT IN NORTHERN LATITUDES

rays is less in Alaska than in the tropics, but because of the total sunlight and twilight received during the summer in these northern latitudes, the radiation effect is fairly close to that received in lower latitudes.

It is noteworthy that light is bent in the direction of increasing air density—that is, cold dense air—and this phenomenon pulls the image of distant landscapes above the horizon. Thus, mountains that are invisible in warm weather may be clearly seen when it is cold. This is called the "looming" effect.

The pattern of the seasons in the north is dramatically different from elsewhere. In the Arctic, the summer is one long day, while the winter is one long night. At Alaska's northernmost point, the sun remains above the horizon for over two and one half months—from the second week of May until early August. But for the two-plus months from mid November to late January, the sun never shows its face; twilight takes its place. Once the sun returns, the hours of sunlight lengthen dramatically from day to day. The seasons—a function of the sunlight, of course—must race to change: with sunlight going from zero minutes to twenty-four hours per day in a matter of less than four months, the passage of spring and early summer is a particularly exciting time.

Even in Alaska's more southern areas, this same pattern of light is felt. Although the sun slips below the horizon in summer, the twilight lingers all night long, and in many places the skies are starless and the only heavenly body to be seen is the moon. In deep winter, the sun barely clears the mountains to slant its light against the snowy ground.

Displays of the aurora borealis frequently light up Alaska's skies. (Near the South Pole an equivalent effect is called the aurora australis.) These stunning light shows are caused by the solar wind—a burst of the sun's particles released when its surface flares up in sunspots—encountering the earth's magnetic field. The energy released in these collisions strikes the molecules of earth's common atmospheric gases, oxygen and nitrogen. When such encounters occur in the upper atmosphere, oxygen reacts by giving off a red glow, while nitrogen glows yellow. Closer to the earth, oxygen ionizes violet, and nitrogen ionizes green. In Alaska, look for the aurora borealis in clear night skies from August through May. The aurora, the subject of many Eskimo legends, can also be seen from a distance of 1,000 miles when you are flying 30,000 feet high; look for it on clear winter nights on the flight from Seattle to Anchorage or Fairbanks. If you have a good show, you may be able to view about a quarter of the entire aurora in the Northern Hemisphere. (Sit on the right side flying north.) If you're in a position to photograph the aurora from the ground, use ASA 400 film, a wide-angle lens, and a time exposure of from 3 to 30 seconds. An object, such as a tree or a lighted cabin in the foreground, will add scale to your picture.

The intense electrical currents generated by the aurora in the ionosphere (70 miles up) induce secondary currents on the earth's surface that have caused interesting effects in the trans-Alaskan pipeline—a particularly good north-south conductor.

Because of the slanting light in Alaska, you will always have a shadow on sunny days. Trees do, too, of course, especially in the sparse forests of the Interior. Flying over these forests on a late summer afternoon, watch for traceries of parallel tree shadows on the ground; they look as though they had been penciled lightly onto the soft green landscape. In the winter, the tree shadows make blue stripes on the snow.

Alaska's flora and fauna—including its people—have adapted to the rhythm of the Nordic sunlight. They cram much of the whole year's living into those months of daylight. The conifers nearly burst with cones, the alders hang out their tassels thickly, flowers bloom everywhere. (Because of the steady light, cabbages grow to be four feet in diameter; delphiniums shoot up as high as twelve feet.) Children play all night and some adults, too. You can find yourself making camp at 1 A.M. with no difficulty or taking off in daylight at 3 A.M. People also take advantage of the long hours of twilight in summer and in winter—thus you will have more hours in the day in which to enjoy the outdoors. Alaskans seem to need less sleep during the summer, and you may find yourself getting by on less than you do in lower latitudes. But remember, Alaskans can sleep it off in their long, dark winter.

The quality of Alaska's slanting light reminds some people of the glowing illumination that seems to flood many paintings of the Dutch school. Photographers are apt to go slightly crazy over it, especially when, around midnight, the sun backlights a field of dryas or the ice floes of the Arctic Ocean or a caribou standing on the riverbank and curiously watching the creatures bobbing by on their strange craft.

Alaskan light is soft: it gentles hard and vivid colors. When you return from Alaska to the Lower 48, you will probably find yourself blinking at the glaring brightness of the colors around you and the newly seen harshness of the neon signs.

HISTORY

No one knows when people first found the land that would one day be called Alaska. Recent discoveries in Canada's Yukon Territory—in the Old Crow Basin not far from the Alaska border—suggest the presence there of human hunters more than 27,000 years ago, and some anthropologists believe that people migrated from Asia to North America as long as 30,000 to 40,000 years ago or more. Others argue that the date of human arrival was closer, perhaps, to 15,000 years ago, when wanderers may have found the place in Alaska now known as Onion Portage. Whenever the actual event occurred, it certainly went unnoticed and unremarked, for the people reaching Alaska were not intent on exploring the world; they were simply pursuing their way of life and following the animals that provided them their food.

These first Alaskans may have arrived during a warm interglacial period when they could easily cross the narrow body of shallow water that separated Siberia from Alaska. It is more likely, however, that nomadic hunters and fishermen first entered Alaska during an Ice Age when the sea level was low and the Bering Land Bridge, extending perhaps 900 miles from south to north, joined what are now Alaska and Siberia into one continuous landmass.

Never glaciated, the land bridge was probably similar in character to regions in western and Interior Alaska today. A grassy tundra community covered broad stretches of gentle plains, or steppes. Low hills delineated the horizon, with a mountain thrusting up only here and there. There were few trees, but streams and braided rivers meandered through the lowlands. The weather was frequently stormy and chilled by icy winds. Then, as now, great mountain walls barricaded the land to the southeast and the north, but then glaciers radiated in every direction from high cirques, and snow fields and ice choked many of the mountain passes.

It was not a particularly hospitable land, but the coastal areas, especially on the south, were exceptionally rich in shellfish, fish, and sea mammal populations. The streams were full of salmon, and there were many land animals. And so the hunters and fishermen came traveling in small bands or family groups, new families forming and budding off to make their way on their own. They came sporadically through many millennia, starting from different places, taking different pathways, and bringing different ways and ideas with them. As the Ice Ages drew to a close and the seas began to rise, these people moved to higher and drier places, the land that would become Alaska.

During times when the ice melted from the mountain passes, some of these first adventurers continued to migrate through Alaska to more distant places, perhaps as far as South America, so that the Bering Land Bridge may have served as man's gateway to both of the American continents.

It was during the colder times, some anthropologists believe, that people were confined to the Interior refugium, or the Arctic (which also escaped glaciation at times), and they settled in and stayed. Whatever the reason, members of four ethnic groups—the Athabascans, Aleuts, Eskimos, and Tlingits and Haidas—that came into North America remained in Alaska and made it their permanent home.

While all four groups shared certain basic similarities—they all hunted, fished, and gathered food; had no written language; and were skillful and ingenious people—there were distinct and sometimes subtle differences between them. Some of these were physical, but, more importantly, as they settled into their different environments, they developed distinctive cultures and sets of skills.

The Eskimos, perhaps the last to come to Alaska, were primarily a coastal people, although some of them lived inland as well. Groups of Eskimos moved both south and north along Alaska's shores, and some continued across the Arctic coast as far as Greenland. Many of them learned to live successfully under the demanding conditions of the Arctic. They developed an extraordinarily fine, almost uncanny, directional sense. Traveling in a straight line, noting which way the wind blew, knowing the features of the terrain as they knew the faces of their families, they could find their way through blinding snowstorms, whiteouts, and dense fogs. They also mastered the art of making their way through ice-choked waters, and they became adept at spearing seals and harpooning the white beluga and bowhead whales long before Europeans brought metal to their culture. Gifted carvers, they fashioned exceptional toggle harpoons and such things as snow masks to protect their eyes from wind-driven snows and the glaring eye-level sun. They traded extensively among themselves—seal oil, walrus, sealskins, ivory—and regularly with the Chukchi of Siberia and the Athabascans. They also fought frequently with the latter who were their immediate neighbors. Some were nomadic, they returned over and over again to favored fishing, sealing and caribou-hunting camps, to such places as Cape Krusenstern, Point Hope, and Shishmaref— where they left their traces in arrowheads, chippings, bones, and the faint outlines of their dwellings—and to Anaktuvuk Pass, the "Place of Caribou Droppings." (It is noteworthy that the descendants of these ancient people are directly involved in current archeological digs in Alaska.) Needing the caribou, as well as sea mammals, for many purposes—food, clothing, to make bone implements or needles and thread—they were skillful at intercepting the animals in their far-sweeping migrations, knowing through which passes the great herds would funnel.

Their neighbors, the Athabascan Indians, may have been the first people to come into and, indeed, to continue through Alaska; some Athabascans went as far east as Hudson Bay, and others filtered southward to become the ancestors of the Apache and Navajo Indians. Like the Eskimos, the Athabascans were skillful hunters, but they depended more on large land mammals, such as caribou and moose, and on salmon and other fish that traveled the Yukon and its tributaries for their major subsistence. The Athabascans became adept at corralling caribou, tracking moose, and using snares, traps, and pits to catch smaller game, which they used for food as well. They also devised ingenious hooks, lures, traps, and nets to snare fish. Generally nomadic, the Athabascans looked for forested land to pitch their camps, seeking the warmth and shelter afforded by the white spruce trees of the Interior.

In winter, bands of related people frequently joined together to spend the long dark months in small settlements, and at these times songs, stories, and dances told the history of the tribes and so perpetuated the past. But subsistence for the Athabascans was never certain: they had to cope with a harsh and often cruel climate and with undependable food supplies. They lived precariously from season to season, needing an inner as well as a physical strength to survive. Believing reincarnation of the spirit was possible into both human and animal forms, they identified closely with the animals they depended upon. They also developed a complex system of beliefs that helped answer the worrisome philosophical questions which arise in the minds of all peoples.

The Aleuts and the Southeast Indians lived under more benign environmental conditions. It is probable that the Aleuts originally populated the rich southern shores of the Bering Land Bridge as well as the Aleutian Islands. The Tlingits and Haidas occupied the lush forested shores of the Southeast, where the food supply was also dependable and easily harvested. The weather in both Alaska's Southwest and its Southeast became what the Russians later described as "surprisingly warm," although fog and rain were part of the daily lives of the people living in both regions; for the Aleuts, storms were commonplace and so were winds strong enough to blow rocks around.

The rich culture that flourished among the Tlingits and Haidas (known collectively as the Koluschan) has been well studied and frequently described. These people developed a complex society, took slaves, gave lavish potlatches, and lived their lives in accordance with highly organized social structures, while observing clan rituals and strictly regulated relationships. Their art-work—magnificent totem poles, beautiful blankets, fine cedar-bark and spruce-root baskets—and their architecture are well known and notable for bold and highly stylized designs.

Less well known is the culture of the Aleuts; it was almost totally changed by a handful of Russians in a matter of a few decades. However, it was evidently as complex and fascinating as that of their neighbors across the Gulf of Alaska. Since their food supply was also rich, varied, and readily available, all age groups in their society could play a role in bringing it in; old people and children, for instance, gathered shellfish while the stronger, more skillful hunters brought in the sea mammals. It is known that the Aleuts practiced surgery and that their elaborate ritual burials included the practice of embalming the dead. They lived in villages, and, although not as aggressive or warlike as the Tlingits, like the Tlingits they took slaves.

Lacking a written language, they left no records themselves, but early European visitors wrote at some length of their charm and well-developed culture. Among those who traveled among the Aleuts (and the Russians) in the late eighteenth century was Martin Sauer, who was greatly impressed by the Aleut people and their artful handiwork. "Their instruments and utensils," he wrote, "are all made with amazing beauty and exact symmetry . . . their darts are adapted with the greatest judgment to the different objects of the chase." (The Aleuts, in fact, used 30 different kinds of harpoon heads for different species of game.) Sauer found their baidars, or boats, especially fine, and said of them: "If perfect symmetry, smoothness and proportion constitute beauty, they are beautiful: to me they appeared so beyond anything I ever beheld. I have seen some of them as transparent as oiled paper, through which you could trace every formation of the inside, and the manner of the Natives sitting in it; whose light dress, pointed and plumed bonnet, together with his perfect ease and activity, added infinitely to its elegance." The Aleuts, he went on to say, maneuvered their baidars with agility and skill, and "paddled in among the breakers which reached to their breasts, and carried the baidars quite under the water, sporting more like amphibious animals than human beings."

Sauer was incensed at the treatment the Aleuts received from the hands of the Russain *promyshleniki* (hunters and traders): "Their behavior," he noted succinctly, "is not rude and barbarous, but mild, polite and hospitable . . . they by no means deserve to be termed stupid, an epithet so liberally bestowed on those whom Europeans call savages."

Father Innokenti Veniaminoff, writer, anthropologist, and priest, lived among the Aleuts for seven years during the first part of the nineteenth century.

He learned their language, and he gained great respect for their intelligence and gifts of artistry. His notes are still among the most definitive made about these people.

By the time European explorers first came to Alaska, a relatively large Native population—perhaps larger than Alaska's Native population today—had become well established there. Some estimates put the number of Eskimos in the early eighteenth century at around 40,000, the number of Aleuts at 25,000, and that of the Tlingits and Athabascans at around 10,000 each. Although relationships between the Native peoples were not always cordial, they had by then more or less defined their respective territories, and their unrecorded boundaries were generally honored. And while other cultures might have developed land use and exploitation and erected sophisticated buildings and monuments, the Alaska Natives had disturbed their land almost not at all, for they lived in profound harmony with it. (What a legacy!) Vigorous, resourceful, and adapted to their various environments, they lacked the metal, guns and gunpowder to defend themselves. Without these, they were helpless before the Europeans.

The first Europeans to claim Alaska successfully were the Russians, who were engaged in exploring to the east just as the English, French, and Spanish were then probing the mysteries of the world that lay to their west. Many of these early explorers were looking for the Northwest Passage, whose mythical location had been described by Sir Martin Frobisher in 1628. A century after this report, Vitus Bering, a Dane sailing under the Russian flag (as did adventurous young men from many countries at that time) became a sort of Alaskan Christopher Columbus. Commissioned first by Peter the Great and then by Anna Ivanovna to take part in an ambitious attempt to find the New World and to chart its coast north of Mexico (and the entire coast of Siberia), Bering was allotted the finding and exploring of the American coast. The expedition he led would change the course of Alaska's history.

Bering made his initial landfall on Alaska after fifteen heartbreaking years of preparation and then unsuccessful sorties from Kamchatka. (On one early trip, he did, however, discover and name Saint Lawrence Island and Big Diomede in what would come to be the Bering Sea.) He set forth from Russia in the spring of 1741, captaining the *Saint Peter* while Lt. Alexei Chirikof captained a sister ship, the *Saint Paul*, and sailed with him. The two soon became separated and Chirikof proceeded on a less eventful course. After poor weather and difficult sailing, on July 16, the birthday of Russia's Saint Elias, Bering found himself near the 60th parallel, with a longitude of 140 east. The day was clear and looming against the eastern horizon was a magnificently high white mountain. Looking at a future major landmark of Alaska, Bering— who was already failing in health and suffering from exhaustion—is reported to have simply "shrugged his shoulders in the presence of all on board the *Saint Peter*." But he did leave the great mountain the name of Saint Elias, and he did drop anchor nearby and put to shore on an island that the Russians

Mount Saint Elias viewed from Icy Bay. Source: National Park Service.

later named Kayak Island because it was shaped like a Native boat. Georg Wilhelm Steller, the headstrong and gifted naturalist who accompanied Bering on this trip, verified the fact that they had indeed found North America because he saw an American blue jay, known to be native only to that continent: hence, Steller's jay.

Although Bering found the New World on this fateful voyage, it was ultimately a disastrous expedition. (Chirikof actually found Alaska—probably Prince of Wales Island—the day before Bering landed on Kayak Island, but he lost at least 13 men in landing attempts and he returned to Russia without having set foot on the North American continent.) Along with many of his crew, Bering came down with scurvy and became weak and ultimately disoriented. Bad luck dogged him, and fierce head winds and storms battered the *Saint Peter* as it sailed for its home port in Siberia. Steller wrote: "The wind seemed as if it issued forth from a flue, with such a whistling, roaring and rumbling, that we expected every moment to lose mast and rudder, or to see the ship crushed between the breakers." The crew became too feeble to man the ship or to stand watch, especially after their water supplies ran out. "Their courage," Steller noted, "was an unsteady as their teeth." Finally the *Saint Peter*, unguided, drifted ashore on what would be called Bering Island, one of the Komandorski Islands, owned by Russia. There Bering and several of the crew members died and were buried. After rebuilding the wrecked ship, the tattered survivors of the crew—Steller among them—managed to limp back home.

The reports brought back by the *Saint Peter's* crew of Alaska's fabulous sea otter and fur seal populations and Steller's excellent and detailed descriptions of these and other animals excited the Russians and prompted bands of adventurous and ambitious *promyshleniki*—the hunters and traders—to set forth into the Bering Sea, seeking their fortunes. Their onslaughts initiated the near extinction of the fur-bearing sea mammals as well as the Aleut people, whom the Russians had subdued and enslaved by 1766. Sauer wrote of them: " . . . the Russian *promyshleniki* . . . are infinitely more savage than any tribes I have hitherto met with." A Russian Naval officer later wrote sadly of the brutality: " . . . wives were taken from their husbands, and daughters from their mothers . . . they [the *promyshleniki*] used not infrequently to place men close together, and try through how many the ball of their rifle-barreled musket would pass." (It should be noted that not all the *promyshleniki* were so brutal.)

Along with the *promyshleniki*, several Russian explorers set out on new expeditions of discovery. They eventually managed to sail as far north as Cape Krusenstern and then up the Yukon River as far as Nulato, where they left their names and religion among many of the Athabascan Indians. (They also eventually traveled southeast as far as California.)

The English, French, and Spanish explorers were not far behind the Russians, however. In 1778, Captain James Cook, with George Vancouver along, reached the Arctic Ocean. (Another Englishman, Captain Frederick W. Beechey, pushed on farther north to Point Barrow in 1826, and the New England whalers soon followed him.) George Vancouver made a second trip to Alaska in 1793; he charted the complicated coastal area of Southeast Alaska so accurately that his maps were used for more than a hundred years afterward. The Frenchman, Jean Francois de Galoup, Compte de La Perouse, explored as far north as Lituya Bay in 1786, searching for the Northwest Passage. He lost 21 of his crewmen to the treacherous waters of Lysianski Strait and died himself on his return voyage to France. Between 1774 and 1792, Spain sent several of its greatest navigators, including Juan Francisco de la Bodega y Quadra, into Alaska's southeastern waters.

By this time, Gregor Shelikoff had established Russia's first permanent settlement at Three Saints Bay on Kodiak Island, and, in 1799, the Russian American Company was formally established with the blessings of the emperor Paul. This company, patterned after the British East India Company, was expected to promote further discovery, expand trading, develop agriculture, and spread Greek Catholicism in the New World. According to William Healy Dall, an American explorer, scientist, writer, and early Alaskan explorer, Alaska's Natives were easily converted to the Russian faith because they believed that a god who could save such cruel souls as the *promyshleniki* must be all-powerful indeed. The Russian establishment, however, was more benevolent, despite occasional warlike incidents.

Under a series of managers—the first, Alexander Baranof and later Admiral Varon Ferdinand von Wrangell—the Russian American Company became in effect the governing body of Alaska for the next 60 years, the directors running things much like lords of a fiefdom.

Baranof started his company operations in Aleut territory, but when the sea otter and fur seal were nearly exhausted, in 1806, he moved from Kodiak and the Aleutian Islands southeast. There he established the first Russian capital, Mikhailovskii Redut (Fort Saint Michael), on Baranof Island. Although the Tlingits succeeded in burning and sacking this fort in 1802, they were not so successful at getting rid of Novoarkhangelsk (later Sitka), especially since the Russians had reciprocated with a devastating reprisal in 1804. For the next two decades, Baranof presided over a lively society in Sitka, which was called the "Paris of the Pacific." During the years the Russians occupied Alaska, there were rarely more than 500 or 600 of them living in their immense colony. (An early census showed that there were more Hawaiians in Alaska than Russians by nearly two to one.)

Despite such a low population, the Russian settlers could not produce enough food to live on. Russian holdings in California also failed to supply the needed agricultural base, and as time went on, the fur seal and sea otter became more and more scarce. Trade became more competitive as well, with both England and the United States pushing northward and vying for the available resources. In addition, Sitka was a long way from Saint Petersburg and a fatherland that was devoting its energies to wars with Napoleon's France. So it was that after little more than a century in the New World, Russia began to find itself overextended. In 1867, Russia sold Alaska to the United States for $7,200,000. (Russia's Baron Stoeckl, who handled negotiations with United States Secretary of State William H. Seward, is reported to have taken $200,000 to reimburse himself for the amount he had spent out of his own pocket enlisting the support of key congressmen for this purchase.) It is noteworthy that no treaties were made with the Native Alaskans at the time of this transaction. Seward changed the name of the territory then known as Russian America; he rechristened it Alaska.

Although he considered the acquisition of Alaska the greatest achievement

Abandoned miner's cabin near the Yukon-Charley National Monument.
Source: National Park Service.

of his life, the Alaskan purchase was not entirely popular with the American people. Some called the new territory Seward's Folly, Walrussia, and Icebergia. The myth of a land locked perpetually in ice and snow, where only an Eskimo or a polar bear could survive, became all too quickly and firmly established. For the thirty years after it was acquired, Alaska—remote and inaccessible—was left virtually alone by the United States, first called "Indian Country," later a district. During that time, the explorer-historian William Healy Dall wrote, it was a place where "no man could make a legal will, own a homestead or transfer it, or so much as cut wood for his fire without defying a Congressional prohibition: where polygamy and slavery and the lynching of witches prevailed, with no legal authority to stay or punish criminals." An early Juneau miner put it more colorfully: "We had an earthquake a while ago, so we know the Lord ain't forgotten us, even if the government has." It took the gold rushes—which brought Alaska its first recorded population boom—at the turn of the twentieth century to establish some semblance of authority and order; and even then the law was often decided by the miners themselves and on their own terms.

In 1900, Alaska's population was estimated to be about 60,000 people, including almost 30,000 non-Natives, most of whom would leave after failing to find gold. One of the 1900 census-takers was an "outsider," who found life in Alaska to be rough and ready; in fact, he described the place as being "the worst country in the world for swearing." He told of meeting one relatively pious Alaskan who named every dog on his team with a four-letter word so he could swear as much as he wanted all winter long without disturbing his conscience. (It is worth reading Robert Service, whose Yukon poems capture the spirit of this period in Alaska's history so well. See Bibliography.)

Alaska may have been far from civilization, but American industry was not entirely idle in the newly acquired district. When whaling declined in Alaska's waters, the whalers turned to taking walrus for their oil and tusks. (It is estimated that between commercial take by whalers and the subsistence take by Eskimos, 200,000 walrus were killed in Alaskan waters between 1860 and 1880.) There were also the rich salmon fisheries in the Southeast and Southwest, and these attracted increasing commercial exploitation too. Canneries went up, first small, then rambling wooden buildings, and stationary fish traps, or nets, were being set across the mouths of the major migratory streams and rivers. Workers came from China, Japan, and the Philippines. (A machine which speeded up the processing of the fish was named the "Iron Chink.") In the meantime, the Americans continued to hunt the sea otter and fur seal. By the early twentieth century, people were beginning to worry more about Alaska's fisheries and the vanishing populations of the sea mammals. Finally, the federal government stepped in to end pelagic seal fishing and to initiate strict controls on the hunting of sea mammals, with a measure of success: both sea otter and fur seal have since become reestablished.

Meantime, in the 1860's Alaska (still Russian America) was chosen as a launching point for the newly developing Western Union Company's telegraph system. This led to a period of major scientific exploration in Alaska, funded by the U.S. Government. However, a preferable route for the cable was eventually found from the east coast to Europe. Copper mining was a more successful venture. Soon after the beginning of the twentieth century, capitalistic tycoons moved in to build a railroad into the heart of the Wrangell Mountains, and the Kennecott operation went into major production. (See the section on the Wrangell Mountains.)

In 1912, Congress finally passed the second Organic Act for Alaska. This one at last gave it its own territorial legislature. (In 1906, it had received a voteless congressional delegate.) Near that time, the U.S. Forest Service was consolidating its Alaska holdings into 24 million acres of the choicest forested land in Alaska's Southeast and Southcentral regions. The federally built and operated Alaska Railroad was authorized in 1914 and completed in 1923. This played a major role in opening up and developing Southcentral and Interior Alaska. (The Alaska Railroad was acquired by the state of Alaska in 1984. It continues to serve a number of homesteads that are inaccessible by road or by air.)

In 1920, a pioneer flight from New York to Nome (by the Army) initiated a new era for "the bush." But it was not until World War II that a major change hit Alaska. At that time, the military constructed numerous airfields and established several large installations there. Soldiers spent long lonesome and dangerous months on the foggy and windy Aleutian Islands; Dutch Harbor was bombed, and Attu and Kiska were both invaded by the Japanese. It took the Americans more than a year to reoccupy these islands, and during the bloody battle on Attu Island, only 28 out of 2,600 Japanese were known to have survived. (This count was possible only because they were taken prisoner.) The island of Kiska had 1,255 tons of bombs dropped on it, and the Japanese managed to evacuate their force of 5,183 men in a record 55 minutes—a somewhat hollow American victory.

Perhaps most significantly for the future, many new roads were built during this time, including the AlCan Highway, which joined Alaska to the "Outside" once and for all. All in all, the military spent over one billion dollars for its various Alaskan efforts between 1941 and 1945, and Alaska's population grew from 74,000 to 112,000.

Alaska continued to grow after World War II. In the fifties, oil was brought in on the Kenai Peninsula, a major discovery. The U.S. Forest Service began to open its forests to "harvest," and the commercial fishing business continued to prosper. Still, the territory felt itself a stepchild. With a growing population, pressures for statehood increased. Congress finally responded with a statehood act. When President Eisenhower proclaimed Alaska a new state on January 3, 1959, the story goes, every church bell in Alaska pealed in celebration. Because Alaska still had what was then considered a meager economic base, Congress was especially generous with the new state (see Who Takes Care of Alaska's Land), but it failed to define and settle any Native land claims.

Of course, it turned out that Alaska's natural resources—particularly its oil—were richer than anyone had dreamed. By bringing in the oil on the North Slope in 1969 (the presence of oil there had been known since before the turn of the century), and the subsequent building of the oil pipeline from Prudhoe Bay to Valdez, Alaska gained an economic base that is the envy of many other states and even nations. With an overall population of about five hundred thousand, Alaska has the highest per capita income of any of the 50 United States—a budget in the billions and in the black.

An important consequence of the discovery of oil was the passage of the Alaska Native Claims Settlement Act, which at long last gave recognition to the rights of Alaska's Native people. Because of this act, Alaska's Natives have been brought into the mainstream both of Alaskan business endeavors and the exploitation of Alaska's resources.

As you travel through Alaska today, you can find traces left by many of its earliest settlers. There are totems, lodges, umiaks and kayaks (many are built of different materials now, but they are still shaped in the traditional way), frames for stretching skins, whalebone enclosures, and subsistence tools such as the Tlingit halibut hook and the Eskimo ulu (a curved blade used as a knife in food preparation). Almost everywhere you go you will find racks for drying fish. The traditional subsistence way of life is still practiced and cherished to one degree or another in many parts of Alaska. (See Visiting Native Villages.)

The artwork of Alaska's Native people can be exceptionally beautiful. You will find it—along with not-so-beautiful (frequently foreign-made) copies—in any Alaskan city and in many of the villages. Look for fine carvings: although Alaska's Natives are legally allowed to gather ivory from walrus tusks (non-Native Alaskans are not) and work with it, you might prefer to buy carvings of fossil ivory, soapstone, and bone. Also look for beadwork and baskets. If the articles seem costly, consider the time spent by the artists in creating them.

Wherever the Russians had traveled, they, too, left their marks. You will find Russian churches and graveyards in many places. Later, the sourdoughs left their cabins, worn-out dredges, picks and shovels and kitchenware. (It is said that more metal has been taken into Alaska by miners than has been taken out.) And, of course, the evidence of contemporary man is proliferating yearly and making new history in everything from plush hotels to pipelines.

HOW TO GET THERE

You can get to Alaska by air, by water, or by highway. Jet service to Alaska's three major cities—Juneau, Anchorage, and Fairbanks, the state's principal gateways—is relatively good. Anchorage, in fact, has one of the busiest international airports in the country, being a way station on the great circle route. The air tariff is high. Airlines are expanding their services, however, and you may be able to find a good package fare.

If you enjoy traveling by water, you'll find Alaska's state ferry-liner system a super way to go—with or without your car. (Without a car, the ferry is a real bargain; there are comfortable staterooms—which you must reserve—and lounge chairs, or you can roll out your sleeping bag topside.) Known as the Marine Highway, Alaska's ferries operate on two separate route systems: one system travels the Inside Passage from Seattle (or Prince Rupert, B.C.), to Haines or Skagway, a distance of 1,130 miles with many stops along the way.

The other serves Prince William Sound, Kodiak, and parts of the Kenai Peninsula. Both routes carry you through not only overwhelmingly beautiful scenery, but also through some of the richest marine and avian wildlife habitat in Alaska. Either route offers fine wildlife viewing opportunities. From Seattle to Skagway, by the way, takes about four days, but you can make it a longer trip if you wish; there's no charge for stopping over along the way. A great plus for bikers and kayakers is that anything you can carry onto the ferry with you travels free. (There are excellent bicycling opportunities in the accessible parts of Alaska.) When you reach the northern end of the Inside Passage, you can continue your journey, if you wish, by bus (in summer), by railroad, or in your car. There are roads from both Haines and Skagway that lead into Alaska's Interior road system.

Driving the Alaska Highway, which you pick up at Dawson Creek, British Columbia, can be a real adventure, but it takes a lot of time (at least five days on the road) and is demanding of both driver and passengers. The Canadian portion of the road includes miles of gravel surface, which is hard on tires and

Moose (*Alces alces gigas*), *the largest member of the deer family. Range: throughout Alaska.*

windshields, and it is incredibly dusty in summer. (Many Alaskans prefer to drive this road in winter when it is frozen, the traffic is light, and there's no dust or flying gravel.) While there are adequate accommodations along the way, you'll enjoy this trip more if you really love the out-of-doors and have a feeling for roughing it.

The principal roads in Alaska, including the Alaska Highway and the access road from Haines (ferry port) to the Alaska Highway, are paved. But it's a small highway system, totaling only a few thousand miles, and the roads are not all contiguous either. Do not expect an Interstate 5 anywhere in Alaska; freeways are few and far between. The Glenn Highway, north of Anchorage, is the best there is, and it's also the most heavily traveled. More moose are killed on sections of this highway, incidentally, than die by hunters' guns in the same area.

WORDS ABOUT THE ALASKAN WILDERNESS

Being Prepared

Expect Alaskan wilderness to be unlike any wilderness you have encountered before. It is different because of its weather, its size and scale, and its wildness. Weather is emphasized throughout this book because it plays such an important part in any Alaskan adventure: not to be repetitious, you will meet unpredictable and cantankerous weather—and on its terms, not yours—on any travels you make in Alaska's wilderness. (Remember, though, that Valdimar Steffanson wrote a book called *The Friendly Arctic*; it is possible to enjoy Alaska's weather.)

As to size and scale, they will color all your perceptions of Alaska. You will find intimate spots in this wilderness—perhaps in an alpine meadow or beside a glossy black lake studded with yellow water lilies or along a clear chattering stream. But when you lift your eyes, the immensity of the landscape will always be around you. Outside of the Southeast and regions around Anchorage and Fairbanks, you will not often be able to drive or walk to a roadhead or trailhead; you will have to fly to your point of departure or to your camping spot in the wilderness. (A few notable exceptions are mentioned in the text.) Once the plane leaves you, you may be several days away from the nearest civilized place, whether you travel by land or by river.

As you travel through this wilderness, you will, for the most part, be in wild and relatively untouched country. Although it is being used more and more by people (and certain areas of it are passing into private Native ownership), your chances are still good of seeing very few other travelers. Instead, for company you will have the wild animals whose territory you are crossing. Respect these fellow creatures, please; wild Alaska is their home. Respect, too, the rights of the Natives whose territory this has been through the millennia (see Visiting Native Villages).

Before you start on an adventure in Alaska's wilderness, it is wise to ask yourself if you are ready not only for the best but for the worst. (This is a worthwhile exercise even before starting on a day-hike in Alaska.) Are you prepared to spend an unspecified length of time comfortably in heavy rain and/or wind and/or cold? Are you prepared—mentally as well as physically— to wait for your bush pilot, especially if the sun is out and you cannot see any good reason for a delayed pickup? If this is your first trip, are you prepared to go with a friend or a group? Most important of all, if in a private party, have you prepared your trip plan and told someone about it and where you expect to be when?

Don't let all of this put you off; it is not much more than common sense in an uncommon wilderness. In Alaska, you will have the rare opportunity to be entirely on your own in one of the most magnificent parts of the earth. If you are prepared and know what you are doing, your adventure here should be one of the great experiences of your life.

Firewood

Firewood is inadequate in many parts of Alaska. It is unavailable above tree level and also in much tundra and coastal country. Where it is readily available—for example, in Southeast—the wood is often damp and difficult to burn. (Under these circumstances, search out dead spruce fronds or red cedar bark, preferably from the protected part of a dead tree.) You may or may not find firewood on sand or gravel bars in the rivers, depending upon the location and the time of year.

For all these reasons, it is a good idea to carry a small stove if you are taking any kind of an extended trip into Alaska's wilderness. Even on a short trip, a quick cup of hot tea or bouillon (made in a Sierra Club cup, if nothing else) can be highly restorative.

If you do build a camp or cook fire in Alaska's wilderness, do so carefully and do not cause a scar. When you leave, be absolutely certain your fire is out; douse it thoroughly with water. Although the countryside can look wet and fireproof, it may not be. If a fire gets started in peat or tundra, it can travel underground almost indefinitely. Forests, even when damp, can burn easily once flames get going. Lightning-caused fires have burned hundreds of thousands of acres in Alaska; so have human-caused conflagrations. Between 1955 and 1980, in fact, an average of 712,855 acres burned per year, and in peak years as much as two to five million acres have been consumed. Firefighting is difficult under the circumstances and very costly (mostly to the federal taxpayer, since the Bureau of Land Management (BLM) is Alaska's principal firefighter). While fire is important to the natural succession of plants and animals in many ecosystems, its role in Alaska is still being studied. Human intervention in this process—one way or another—can be disastrous.

Stream Crossings

If you plan to cover much Alaskan territory on foot, it is almost certain that you will be fording one or more streams or rivers. Your former wilderness experience elsewhere may not have prepared you for Alaska's waterways. The water here may be icy; the currents, swift and strong. Streambeds may be covered with unstable or rolling rocks, and if the waterway is glacial in origin, its depth may be difficult to gauge. Here are a few tips that can help speed your crossings.

If it is not feasible to build a ford of logs or big rocks—and it rarely is—look for the widest place you can find to cross the stream or river. Usually, the farther downstream you go, the wider and more shallow the water is apt to become, and many rivers break into braids in their lower courses. When you have chosen a spot, see if you can find a long stick to help you gauge the depth of the water and to keep your balance. If the water is swift and deep and you are wearing a large pack, uncinch your waistband so that you can shed your pack easily if necessary. With several people along, you have certain advantages crossing rivers; you can string a rope across the water, which will give you both physical and moral support. You can hold hands as you wade across, or you can pair off and travel tandem, the stronger person behind, with his or her hands on the shoulder of the person in front. (Some people put the stronger one in front.) As much as possible, angle into the current and keep your feet as wide apart as is comfortable.

As to what to do about your feet when fording Alaskan waters, you have four choices. You can carry old sneakers or running shoes and wear them on bare feet, hauling your boots and socks across in your pack: since your feet will probably get very cold, dry shoes and socks will feel wonderful when you put them back on. Or, as many Alaskans do, you can remove your socks and wear your boots on your bare feet: this means you will have damp, if not wet, feet when you continue hiking. The other two obvious stream-crossing methods—neither of which I recommend—are to simply leave on your shoes and socks and walk across, or to wade across barefoot. The latter option can be disastrous if you encounter poor footing, big rocks, or have tender feet.

It is not smart to try stream crossings wearing a long rain poncho or cagoule. The water can catch in such a garment and act like strong wind against a sail, tipping you off your feet and into the water. I had this happen twice in a matter of minutes trying to cross the Toklat River in Mount McKinley Park one July day. I ended up initiated into one of the rites of being an Alaskan but also with a not-so-mild case of hypothermia.

I learned another lesson from this particular venture on the Toklat. Alaska's rivers, especially those that flow through areas with permafrost underneath, can rise several feet during the day in both fair and foul summer weather. When the weather is hot and sunny, snowmelt can add measurably to the stream flow. During rains, the volume of the rivers is likewise increased. On our Toklat outing, we had started about 4 A.M. and had easily crossed and recrossed the river. Then we hiked several miles downstream during a day of drizzly rain. When we returned in the late afternoon, we found that the river had risen at least two feet in the area where we had made our crossings.

Hypothermia

The word *hypothermia* derives from two Greek words: *hypo*, meaning under or beneath; and *thermé*, meaning heat. It accurately describes a condition brought about by the abnormal decrease of body temperature.

The human body can lose heat outdoors from at least three causes: cold, wind, and moisture. The combination of any two of these speeds up the cooling process, and the combination of all three compounds it even more. Add fatigue to this, and you can be in real trouble.

The first symptoms of hypothermia are shivering, the presence of goose bumps, and an accelerated heart rate. (These are all automatic body reactions to compensate for heat loss.) Then comes clumsiness, loss of body functions, loss of judgment, and finally disorientation. Even when arrested, hypothermia can lead to serious complications; if not arrested, it can lead to death. Hypothermia can almost always be avoided.

The first way to avoid hypothermia is to be responsible for your own clothing needs. Travel with enough clothing to protect yourself under any possible adverse situations you could encounter. Enough clothing includes warm headgear, handgear, and footgear, since the body loses heat first from its extremities. The head, in particular, should be protected. Enough clothing also includes enough layers to keep yourself warm, and a windproof and/or waterproof shell to protect you against rain and wind. Second, avoid getting overheated and sweaty; damp clothes can act as a refrigerating agent. Third, do not push yourself when you begin to feel exhausted.

If a member of your party shows symptoms of hypothermia—slurred speech, a slowing down of pace, apathy, unusual behavior, or poor judgment—stop traveling immediately and build a fire if possible. Get the victim as warm as you can and give her or him a hot drink (*not* alcohol). If the hypothermia persists, get into a sleeping bag with the victim and warm her or his body

EQUIVALENT CHILL TEMPERATURE

Wind Speed Miles per Hour

Temperature (°F)

Wind Speed (mph)	40	35	30	25	20	15	10	5	0	-5	-10	-15	-20	-25	-30	-35	-40	-45	-50	-55	-60
Calm	40	35	30	25	20	15	10	5	0	-5	-10	-15	-20	-25	-30	-35	-40	-45	-50	-55	-60
						Equivalent Chill Temperature															
5	35	30	25	20	15	10	5	0	-5	-10	-15	-20	-25	-30	-35	-40	-45	-50	-55	-65	-70
10	30	20	15	10	5	-5	-10	-15	-20	-25	-35	-40	-45	-50	-60	-65	-70	-75	-80	-90	-95
15	25	15	10	0	-5	-10	-20	-25	-30	-40	-45	-50	-60	-65	-70	-80	-85	-90	-100	-105	-110
20	20	10	5	0	-10	-15	-25	-30	-35	-45	-50	-60	-65	-75	-80	-85	-95	-100	-110	-115	-120
25	15	10	0	-5	-15	-20	-30	-35	-45	-50	-60	-65	-75	-80	-90	-95	-105	-110	-120	-125	-135
30	10	5	0	-10	-20	-25	-30	-40	-50	-55	-65	-70	-80	-85	-95	-100	-110	-115	-125	-130	-140
35	10	5	-5	-10	-20	-30	-35	-40	-50	-60	-65	-75	-80	-90	-100	-105	-115	-120	-130	-135	-145
40	10	0	-5	-15	-20	-30	-35	-45	-55	-60	-70	-75	-85	-95	-100	-110	-115	-125	-130	-140	-150

Winds Above 40 Have Little Additional Effect

Little Danger

Increasing Danger (Flesh may freeze within 1 min.)

Great Danger (Flesh may freeze within 30 seconds)

directly with yours—without clothing. Send for help if you can, but if there are only two of you, stay together: a person in this condition should not be left alone.

Insects

According to the Koyukon people, when the Raven finished creating humans, a man came and stole Raven's wife. So Raven went out and found some rotten willow wood, ground it into a fine dust, and tossed it high into the air. The powdery specks all became mosquitoes, which from then on would torment humankind.

Chances are that you have heard horrific stories about Alaska's insects. Sadly, they are probably true. Alaska is something like a giant sponge: it freezes solid in winter, but in summer its top layer thaws and water gathers everywhere to make hundreds of thousands of ponds and puddles. Add to this lakes and overflowing rivers, once spring breakup occurs. All that shallow stagnant water is heaven for breeding insects. These conditions do not persist, but while in effect, the bugs mass in the billions (or so it seems). This is one reason, of course, why birds come from all over the world to Alaska. The insect food supply is unsurpassed.

Like humans, Alaska's insects thrive in the best weather. May, June, and July are the months for mosquitoes. July and August are the months for the midges (no-see-ums) and black flies (whitesox). Here's what you're up against with these pests.

Mosquitoes, midges, and black flies are all flies, although each belongs to a different family. While each has its own characteristics, they also have similarities. Among all of them, the female requires blood (for protein), and the male gets by on either nectar or other vegetative material. All require still water for their larval stage, and all the females feed by inserting a tiny stylus into the skin of an animal and sucking blood. Compounding this outrage, they also inject an anesthetizing agent—which varies in degree of toxicity— that numbs you to the attack. It is this little squirt of poison that causes complications.

Mosquitoes belong to the family Culcidae, subfamily Clucinae (there are hundreds of species). They are, of course, familiar to people all over the world. In Alaska there are some 25 to 40 species, the principal ones being *aedes*, *anopheles*, *culex*, and *psorophora*. None of them carry diseases, and—if it's any comfort—they feed on animals and birds as well as people. Some large adult mosquitoes hibernate during the winter in places such as leaf litter. These are the ones that are ready to pounce at the first sign of warm weather.

Since Alaska mosquitoes tend to stay in the general region they originated (puddle, pond, lake, or overwash of stagnant water), you may be able to avoid major confrontations by moving out of a heavily infested area. But don't count on this; swarms will often simply follow you, even down the middle of a river.

Higher ground with a breeze is usually less populated by these small creatures.

Biting midges (commonly called no-see-ums or punkies) belong to the family Ceratopogonidae. These insects are so tiny that it is hard to see them, and they can usually get through a standard mosquito net with no trouble. They announce themselves by a high whine and a swift, light sting. Later, you may develop a fine case of welts or hives from their poison. Since these minute pests are even more home oriented than mosquitoes, they can sometimes be avoided by moving just a few yards away. Watch out for them along streambanks and around the edges of lakes.

The most poisonous of Alaska's winged and stinging insects are the black flies, also called whitesox and buffalo gnats. (A Yupik story tells how two young orphan boys became so frightened by a higher-than-usual tide that, to save themselves, they turned into little flies, and that is why we have gnats today.) These tormentors belong to the family Simuliidae; they are small, dark, and have short legs (sometimes white), broad wings, and a humpbacked appearance. They breed in streams and tend to remain close to their home base but not always; some of them travel widely. The bite of one of these insects can not only be painful but can draw blood. Frequently it will cause major swelling, as many people are sensitive to the toxic agent injected. As with wasps and bees, certain people react violently to the toxin, and a bite can be, though very rarely is, fatal.

Covering up is your first line of defense against Alaska's stinging insects. Since they seem to prefer dark colors, you can wear outer garments that are light colored but not light in thickness! The stinging apparatus of all these bugs—or the tinier bugs themselves—can go right through thin or loosely woven clothing. A cotton flannel shirt is good armor; you can get one that is light colored and thick enough to give you protection. Of course, you will also want long sleeves (and long pants) when you are in bug country.

Net jackets with hoods are now available (some impregnated with repellent), but they are not cheap. A head net is a simpler solution, and I would consider it a necessity if insect bites bother you and you are going into the Alaskan bush. You can find head nets at army surplus and sporting goods stores. You should also be sure that your tent has a good tight mosquito screen—it can be a marvelous haven when you are under attack. You can get tent screens with a small enough mesh to keep out midges, but they will also cut down on the airiness of your tent.

Insecticides are another line of defense. Jungle juice, bug juice, Cutter's, Off, Muskol, etc.—people swear by all of these. All contain diethyl-meta-toluamide in varying amounts. You can look for lotion, liquid, stick, aerosol spray, or towelette. (Interestingly, the repelling agent does not send mosquitoes away because of its bad smell or taste; instead, its heavy and irregularly shaped molecules befuddle a mosquito's sensory functions and send her buzzing off in confusion.) If you don't want to cover yourself with chemicals, you can try taking large doses of vitamin B (or another "systemic repellant") or using an electronic device, but most researchers are skeptical about the effectiveness of these methods.

Just keep in mind that there are few wildernesses anywhere that do not have pests of one kind or another. Alaska makes up for a spectacular insect population by having few large stinging insects such as hornets and wasps, no plants that are poisonous to the touch, no scorpions, and no poisonous snakes (in fact, no indigenous snakes at all).

The Good News

Despite the inconveniences and possible dangers you might encounter in Alaska's wilderness, there are unexpected pluses that are quite apart from the magnificence of the scenery and the wonders of the wildness and wildlife. Although it can be cold, wet, and muddy—or warm, sunny, and dry—Alaska's wilderness is relatively clean to travel through compared with, for example, the wilderness of the Sierra Nevada where your socks turn grimy your first day in. You may sometimes slog through mud or sand, but you are not likely to encounter heavy dust on the wilderness trail (if you find a trail, that is). An exception to prove this rule is glacial country where the wind whips up deposits of glacial silt. (Also note that if you fall into a glacial stream, it will take you several washings to get all the silt out.) With certain exceptions, which have been well emphasized, you will find the temperature generally pleasant for summer hiking or backpacking, and you won't, as a rule, find yourself working up a great sweat. And last, but not least, while some tundra is rough going, a lot of it is such good walking that you feel as nimble as a ballet dancer or, perhaps more appropriately, a Dall sheep or mountain goat.

EQUIPMENT

What to Wear

The kind of clothing you choose to take to Alaska will depend, of course, on which part of the state you plan to visit, the time of year that you visit, and what you want to do while you're there. Clothing needs and gear lists for wilderness travelers follow. For general travel, be guided by the fact that Alaskans for the most part are not only very informal but completely unpretentious. In Juneau, Anchorage, and Fairbanks, you will see people in business clothes, but you will also see business people in the most casual kind of dress. You will look—and feel—more at home in these Alaskan cities if you dress primarily to be comfortable. Jeans or informal slacks or skirts, sweaters, open-neck shirts, parkas, crepe-soled shoes or boots are acceptable almost anywhere. (There are elegant and excellent restaurants in Alaska, but almost none that requires ties and/or jackets for gentlemen.) Try to stay away from traditional tourist garb if you want to fit in; the polyester pantsuit for women or the loud colored leisure suit for men can brand the wearer a Cheechako, or rank newcomer. While this may make little difference in Alaska's larger towns, it may set you apart in smaller communities, especially in Native villages.

The great guiding principle to follow when choosing travel clothes for comfort in Alaska is to be prepared for changes in the weather. In the summer, you can encounter real heat, so take at least one change of light clothing. You can, on the other hand, also encounter chilly weather, so take along at least one change of warm clothing. And, always—always—be prepared for rain. A light, waterproof (well, water-repellent) hooded parka with a full zipper opening that is easy to get into and out of is an excellent all-around piece of summer clothing.

If you are headed for Alaska's cities in the winter, you can use the following rules of thumb: Juneau, dress for wet snow and soppy streets; Anchorage, dress as for Chicago; Fairbanks, carry a down parka with a hood, warm gloves or mittens, and insulated footgear.

Some Thoughts About Clothing and Equipment

Get the Best You Can Afford

Whether you are buying boots, bandannas, or sleeping bags, get the best you can afford for your Alaska travels. You might be able to economize in the Sierra Nevada or Great Smokies with a cheap air mattress that you plan to discard after your trip, but this system—a wasteful one under any circumstances—will definitely not work for Alaska. If you are going into the Alaskan wilderness, you will need the sturdiest and most reliable equipment you can manage to obtain—not only for your comfort but, possibly, for your survival.

Be Sure Your Equipment Is in Good Shape

You won't find shoe-repair shops outside the larger communities, and you might even have trouble finding new shoelaces. It is even harder to find sporting goods shops that will repair a tent or backpack once you leave Alaska's three main cities. You can avoid a lot of headaches by getting all your equipment into top condition before you leave home.

SUMMER CLOTHING LIST FOR ALASKAN WILDERNESS ADVENTURERS

Item	Wilderness Foot Travel & Camping	River Running & Kayaking	In SE	SC & SW	Int. & Arctic	Comments
Warm underwear top and bottom	X	X	X	X	X	Can double as pajamas.
Three pairs inner and outer wool socks	X	X	X	X	X	Four pairs of each is better, if you can find the room. There is nothing like warm, dry feet.
Wool pants	X	X	X	X	X	I would rather be too warm in wool pants than cold and wet in jeans, but lots of people wear jeans anyway.
Cotton flannel shirt	X	X	X	X	X	A good all-purpose garment. Be sure it has plenty of pockets.
Wool shirt or long-sleeved warm sweater	X	X	X	X	X	A wool shirt is easier to get into and out of, but suit yourself.
Down vest or down sweater	?	?	?	?	?	I happen to like down (well-protected), but for wet environments, you might prefer a synthetic.
Windproof hooded parka	X	X	X	X	X	The Eskimos discovered the advantages of this design long before we arrived on the scene.
Hooded down parka	X	?	?	X	X	You will not need a down vest or down sweater, of course, if you carry this warmer item.
Wool hat or wool stocking cap	X	X	X	X	X	Wear it to bed if it is really cold.
So'wester hat		X	X	?		Introduced by early whalers and beloved of Southeasterners.

Item	Wilderness Foot Travel & Camping	River Running & Kayaking	In SE	SC & SW	Int. & Arctic	Comments
Rain parka	X	X	X	X	X	Stay away from long ponchos and/or cagoules if you plan to cross any streams or rivers.
Rain pants or rain chaps	X	X	X	X	X	Although you may not need these for rain in Interior or Arctic, they are good everywhere for wind and cold protection, and for traveling through wet vegetation.
Warm gloves	X	X	X	X	X	If you can get tight-knit wool gloves, do so. Leather is good until it gets wet. Also consider fishermen's hand gear or leather mitts with wool or silk liners.
Knee-high rubber boots	X		X			The standard footgear of most Southeasterners.
Shoepacks				X	X	Good for light use outdoors.
Hip boots		X	X	X	X	Unless you plan to wear a wet suit.
Sturdy hiking boots	X	X	X	X	X	Hopefully, yours are tried and true friends. Be sure to wear good innersoles as well. Waterproof the seams and carry extra laces.
Sneakers or old running shoes	X	X	X	X	X	My recommendation for stream crossings and for kayakers to use as a change of footgear, although you may want boots instead, particularly if you plan to hike on your river trip.

Backpacking near Nikolai Pass, Wrangell Mountains. Source: *National Park Service.*

Some Thoughts About Tents and Such

A good tent is essential. There are some campers, notably those who have traveled frequently in the Sierra Nevada, who like to carry only a lightweight tarp that can be used as a ground cloth or rigged as a shelter. I strongly recommend against this practice in Alaska. You may get by with this arrangement for one or two trips, but almost certainly you will eventually wish you had brought along a snug tent. If you encounter severe winds and weather or have an accident, such a tent could mean the difference between life and death.

Your tent needs to be lightweight, waterproof, as windproof as possible, and you will need a fly. I prefer a freestanding tent that can be rigged and then moved easily to the optimum level and sheltered spot. Be sure, however, that you have good strong stakes with which to nail it down and extra line to tie it down more securely, if necessary. I travel with a geodesic-dome-type tent, but many friends use standard teepee types or the caterpillar type as well.

You should be prepared to whisk wet sand off the bottom of your tent in Alaska's backcountry and to sponge moisture off your tent fly even after a clear night; there can be heavy condensation. A small, lightweight whisk broom, a good-sized sponge, and a piece of old lightweight canvas big enough to sit on always go inside my tent bag. This canvas porch is extremely useful. You can sit on it to remove your boots before entering your tent and so avoid tracking in mud or caked dirt; or you can clean your wet boots off on it before diving into your tent during rains.

Although certain tundra communities in Alaska are wondrously soft and springy and a delight to sleep on, you should always have some kind of mattress or pad to go under your sleeping bag, and a waterproof tent floor is a great comfort. In Southeast, I prefer a good old-fashioned air mattress, since it keeps one well off the tent floor, which may become clammy. Many people prefer a foam or other composition pad because it is lighter and provides good insulation when the weather is cold. You can also get a combination type.

The question of down versus man-made fibers for sleeping bags (as well as for vests, sweaters, and parkas) gets lots of going over among people who travel in the Alaskan bush. I prefer down (and, generally speaking, other natural materials). There's nothing like a down sleeping bag (inside a snug tent, of course) to crawl into after a cold, hard day. Remember, though, that it can get very hot in Alaska during summer in some places, and a down bag that feels only mildly toasty in the Arctic can roast you alive in the Interior heat. Since you are probably going to carry only one sleeping bag, you will have to decide whether to go light or heavy. I would rather unzip my warm bag (a twenty-plus-years-old, three-pound down bag) on a hot night or even sleep on top of it than be caught cold. You may belong to the school that keeps adding clothes inside a light bag when it gets chilly. Take your choice.

If you do decide to take down, remember that it is practically useless when it is wet. Carry your sleeping bag inside a good heavy plastic bag—I line my stuff sack with a heavy-gauge garbage bag (and I carry a spare garbage bag in case the first one tears). Man-made fibers do provide greater insulation when wet, and you should give them your careful attention if you are thinking of acquiring a bag.

Backpacking Equipment

If you are into backpacking, you probably have a pack of your choice, and any good design that is sturdy and comfortable (and relatively waterproof) is fine for Alaska. However, if you are starting fresh, you should consider the pros and cons of the rucksack-type pack with internal frame versus the pack with an external frame. In Southeast and in other areas of heavy brush, the pack with an inside frame has certain advantages because it will not hang you up. However, for open country, a pack with an external frame is my choice, and I recommend getting the kind that will stand up alone when you put it down. Of course, try to select material as waterproof as possible for the body of the pack.

Carrying different items in plastic bags inside your pack will add to your chances of keeping your stuff dry, and this is a good way to see what you've got where. Be sure the plastic bags you carry are reasonably sturdy. I usually get two sizes of bags that snap shut. (By all means, reuse them year after year.) Heavier-gauge plastic bags are available in outdoor equipment stores.

Heavy-gauge plastic garbage bags are also useful for protecting the outside of your pack, but be sure to take along one or two extras since even the best of them will not hold up well with heavy wear. You can also look for a pack that comes with its own separate raincoat. A brightly colored day pack is a good item to carry if you plan to do any day-hiking on your trip.

Footgear

Rubber boots of one kind or another are standard equipment for most Alaskans who live in the bush or anywhere in the Southeast. They have a special, invaluable place in a country that is full of wet places. However, waterproof footgear is not ideal for most real hiking, and it can certainly add a lot of weight to a pack. But if you are going to spend your time in Southeast Alaska, by all means consider getting a pair of knee-high rubber boots, sometimes known as "Southeast sneakers" or "dancing shoes." They are ideal for slogging around on bird-watching outings, traveling in the low country, exploring muskegs, and general wear on wet days. A good pair will be worth the money, and several stores in downtown Juneau carry the best.

For kayaking or river-running, you will probably want hip boots for at least a few members of your party, unless you decide to use wet suits and sneakers. (Or you can just decide to get wet when you have to line your river craft, which you will probably have to do a time or two since even the finest of Alaska's rivers may require lining when the water is high.)

Assuming that you're going to hike a lot also assumes that you have a good pair of boots with which you're well acquainted and on—shall we say—a good footing. Just be sure your boots are sturdy and remember to waterproof the seams and oil the leather well. (Completely waterproofed boots, even if you can achieve them, have the same drawback as rubber boots, and you will end up with wet feet in them.)

If you plan to do only light hiking—you might, for example, be going to visit a wilderness lodge such as Camp Denali and plan to wander only locally— you may find shoepacks (that is, boots with rubber bottoms and leather tops) both adequate and comfortable. A great many Alaskans wear this kind of footgear, too. You can purchase shoepacks in Alaska or obtain them by mail from L. L. Bean, which sells them as "Maine hunting shoes." Whatever your footgear, good insulating innersoles will add to your comfort, as will, of course, two pairs of wool socks.

The Merits of Wool

Most Alaskans swear by wool clothing of all kinds for outdoor wear (or for any kind of wear). Wool is not only warm, but it also sheds water, and if it does get wet, it is still good insulation. Except for the already mentioned Interior summer heat, there are few places in Alaska where a pair of wool pants and a wool shirt will not feel good year round. You will see some old-time Alaskans wearing dark green wool whipcord pants and matching battle jacket, a light wool shirt, and a bolo tie with a gold or ivory Native artwork clasp: this was once known as the "Alaska Tuxedo." Another popular piece of clothing, especially in the Southeast and other fishing areas, is referred to as a "Halibut Jacket"; this is simply a heavy wool shirt. If wool is hard to come by where you live, you'll find a good selection of wool clothing in places like Juneau. (If you can find a pair of tight-knit wool gloves, they will give you a lot of comfort in Alaska's summertime.) Remember not to wash or dry-clean wool any more than is absolutely necessary: lanolin is removed by cleaning processes of any kind, and the lanolin is what gives wool some of its marvelous qualities. Since good wool has the property of shedding dirt as well as water, quality wool clothing can be kept clean without washing or dry-cleaning for a surprisingly long time. When you get it home from a trip, give your wool clothing a good brushing, spot clean it with a cloth wrung out in cold water, and hang it in the sun. Store it, of course, with mothballs.

The Onion or the Artichoke

When you dress for the outdoors in Alaska, use layers of clothing. (Some people refer to this as the artichoke method, some as the onion; take your choice.) The air trapped between the layers provides excellent insulation; it also allows condensed body heat to dry, thus avoiding the dampness of perspiration. A further advantage is that it is easy to regulate how much clothing you want or need for the current temperature. The best outer layer for summer is a light, windproof (and, if possible, breathable) waterproof parka with a hood and a front zipper that makes it easy to get into and out of. A hood avoids drafts around your neck and, if it is cold, you can add a snug wool cap. If you are carrying a sweater, a cardigan is convenient. In harsh weather, you can let the layering system help keep your hands warm: wear your wool gloves inside a pair of ski mitts, or, if the weather is wet, wear your gloves inside a large pair of fisherman's gloves (available in marine supply shops).

Other Tips

Try replacing the buttons on your shirt sleeves with Velcro tabs; this makes it easy to roll your sleeves up and down if you want to. Buy shirts with enough pockets; pockets can provide many needed places to keep "everything in its place." Be sure your shirt pockets have fold-over flaps and buttons (or Velcro tabs) to keep things from falling out when, for example, you lean over a swift-flowing stream to get a drink. When you are wearing rubber boots, pull your socks over the bottoms of your pants—this is not only tidier, but it makes getting boots on easier. Use large rubber bands to cinch your pants around your ankles when hiking through brush. Avoid pants with cuffs; cuffs collect debris that falls out inside your tent.

Waterproofing

Seam-sealing is a real necessity for tents and rain gear if you are going into country where it rains, so don't stint on it.

What raingear you use in Alaska will depend upon the kind of outdoor activity you will be doing. For canoers or raft travelers who aren't going to be getting steady or heavy exercise, a good fisherman's waterproof outfit may be the answer. You'll find a selection at Alaska stores, especially in Southeast. Hikers and backpackers who want a lighter garment have more of a choice. There are several companies making lightweight raingear that is supposed to be both waterproof—and to breathe. For a while, I found Goretex to be unreliable, but some of my friends now swear by it. Others prefer Peter Storm, which I have not tried recently. You may want to shop around, but for Alaska, just be sure that you have rain protection that you can depend on.

Important Incidentals

Someone once said that to really see and appreciate Alaska, you need both a telescope and a microscope, and it is true that you will enjoy your travels more and certainly add further dimensions to your Alaska experience if you carry field glasses and a small magnifying lens. The magnifying lens is perfect for looking closely at the incredibly beautiful structure of flowers and examining other small flora of the tundra and forests. Both glasses and lens should be lightweight, inexpensive, and, if possible, waterproof. If you are going to do any kayaking or river-running, field glasses that float are a good idea. If you cannot find bright orange binoculars—they are available—be sure to tie or stick bright orange tape on your binoculars and tie bright orange yarn on your small lens so that they will be easy to see if dropped on the ground. A brightly colored string or a leather thong makes a good necklace on which to wear your small viewer.

Tips for Photographers

Unless you're a professional photographer, you'll find a small lightweight single-lens-reflex camera more than adequate in Alaska, and it will certainly add pleasurable freedom to your travels. Remember the telescope and the microscope idea. It is worth carrying a long lens (minimum 200 mm with a 2× ring) and a macro or micro lens, or you can opt for a zoom lens. A wide-angle lens is also desirable, indeed, a necessity for many scenic vistas. (Either a 28 mm or 35 mm is a good choice.) Since it is all too easy in Alaska to get your photographic equipment wet, especially in the Southeast, a good waterproof camera bag is an excellent investment. If you can't afford one, then heavy plastic bags are a must.

Again, be sure to tie string or stick tape that's bright orange onto your camera, camera equipment, and camera bag. It can be virtually impossible to find a small dark object like a camera, field glasses, or even a camera bag in Alaska's wilderness. I learned this the hard way on a foothill of Mount

McKinley when I put my camera down in the tundra during a lunch stop and inadvertently went off without it. A two-hour search, initiated almost immediately, proved unsuccessful, and my camera (a beloved Nikkormat with a Micro lens) was gone forever.

If you like to work with high-speed film you will find it well suited to many situations in Alaska where the light is often not very strong. I always take along a few rolls of ASA 100, 200, and 400. ASA 64, however, is a good all-around film and is preferable in glacier country and on bright winter days. Note that in extremely cold weather, film and/or fingers can freeze.

Carry your unexposed film in a bag of one color and your exposed film in a bag of another color. This helps to keep things separate and readily identifiable. I like to buy prepaid-development film, or prepaid-development mailers (available at Recreational Equipment Inc.) and send my exposed film off when I get to a post office. This has several advantages: it lightens the weight I carry, lessens the chance of losing or damaging exposed film, and my developed pictures or slides are waiting for me when I get home.

Travel Light

A final word of advice: keep your gear to a reasonable minimum. You will want to spend your time and energy in Alaska doing other things besides packing, sorting, and hauling gear. Always keep your things organized. This will save you a remarkable amount of time and trouble.

TWENTY NECESSITIES FOR ALASKAN ADVENTURING

PLEASE NOTE: Except for the extra clothes, all of the following items are small, lightweight, and easily carried in a day pack. (You can separate them into plastic bags, if you wish.) The dozen starred (*) items are an absolute must whenever you leave civilization in Alaska; I recommend that you carry these items with you routinely.

Item	Comment
*Knife	Swiss Army knife with scissors (recommended) or hunting knife.
Space blanket	Use for wind, rain, and/or cold.
*First aid kit	If nothing else, carry Band-Aids and a small piece of soap to clean any wound.
Bandana or diaper	Wonderful multipurpose item. Can be used for bandage, sweatband, towel, hot pad, napkin, scarf, head net, and so on.

Item	Comment
Safety pins	Pin a couple into your hatband or along an inner seam of your parka.
*Sierra Club cup or one similar to hang on your belt	Another multipurpose item, useful for noisemaking to keep bears away, and for washing small wounds, heating water for tea or bouillon, etc., and, incidentally, for scooping water from a stream to drink.
*Extra candy bars and/or nuts and/or gorp; a tea bag or two and/or bouillon cubes	Survival fare.
*Extra clothes	Wear a tee shirt and shorts, if you like, but *always* have wool pants, a warm shirt, parka (if possible, waterproof), and warm headgear and handgear in your pack—*survival items*.
*Waterproof matches	Dip big kitchen matches in melted wax.
Old candle stub	Fire starter deluxe.
*Flashlight	Check batteries before starting or carry a flare.
*Maps	So you'll know where you're at.
*Compass	Know how to use it in the higher latitudes.
*Toilet paper	Please cover it with rocks, or bury it; think how you feel when you find someone else's.
*Sunglasses	Requisites for snow or water travel. In fact, the sun's angle in winter makes these a year-round necessity.
Bug juice or other insect repellent	People swear by Muskol and good old U.S. Army bug juice. Cutter's Insect Repellent stick has the advantage of not leaking.
Head net	A small, priceless item.
Gray tape	Roll up a foot or two to carry for emergency repairs. I have friends who use it for blisters.
Waterproof watch or cheap pocket watch	Although you may want to get away from it all, knowing the time can be extremely useful once in a while.
*A general trip plan discussed with at least one other responsible person	Perhaps the most important item of all.

EQUIPMENT LIST FOR KNAPSACKING AND-OR CAMPING IN ALASKAN WILDERNESS

Item	Comment
A good tent, preferably freestanding, with a fly and plenty of stakes	Carry a big sponge, small whisk broom, and a scrap of canvas for a "front porch."
Extra line	
Sleeping bag	Down, or synthetic.
Air mattress or pad	
Backpack	
Small day pack	Brightly colored.
Plastic bags	They keep clothing dry and easy to find.
Toilet kit	Small and light.
Sunburn lotion	Believe it or not!

See lists for Twenty Necessities and Optional but Useful Items.

OPTIONAL BUT USEFUL ITEMS OF CLOTHING AND EQUIPMENT

Light underwear

Light shirt

Broad-brimmed hat

Dental floss

Nail file

Sleep shade

Jeans

Shorts

Wet suit

Bathing suit

Waterproof notebook

Binoculars

Magnifying lens

I make these last two optional reluctantly; they will add so much to your experience.

The Compass

The farther north you travel, the more the needle on your compass will point upward—at Fairbanks it will be only 11 degrees from vertical. The magnetic force centered in the North Pole will also skew your needle to the east of north. Thus in Southeast Alaska, your compass needle will point to between 28 and 31 degrees east of true north. If you're using a USGS map, this difference between magnetic north and true north, or declination, will be shown for the area the map covers; look at the bottom of the page and use your compass accordingly. (Margaret Piggott's book on the Southeast is particularly helpful in this matter, since all of her maps indicate the degree of declination. See Bibliography.)

TRAVELING IN SMALL BOATS

Before the Great Flood, the Koyukon People believe, the rivers in the world ran both upstream and downstream, like two-way highways, and it was possible to travel them in both directions. But after the Flood, Raven took a good look at things before restoring order. He decided that humans had been having too easy a time of it, so he directed the rivers to flow in only one direction, as they do today.

There is no better way to experience the ultimate beauty of Alaska than to travel its waterways in a small, motorless boat, a canoe, a kayak, or perhaps an inflatable raft. As the buoyant waters cradle and carry you, you become an integral part of this great land and move with the flow of the river or with the rhythmic motion of the tidal waters and their currents. Or else you propel yourself naturally, dipping your paddle into the water, and, as you lift the blade, watch the drops fall like small crystal worlds to float briefly before they disappear. The shore slips by, sometimes deeply forested, sometimes a bare sharp cliff or wedge of earth, sometimes a drape of tundra. The air smells clean, perhaps fragrant with lupine or, near the coast, with the faint pungent scent of salt.

The silence of your passage may be broken by the sudden distant roar of rapids, the pure sound of adventure, or the soft sigh of waves meeting the shore may invite you to land and explore unknown territory. You may hear the elemental crash of an iceberg as it leaves its parent glacier or an avalanche of earth crumbling from a riverbank. If the river you travel is glacial, the sibilant hiss of silt against your craft will sound like the cool rustle of silk.

On a clear river, there will nearly always be a mother merganser to race ahead of you with her brood, at first traveling immense distances in an effort to escape you and then, finally, giving up and huddling near the riverbank as you sail by. Eagles may soar above you—or osprey or peregrine, rough-legged hawks, or perhaps a rare horned owl. On any river, you are likely to find shorebirds of one kind or another who have come, like yourself, from a distant place. They will dip and bow, performing deep knee bends on the sand bars. A bear may amble along the shore unconcernedly until, abruptly aware of you, it bolts into the nearest brush. You may pass the neatly constructed lodge of a beaver or see a mink scoot sleekly through the water. Near the coast, you may watch a whale blow, then arch powerfully but easily as it sounds.

To really enjoy traveling by small boat in Alaska, you should be familiar with the kind of craft you'll be using and know what you are doing. Can you right a boat that has capsized—or gotten hung up in midstream—especially if the water is cold and/or rough and the current is swift? Do you know how to get back into your righted boat quickly under such circumstances? If you are kayaking, can you do an Eskimo roll? Can you avoid sweepers in a hurry? Does swift water faze you? If you're traveling in tidal waters, can you read a current table as well as a tide table?

You can find almost any kind of a small-boating experience you want in Alaska, since Alaskan waters vary enormously. The moods of these waters and the Alaskan weather, however, are not predictable. Even the slowest stream or the most placid stretch of a lake or a channel can be suddenly roiled and roughed up by winds or a storm. Therefore this is really not the place for neophytes or would-be small-boaters to venture out for the first time on their own. If you're not experienced in such things as I have mentioned, consider learning about them (whichever ones apply to the kind of boating you have in mind) before you go to Alaska. If this is not possible, then go with someone, or several people, knowledgeable about small-boating in Alaska. Or you can go with an organized commercial outfit; there are some excellent small-boat outings now being conducted in many parts of Alaska that can introduce you to the wonders of this great land in a small, silent craft. (See references throughout this book.)

Some Thoughts About River Travel

Alaska's rivers are still the most magnificently wild rivers remaining in the United States, and there is extraordinary variety among them. You should be able to get a broad overview of them, as well as some idea of the many river-running possibilities they offer, from this book. For further information, you can write the state or federal agency administering any area you are interested in and ask for details about its riverine system. Most of Alaska's rivers have been described for river-running only very recently; some of the information from the public agencies may be based on the experience of only one or two parties—or even on an aerial overview, and this can add to your sense of adventure.

Alaska has rivers that are deep and crystal clear, so clear that flowering

plants can fasten themselves to the riverbed and thrive on the sunshine coming
through the water. These rivers are a particular delight to travel. Alaska also
has rivers that are dense with gray glacial silt and therefore difficult to read.
It has other streams like the Yukon, as well, which are fed by such a mix of
waters from such a variety of watersheds that, like the Mississippi, they are
"too thick to drink but not thick enough to plow."

Like proper rivers anywhere, Alaska's rivers have characters of their own
and they're also very changeable. In high winds, their waves can slow you
down, and, if the wind direction is upstream, you may feel that you're actually
traveling backwards. Summer weather, whether it's heat or storm, can also
change rivers radically, particularly in streams flowing over impermeable
land—be it rock or permafrost. Such waterways can flood dramatically in a
remarkably brief time from either the melt-off of snow in their headwaters,
from rainfall, or from both combined. I once traveled the Alatna River, usually
as clear blue as a fine aquamarine, through a day of rain. That night we made
a very late camp on an island at a place which was at least four feet above
water level. The next morning, the river was lapping at our tent doors; in a
matter of a few hours it had risen a good four feet, doubled in width, and
engulfed the lower riverbanks, drowning the mouths of smaller streams.
Indeed, it looked something like the Mississippi: majestic, roiling with mud,
with flotillas of foam and tree branches sailing down it.

This kind of flooding (also described by Bob Marshall, see Bibliography)
can pose problems for your safety and should always be taken into account on
Arctic and Interior rivers when there is rain or melt-off. It can also be a
nuisance as far as drinking water goes. True, you can let the mud and grit
in the water settle out, but it takes time, and the taste is not likely to be
wonderful.

Braided rivers—there are many of them in Alaska—pose other problems.
You need to travel the main channel if you don't want to get hung up on
barely covered river bars. The explorer Frederick Schwatka told hilarious
accounts of many such happenings when he explored the Yukon in a large
home-made sailing raft. Even experienced river people can be fooled by glacial
waters, and you should be prepared to get in and out of your small craft many
times when you travel in low water on such a stream. Glacial streams are
often swift flowing and always cold; they need to be treated with respect and
good sense.

BEAR ESSENTIALS

If you are very lucky you may get to see one or more of the great Alaska Brown Bear. What a fascinating creature he is! So very human, so concerned with "face." So playful. Watch one climb repeatedly up a steep rocky slope in order to slide on his butt down a snowfield. Watch a sow teaching her cub how to fish in a stream, catching one in her jaws to show how it is done, then carrying the fish ashore to demonstrate that delicious eating and the fun of fishing are closely related. Watch a sow discipline a disobedient cub with a spank which may send it flying through the air. Watch two boars telling each other off.

But aren't bears frightfully powerful and dangerous? Powerful: oh my yes. A bear's great muscles move so smoothly that he seems to flow, and he can run maybe twice as fast as a fast human runner. Dangerous: of course. Dangerous like a car hurtling along the highway. People who cannot accept the chance of meeting sudden death on the road have no choice but to stay out of cars and off the road. People who cannot tolerate the probably more remote chance of being mauled by a bear can simply stay out of the bear's country. No problem at all.

The single most important rule for moving safely in bear country is to let the bear know you are there, bearing in mind always that it is his country; you are the intruder. If you want to see and watch bear, however, then you must move quietly, thereby somewhat increasing the chance of an unexpected encounter. But not to panic. In a secret bear-watching spot where we take people we have several times, while watching bear in a river bottom out in front of us, discovered that there was a people-watching bear behind us having as much fun as we were.

Jack Calvin, Sitka

Almost anywhere you travel in Alaska, you will be sharing the rightful territory of one or more wild animals—great animals like wolves, wolverines, Dall sheep, deer, lynx, arctic foxes, mountain goats, bears, moose, and caribou. This is a rare experience that cannot be duplicated in many parts of the world. Treat these animals and their habitat with respect. As Alaska becomes more and more developed, these animals will become increasingly threatened, and you will not want to add to the pressures being put on them. In certain heavily visited areas, limitations on human use of the animals' habitat have been initiated by federal and state wildlife agencies; these, of course, must be observed. If you plan a wilderness outing elsewhere, you should also check with the appropriate agency to find out if there are sensitive wildlife areas where you plan to visit; avoid these areas. Walk lightly where you do travel; keep your distance, and you may be privileged to see—and to coexist with—some of the most magnificent wildlife remaining on earth.

Always travel with caution but never with fear. Most of Alaska's wild animals, like the wolves and wolverines, lynx, Dall sheep, and foxes, are more anxious to stay out of your way than you are to stay out of theirs. Chances are they will do their best to avoid a face-to-face meeting with you at any cost. (How many times have I framed a perfect wildlife shot in my camera, inadvertently made some small sound, and watched my subject leap from sight.) A small animal like the ground squirrel might not be so spooky and will probably even pose for a portrait. Caribou, especially the males, are not notably timid either. On more than one occasion when floating an Alaskan river, I have watched a fine caribou bull watch me, first with curiosity, then with indifference.

Moose and bears, however, are another matter. When encountered at close quarters, both of these great animals can be dangerous. It is up to you to stay out of their way. Moose are so large and frequently make so much noise that they can usually be easily avoided. The idea is not to get close enough to be kicked or charged. They are also often found in places that are wetter and sloppier than you would probably want to travel through. Females, especially when they have a calf or calves with them, are very protective, but they are also anxious to get away from you as soon as possible.

Bears demand special respect. Remember that they are the top predator in this particular wild animal community. Although they are seldom the active aggressor against a human being, they are unpredictable. Unwanted encoun-

Brown bear (Ursus arctos); *the grizzly is considered to be the same species. Range: throughout Alaska. The smaller black bear* (Ursus americanus) *is more abundant, and is the most widely distributed bear in Alaska. Its color ranges from jet black to brown or cinnamon, with the blue or glacier phase found rarely.*

ters with bears can occur when the bears are surprised and/or when their territory is intruded upon.

I learned this firsthand one late June afternoon on West Chichagof Island. Five of us had been traveling by boat along the coast of this magnificent wilderness island, and we had come ashore for a stroll through an area that had been logged a few years before. It was a soft rainy afternoon, a little misty and mysterious, with big old stumps looming out of the fog. We fell silent as we spread out along the road, musing over the way the forest had been removed or simply thinking our own thoughts. I was second in line, walking behind a young man of considerable strength and size who had a longer stride than I, and he soon disappeared from sight ahead of me. After rounding a bend in the road, he suddenly reappeared, racing toward me and yelling, "Bear—get out of here." Then he disappeared as he sped back down the road.

Without thinking, I turned and sprinted after him, passing his wife who, in turn, followed me. Down around another curve, the only Alaskan in our party was standing with my husband in the middle of the road waving his arms and yelling a stream of imprecations that quite surprised me, even in my state of shock, for he is one of the most gently spoken people I have ever met. My husband was doing a good imitation as well and, stopping to join them and the other two in our party, I looked back and saw the bear.

It was a brownie, a creature so large that I thought he was standing on his hind legs until I realized that he had halted on all fours to survey the situation. He was making sounds which, to me, sounded like the roaring of a lion. (I have since learned that bears are properly said to "woof" or to "bellow.") The two men were making a real racket by now, and finally the bear grew quiet. After what seemed an eternity, the bear turned and ambled off in the opposite direction. We made a quick and quiet retreat to the boat and, thoroughly shaken, congratulated ourselves on being alive.

We were, of course, lucky to have escaped unscathed from such a face-to-face encounter with a brown bear, but the incident took place only because of our own thoughtlessness. We were the intruders, the uninvited guests in the bear's territory, and we had failed to make our presence known. The first member of our party had come unexpectedly upon the animal. Walking quietly around the bend in the road, he had met the brownie practically head-on—and he had made the mistake of running. Two other members of the party (including myself) had compounded this mistake, quite understandably, because there was no place to hide, no tree to climb. Except for the presence of mind and the bear expertise of our Alaskan friend, who is an old hand in the Alaskan wilderness, we could easily have had at least one serious injury among us. (Recent studies also suggest that a large group has a better chance of bluffing a bear successfully—another reason not to travel alone.) We learned our lesson and added another bear story to the Alaskan anthology of bear encounters with happy endings.

The lesson was, of course, that you must announce your presence when you travel in bear country and cannot see or be seen easily. Make some kind of noise as you walk. Some old-time Alaskans strap a tin can half full of pebbles onto their packs; others tie a bell to their belts or bang on a tin can as they walk. (A Sierra Club cup makes a good loud clang, especially when struck with your spoon.) You can lace bells onto your boots or you may want to sing, or even play your harmonica. Field biologists working for the Alaska Department of Fish and Game have been known to set off firecrackers when they were working in areas with high bear concentrations along salmon streams. You can also, when possible, walk with your back to the wind. This gives the bear the added warning of your scent. Whistling is not recommended since it may inadvertently suggest that you are another wild animal.

If you are traveling cross-country, as you will be in most wilderness areas of Alaska, choose where you walk with care. Avoid willow patches and other brushy places, especially along salmon streams when the salmon are running. Keep a sharp eye out in rolling terrain where there are berry patches. A browsing bear can be invisible in a hollow while feasting on blueberries. Also, beware if you smell decomposing meat; avoid the source of the smell, for it is likely that any bear in the vicinity will be at work on the carcass.

Travel with care on any game trail through brushy country or through forests or any other area where you cannot be easily seen. Never, *never*, make your camp on a game trail; this simply invites disaster. Game trails used by bears are easily identifiable. They are likely to run along the banks of rivers and every now and then down to the stream. There are almost always several near salmon streams. These trails may also lead into berry patches, and they frequently cross the low points of ridges. Bear trails usually have been worn into two well-traveled lanes, about the distance apart of a bear's legs, and you may find occasional large bear footprints, as bears like to step in the same place over and over again.

When you camp in the wilderness, you should pitch your tent downwind from any evidence of bears, such as scat or dug-up earth. The most effective bear insurance of all for campers is to keep an immaculate camp. Despite what you have been taught in the lower 48, do clean your fish into the stream or river in Alaska, being sure the offal gets into the current and is carried away. (Decomposing fish contribute important nutrients to Alaska's fast-running streams.) Burn or pack out any garbage you have left after eating, and wash your dishes well. The U.S. Forest Service says that improper waste disposal is a primary cause of "problem bears."

Never keep food inside your tent, and never leave food lying around. If there are trees around, wrap your supplies in double plastic bags; if you have a heavy cloth or burlap bag, use that too for added strength. Tie this bundle on a rope and sling it over a branch out of the reach of bears. If there are no trees, wrap your food as described and stash it as far away from your tent as is practical. Well-packaged, dehydrated or freeze-dried food and canned food are less attractive to bears than fresh food and meat. The National Park Service advises campers to cook and eat 200 feet or more away from their tents.

If you camp in a frequently visited area where the bears have become relatively tame and accustomed to being fed, your bear problems may be worse than when you are in the wilderness. Keep in mind that in Alaska it is illegal to feed bears (and other wild animals). It is also extremely dangerous—both to yourself and to the bear. Expecting food and being inadvertantly provoked, a bear may injure you and end up being shot for the "offense". If you care about your own safety and the animal's right to survival, don't treat a bear like a pet. It is a wild animal.

It is particularly important to avoid close encounters with a female bear (sow) that has her cub or cubs with her. These charming animal families are safely viewed only from a long way off—through your field glasses or the telephoto lens of your camera. Never make the mistake, which has cost more than one eager photographer serious injury or even a life, of trying to get a close up of bear cubs. If you're into wildlife photography, keep in mind that a good telephoto lens is a lot cheaper than a stay in the hospital.

If, despite all precautions, you do surprise a bear at close range, try not to panic. A startled bear will frequently simply let out a "woof" and run. (If this sound reminds you of a dog, remember that dogs are evolutionary descendants of bears.) The bear, however, may stand its ground, rear up on its hind legs, and swing its head from side to side; this is an effort to try to see what and/or who you are. This is the time to yell and wave your arms. Bears have generally poor eyesight, but they can distinguish motion easily, and they have sharp ears. Sometimes a bear will turn sideways and pose, as though showing off its muscles. This is supposed to intimidate you (it undoubtedly will), and it is a signal that you should leave. Another signal is when a bear pops its teeth or lets out a series of loud "woofs" in a sound that is routinely described as being "like air being forced out of a bellows." Never "woof" or bellow back at a bear or imitate its actions, which may well be body language indicating hostility. *Do not run.* Bears have a critical range of up to 50 yards and, if you possibly can, back slowly out of it, always facing the bear. Or, if it's a grizzly or brown bear, climb a tree if one is handy and you have time. (Black bears are tree-climbers.) If there is no place to go and the bear comes toward you, drop your hat or jacket for it to smell. Should all your cool-headed efforts fail to deter the bear, and it decides to attack you, drop to the side of the trail onto your stomach or curl up into a ball, clasp your hands behind your neck to protect your head, and stay as still as possible. Play dead. Bears which attack when they feel threatened usually won't bother someone they think they have killed.

If you are familiar with guns, you may consider packing one with you to protect yourself against bears when you travel in Alaska's wilderness. There are two distinct schools of thought among Alaskans about carrying weapons into the bush. One school argues that a gun is not only heavy and dangerous but also unnecessary. Our Alaskan friend who fended off the bear on West Chichagof Island shares this opinion. He believes that by the time you can get ready to shoot a charging bear, for example, it will probably be too late. If you succeed in only wounding the animal, you will be in an even more serious situation with a wounded, infuriated bear for an adversary. Those who do not tote guns also point out that too many bears are killed needlessly by trigger-happy people who are unfamiliar with these great animals. There is the further chance that people not thoroughly used to high-powered weapons will kill or injure themselves or another person instead of the bear.

In the opposite camp, there are many Alaskans who would not think of going into the bush, or at least into known bear country, without a gun. These people feel that a firearm not only gives them control over many risky variables in potentially dangerous situations, but it adds greatly to their confidence— an important factor since body language may influence whether or not a bear will attack. They feel, too, that in camp situations where a bear chooses to invade human space in search of food, a gun is essential. On long, cross-country treks, they point out, the loss of your food supply could be disastrous. They grant that guns are cumbersome and potentially dangerous, but argue that knowing how and when to use a gun can effectively remove the hazards. They recommend a twelve-gauge shotgun loaded with either 00 buckshot or rifled slugs, rifles larger than 30-06 or pistols chambered for .357 magnum or larger cartridge. And they emphasize being familiar with your firearm and understanding how to use it.

If you do decide to carry a gun for protection, you will not need to get a hunting license in Alaska. (You are not permitted, however, to carry a pistol into Canada.) If you should be forced to kill a bear to save your own or someone else's life, do not just leave the dead animal. Alaska law requires that you turn over the skin and skull of a bear killed in self-defense to the Alaska Department of Fish and Game.

All public land agencies in Alaska are anxious to help you avoid a human-bear encounter. Consult them when you travel Alaska's wilderness. The pamphlet, *The Bears and You*, published by the Alaska Department of Fish and Game (ADF&G) is also recommended reading: it is available at many federal as well as state information centers in Alaska, or you can write for it to ADF&G, Subport Building, Juneau, AK 99811.

With all these warnings, it is important to remember that you are far less likely to be injured or killed by a bear in Alaska's wilderness than you are driving on an Alaskan highway. Odds of being in a serious auto accident in Alaska are fifty times greater than those of being in a serious bear encounter, and Alaska's highway accident rate is lower than those of many other states. While a bear incident makes headlines all over the country, an auto accident is usually just one more statistic. As noted earlier, be cautious in Alaska's wilderness, but do not be afraid.

THE BUSH

Alaskans refer to the great roadless area that comprises most of their state as "the bush" and to small isolated communities as bush communities or bush villages. (The federal government actually classifies the entire state of Alaska except for Anchorage as "rural"—Fairbanks and the capital, Juneau, notwithstanding.) The bush is homeland to most of Alaska's Native people and to many sturdy emigrants who have homesteaded (in past decades), mined, or acquired land by other means, choosing to leave the pressures of urban life to adopt an elemental life-style.

You will find some of Alaska's most interesting residents living in the bush. Some may have migrated from universities or businesses or simply have been ambitious and rugged individualists who succeeded in making it on their own in an extraordinarily beautiful if difficult and demanding environment. (It's too bad that there isn't enough of Alaska to go around for all the people who might have the same idea!) People in the bush are routinely strong, independent, and careful—or they wouldn't survive. Many are also extremely ingenious and add many gracious amenities to their basic subsistence in the midst of the wilderness.

Many bush families make their living by being outfitters, professional guides (hunting or otherwise), and/or bush pilots, or by operating wilderness lodges. If you stay at a wilderness lodge, therefore, say at Thayer Lake Lodge on Admiralty Island or the Hornbergers' Koksetna Camp at Lake Clark or at the Coles' Camp Denali in Denali National Park, you will have a chance to get acquainted with the uniquely Alaskan bush way of life. This can give you insights into Alaska and a feeling for it that you otherwise could not have. It is highly recommended if you can afford it.

THE ALASKAN BUSH PILOT AND HIS REMARKABLE FLYING MACHINE

In the wonderfully vast roadless area that is most of Alaska, the way people get around is by air, usually in a small airplane. This explains why Alaska sets the record for small-plane use in the United States and on several scores. Of any state, Alaska has the highest per capita ownership of small planes; there is one plane for approximately every 75 Alaskans. It has the greatest percentage of pilots, by far; one out of every 45 Alaskans is a licensed aircraft operator, twelve times the national average. Alaska has the greatest number of float-planes (planes equipped with pontoons rather than wheels). Lake Spenard in Anchorage is not just the busiest floatplane base in the United States but in the world, and Merrill Field in Anchorage, used by small-wheeled aircraft, is just behind San Francisco International Airport in volume of traffic (in 1977, there were 348,000 takeoffs and landings). Merrill ranks twentieth among the nation's most heavily used airports. Small wonder that if you stand on an Anchorage corner on a clear summer day, you will probably see a small plane almost anywhere you look in the sky.

From all of this, you will gather that most Alaskans, particularly those who live in the bush or find their recreation in it, get in and out of small airplanes as casually as you do your own automobile or the corner bus. If you're to do any off-the-track travel (or even on-the-track travel in places) in Alaska, you will have to go by small plane, too. If you have not flown much in small planes, it might take some getting used to, but it's worth it. Small planes can not only take you where you want to go in the wilderness and bring you back, but they can also give you the opportunity to view the country from a relatively low altitude, traveling at a relatively slow speed. You can see the grandeur of the country much more intimately than you would from a jet, and you can also put things into a manageable perspective. Furthermore, flying in a small plane offers you chances to see animals like bears and moose, as well as nesting pairs of trumpeter swans and other birds, which you might not see as comfortably on the ground—or might not see at all. (It's pretty exciting, too, to fly with and past a bald eagle, as you very well may do.) I fly in a small plane

Merrill Pass, near Anchorage, the kind of landmark pass crossed routinely by Alaska's bush pilots. Source: National Park Service.

in Alaska whenever I have the chance; flights in small aircraft have given me some of my most memorable views, and best photographs as well.

Although Alaska's small planes may look fragile and as if they have been around for a long time (they probably have), they are usually sturdy, reliable vehicles. As noted, many are on floats, which lets them land on Alaska's many lakes and the wider rivers throughout the state, and some are amphibious. But even when they are equipped only with wheels, they can and do land in a remarkable variety of places under a truly remarkable variety of conditions.

If you are any kind of a small airplane buff, you'll have a field day in Alaska. You'll find Widgeons, Beavers, Otters, Grumman Goose, Beechcraft, Cherokees, Cessnas, Piper Cubs, and Supercubs routinely. D-C 3s—among the greatest airplanes ever built—still fly the Aleutian chain, and not too long ago, an old PBY bomber from World War II was carrying passengers in its bomb bay on scheduled flights in the Southeastern part of the state.

In the Arctic regions, you'll find that most of the small planes, even those used for scheduled flights, have a single engine. This is because it saves a lot of time (and is cheaper and easier) to warm up one engine in minus-50-degree weather than it is to service two. Single-engine planes haul around a lot besides people: furniture, groceries, cases of beer, game. I once was the next passenger after a moose in a Piper Cub, and I still haven't figured out how the pilot got the moose into and out of a plane so small it crowded even me. Sometimes you will see various things strapped on the outside of small planes, but large items such as canoes are generally taboo (according to FAA regulations, that is). Be sure to check with your bush pilot, now frequently known as an air-taxi pilot, if you need to transport this kind of gear.

Chances are that you will find your bush pilot—particularly if he has been around for a while—an especially interesting Alaskan. Alaska's bush pilots are members of a legendary fellowship and hold a special place in Alaskan history.

The first bush pilot to arrive in Alaska was Roy F. Jones, a World War I aviator for the U.S. Signal Corps. After the war, he picked up a surplus Curtiss flying boat and outfitted it in Seattle with a 90 horsepower Hispana Suiza engine, christening it the *Northbird*. In 1922, he flew the *Northbird* up the Inside Passage, and, on July 17, he landed it on the waters of the Tongass Narrows, right outside of Ketchikan. Without knowing it, Jones thus initiated a new era in Alaska. The *Northbird*'s battered, brass-feathered propeller now hangs on the wall of Ketchikan's air terminal.

During the next decades, the bush pilots—often flying for the U.S. Fish and Wildlife Service or on other federal missions—explored Alaska's territory as it had not been explored before. They were the first to see what today has become commonplace for the thousands who fly around Alaska. They saw the immensity of the frozen land and how intricately the frost action had patterned it—pitting and pocking it, drawing it into scallops on steep slopes, and fracturing it into laceworks of polygons. They discovered the vastness of the southeastern snowfields, the beauty of hanging glaciers cupped in dark ragged rock, the incredible size of the Malaspina Glacier with its pattern of black and white stripes. They were the first to see the extent of the Kobuk and Koyokuk dunes, sand dunes that lie far inland from the ocean. They saw the thousands of lakes that dot the Arctic Slope and the wind-blown silt from Arctic rivers smoking against the pale skies. They saw the slow rivers of the Interior winding across the land in sinuous curves.

They flew in every kind of weather, by moonlight, through darkness (carrying a lantern to mark their location should they lose their way and a friend need to find them), and past erupting volcanoes when the cinders rained around them like hail. Of necessity, they flew by the seat of their pants, for there were no maps and no weather reports to guide them; they followed the great rivers—the Yukon, the Porcupine, the Kuskokwim, the Copper, the Yentna—even as earlier wingless explorers had.

Bush pilots flew to the most distant and smallest Native communities, performing amazing takeoffs and landings and using any near-level spot they could find. They brought not only access but change everywhere they went. Early on, they began to carry the mail, ending the legendary dog-team mail service in Alaska. They hauled in not only mail and food supplies, but also missionaries and doctors, some of whom became bush pilots themselves. They brought, often for the first time, news from around the world—along with sport hunters and many other people from Outside (even as they do today).

From the early twenties until the mid fifties when the Distant Early Warning Stations (DEW Line) went in (with time out for World War II), the bush pilots seemed to own Alaska. There were almost no rules and regulations to check their adventures, and they could fly where and very much how they chose. They became folk heroes of a sort, and rarely have there been more romantic heroes. Expert flyers, they wove tenuous lifelines into the bush and were often willing to risk their lives for the people who lived there—daring to land in the most inaccessible places to rescue a stranded hunter or to save the life of a dying child. Many died, themselves, as a result.

The stories about Alaska's bush pilots are legion. Noel Wien, one of the greatest, refused to use a map even when maps were finally available: he carried the physiognomy of Alaska around in his head until he died. Archie Ferguson from Kotzebue loved to fly and yet he never learned how to land a plane: "Every landing he made was a controlled crash." During World War II, when the Army took over in Alaska and tried to lay down the law, Ferguson flew merrily into Nome, which was off limits. When the control tower challenged him he replied hoarsely: "I got only one engine," and they let him land. He always flew, of course, a single-engine plane. Jay Hammond, the governor of Alaska, broke both ankles landing a Piper Cub at King Cove rather than endanger children skating on the frozen lake that was the landing field.

Over the years, many pilots homesteaded land and patented hunting and fishing camps in some of Alaska's choicest wilderness. They made their living in part as hunting and fishing guides, and some still do. In the process, they managed to more or less divide Alaska up into their own territories: thus if you flew out of Kotzebue in the 1930s, chances were you would have flown with a Ferguson (and you still might); if you flew out of King Salmon in the 1950s or 1960s—or even the 1970s—you would likely have flown with Dick Jensen or Jay Hammond. The tradition continues, particularly in the more remote parts of the state. If you're going into the Arctic Wildlife Range, for instance, you'll probably fly with Walt Audi's outfit out of Kaktovik (Barter Island), which services this region of Alaska.

Whenever I can, I fly with an old-timer, for there are still quite a few of them around. (There are old pilots and bold pilots, the saying goes, but no old bold pilots.) Pilots like Walt Audi are so familiar with their country that they know where they are even when the fog is so thick you can't see ground. There are many good newer pilots, of course, flyers who have gotten bored with piloting jets or who are fresh from the armed services or who have simply fallen in love with Alaska. Sooner or later, they learn their way around the bush, but it may take a while. I once flew in a helicopter with an ex-marine who had just arrived from Texas. He got lost the minute he left the road between Fairbanks to Circle, which is where the road ends. Heading for the Charley River, we flew instead within sight of the Wrangell Mountains and had to set down on hillsides twice to lay out the maps—and eat blueberries—before we finally ended up using the Yukon River for navigation.

Experienced bush pilots may fly in conditions that may petrify you if you have not flown before in Alaska. However, they will usually know what they are doing, and you have to respect their judgment (and remember that they, too, want to keep on living). Accidents happen most often when the pilot is pushed too hard. People have lost their lives trying to keep a particular engagement that seemed more important than dangerous flying conditions. When you travel in a small plane, don't be in a hurry and do keep your schedule flexible. If your pilot doesn't want to fly because of one reason or another, abide by his decision.

When you fly around Alaska in the summer, expect to wait at both ends of your trip. Bush pilots do most of their year's business during the summer season, and they try to pack in as much as possible. This usually works fine if the weather is good. Poor flying conditions, however, can cause major delays. I once waited for days in Kaktovik when a wintry storm hit the area in early July—but I was lucky. There were twenty people stacked up behind me who waited even longer. We went out in our proper order, and our party finally took off one midnight and flew into the headwaters of the Kongakut River in the very early morning, delighted that we could make it. You are even more likely to wait on the other end of your trip. Don't worry if your pilot fails to show up on time, and rejoice if he does. Carry extra food, a pack of playing cards or an extra paperback or two, just in case. He'll make it when he safely can.

If you're laying out the logistics of an Alaskan wilderness trip on your own, plan to fly commercial as far as you can before you charter. Try for a scheduled mail carrier to more remote places. You will want to rent the smallest air-taxi you can that can still handle your gear. If you have a lot of gear, balance the cost of a larger plane versus two trips in a smaller plane—assuming, of course, that your air-taxi operator gives you a choice. Keep in mind that you will have to pay for a round-trip unless you're lucky enough to find passengers to take your place.

In many parts of Alaska, you'll need to carry your own stove because of lack of wood. It is, however, against federal regulations to carry gasoline on any commercial flight, so choose your cooking equipment accordingly if you're flying a scheduled carrier on any leg of your Alaska trip.

Chances are you'll travel in a floatplane on most of your air-taxi journeys into the bush. If you're in a Beaver for the first time, don't panic when, at takeoff, the plane appears to be going underwater; this is only an illusion. If you're not wearing hip boots on such an outing (and you probably won't be), expect to get a ride, piggyback, on your pilot's shoulders from the plane to the shore if you land in fairly deep water. (Bush pilots of floatplanes routinely wear hip boots.) This is standard practice when the plane cannot be brought close enough in to a reasonably dry landing spot.

Enjoy your travels in Alaska's small planes. They can provide you with some of the best memories—and best stories to tell—of your wilderness adventure. Even though times are changing in Alaska, the bush pilot with his remarkable flying machine still plays a very special role in the Alaska experience.

WHO TAKES CARE OF ALASKA'S LANDS

Your travels in Alaska will take you for the most part through lands administered by the federal or state government. These lands have recently been the subject of much, and often bitter, contention. Indeed, public land ownership and administration in Alaska remains a primary concern and is a frequent and lively topic in the news media and in a good deal of conversation. You're apt to hear the phrase "D-2 lands" spat out with disgust or mutterings about the "feds' big lock-up" or how the freedom of the hills is a thing of the past. The following will provide some background for understanding what this is all about.

Historically, the Native people of Alaska had a sense of territory, but the land in general was looked upon as a kind of vast commons—nobody owned it. The Europeans who started appropriating Alaska in the mid-eighteenth century had, of course, a very different land ethic, but they failed to make any treaty with the Natives spelling out just how different that ethic was. Nor did the United States make any final land settlement with the Natives when it acquired Alaska in 1867—beyond guaranteeing them their "historic rights." Thus the 375 million acres of Alaska purchased by the United States simply became part of the "vacant and unappropriated" public domain, and—although nobody thought about it that way—the stage was set for the eventual subdivision of these acres.

A few communities, homesteads, mining claims, trade and manufacturing sites (five-acre parcels), etc., took a nibble here and there out of the whole, but no major federal land withdrawal from Alaska's public domain occurred until the national forests were roughly delineated and set aside soon after the turn of the century. Further withdrawals continued during the following decades with the establishment of the first national parks, the Navy Petroleum Reserve (Pet 4) in the Arctic, military reservations, Indian reservations, the U.S. Fish and Wildlife Service refuges, and large power withdrawals. By the time statehood was decreed for Alaska in 1959, the disposition of the land had come this far:

Federal Land Reserves	Acres
National Forests	20,700,000
National Parks and Monuments	6,900,000
Wildlife Refuges and Ranges	7,800,000
Navy Petroleum Reserve No. 4	23,000,000
Power Reserves, etc.	27,400,000
Indian Reservations, School Reserves, etc. (BIA)	4,100,000
Military Reservations	2,300,000
Other	200,000
	92,400,000
Private ownership, patented and certified	700,000
Unperfected entries	600,000
Vacant, unappropriated public domain lands (BLM)	271,800,000
Total Alaska land:	365,500,000*

*From: Alaska, A Challenge in Conservation by Richard A. Cooley. Estimates of total land acreage vary.

The Statehood Act gave Alaska 104 million acres to be selected out of this enormous reservoir of public domain, as well as the rights to all tidelands (35 to 40 million acres) and navigable waters (another 8 to 12 million acres). The first state selections, however, ran head on into Native resistance, and the Native people in turn began to lay claim to land that they identified as belonging to them historically and legally, in light of the failure of Congress to settle their legitimate claims. (At one point during the 1960s, because of overlapping claims, more than 375 million acres of Alaska land had been spoken for by the Natives.) In 1966, Secretary of the Interior Stewart Udall froze all land disposition in Alaska pending settlement of the Natives' claims. Among other things, this brought an end to homesteading, which—based as it was on land laws drawn up with the east coast of America in mind—had always been an incongruous, frequently destructive, and prohibitively expensive method of acquiring Alaskan land.

In 1971, the Congress passed the Alaska Native Claims Settlement Act (ANCSA), and a huge step was taken in the subdivision of Alaska. Under terms of this exceedingly complicated act (which has made Alaska a lawyer's paradise during the past few years), the state was divided into twelve Native Regional Corporations, each of which would receive acreage according to its historic land use and the number of its corporate members. (One region, Doyon, in the Interior, ended up with over twelve million acres, the largest corporate holding in the United States.) Every Native village was also mandated to be a profit-making or non-profit-making corporation (or both), which would receive from one to three townships of land according to the number of its stockholders, that is, Native villagers. (To qualify as a Native one had to be born before December 1971 and have at least one Native grandparent.) In all, some 44 million acres would pass into Native ownership—as private property—as would nearly one billion dollars from the federal government and from state oil royalties.

The terms of this act also decreed, under its section 17: d-2, the setting aside of at least 80 million acres of "national interest" or conservation lands for the protection, more or less, of their unique and superlative values. (These are the d-2 lands.) Congress implemented this measure in December 1980, after nine years of struggling to identify these lands, with the passage of Public Law 96-487, the Alaska National Interest Lands Conservation Act (ANILCA). The land situation in Alaska now looks something like this—subject to final conveyances under ANILCA:

Federal Land Reserves	Acres
National Forests	22,900,000
National Parklands	52,000,000
Wildlife Refuges and Ranges	76,100,000
Wild and Scenic Rivers	1,200,000
Military Reservations	3,000,000
	155,200,000
State Selections: does not include tidelands (Not yet completed)	104,500,000
Private Ownership	
Native Selections (Not yet completed)	44,000,000
Other	1,300,000
Vacant Unappropriated Public Domain Lands (BLM)	70,000,000
Total Alaska Lands:	375,000,000

Acreages are approximate.

Each federal agency that administers lands in Alaska (and elsewhere) has a different charge and a different emphasis in the way it handles its lands. Thus the U.S. Forest Service is dedicated to "Multiple Use" (harvesting timber, protecting watersheds, recreation, wilderness, wildlife, and so forth, and it allows for mining, hunting, gathering firewood, and such). The National

Park Service is dedicated to the preservation of its lands "in perpetuity" and, simultaneously, to making the lands available for the use and enjoyment of the general public. (This dual purpose has led to many conflicts in land administration, and the National Park Service has been charged with both overprotection and overdevelopment.) Hunting, mining, and the use of motorized vehicles off the beaten track are traditionally prohibited in national parks; however, the legislation placing some 43 million more acres of Alaska's lands into the National Park Service has established numerous "preserves," which allow for sports hunting and, in places, the use of snowmobiles, and all of the new National Park Service lands in Alaska allow for subsistence use by Alaskans where it has been established historically.

The U.S. Fish and Wildlife Service is charged with the management and enhancement of the habitats of the fauna living on its lands (the state manages the fish and game, per se, except for sea mammals, which are under the protection of the U.S. Departments of Commerce and Interior). The Fish and Wildlife Service also allows for hunting and mining under its regulations. The Bureau of Land Management, which for so long had almost no strings tied to the uses of the land under its aegis, has less stringent land-use restrictions than any other federal agency, although under the terms of its 1975 Organic Act, it has new powers and opportunities for protecting as well as managing the public domain. All of these agencies—except for the U.S. Forest Service, which is part of the Department of Agriculture—belong under the Department of the Interior.

Note that while the acreage of the National Park Service has increased about sevenfold in the past few years, the BLM-administered public domain has shrunk to less than a third of what it once was. This is one thing that has upset certain Alaskans who feel they should be able to use "their" land however they want to, as they have in the past. Of course, all public lands are the property equally of every United States citizen.

Each of these federal agencies has recreation as one of its primary, specific uses. As you adventure in Alaska, you can get a great deal of information and help from the agency administering the land you visit if you will call on it. Since this is your land, you should avail yourself of their services and you should also, it goes without saying, do your part to take care of Alaska's wilderness lands.

This book tells of the superlative recreational opportunities you will find on Alaska's publicly administered lands. It may, however, be necessary for you to pass through Native-owned private property or to fly into or out of Native-owned villages to reach these lands. You should, of course, respect the property rights of these new landowners as you would those of anybody else. Permission to use Native lands should be requested. (See section on Visiting Native Villages.)

Note: the Heritage, Conservation, and Recreation Service (HCRS), a bureau of the Department of the Interior, was abolished by Secretary James

Watt in 1981. Before its dissolution, HCRS had been charged with studying the rivers of Alaska and evaluating them for possible Wild River classification. During the past several years, HCRS published two guides to river-running in Alaska: *Alaska Float Trips, Southwest Region*; and *Alaska Float Trips, North of the Arctic Circle*. These guides are the best available for river-running in these regions in Alaska: write the National Park Service 2525 Gambell, Anchorage, AK 99503.

VISITING NATIVE VILLAGES

One summer afternoon a few years ago I was in Fort Yukon when a flying club from the lower 48 arrived—28 planes strong—on an unannounced sight-seeing visit. One after another, the little Cessnas and Pipers landed on the small airstrip, and their passengers, amounting to 56 or more people, jumped out and took off for the village. Roaming the dirt streets in crowds, they gawked at the little log cabins (some only one room in size), wondered out loud where the toilets were, stared at the Native people (whom they almost outnumbered), photographed them without the least thought of asking permission, and muttered audibly: "Imagine living like this!" After a cursory once-over of the town's eating place, no purchase of the really beautiful beadwork done by the Athabascan women who live in Fort Yukon, and scarcely a word, friendly or otherwise, to anyone in the village, the crowd trotted back to the airstrip en masse and took off. It is small wonder that this kind of rude visit—too often typical of thoughtless tourists—has left a lingering bad taste in many Alaska villages.

Add to this the fact that Native people in villages have, historically, been the subject of other kinds of unannounced, and often unwelcome, visits. In recent years, as a friend of mine once said: "People just dropped down out of the sky all the time and started asking us what we eat, how many teeth we have. Or what we wear under our parkas. Or how come our kids have runny noses." Many such visits were made—and to virtually every village—by government agencies with the best of intentions. Or they may have been made by anthropologists or other scientists who were sincerely concerned about their subjects. But the Natives were rarely consulted beforehand; their permission was simply taken for granted, and they were, in fact, treated arbitrarily.

With the passage of the Alaska Native Claims Settlement Act (ANCSA), the situation has, of course, changed. The Native villages are now privately owned and the village corporation must be consulted before any outside agency takes actions affecting the residents. You, too, should get permission before staying in a small village or using any village-owned facilities.

In subsistence use, every part of the animal is utilized. This Eskimo is trimming seal intestines. Source: National Park Service.

Also keep in mind the fact that Alaska's Natives are presently in a period of major and profound change. Although the impact and influence of white cultures have been felt for nearly a century and a half, many traditional ways have survived until recently. In the past decade, however, these ways have been more strongly challenged than ever before. As each village has made the quantum leap from a more or less traditional enclave to a corporate entity, new ways of looking at things and doing things have had to be incorporated into a deeply rooted life-style. Inevitably, there have been difficult choices and conflicts in values; for many of Alaska's Native people, this has not been an easy time. There are some 65,000 in-state Natives.

Subsistence hunting, a cherished way of life, has become a particularly sensitive subject as new uses have been spelled out for the land. The new federal Alaska land laws allow for established subsistence use throughout all public lands, including the new federal reserves; anyone traveling in Alaska should respect the Natives' (and non-Natives') rights to pursue it. This means that you should not intrude when subsistence hunting or fishing is taking place, and you should never touch a fish net, fish wheel, traps, or any other subsistence gear that you might come across. (Natives on the Kobuk River were recently appalled—and outraged—to find that their set nets had been removed by kayakers who were trying to help keep the wilderness clean.) Of course, you should never occupy a vacant fish camp . . . it belongs to someone; and do not walk in, uninvited, on one in use. A friendly wave is in order.

Another sensitive point to some Natives is the increasing number of people who are using land that historically has been used by themselves. The idea of boundaries is not easy to accept in a culture that has lived so long without them, and it is hard for some people to see the difference between a group of backpackers (nonconsumptive and noncompetitive recreational users) and an oil crew about to dig for an exploratory well. If you should encounter hostility on your travels, a friendly approach and discussion of why you are there can usually clear the air and can certainly help establish long-range good relations at a time when many new attitudes are taking shape.

All of this should make it clear that you should never descend, unannounced, upon a small Native village that has limited—if any—facilities and expect to be welcomed with open arms. Also, it will pay you to do some homework, as well as to exercise courtesy, with regard to any village you wish to spend some time in, or whose land you wish to pass through or over. (Some communities, like Kotzebue and Point Barrow, are on the tourist circuit and you will routinely be treated like a tourist if you travel like one. Some villages, like Hoonah in Southeast, are interested in developing tourism and will welcome your business. A few villages, such as English Bay, prefer not to be visited.) You can get background information on any Alaska village by writing the State Department of Community and Regional Affairs, 225 Cordova Street, Building B, Anchorage, AK 99501 and requesting a Village Profile, which will convey some flavor of the particular village and show what lands it owns and what its particular interests are. Further, if you are going to be traveling through village lands or if you want to spend any time in a village, write ahead and ask permission and/or inquire about accommodations. (The Appendices include a list of villages: address the president.) If you do not receive a reply, your letter—and your courteous intent—will be on the record.

When running a river, it is good wilderness manners to keep a low profile. Not only does this respect the rights of others in the area, but it gives you a much better chance to experience the wilderness fully. If you spread out your gear all over a river bar, you will not only offend any people around you, but scare off any local wildlife. If you feel it necessary to carry a gun (and many do not—see section on Bear Essentials), do so discreetly. If your route passes several villages, it will make your trip more pleasant if you advise the village presidents of your plans. (A friend of mine suggests writing the regional non-profit corporation as well; see the Appendices.) Easements for public camping have been established in areas of private property and should be used accordingly. The agency administering the river you run can advise you of the status of land ownership along your route. (You can expect a good commercially run river-trip to take care of all of this.)

When in a Native village, keep in mind that you are in the home community of people whose ancestors settled Alaska many millenia ago. Their way of life may be different from yours, but it has succeeded in a particularly difficult environment. Please respect it, and respect the people who have learned to get along under conditions that might easily have long since done you in. By far the greatest majority of these people will return twofold the friendship that you offer them.

TANANA MOON CALENDAR

The year begins with October, is 13 months long, and there are 29 days 12 hours and 44 minutes in a month. Not to worry if there are more than 365 days in a Tanana year: the day of the month need not be exact.

Month 1	Moon when the bull moose ruts
Month 2	Moon when the sheep ruts
Month 3	Hook Game month (a time of games and social activities)
Month 4	Moon when the sun appears again after long sleep
Month 5	Moon when days grow longer
Month 6	Moon of the cold winds, or Eagle Moon
Month 7	Hawk Moon
Month 8	Moon when snow is soft by day and freezes by night
Month 9	Moon when young animals are born
Month 10	Moon when moose comes down off the hill
Month 11	Moon when the moose fat is ready
Month 12	Moon when the animals take on their winter coats
Month 13	Moon when the leaves turn red

With thanks to Neil Davis of the Geophysical Institute, University of Alaska

Part II

SOUTHEAST

INTRODUCTION

Southeast is a very special part of Alaska. Stretching from the Portland Canal in the south to Icy Bay in the north and arcing gently from southeast to northwest, it is a long (540 air miles) narrow (140 air miles at its widest) area of land and water lying between roughly the 55th and 61st parallels north latitude. Geographically, it consists of a slender strip of mainland territory and, except at its northern end, of an extraordinary assembly of countless islands—the Alexander Archipelago—which account for the impressive mileage of the Southeastern coastline. Although its acreage comes to about the size of Massachusetts, New Hampshire, Connecticut, Delaware, New Jersey, and Rhode Island put together, Southeast comprises only about 6 percent of the state and is a relatively small and compact area compared to the rest of Alaska. Southeastern Alaska is also more intimate, and its wilderness is more readily accessible.

Delineated on the west by the Gulf of Alaska, its eastern boundary runs along the tumultuous crest of the tallest coastal mountains on earth, a section of the two-continent cordillera that approaches its most splendid northern climax here. This section is tied to the main body of Alaska by only a sliver of land that at one point stretches less than eleven miles from the coast to the Canadian border. Southeast is frequently called Alaska's panhandle, and it is a world of its own. Not only are its scenery, climate, and biota distinctive, but its way of life is as well. This is a place of flower-filled alpine meadows, shining glaciers, island-studded channels, waterfalls, dark green forests, and clear cold ocean waters. It is a place of soft rain and brilliant sunsets, of snow stained the color of ripe apricots by the winter sun, of fishermen and poets, and of people with a culture so ancient it predates the coming of white men by millennia. It is a place for those who love bird song, snow, silence, storms, small deep blue lakes, wetness, and wilderness. (It should be noted that similar country extends west along the coastal mountain area around Prince William Sound and on the Kenai Peninsula and easternmost Kodiak Island.)

Despite its many intimate qualities, the Southeast is put together on a scale that's overwhelming. Consider the uplift of the mountains that rise almost directly from the sea. In places they brush the 20,000-foot level. Snowy peaks of 10,000 feet appear as mere foothills next to giants like Mount Fairweather and Mount Saint Elias. When seen from the sea, such mountain complexes fill up half the sky.

This remarkable upthrust of the earth's crust is currently believed to be related to the massive collision between two major tectonic plates—the Pacific

Southeast Alaska

and the North American plates—which has occurred and is continuing to occur in this part of the world. In this area, the Pacific plate is presently moving generally northward, and from Yakutat to the north it is plunging under the continental plate. (This is termed subduction.) As it does this, it acts like a giant bulldozer, heaping the land up higher and higher. Evidence indicates that in the past the Pacific plate was being subducted in a more northeasterly direction so that it bulldozed up the great mountains of the Southeast. However, the present tectonic action seems to be dragging the Pacific plate along the continental margins in this area in a series of strike-slip faults, which would account for earthquakes like the one that wracked Lituya Bay in 1958.

Geologists continue to study the Southeastern coastal region for further answers, as many questions remain and new information keeps surfacing. Until recently, for example, many geologists were puzzled by the curious disparity between vast chunks of Southeastern rock formations. Earlier theories had explained these disparities as being part of the jumble of earth associated with plate collisions. More recently, intriguing new theories propose that blocks of Southeastern Alaska have been "rafted" in from distant areas of the Pacific, being swept up and carried along by the moving crustal segments of the planet. One such block has been christened Wrangellia (after the Wrangell Mountains); Wrangellia matches up with regions in British Columbia, on the Queen Charlotte Islands, and with the Hell's Canyon region of Oregon and Idaho. Another block, christened Stikinia, has fossils that are associated with China, Japan, and Indonesia. It has been proposed that this area was transported across the ocean and pinned against the North American continent. The evolving science of paleomagnetics, which identifies what the direction of the earth's magnetic field was that has been locked into certain rocks at times past, helps to confirm these somewhat radical new ideas.

The mountains of Southeast, in places, contain rocks that date back to Paleozoic times. It seems likely that the forces of uplift, erosion, and downthrust have created many landscapes here that have been worn away, drowned, or long since lost in time. Today's rugged terrain has been—and is still being—actively uplifted over a span of time much shorter than the age of the older rocks that formed it.

Along with the vigorous and continuing earth movements in the Southeast, the immense powers of water and ice have helped to shape this land. Great rivers—the Alsek, Stikine, Taku, and Unuk—drain the coastal and interior mountains. Gathering and carrying along enormous volumes of water, they have worn the earth into great canyons and valleys and have formed vast deltas and marshlands along the coast. Working with them and contributing to the profile of this unique landscape as much as any single earth force have been the glaciers.

Glaciers

Southeast's glaciers rise from some of the world's most impressive ice fields, which are cradled among the high ridges and peaks of the coastal mountains. They clothe hundreds of square miles, and, when you fly in a small plane over the shimmering high landscape, you can get some idea of how the North American continent must have looked during the millennia of the great Ice Ages when snow and ice engulfed everything except the highest peaks and pinnacles and the open sea itself. There may be remnants of these ancient glaciers buried deep beneath Alaska's present ice fields, but the snow and ice you see blanketing the land today are estimated by geologists to be much younger, at most 3,000 years old. Because these ice fields are being constantly renewed and replenished, they constitute a sort of small-scale living Ice Age and offer a bonanza for scientists studying glacial phenomena.

Glaciers require a particular set of meteorological and geographical circumstances for their formation and continuing existence. Interestingly enough, extreme cold is not a prerequisite, and while heavy precipitation is required, it is not sufficient by itself. A delicate climatic balance is needed. It must be just cold enough and just wet enough, the average summer temperature must be just low enough, and there must be just enough average persistence of cloudiness so that over a long period of time more snow and ice will accumulate in an area than will be lost through melting and evaporation (and the calving of glaciers). There must also be, of course, terrain on which snowfields can form and grow and over which glaciers can flow. The unique landscape and climate of Alaska's Southeast fulfill these special requirements, as do only a few places on this planet. Even a minor climatic change could disrupt the present dramatic glacial conditions.

The Japanese current is primarily responsible for the amount of precipitation that falls in the Southeast. This great stream of warm water surges through the Gulf of Alaska, and, swung counterclockwise by the Coriolus force, it heats the cool water and causes warm wet air to rise. Borne by offshore winds against the immensely high wall of the coastal mountains, the warm air condenses, falling as frequent and often steady rain and becoming heavy snow at about the 5,000-foot level year round. (In winter, you can watch the snow level inch down the southeastern mountains, storm by storm—sometimes hour by hour—until it touches the water and all the world is white.) The 1,500 square mile Juneau Icecap, which rises to six thousand feet above Juneau, may receive more than 100 feet (1,200 inches) of snow a year. The long hours of sunlight during the summer months can cause heavy melt, but the high altitude acts as a refrigerant and slows the melting. Added to this, in winter frigid air masses formed in the sunless Arctic regions flow across the continent to be stopped by the rim of the high coastal mountains. Pressing against this mountain barrier, the intensely cold and heavy air mounds up into a dome. Ultimately, it must breach the mountain passes and pour through as fierce cold gales called *Taku* winds. (*Takus* have been known to blow away the anemometers set up to measure their speed—after registering wind speeds of more than 100 miles an hour near Juneau. (At Wrangell, these winds are known as *Stikines*; at Prince Rupert, as *Skeenas*.) The *Takus* race through the mountains and set the snow streaming off the high peaks in glittering white banners, but these frigid winds also send the temperatures plummeting at every level of altitude.

As the snow piles higher and higher in the ice fields, certain phenomena occur below the surface. At a depth of about 200 feet, the immense weight of the overburden brings about structural changes in the buried snow. The snow crystals are compressed into extremely hard ice which, paradoxically, has the ability to flow like viscous water. As it gathers mass, this plastic glacial ice moves of its own weight, being pulled downward by gravity. It can travel at remarkable speed, sometimes several miles a day. It stops only when melt-back literally brings it to an end or, in many places in the Southeast, when it encounters the warmer saltwater of the sea.

Glacial ice is formed under such intense pressure that air bubbles are completely squeezed out of it and all cracks are obliterated. The resultant dense ice can admit light but absorbs the reds and yellows of the spectrum, its prisms reflecting only the shades of blue: hence, the marvelous intense blues that you see in crevasses and on the face of many of Alaska's glaciers, especially when they have just "calved" or dropped large chunks of ice.

A glacier is actually a river of ice, and, like any proper river, as it travels it follows the lines of least resistance in the terrain, bending around areas of tougher rock (though scouring away at them the while), plucking off loose rocks, and wearing away the ground it moves over. In the Southeast, glaciers also gather and transport a great deal of loose dirt and debris from the fractured rocks of this heavily faulted area. This debris gathers along the sides, or lateral moraines, of the glaciers, making black borders. When glaciers flow together and coalesce, as they do frequently in the Southeast, they form a massive river glacier, and the debris from each of them forms a black ribbonlike stripe. Each stripe originated on and marks a different glacier. On the Malaspina, a vast piedmont glacier, there are multiple stripes that have been curved and formed into intricate and extraordinary designs—a breathtaking sight from the air. You will also have some incredible aerial views if you "flightsee" over the Juneau Icecap on a clear day: thirty-six different glaciers radiate from this great mass of ice and snow. (A flight-seeing trip anywhere you can take it in Southeast is recommended.)

During earlier Ice Ages, glaciers were much more extensive than they are today. They covered the Southeast completely, burying virtually all of what is now the Inside Passage under ice and snow. A few places here and there remained ice free: these were the places of refuge, or refugia, where plants and animals could survive. The sea level was probably at least 300 feet lower during these cold eons because so much of the earth's water was locked into ice. During those Ice Ages, glaciers shaped the unique landscape you see today, including such features as the fjords that incise the mainland (and may, like the Endicott Arm, still have glaciers at their heads) and the cirques and high U-shaped valleys. The long straight channels in the Inside Passage—for example, Lynn Canal—were also the work of those early glaciers, marking major earthquake faults where the rock was unstable and easily quarried out. The Southeast's myriad islands, too, were carved by ice, being the tops of mountains and nunataks—or islands of resistant rock—that were drowned when the ice melted and the seawaters rose. (You can see nunataks in Glacier Bay today.)

Actually, not many decades ago the Southeastern glaciers were more extensive than they are today. When Captain James Cook visited what is now Glacier Bay in 1778, it was entirely under ice. Mendenhall Glacier, near Juneau, covered much of the forested area below its snout as recently as 1940. (The Mendenhall is the most visited, and the most easily visited, of the glaciers in the Southeast. See the Juneau section, Day Hikes.) A recent warming trend in the climate has caused a great many of the Southeast's glaciers to shrink. Despite the fact that they continue to be fed by heavy snowfall and can travel very rapidly, most of them are melting more rapidly than they can grow in their terminal portions. As noted, however, only a very slight change in any of the variables responsible for the formation of glaciers could send one or all of those in the Southeast surging ahead once more—with some interesting results. (Some glaciers are, in fact, presently growing.) Imagine the Mendenhall Flats or Glacier Bay once again under ice. It could happen and very well may.

The Forest, the Waters, and the Rain

Because Southeastern Alaska has been formed by such stark and elemental forces, it is pleasantly surprising that it is not entirely a bare and frozen though dramatic land like Antarctica. The lowlands and thousands of islands here are clothed with deep sweet-smelling forests of spruce, hemlock, and—to the south—cedar. The understory of these dense forests glows with a soft green light like an underwater scene. (Sometimes it feels like one, too!) Parasols of devil's club (admire but don't get too close) and the big, handsome leaves of skunk cabbage fill the shadows, and dwarf dogwood and delicate white saxifrages star the forest floor. Succulent blueberries may reward a hungry hiker in summer but also tempt the resident brown and black bears. Streams lace through the Southeast forests, and the lakes and the wet meadows of muskegs break the dense forest canopy into pleasant openings. In the Southeast the tides are immense, lifting and dropping the channel waters as much as twenty to twenty-five feet; in many places the tidal water floods the low-lying lakes and streams. These spectacular places of encounter are known as salt chucks. At low tide, you can be sitting next to a silvery cascade of fresh water, but as the tidal waters lift, you may see it drowned before your eyes. (Watch where you sit.)

   If you're traveling on the water in a small boat or kayak, you can nearly always find a bay or easy shore for landing in the Southeast. Beaches are sometimes formed of sea-smoothed rock, or they may be cobbled with small rounded stones and pebbles that are elegantly patterned and make for pleasant walking at low tide. Kelp and other seaweeds festoon the high-tide mark, perfectly outlining the parameter of the last high water. The tidepools hold fascinating sea animals, shelled creatures, brightly colored starfish, sea urchins, and sea anemones.

   When flying in a small plane over the Southeast, you'll see swirling patterns of opaque jade and turquoise where silt-laden glacial meltwaters pour into the clear, dark green channel water. There may also be whole flotillas of small icebergs spewed from the glaciers riding the tides. From the water, you can frequently see seabirds or seals riding the icebergs.

   All in all, there are few places on earth that can match the particular beauty of Southeast Alaska. Along with the sheer magnificence of the landscape, there are the changing waters, the lift and sigh of the tides, and always the special quality of the light. On blue days in the summer, the colors—all greens and blues, gold and white—glow with a special intensity. In winter, the late and early sun paints the blank canvas of the snow-covered landscape with orange and rose; the snow shadows are deep blue.

There is also a special magic here on days that are gray. In summer, the air is cool and soft, and the waters shine with a smooth patina like old, well-polished silver. Suddenly the quiet surface of the channel breaks with the rising curve of a whale. A raven cries. Bald eagles spiral overhead and disappear into the low clouds. When the rain comes, it makes music on each leaf and the streams sing louder. Islands loom dark and mysterious in the mist. In winter, snow outlines every bough of every spruce and alder; you can watch a pair of old squaw ducks glide past in the dark clear water, and the glaciers gleam, illuminated from within by a deep blue light.

Because rain and snow are so much a part of Southeast, it is a good idea to accept the fact that the weather will probably be rainy or snowy or misty for at least part of the time you visit there, whatever the season. May and June, on the average, are the driest and the sunniest months, and the sea, as

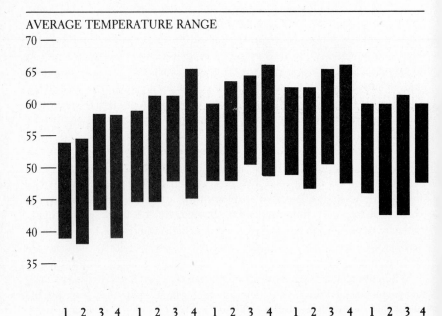

AVERAGE TEMPERATURE RANGE

1. Sitka
2. Juneau
3. Ketchikan
4. Skagway

well, tends to be the calmest during these months. Still you should always be prepared for wetness, remembering it is responsible for the lush forests, green alpine meadows, and blue faceted glaciers, as well as for the unique mood of the place. At the same time, the amount of precipitation does vary quite dramatically in different parts of the Southeast. Thus in places on Baranof Island, rainfall can average over 220 inches a year; in Ketchikan it is 154 inches; in downtown Juneau, 92. Haines, however, receives an average of only 53 inches and Skagway, just 26.3. Snowfall varies as well: Haines, for example, averages 139.6 inches of snow a year, while Ketchikan catches only 32. Remember the ice field above Juneau, with 100 feet of snow falling in a single winter!

TRAVELING BY FERRY

Southeast Alaska does not have the usual highway system. While each of its fourteen communities has its own larger or smaller network of streets and service roads, there are no connecting roads. (Juneau has the most extensive system of paved highways—about 54 miles in all, and only eight miles of it are four lane, from the airport to downtown.) Therefore, you travel by air or by water, and the grand waterway you travel is the Inside Passage. You can start your voyage up the Inside Passage at Seattle, Washington; Vancouver, British Columbia; or Prince Rupert, British Columbia, and go for more than 1,000 miles among forested islands, alongside breathtaking cliffs that tower as high as 4,000 feet above you, and past picturesque towns on the shore.

If you have a small seaworthy boat of your own, the lore of the Inside Passage has probably already reached you. Everyone I know who has traveled it in such a craft has had memorable and beautiful experiences. There have also been legendary canoe trips from Seattle up the passage: one—a honeymoon journey—was taken by friends of mine in a hand-made wooden canoe, but such a trip is recommended only for intrepid, enthusiastic, and experienced canoers. Kayaking in various parts of the Inside Passage is superb, but more of this later.

If your time is short and you enjoy organized tours, you have a good choice of well-run tour ships, many offering reasonably priced trips through the Inside Passage. They sail from United States west coast ports as well as from British Columbia. These tours usually run from one to two weeks with stop-offs at most of the principal towns in the Southeast.

If you can take your time, however, and want a less programmed, more active Southeast adventure—and if you really want to see the country—the way to travel the Inside Passage is by public transportation, that is, to voyage up the "Alaskan Marine Highway" on a state-operated ferry liner. Alaska's ferries are, generally, the most comfortable (and always the most fun) of any I have ever traveled on. Two large ships (over 350 feet long), the M.V. *Columbia* and M.V. *Matanuska*, service the Southeast from Seattle; another two, the *Malaspina* and the *Taku*, sail from Prince Rupert, British Columbia. (Alaska's ferry liners are named after glaciers.) In summer, from May through September, these ships travel their weekly routes, stopping at Ketchikan, Wrangell, Petersburg, Sitka, Haines, Skagway, and, of course, Juneau. (Smaller ferries, the *Aurora* and the *LeConte*, make local runs, servicing the smaller communities such as Kake on Prince of Wales Island, Angoon, Hoonah, Metlakatla, Hollis, Tenakee, and Pelican—although not necessarily daily.)

There are several wonderful things about Alaska's ferries. First of all, you can take aboard free anything that you can carry. This means that you can tote not only a large backpack, but you also can take your bicycle, canoe, or kayak. (You will keep your backpack with you aboard, but you can park your bike, canoe, or kayak in a special section on the vehicle deck.) Secondly, the ferry liners are not only spacious but also generally comfortable. The berths on the larger ships (the smaller boats have no sleeping cabins) are clean and comfortable, although you'll have to share a double or a four-berth accommodation, and you must make your reservations well ahead of time. There are also banks of lounge chairs where you can stretch out and sleep inside, although these get taken early. Most of the ferries have a solarium or sundeck, where there are deck chairs and a radiant heating system that keeps you cosy even in frigid weather, and this is where I prefer to sleep. (My last ferry trip from Juneau to Haines took place during a lovely December snowfall, and I was almost too toasty in my down sleeping bag sleeping topside beneath the overhead heater.) Unfortunately, the solaria are apt to be very crowded in the summer; if you want a deck chair, you have to board early and mark one for your own. Although I have never been wet in a solarium, I am told that under some conditions they can be "wet above and marshy on the floor."

On the larger ferries, there are two restaurants—one a snack bar, the other a dining room—and there is a bar. On the smaller boats, there's one cafe and a small bar. However, you can bring along your own food as long as you don't mind eating cold.

If you like to bike, the ferries offer you an ideal vehicle to travel to numerous interesting destinations in the Southeast. If you are after a more extensive bike trip in Alaska, the ferry is a great way to start it. You can ferry your bike to Haines and, in summer months, transport it by bus until you're home free on the Alaska section of the AlCan Highway. Or you can take your bike off at Skagway and carry it on the White Pass and Yukon Motor Coaches or other motor coach (in the summer) to Whitehorse and from there—again by bus— back into Alaska. The unpaved Canadian section of the AlCan Highway is not recommended for biking during the summer as it is heavily traveled then; when the gravel is sprayed onto you by passing vehicles, it's terrifying. (Gravel on less-traveled Canadian and Alaskan side roads is not such a problem.)

If you can arrange your time in Alaska out of tourist season, you'll find ferry-liner travel especially attractive. During peak tourist months—from mid June through August—the ships are apt to be full if not over-crowded, although you will probably have no difficulty getting on without a car (except for the Alaska State Fair Days in Haines in mid August). But in May, September, or early June (before school is out), you'll find fewer passengers on board. Further, if you like crisp weather and don't mind some snow, you can take a ferry trip from October through April at a 25 percent reduction in fare, and you are likely to have the ship more to yourself, although the number of people, even in December, may surprise you. (If you should be bringing a car along during these months, you will only pay for your vehicle: auto passengers ride free.) The schedule does slow down during the off season, with the big ferries making the long round trip only once a week. (Anyone 65 or older can travel on the ferries inside Alaska free from October 1 through May 15.)

It is also worth noting that the ferries traveling south are more apt to be less crowded than those heading north during the summer. If it fits into your summer plans, you might want to finish—rather than start—your Alaskan adventure on the ferry.

All of the large, and some of the small, ferries on the Alaskan Marine Highway in Southeast, incidentally, have U.S. Forest Service (USFS) ranger-interpreters aboard in summer. Forest Service movies and slide shows are routinely shown in the main lounge. Most of the Forest Service people are well-informed, friendly, and helpful. They can give you tips about USFS facilities that you'll find on shore and possibly about road conditions for biking and so on. Ask them for anything you need to know.

Using the Ferry for Your Small Boat Trip

Almost any community on the regular Southeast ferry run will offer interesting opportunities not only to hikers (see following sections) and bikers but also to kayakers and canoers. These communities can also be ideal "road-heads" and "pickup points" using the ferry as your "shuttle vehicle." For example, you can put your canoe or kayak in the waters in the Inside Passage at Ketchikan and take it out at Wrangell. Sightsee and stock up at Wrangell and continue on to Petersburg, and so on, reboarding the ferry when you wish. Or you can take the main-run ferry, say to Sitka, and then plan a kayak trip to take out at Tenakee—or, if you have more time, at Hoonah—on a day when a smaller ferry calls at one of these little communities. (Either of these suggested trips will be a fine one if you're an experienced kayaker; you will have to cope with a stretch of open ocean on the way.) Or you might take the regular ferry to Juneau, then take the small ferry to Angoon and canoe or kayak across

Admiralty to Mole Harbor and have a charter air-taxi pickup to get back to Juneau. (This is another lovely trip that does not call for super expertise, but it does require a strong back for some of the portages.) If you decide to use the ferry this way, it's particularly important that you obtain the schedule since not all runs serve Sitka, and the service to many of the small villages is only weekly, and sometimes monthly. When planning trips of this kind, you should also write the USFS for suggestions on routes and camping spots along the way.

For further information about Alaska's ferries and for the latest fares and schedules, write Alaska Division of Marine Transportation, Pouch R, Juneau, AK 99811. For reservations, phone (Seattle) 206-623-1970; (Juneau) 907-465-3941; (Anchorage) 907-272-7116; (Prince Rupert) 604-627-1744.

When you travel Alaska's ferry liners, keep in mind that, as with all things in Alaska, the time frame is elastic. You may have to wait an hour or so, or possibly longer, for your boat. Sometimes the weather holds things up—for example, fog in the Wrangell Narrows is a frequent cause of delay. Or a ferry may get flagged along the way for one reason or another, or it may have to deliver something. My husband and I once waited all day in Juneau for the ferry, which had stopped en route from Ketchikan to leave an axe off at somebody's house and then had gotten caught by the tide. Mechanical difficulties can also slow operations: one year the *Malaspina* broke down so often that some wag suggested it be renamed the *Lemon*—for the Lemon Glacier, of course! However you travel in Alaska, don't bind yourself to a rigid time schedule if you want to enjoy yourself and avoid frustration.

TRAVELING IN SOUTHEASTERN WATERS

The great tides of Southeast Alaska are a part of the magic of the place. To experience their lift and fall in a small boat and to be carried by them is a special and elemental experience. Understanding these tides and some of their effects can add to the dimensions of that experience and also help you to enjoy it safely.

Tides are caused by the gravitational pull of the celestial bodies closest to the earth, our sun and moon. Tides vary according to the distance of these bodies from our planet, so that when the moon, for instance, is closest to us— at perigee—the tides will be subjected to greater pull and will be higher; when the moon is farthest away—at apogee—its effects are less forceful. Tides are also affected by the size of the body of water in which they occur, by the depth of the water, and by the configuration of the land that surrounds the water. Thus, in mid ocean, where the waters are vast and very deep and there is no immediately constraining landmass, the tides are little noticed. Along the shores, however, the tides make themselves felt to one degree or another, and they can vary markedly within a fairly narrow range. In Alaska, the tides reach extremes: Some of the greatest recorded tides on earth occur in the Cook Inlet (36 feet), and some of the weakest (less than a foot) occur along the Arctic Ocean. In northern Alaska, the tides occur only once a day; in the Southeast, they rise and fall twice a day (on a 25-hour cycle). They can exceed 25 feet in range in narrow channels distant from the sea.

Such tides require your respect and a strict observance of their rhythm. Even a one-foot tide can wash away gear left too close to the tide line: you will have to think in terms of much higher tides in the Southeast. When you camp or even when you stop for a brief exploratory wander along the shore, keep in mind the tidal schedule. (You can get a tide book at any sporting goods store in the Southeast and in other stores as well. It is among the most-read publications in the region.) Obviously, you should make your camp well above the tide line; you should tie your boat securely; and be sure that all of your gear is stowed out of danger. (Note: grasses fringe many Southeast beaches, making the territory look safely above salt water—but it isn't. Tidal waters frequently invade this part of the shore. It's best to park your boat and gear among trees whenever possible.) You will also want to take the tides into account when planning the put-in as well as the take-out of your boat. There's no point in hauling your craft up and down the beach if the tide can do it for you.

Apart from their effects on the shorelines, the Southeast tides have a powerful effect on the speed, volume, and character of the water. A great deal of the ocean is pulled back and forth irresistibly through some very narrow channels in this area, and the resulting currents can build up to what my friend, Jack Calvin of Sitka, described as "furious torrents." That is why you may come across a number of boats of various shapes and sizes waiting just short of certain narrows. If you do, by all means, wait with them for slack water or a favorable current. As Calvin put it: "Swift-water narrows must be traversed 'by the Book,' and the book is not the tide tables; it is the *Current Tables of the West Coast of North and South America* (of the current year), published by the National Oceanic and Atmospheric Administration (NOAA). I believe that *Current Tables* should head the equipment list of anyone traveling by boat in the Southeast."

Along with paying attention to and enjoying the tides and currents in Southeastern waters, there are a few other things to be aware of. At least part of the time, you will probably be traveling through glacial waters, and they are really cold, particularly so in fjords and inlets where the terrain tends to contain the water that is pouring from ice. In such places the water temperature ranges between 34 and 42 degrees Fahrenheit. Dress to keep yourself snug in your small boat and try to keep your boat upright. These are waters you don't want to spend any time in.

Ice can be gorgeous, whether in glacial or iceberg form, but it is also unpredictable. Do not get too close to a tidewater glacier; the National Park Service advises that a half mile from the glacier's face is a safe distance to observe. A tidal glacier can "calve"—cast off a huge building-size chunk or chunks of ice from its snout—most unexpectedly, particularly at low tide when its lower ice is exposed and melts more readily. Tons of ice smashing suddenly into inlet waters that have no place to go can cause waves which can easily swamp your boat. (Waves 30 feet high have been recorded under these circumstances.)

Along with the tidal range, keep the above in mind when you stop or camp along the shores of an inlet. Your gear can be drenched or washed away if it is left too close to the waterline and a nearby glacier suddenly decides to calve. Your kayak, too, is vulnerable; be sure it is secured. In other words, always keep a safe distance from the terminal faces of glaciers, on land as well as in the water; don't linger too close to the water's edge with unstashed gear; and make your camp well above high-water level.

Icebergs pose other, equally interesting, problems. While little boats can make their way through smaller pieces of ice safely, larger bergs can be hazards and should be avoided if possible. Don't leap onto one to get your picture taken! They are unstable and can tip over without warning, taking you with them. They can also disintegrate with extraordinary suddenness. Keep an eye out, as well, for icebergs just below the surface of the water. Sometimes they're so heavy with glacial silt that they travel around slightly submerged and out of obvious sight.

Once in the water, ice moves almost continuously. Tidal action carries it back and forth. A good stiff wind can push an iceberg around even as it can a small boat. Sometimes, ice floes will jam up to block your passage. Since you don't want to be inside an inlet when such a thing happens, pay particular attention to your tide schedule and wind direction when you're venturing around.

Winds and weather in general are as unpredictable as the ice in Southeastern waters. Mornings can start out with the water as smooth as a well-waxed table, but around eleven or noon, the winds can rise, and the going can get much less comfortable. (Traveling early in the morning is good technique and early morning is a beautiful time to experience the water world of the Southeast.) Sudden squalls can also occur on blue days when the water is calm and there is absolutely nothing to give you a warning. A squall can be particularly dangerous if you're close to a glacier and the wind slams you into it—another reason to keep your distance from the tidewater glaciers.

Keep in mind that the climate in the Southeast is maritime and apt to be

Icebergs; Tracy Arm. Source: U.S. Forest Service.

damp. This, too, is part of the magic of the place. You may travel through rain and fog with near-zero visibility (and a wonderful sense of mystery) for hours at a time—and then the weather can clear with total unexpectedness, and the beauty of the day will almost stun you. By the same token, on a crystal-clear blue day, a sudden storm can roar in from the Gulf of Alaska. (High drama!) You should be prepared for anything. (See section on Equipment.)

Although seals can be the most enchanting of animals as they watch you with their round black eyes and their sleek wet heads dipping into and out of the water, try to keep your distance from them. When they need to make a quick getaway from a predator, they have been known to clamber aboard a kayak as though it were an iceberg or a tiny island. Take care, as well, when approaching or traveling among whales and/or sea lions; any large mammal can inadvertently upset a small boat. (Be sure to keep your eyes out for sea otters—these enchanting animals are returning to Southeastern waters.)

Numerous large cruise ships sail the Inside Passage during the tourist season. They have—and take—the right of way, and you surely don't want to argue with them. In narrow stretches of water, they usually travel down the middle, so you can chart your course accordingly.

As always in Alaska, don't try to keep to a tight schedule. Be prepared to wait out bad weather, take time to repair a paddle or whatever, or especially linger in a place you find particularly lovely. Allow for at least a day or three extra when you plan a small-boating trip and take along enough extra food to let you enjoy it. An alternative, of course, is to use the fish and shellfish of this richly endowed region of Alaska for at least part of your subsistence. Bottom fish are plentiful, and you can jig for them from your boat. In season, salmon practically leap onto your hook. Abalone, snails, limpets, and crabs are all delicious and easily gathered. Clams and mussels should be taken only during safe months; check with the National Park Service or the Forest Service to be sure that there are no red tides before you risk a feast on these filter feeders.

What kind of small boat will serve you best in the Southeast? If possible, use one that you can carry on and off the ferry. That way you can go least expensively, and you will have the greatest mobility. This means, of course, that you will choose a lightweight canoe, a kayak, or a rubber raft. The National Park Service recommends a touring kayak with a spray cover or a closed-deck canoe. A raft that will take oars is also a good choice.

HIKING AND BACKPACKING

Although caveats apply to many of the trails in the Southeast, they should not discourage strong hikers and backpackers from trekking in this area. You should be prepared for some of the realities and eventualities you can encounter if you decide to explore in the Southeast on foot. It takes strength, skill, and good sense to get around in this country. The rewards, however, can be great. The forests are lovely to walk through; the meadows are full of wildflowers; the muskegs are very special places; and the views from high places are breathtaking. Where else would you have the chance to so readily explore among major and gorgeous glaciers, look for mountain goats, perhaps see a wolf or a brown bear? And where else can you hike (or ski) from a downtown area into superb wilderness in a matter of minutes?

If you do decide to go it on foot, start with the fact that the number of maintained trails in Southeast is limited, which means that so are your opportunities for a relatively easy backpack. You will be traveling generally over wet and fragile terrain that is not suited to the building, or the maintenance, of trails. Trails erode easily, quickly turning into stretches of soggy and slippery mud. Not infrequently they develop potholes that are potential ankle breakers. During heavy rainstorms, trails are more like waterways than passages over land.

The U.S. Forest Service, which administers most of the land through which you will hike in the Southeast, is confronted with the choice of boardwalking trails through continuously wet areas (thus detracting from the wilderness experience), damaging the land by building a regular trail, or just not building a trail at all (in the past, this has too often been the choice). The Forest Service is further confronted with the fact that maintenance must be constant to be effective, and this is costly. One major problem of maintenance is the rapid regrowth of underbrush in this lush country. Trails can choke up in a matter of weeks it seems, particularly if they are not heavily used and some are not. There is also frequent windfall; in fact, you'll find whole blocks of forest that have been leveled by what are locally known as williwaws—sudden, localized brutal windstorms.

Animals can also add to the difficulties of trail maintenance. Along with hiking in different places on Admiralty, I have taken two of the better known cross-island routes. The first is a canoe trip that involves portages between several lakes across trails where one slips and slides through mud and climbs in and out of potholes. (Despite this, I recommend this trip most highly.) The second is a foot trail that travels less than two miles from the east side of the island to Hawk Inlet on the west. The last time I took this route we found that beavers had dammed up a creek and flooded out a sizable section of the trail, which wasn't in the greatest shape to begin with. The water was deep enough for a small boat, so we had to hike around the beaver pond through heavy brush and tangles of fallen trees, all of which slowed us down considerably.

Some of the better trails are old logging roads, routes of old tramways, or abandoned mining roads. Along mining roads, you may be tempted to wander off and explore the ghostly weather-beaten buildings that are still standing in places. Keep in mind that they can be unsafe, and, just as dangerously, they can obscure the location of mine shafts located around them. Watch your step, literally as well as figuratively, in such places. Preferably, stay on the trail.

In the lowlands, you'll be hiking primarily through forests (or cutover land) and muskegs. Note that there is considerable sameness to the forests. The Southeast forest species are, in fact, limited, although each one thrives in this habitat. (You will find gorgeous skunk cabbage, for instance, much larger and lusher looking than that of the northwestern lower 48 states.) It is not easy to establish good landmarks even along the trail through many forests; once off the trail, it can be extremely difficult to get back on. Stay on the trail unless you are in the company of an Alaskan who knows the terrain through which you are traveling. Bushwhacking is also difficult and not recommended, even if you carry a machete. Not only is the heavy growth a formidable barrier to progress on foot, but willow and alder stands are places where bears like to relax and snooze.

Muskegs—or peat and sphagnum bogs—are quite extensive throughout Southeast and are especially interesting parts of the terrain. They are prime wildlife habitat for many animals and are used by several species of birds for nesting and feeding grounds. They are also fragile and easily damaged, and they can be difficult to travel through, since they are wet and soppy, possibly leading to drenched boots, socks, and feet. (They can also, in places, have areas of quicksand.) For all these reasons, watch where you step. It may be possible to find your way on the higher ground in and around muskegs, or, if there is a boardwalk, stay on it.

Beach walking in Southeast can be a particular delight. There are tidal meadows and glacial forelands as well which may offer good wildlife viewing. But, watch the tides!

While the alpine country in the Southeast may be open and a delight to travel through, it is also quite often extremely steep. The grass can be unbelievably slippery, and many of the drop-offs are literally deadly. People have lost their lives when they have lost their footing, or their balance, and have fallen nonstop down one of these precipitous slopes. A good friend of mine, and an excellent mountaineer, was killed on Mount Juneau when he tried to help another hiker across a slippery exposed spot. The other hiker made it safely, but my friend's boots did not hold on the grass, and he plummeted to his death. These two people were off the trail, traveling cross-country, and so are many of the people who get into trouble on steep grades in the Southeast. If there is a trail, stay on it. If you reach a spot that makes you uneasy, turn back. If there is no trail, you're better off in the company of an experienced Alaskan who knows that part of the country, or else you should have a clear idea (from Forest Service or National Park Service people) about what you're getting into.

Rock slides and avalanches are also dangers in alpine country. Move quickly and carefully across the obvious paths of rock slides if you must traverse them at all. If you are cross-country skiing during the winter or in spring, watch out for areas of snow avalanches. Even in summer, you will find patches of snow in many places at higher elevations: these may not pose avalanche problems, but they may be extremely slippery, and you will find that an ice axe is useful.

Even if you plan a day-hike only, be prepared for the contingency of staying overnight. Essentials in your backpack include: waterproof matches, topo map, flashlight, first aid equipment, compass, bug juice, extra food, knife, enough warm clothing, rain gear.

If you are a seasoned hiker in good shape and want the adventure of backpacking in Southeast, it is a good idea to write the appropriate state or federal agency before you plan your trip. You should also invest in a copy of Margaret Piggott's book on Southeast trails. (See Bibliography.) If you have not visited the Southeast before, do not plan on a cross-country trip. Even if you're a dyed-in-the wool loner, don't backpack alone; it's a lot easier to have one or more friends help carry the weight, and it's immeasurably safer.

Once your plans are made and you arrive on the scene, check with the local agency people again to get last-minute information and advice on your proposed itinerary. If this all seems like too much trouble, why not take a hiking or backpacking expedition with an organized group? This way, on your first Southeastern outing, you'll save yourself a lot of headaches as you learn the ropes and prepare yourself for future adventuring on your own. You can contact any one of the following: **Alaska Discovery**, 418 South Franklin Street, Juneau, AK 99801; phone 907-586-1911 or c/o Bonnie and Hayden Kaden, Box 26, Gustavus, AK 99826; phone 907-697-3431 (kayak rental as well as guided trips); **Alaska Travel Adventures**, 200 North Franklin, Juneau, AK 99801; phone 907-586-6245 (elsewhere 800-227-8480). You can also write or call the **Alaskan Backcountry Guides**, Box 81533, College, AK 99708; phone 907-456-8907. Although headquartered in the Interior, this organization may be able to put you in touch with wilderness guides in the Southeast. The National Park Service people keep a list of current guides, too, and you can contact them in Glacier Bay. (See Glacier Bay: Useful Information, for address and phone.)

MUSKEGS

As you travel through the countryside of Southeast Alaska, sooner or later you will come upon a muskeg. Muskegs, like glaciers, are unique and interesting natural phenomena that are common in Southeast. Put simply, they are open peat bogs that may occur in the midst of forested land, on more or less level areas throughout the subalpine terrain, and even on slopes as steep as 60 degrees. Actually, they are quite complex small ecosystems which scientists are still exploring.

The Southeast muskegs form in areas of heavy rainfall (where precipitation is generally greater than evaporation), where the substrate is uneven, with dips and declivities, and where there is poor drainage; that is, the substrate is either composed of hard bedrock or of impermeable soil that can hold water like a big saucer. Over the centuries, bogs form in the depressions and build up layer by layer. Muskegs can become as much as 40 feet thick, as one plant community succeeds another.

Since conditions for the formation of muskegs are so frequently ideal in the Southeast, these lovely landforms are abundant. Rainfall and snowfall nourish them year round. They rest in the deep or gentle depressions that past glaciers have scooped out and paved in many places with water-laid glacial flour or compacted till that, through the millennia, have become as hard as concrete.

Muskegs have, in fact, been around in the Southeast for a long time. When a muskeg plant community reaches its climax of growth, it may give way to invading conifers, and what was once a thriving peat bog will become a forest. The U.S. Forest Service estimates that about 10 percent of the forest land in the 16 million-acre Tongass National Forest was muskeg in the recent geological past. (Perhaps another 10 percent of this forest is presently living muskeg.) Interestingly, it is also suspected that mature spruce forests can eventually degenerate into muskegs, which makes this unique landform unusual ecologically as well as aesthetically.

Muskegs come in various shapes and sizes and vary greatly in appearance. (Scientists identify four quite different types in the Southeast.) You may come upon one that looks like a dying lake choked with sedges and rushes or another that you think is only a thick patch of blueberries. More frequently, you will see something that looks like a floating community of several different kinds of plants. Typically, the water level of muskegs is at or very close to the surface, and there are many little pools of standing water, hence the illusion that things are afloat. Actually, the muskeg plants are fastened into a layer of drenched sphagnum moss, which may be four to twelve inches thick. The plants may include, among many others, such familiar ones as Labrador tea, bog rosemary, skunk cabbage, highbush cranberry, salal, marsh marigold, shooting stars, and sundew. Here and there may be a small grove, or scattered individuals, of lodgepole pine, mountain hemlock, or—more rarely—of the graceful yellow (Alaska) cedar, these trees having found precarious footholds and assumed a shrubby growth. If you're fortunate to find a muskeg where spruce has taken hold, you will enjoy a Japanese-printlike scene of exceptional loveliness—totally unlike the black spruce–tamarack muskegs of the North Woods or those of Alaska's Interior. Sometimes a single plant species will dominate a part of the muskeg. I once explored a muskeg near Thayer Lake on Admiralty Island which was so thickly studded with sundew (*Drosera rotundiflora*, one of the carnivorous, insect-eating plants) that in places it looked as though splotches of rose-colored paint had been splashed onto it.

Underlying the sphagnum moss in a muskeg there will probably be layers of older moss and woody peat. Here the air has been pressed out, and the soils have become highly acidic, but even in this strange dark anaerobic world, there are forms of life that have adapted. The peat layers, incidentally, may be between four and forty feet deep. They will be resting, of course, on a base of hard glacial till, or silt, or bedrock.

Muskegs provide important habitats for several species of animals as well as plants. You might surprise a black bear or a Sitka black-tailed deer as you hike past a muskeg or see the quick flash of an ermine, wolf, or even a wolverine. Shorebirds such as the greater yellowlegs and the northern shrike can often be seen among the sedges and rushes that surround the little muskeg pools or in the shrubby or grassy areas that surround the muskeg. (The northern shrike will typically breed in Interior muskegs and come south for the winter; even as a hibernal visitor, it may sing for you.) Or you could hear the pleasant call of a pine siskin as you pass by or the lilting, finchlike song of the Lincoln sparrow. Try to put up with the mosquitoes that may also be part of the muskeg community and take the time to look and listen. (Also, be sure to keep your feet dry.) The Southeastern muskegs are unique, important, and fragile parts of the landscape, definitely worth a few moments of careful observation. You won't find anything like them in the Rockies or the Sierra Nevada!

KETCHIKAN

The name *Ketchikan* is Tlingit, but just what it means or where it came from is unknown. Perhaps it honors a Tlingit fisherman named Kitschk who found a superb salmon run in the creek (*hin* is "creek" in Tlingit), settled here and left his name behind him. Or perhaps it means "eagle wing river" and was given because a particular bend near a particular waterfall in Ketchikan Creek looks like an eagle with outstretched wings. No matter. Ketchikan today means a small Alaskan city with a certain character and charm all its own. It means lush Southeastern forests of spruce and hemlock and superb Southeastern scenery in general—to which it is a major gateway. It once also meant an unequaled salmon fishery and was known as the salmon capital of the world, but in 1977, its fish catch was only a third of what it once had been. And, surely, Ketchikan means water, whether it's falling from the sky, rushing in streams or waterfalls, lying at your feet in the Tongass Narrows, or keeping you afloat in your kayak. Ketchikan gets measurable precipitation for 224 days of the year, on an average. For another 100 days, it's apt to be cloudy. But for 42 days, it has clear skies, and if you're lucky enough to be there then you'll see the beautiful snow-streaked mountains that form this city's backdrop. The people who live in Ketchikan are not bothered much by the wet weather (as a Ketchikan friend once told me: "Southeastern Alaskans don't tan, they rust.") and you'll enjoy the place more if you adopt the same attitude.

You can get to Ketchikan by ferry liner or by jet service from Seattle and Juneau. Appropriately enough, even if you travel by air, you'll have to make your entrance into town across water. Ketchikan and its airport are on adjacent islands with a five-minute ferry ride across the Tongass Narrows that separates them. The Ketchikan Airport on Gravina Island, incidentally, is one of the more interesting jet airports in the state. It has a runway that doubles back on itself to get you downhill from your point of touchdown to the air terminal.

Gravina Island was named in 1792 for a Spanish naval officer, Frederico Gravina, by the Spanish explorer Caamaño, who was among the first Europeans to sail through this area. Ketchikan's home island is seven-hundred-thousand-acre Revillagigedo (ruh-vee-yah-guh-*gay*-do); it is larger than Rhode Island, and got its Spanish name from Captain George Vancouver in 1793 when he chose to memorialize the then-viceroy of Mexico, Count Revilla Gigedo. Today, most people simply call the island Revilla and anglicize the pronunciation. Revilla is separated from the mainland and encircled by the Behm Canal, also named by Vancouver in 1793. (Magnum Carl von Behm, in the service of Russia, helped out the 1779 Cook expedition.) This 150-mile canal is one of the most breathtakingly scenic waterways in Southeastern Alaska and a paradise for fishermen. Part of its eastern section is now properly within the boundaries of Misty Fjords National Monument.

The short ferry ride from Gravina Island to Ketchikan doesn't begin to give you the overall view of the town that the ferry liner does. Although it's only a couple of blocks wide (sometimes less), the town strings along the water for nearly six miles. Its colorful houses and buildings, many of which are built over the water on pilings, come in a variety of styles and vintages, offering photographers many picturesque shots. Along Ketchikan Creek, Ketchikan climbs up the lower part of Deer Mountain, which rises 3,001 feet above it. (It's a local saying that if you can't see the top of Deer Mountain, it's raining, and if you can see it, it's about to rain.) You'll notice that a number of the houses are perched on the mountainside and can only be reached by stairs.

Ketchikan is called "Alaska's First City" and so it is, physically, being the first large community you encounter north of the Dixon Entrance as you travel the Inside Passage. It was actually settled, however, several years later than Juneau and did not get its post office until a decade after Juneau did. Although it likes to call itself Alaska's third largest city, it is in fact the fourth.

Until the mid-fifties, Ketchikan was primarily a fishing town with first a saltery and later canneries and cold-storage facilities for salmon and halibut. In 1954, the Ketchikan Pulp Company, one of the largest dissolving-pulp mills in the world was completed and opened. (It is now the Louisiana Pacific Ketchikan Pulp Mill.) Ketchikan became a center for logging operations being initiated in Southeast Alaska by the U.S. Forest Service. Presently, local Native corporations are also conducting logging operations around Ketchikan.

Commercial fishing remains an important part of the Ketchikan economy, and articulate fishermen are fighting to preserve and restore the once-fabulous fishery habitat of the area. If you're going Outside directly from Ketchikan during the fishing season, it's worth trying to find a fresh salmon and/or halibut to take with you. If you don't meet up with someone who can help you do this, inquire at the Chamber of Commerce, address below.

Ketchikan is a most pleasant place to wander around in. Unless you decide to go uphill on Deermont, you'll find yourself taking a long stroll along the waterfront, sometimes on boardwalks. It's likely to be misting a light rain and, as you pass the old houses along Creek Street, you can get the feeling of stepping back in time. In fact, there is lots of history, Alaskan as well as Indian, in Ketchikan. The town was a major supply center for sourdoughs heading north during the gold rush periods around the turn of the century. Look for the site of Fort Tongass on the bluff above Creek Street; this is a relic of one of the earliest United States military outposts in Alaska. The area around Ketchikan was also the heartland of Tlingit and Haida country, and there are many traces remaining of the these peoples' rich culture. If you're interested in fine Native crafts, you will probably be able to find a contemporary hand-made spruce-root basket here—expensive, but worth it. I find the work of Selina Peratrovich especially beautiful.

The largest collection of totems in Alaska can be seen in and around Ketchikan. At the city-maintained Totem Bight Park, about eight miles north of town, there are many brightly painted and completely intriguing totems that

Sun and Raven totem. Saxman Park, Ketchikan. Source: U.S. Forest Service.

tell Tlingit stories and legends. There is also the replica of a Tlingit community lodge. Less than two miles south of town, there is another display of totems at Saxman Village and Totem Park. Many local people think this has the more interesting totems; for instance, you'll find the famous Abraham Lincoln totem here. I recommend visiting both parks if you have the time. Photographers with an interest in Tlingit art will have fine opportunities.

Most of these totems are restorations of old totems brought in from such places as Tongass Island and Old Kasaan. (*Kasaan* is a Tlingit word meaning "pretty town," and it was given to this village, which happens to be Haida, because of its many beautiful and ornate totems.) The restoration work was done under the direction of the U.S. Forest Service during the 1930s in an attempt to gather together and preserve local Indian artwork. Most of the people working on the project were members of the Civilian Conservation Corps. You may see Indian artisans presently at work on totems, if you visit the Cultural Heritage Center up the hill on Deermont Street.

You might also like to visit the Centennial Museum and Library, which is downtown near Ketchikan Creek on Cock Street. There are Indian artifacts here as well as local history items: open Monday through Saturday from 8:30 A.M. to 5 P.M. Another museum (private) is Dolly's House on Creek Street; it is filled with the memorabilia of a near-legendary Ketchikan madam.

Ketchikan's hotels and restaurants are not remarkable, although they are clean and generally reasonable. If you have wheels of any kind, however, there's very pleasant camping about six miles north of town at Ward Lake Recreation Area, a Forest Service facility. The whole town uses this area as it's particularly good for picnicking; it has two large shelters where you can cook over an open fire and stay reasonably dry if it's raining. The Forest Service also maintains a rain-forest nature trail here, which makes for a pretty .7-mile walk. Last Chance Campground at the Ward Lake Area has 23 units, and Signal Creek Campground has 25. There is also a walk-in campground called Three C's, which has only four units but almost all the comforts of home—water, toilets, tables, grates, and firewood. Signal Creek Campground, on the shore of Ward Lake, has a one-dollar-per-day fee, but the other two are free. There are another nine units at Settler's Cove Campground on Mile 18.2 of the North Tongass Highway south of town. This is a beautiful site, and there's good berry picking in August.

Like Juneau, Ketchikan offers you the chance to hike from downtown to the top of a mountain, and, although Deer Mountain is not quite so high as Juneau's backdrop peaks, it's still a good hike that enables you to experience the beauties of the Southeastern spruce forests just a few steps from civilization. It will also take you through a magnificent stand of Alaska cedar. The trail takes off at the end of Deermont Street, has stretches of boardwalk and several switchbacks. There's a fine view from the 1,500 foot elevation. You can continue to the top of the mountain without technical difficulties, and, if you want to make your trek into an overnight, two- or three-day trip, you can go on to Blue Lake where there is a most attractive Forest Service cabin. Information is available from the Forest Service. The distance up Deer Mountain is three miles one way. To Blue Lake, it's another two miles. Elevation gain up Deer Mountain is 3,000 feet; total gained to Blue Lake is 3,400.

There is another beautiful and more strenuous outing you can take from Beaver Lake, about fourteen miles south of town, up Twin Peaks, but you will have to get yourself to the roadhead. There are also short hikes out of the Ward Lake Recreation Area that are very lovely and that will give you a good sampling of the local flora and fauna. There's a loop all the way around the lake, and there's a stroll up the Perseverance Trail that takes you to Perseverance Lake. This is a less than two-mile hike, one way, and is easy walking in the summer, being largely over boardwalk.

Ketchikan offers some good opportunities for bikers as well as hikers. There are several miles of paved highway around the town and traffic is light. It is also a good place for kayakers to put their boats in the water for trips into the Behm Canal and through other local waters.

Ketchikan is the takeoff point for a large number of U.S. Forest Service cabins. If you're on wheels, you may want to take advantage of the biweekly ferry service from Ketchikan to the nearby Prince of Wales Island where there are several of these unique cabins accessible by car or by bicycle. There is also a Native-operated lodge, the Haida Way, which has good accommodations in the village of Craig on Prince of Wales Island. (Write Box 90, Craig, AK 99921.) Prince of Wales Island also offers good camping. You might work out a kayak trip to tie into the ferry schedule in this part of the world.

The Forest Service can provide you with up-to-date information about these and the numerous other recreational opportunities available out of Ketchikan. As of this writing, many are still in process of being developed.

Some Useful Information About Ketchikan

Ferry
Runs daily in summer. The ferry terminal is about 1.5 miles north of downtown and adjacent to the Ketchikan Airport ferry-taxi.

Airport Ferry
This departs every half hour, at fifteen and forty-five minutes past the hour, from town. Remember, if you miss one, you'll lose a half hour on your flight departure time. Note: You must walk a long ramp to the airport.

Bus Service
Available from the ferry terminal and from south of town. Buses run about once every half hour.

Taxi

Alaska Cab, phone 907-225-2133. **Sourdough**, phone 907-225-6651. **Yellow**, phone 907-225-3900.

Car Rental

Available at the airport: **Avis**, phone 907-225-4515; **Hertz**, phone 907-225-5000; **Payless**, phone 907-225-6609. **National** is available at the Marine View Plaza Hotel (see below), phone 907-225-6601.

Air

Alaska Airlines provides regular jet service inside and outside of Alaska; phone 907-225-2141. **Western**, phone 907-225-3693.

Air Charters

Ketchikan Air Service: Write Box 6900, Ketchikan, AK 99901; phone 907-225-6608; **Revilla Flying Service**: Write 1427 Tongass Avenue, Ketchikan, AK 99901; phone 907-225-4379. **Temsco Helicopters**: Write Box 5057, Ketchikan, AK 99901; phone 907-225-5141. **Todd's Air Service**: Mile 1.25 S. Tongass Highway, Ketchikan, AK 99901; phone 907-225-4267. **Tyee Airlines**: Write Box 8331, Ketchikan, AK 99901; phone 907-225-6118. Flies scheduled air service to local towns including Craig, Klawock, Hydaburg, and Metlak-with connections to Yes Bay, and Bell Island.

Many charter services take off and land along the Ketchikan waterfront. All serve local Forest Service cabins.

Hotels

(There is a 7% room and sales tax.) **Clover Pass Resort**: Mile 15 North Tongass. Write Box 7322, Ketchikan, AK 99901; phone 907-247-2234. Lodge and cabins, on the water, restaurant, trailers and campers, reasonable fishing package. From May 15 to September 15. **Gilmore Hotel**: 326 Front St. Ketchikan, AK 99901; phone 907-225-2174. Downtown, reasonable. **Hilltop Motel**: across from the ferry terminal, 3434 Tongass Avenue, Ketchikan, AK 99901; phone 907-225-5166. Restaurant, moderate. **Ingersoll Hotel**: 303 Mission Street, Ketchikan, AK 99901; phone 907-225-2124. Downtown, reasonable. **Knickerbocker Hotel**: 421 Dock Street, Ketchikan, AK 99901; phone 907-225-2923. Downtown, light housekeeping, very reasonable by the week. **Marine View Plaza Hotel**: 2415 Hemlock, Ketchikan, AK 99901; phone 907-225-6601. Converted apartments, some with kitchenettes. Views, downtown, moderate, reasonable for families. **Youth Hostel**: In the First Methodist Church, 400 Main Street, Ketchikan, AK 99901; phone 907-225-3780. Registration from 8:30 to 11 P.M. Open Memorial Day to Labor Day. Two dollars per day or one dollar for American Youth Hostel members.

Wilderness Lodges

The ones near Ketchikan include those at Bell Island Hot Springs, Waterfall Cannery, and Yes Bay. Air taxi needed. Inquire at the Chamber of Commerce or Visitor's Bureau or consult *Worlds of Alaska.* See Bibliography.

Campgrounds

Signal Creek, Three C's, and **Last Chance** campgrounds at Ward Creek Recreation Area off Ward Lake Road north of ferry approximately six to seven miles. U.S. Forest Service administered. **Settler's Cove:** Mile 18.2 North Tongass Highway. Alaska State Division of Parks administered. **Clover Pass Resort:** See above, Hotels.

Boat Charters

Outdoor Alaska: Write Dale Pihlmann, P.O. Box 7814, Ketchikan, AK 99901; phone 907-247-8444. Misty Fjord trips and other wilderness river expeditions; will carry your canoe, kayak, or raft. **M. V. Lehua:** Write Jess Edwards, Box 5911, Ketchikan, AK 99901; phone 907-225-3702. Forty-seven foot trimaran, sleeps party of six (plus crew). For photographing wildlife, glaciers, and wilderness.

Fishing Charters

Consult *The Worlds of Alaska.* (See Bibliography.) Folks looking for fish to take home should inquire at one of the cold storage plants.

Laundromats

At the north end of town in the **Market Basket Shopping Center,** open 7 days a week, 2515 Tongass Street, and at the south end of town in the **Ayson Hotel** on Stedman Street.

Useful Names and Addresses

Chamber of Commerce: Write P.O. Box 5957, Ketchikan, AK 99901; phone 907-225-3184. **Ketchikan Visitor's Bureau:** Write Box 7055, Ketchikan, AK 99901; phone 907-225-6166. During summer, the Visitor's Bureau has a kiosk at the ferry terminal and one on the downtown dock where cruise ships come in. **U.S. Forest Service:** Write c/o Federal Building, Ketchikan, AK 99901; phone 907-225-3101. There is an information center in the lobby of the Federal Building. You'll find a good brochure here on Prince of Wales Island.

USGS Topo Maps Ketchikan quandrangles B-5 and B-6. Available at **Service Electric Co.,** 744 Water Street; phone 907-225-2168.

MISTY FJORDS

Ketchikan is the gateway to the new Misty Fjords National Monument, a magnificent complex of fjords and mountains rising sheerly from the water, with dense rain forests, wild rivers, waterfalls, and high alpine lakes.

Until recently, you could get to Misty Fjords only by boat or air taxi, and you might still want to take advantage of these means of transportation. You can charter either. (Dale Pihlmann runs special boat tours into Misty Fjords throughout the summer; he can also drop you off to camp and pick you up at the end of a special wilderness experience. See Ketchikan Information for his, and other addresses.) But now you also have the choice of taking a day's outing to the monument and back on board the *Aurora*, one of the smaller ferries of the state ferry fleet. This weekly ferry outing is ideal if you can be in Ketchikan on a Friday. The boat leaves from the ferry terminal at 8 A.M. and returns at 4 P.M. (As of this writing, that is; better check.) You can take

Misty Fjords National Monument. The cliffs rise higher than those in Yosemite Valley. Source: U.S. Forest Service.

your own lunch or eat in the coffee shop aboard. Be sure to travel on the top deck. You may see seals or whales en route, and you're sure to see many bald eagles.

Even if the weather doesn't cooperate entirely, you'll see—and feel—some of the most superb country in Southeast in this new monument. Sometimes you can travel through rain into blue-sky weather, so don't give up. When Henry Gannett wrote the following in 1902, he could have had Misty Fjords in mind:

"There is one other asset of the territory not yet enumerated; imponderable and difficult to appraise, yet one of the chief assets of Alaska, if not the greatest. This is the scenery. There are glaciers, mountains, fjords elsewhere, but nowhere else on earth is there such an abundance and magnificence of mountain, fjord, and glacier scenery. For thousands of miles, the coast is a continuous panorama. For one Yosemite of California, Alaska has hundreds."

Recreational use of Misty Fjords National Monument is presently restricted largely to boat use or to fly-in campsites, but trails may be put in by the Forest Service or further camping opportunities may be developed. (There are several Forest Service cabins in the monument.) The future of the molybdenum mine in the heart of the monument—about a 150,000 acre piece of land that may be developed—will also determine the use of a sizeable area of this extraordinary place.

For further information, contact the Monument Manager, Misty Fjords National Monument, Tongass National Forest, 1817 North Tongass Highway, Ketchikan, AK 99901; phone 907-225-2148.

WRANGELL

Wrangell lies about six hours north of Ketchikan as the ferry sails and is located close to the mouth of the Stikine, a great river that rises in Canada and has been an important—and spectacularly beautiful—waterway for people for many millennia. Northwest Indians probably used the Wrangell area extensively as long as 8,000 years ago; the legends they carved into the argillite along the waterfront are believed to date back that far. When the Russians found the place in the early 1830s, they considered it important enough to build Fort Saint Dionysius there to prevent trespassing by the Hudson's Bay trappers who were after otters. The Americans gave the town its name in honor of Baron Ferdinand Petrovich von Wrangell, a vice admiral in the Imperial Russian Navy and governor of Russian America from 1830 to 1835. Many other nearby place names, including Woronkofski, Mitkof, and Kupreanof islands, also reflect the region's Russian history.

In 1839, the British managed to lease the area from Russia and to rechristen the town Fort Stikine. After the United States acquired Alaska in 1867, it established a military post known as Fort Wrangell, which survived about a decade. Later, sourdoughs bound for the Klondike and the Cassiars headed through Wrangell up the Stikine, and the town became a busy supply and trading center.

John Muir made Wrangell his headquarters for his 1879 adventures in Southeastern Alaska, traveling from there to Haines (then known as Chilkat) by canoe with his missionary friend, S. Hall Young, and a party of Tlingit Indians. Of Wrangell, Muir wrote: "No mining hamlet in the placer gulches of California, nor any backwoods village I ever saw approached it in picturesque devil-may-care *abandon*. It was a lawless draggle of wooden huts and houses, built in crooked lines, wrangling around the boggy shores of the island for a mile or so . . . without the slightest subordination to the points of the compass or to building laws of any kind." This last part of Muir's comment would apply to many towns in Alaska for many decades afterward as well.

Wrangell has become far more orderly and circumspect since Muir made his visit. Today, it is the site of two canneries and two sawmills and is a busy port for the export of local lumber. (You'll probably see several enormous Japanese lumber ships—murus—loading from the sawmill that is visible from the ferry.) Wrangell is also the departure point for adventuring up or along the Stikine River.

The ferry stopover in Wrangell is usually only a half hour, but the tides may stretch the time you'll have in town. If you visit the Wrangell Visitors' Center in the A frame on Front Street near the Stikine Inn, you can get a local Visitor's Guide, published by the Wrangell Sentinel. This contains a city map which is very useful. (You can also get this in the ferry terminal.) Since there are 23 U.S. Forest Service cabins in the Wrangell Ranger District, you might also want to stop by the Forest Service office across from City Hall, just off Front Street, to inquire about them. If you want to buy some local shrimp (excellent), ask at the Visitors' Center or the ferry terminal. If you stay around the terminal when a boat comes in, you'll likely meet the local children selling garnets from the nearby Garnet Ledge. This claim was willed to the town's children and the Boy Scouts of Southeast Alaska by a resident miner. For more local color, you can admire the totems that ornament the town.

If you have a few hours to spend in Wrangell, you can enjoy a couple of strolls from the ferry terminal or from the town. A mile and a half round-trip walk can show you the best of the Indian petroglyphs. It is illegal to use chalk on the petroglyphs to outline the designs or to deface the carvings in any way. They should of course be treated with respect. Wet or dry, however, they are good subjects for your camera, and—perhaps even more interesting, as Margaret Piggott suggests, you can make beautiful rubbings of them if you carry along paper and charcoal or crayons or even a pencil.

Another stroll in Wrangell will take you to Chief Shakes Island, less than a mile south from the ferry terminal. Ask at the Visitors' Center for directions for these worthwhile outings.

If you have longer to stay in Wrangell, you might want to visit the museum on Second Street (open 1 P.M. to 4 P.M. every day during the summer) or if you're feeling more energetic, you could hike a mile up Mount Dewey to see the view. You start up from Second Avenue and Mission Street. If you have your bike, you can ride south down the Zimovia Highway. The traffic is light, and the road hugs the shore most of the time. This is also a pleasant road to walk along. Look for whales and shorebirds. There is a free campground at City Park (Mile 1.7) and another at Pat's Lake (Mile 11.2). At Mile 4.6, there is a Forest Service trail up to Rainbow Falls. The trail is through about a mile of forest and much of it is wet, so wear good boots or your Southeast sneakers, if you have a pair. The views are lovely on this trail, and you'll likely hear bird song as you walk. You may even see a black-tailed deer or a black bear along the way. This walk should take less than two hours.

The Stikine River, which rises in Canada, pours its swift-flowing waters through the Coastal Range and into Alaska, spreading into a beautiful tangle of braids as it forms its delta near Wrangell. It is navigable for a good 150 miles upstream and is considered to be the fastest flowing (six to eight miles per hour) navigable river in the United States.

The Stikine passes through some exceptional Southeaastern scenery. Its grand canyon, which is over a hundred miles long and has cliffs that soar upward over 4,000 feet, reminded John Muir of Yosemite when he visited there in 1879. He wrote, "The majestic cliffs and mountains forming the canyon walls display an endless variety of form and sculpture, and are wonderfully adorned with glaciers and waterfalls while throughout almost its whole extent, the floor is a flowery landscape garden . . . "

Although a swift-running river, the Stikine presents no major difficulties for an experienced river-runner. The put-in at Telegraph is a short flight from Wrangell and, as noted, air service is available. If you're interested in running the Stikine River with a guide, you have several choices. Stikine River Song (write General Delivery, Telegraph Creek, B.C., VOJ 2WO; phone via Fort Nelson 403-235-3301 or 3451) conducts tours as does Alaska Discovery (see Juneau) and Traylor Enterprises, Inc., Box 1381, Wrangell, AK 99929.

Some Useful Information About Wrangell

Ferry
Runs daily in summer.

Air Service
By **Alaska Airlines.** Serves Wrangell daily year round. **Le Conte Airlines** provides scheduled service in Southeast. See below.

Air Charter Service
Write **Stikine Air Service,** Box 631, Wrangell, AK 99929; phone 907-874-3327.

Taxi
Service is provided by **Star Cab**; phone 907-874-3622. There is no scheduled bus service.

Car Rental
Etolin (National), phone 907-874-3314 or 874-3203 evenings and weekends.

Hotels
Hotels include the **Stikine Inn** (phone 907-874-3388) and the **Thunderbird Hotel** (phone 907-874-3322) in town and the **Roadhouse** (phone 907-874-2335 or 874-2336), which is four miles from the ferry down the Zimovia Highway. You can write any of these in Wrangell, AK 99929. The Roadhouse runs bus tours and rents ten-speed bicycles, including one tandem.

Laundromat
In the **Thunderbird Hotel,** five blocks from the ferry on Front Street. Open seven days a week.

Boat Charters
Ask at Visitors' Center.

Useful Names and Addresses
Chamber of Commerce: Write Box 49, Wrangell, AK 99929; phone 907-874-2056 or 874-3327. **U.S. Forest Service**: Write Box 51, Wrangell, AK 99929; phone 907-874-2323.

USGS Topo Maps Petersburg quadrangles B-1 and B-2.

PETERSBURG

Located on the tip of Mitkof Island and at the northern end of the Wrangell Narrows, Petersburg lies about halfway between Ketchikan and Juneau. It is tucked between the almost 10,000 foot snowy mountains on the mainland and the much lower but green-forested mountains of Kupreanof Island. The neat Norwegian-style wooden buildings of Petersburg make a picture-postcard scene in the midst of this magnificent setting.

Petersburg was named for Peter Buschmann, a Norwegian who founded the town in 1897. He selected the site because of its superb fishery, its forests, and its good harbor. After building himself a saltery, he anticipated later generations by building a sawmill. The LeConte Glacier (which was named for Joseph LeConte, a University of California professor of geology and founding member of the Sierra Club) lay conveniently just across Frederick Sound from Petersburg and provided the new little town with plenty of ice. LeConte ice was also exported by ice ships south to the burgeoning city of San Francisco until the early twentieth century. The LeConte, incidentally, is the southernmost tidewater glacier on the North American continent. It is very lively and launches many icebergs into Frederick Sound, some of which you can see from the ferry.

Petersburg today is a thriving community with the largest homebased halibut fleet in Alaska. It is, as well, the principal fish processing port for the Southeast, handling at least four kinds of salmon—silver, pink, chum, and sockeye—along with crab, shrimp, herring, and of course halibut. (It is famous for its succulent shrimp.)

Petersburg celebrates its Scandinavian heritage with a three-day Little Norway Festival that includes dancing, costumes, Viking ships, and delicious food and is held every year around May 17, Norwegian Independence Day. The colorful Norwegian influence of its founders permeates the houses and gardens as well as the boats of the town.

There are two beautiful hikes accessible from Petersburg, but you will have to find a boat or an airlift to get yourself across the Wrangell Narrows to Kupreanof Island. One trail will take you along Petersburg Creek to Petersburg Lake, a distance of 5.5 or 6.5 miles one way, depending upon where you start. The elevation gain is only 200 feet, and there is excellent and varied fishing along the way, and you are likely to see lots of bald eagles; this is their home territory. The second trail, up to Petersburg Mountain, is considerably more strenuous but will give a strong hiker some unmatched views of the

Wrangell Narrows and, on a clear day, of the spectacular mountains and ice fields on the mainland. This a five-mile round trip, with an elevation gain of about 2,800 feet. You should allow a full day for either of these hikes and take along your lunch. On the Petersburg Mountain Trail, it is also wise to carry a canteen unless it's raining. Ask the U.S. Forest Service people (address below) about further details as well as current trail conditions.

If you're traveling in your own small boat, you can make the run across the Wrangell Narrows yourself. (Whoever's boat you travel in, dress warmly for this short—twenty minutes or so—but chilly crossing.) Be sure to check the tides; and check with the Forest Service (or Piggott's book) about this adventurous trip. Watch for humpback whales, sea lions, and porpoises on the way, and keep your eyes out for deer along the short.

If you have your bicycle (or your car) with you and want to spend some time around Petersburg, the Mitkof Highway runs south for 35 miles, and there are three Forest Service sites along it: Blind Slough Recreation Area at Mile 17.5, Ohmer Creek Campground at Mile 22, and Sumner Strait Campground at Mile 26.8.

Experienced mountain climbers with proper equipment may want to investigate the climbing possibilities on the mainland near Petersburg. It is the takeoff point for peaks like the Devil's Thumb and others. Check with the Forest Service for details.

Some Useful Information About Petersburg

Ferry
Runs daily in summer. Dock is at south end of town.

Air Service
By **Alaska Airlines**, daily jets, serves Petersburg year round; phone 907-772-4255.

Bus Service
Available: Check at ferry terminal for schedule.

Car Rental and Taxi
Petersburg Cab and Car Rental: phone 907-772-3811.

Air Charter
Alaska Island Air: Write Box 508, Petersburg, AK 99833; phone 907-772-3130. Also consult Chamber of Commerce; see below.

Boat Charter

Fish Alaska: Write Box 316, Petersburg, AK 99833; phone 907-772-4288. Inquire above boat rentals and other charter operators at Chamber of Commerce; see below.

Hotels

Beachcomber Inn: Write Box 1027, Petersburg, AK 99833; phone 907-772-3888. This is an old cannery located on the Narrows about three miles from the ferry. Restaurant. **King Salmon Motel**: Write Box 869, Petersburg, AK 99833; phone 907-772-3291. Close to ferry, restaurant. **Mitkof Hotel**: Write Box 689, Petersburg, AK 99833; phone 907-772-4281 or 772-4282. A mile from ferry. Older, quiet, serves coffee and rolls. **Tides Inn Motel**: Write Box 1048, Petersburg, AK 99833; phone 907-772-4288. Coffee and rolls.

Showers

The Spa, Main Street next to Mitkof Hotel (also hot tubs and sauna). **Van Vleck Recreation Vehicle Park**, 4th and H Streets.

Useful Names and Addresses

Chamber of Commerce: Write Box 649, Petersburg, AK 99833. Located adjacent to the Mitkof Hotel on Main Street. **U.S. Forest Service**: Office in National Bank of Alaska building, Main and F Streets; phone 907-772-3871.

   USGS Topo Maps Petersburg quadrangles D-3 and D-4.

JUNEAU

All of Southeast Alaska's communities share essentially the same geography, flora, and fauna, but the weather in each one varies and so does the character. Ketchikan, Alaska's southernmost "port of entrance," for instance, has the flavor of a fishing and logging community, while its fine totems tie it vividly to its Indian heritage. Petersburg has a distinctly Norwegian atmosphere, and the Russian influence in Sitka is inescapable. Skagway has kept enough of its gold mining history intact to have most of its main street designated as a national historical monument. Juneau is not only the picturesque population center of Southeast and full of Alaskan history, it is also a cosmopolitan little city.

Juneau was the first American settlement in Alaska that succeeded; for many years it was the first port of call north of Seattle. (It is still an active port.)

Juneau started out as a mining town, has been a center for local commercial fishing of salmon and halibut (in 1936, there were fourteen salmon canneries in the area), and has become today the home of some of Alaska's most creative people—artists, writers, scientists, and scholars. It has been the state capital for more than seventy-five years, the heart of Alaska's political arena, and the place where the state of Alaska does much of its business with Washington, D.C. In 1974, Alaskans voted to relocate their capital to a site to be chosen somewhere between Anchorage and Fairbanks. However, three years later, they voted down the bonds for a capital move and, in 1982, they rejected Willow as a site and nullified the 1974 vote. To date, Juneau remains the capital.

Juneau is the city where, at one time or another, for one reason or another, most of the people involved in Alaska's present, and future, will come. If you stand around in the lobby of the Baranof Hotel, which is located a couple of blocks down the hill from the capitol building, chances are you can rub shoulders with Alaskan decision makers such as the governor and members of his cabinet, Native leaders, directors of major oil companies and lumber companies, businessmen from home and abroad, experts in the fields of geology, fisheries, finance, and more. If you happen to be around when the legislature is in session, you will be able to see a good sampling of Alaska's population—not only the lawmakers themselves—who may be prospectors, hunting guides, fishermen, construction workers, or writers—but also people from every part of the bush. In summer, of course, you'll encounter tourists from all over the world.

If you're interested in adventuring in the out-of-doors, Juneau is the point of departure for some of the best country in Southeast Alaska—Admiralty Island, West Chichagof Island (also see Sitka), and Glacier Bay National Monument included. It is also the gateway to some of the finest Southeastern waters for canoeing and kayaking. In the winter, Juneau is close to one of Alaska's major downhill skiing facilities, Eaglecrest, and the cross-country skiing opportunities around it are fabulous. (Many people simply ski cross-country from their back doors.) And where else can you hike from a downtown corner through forests and fields of wildflowers to the top of not one but two nearly 4,000 foot mountains and some of the loveliest views anywhere? For all of these reasons, if you are only able to visit one of Alaska's three principal cities, I recommend Juneau.

Juneau began life as a tent city that was located as close as possible to the site of the 1880 strike on Gold Creek in Silverbow Basin. (Gold Creek now flows encased in a concrete culvert through the center of town.) In terms of good weather, this was not the optimum location, and the tents are said to have been flattened at least twice by *Taku* winds before more permanent buildings could be erected. Only a few miles north of Juneau on the Gastineau Channel, the climate is more moderate, the winds are less fierce, and the total precipitation is 36 inches a year less. Despite its less-than-ideal climate, Juneau has a setting that turned out to be superlative. Situated on the shore

Mendenhall Glacier, near Juneau. Source: U.S. Forest Service.

of the Gastineau Channel, it has a backdrop of two snow-topped mountains, Mount Roberts (3,819 feet) and Mount Juneau (3,516 feet). Dark spruce forests streak their precipitous slopes, and long white streamers of waterfalls sway through their avalanche canyons. In summer, the slanting sunlight backlights the trees and makes the high green-napped meadows glow like the best velvet.

It was John Muir, founder of the Sierra Club, who is credited with having initiated Alaska's first gold rush when he was indirectly responsible for sending Joe Juneau and Richard Harris to their find in Silverbow Basin. Muir was on his second trip to Alaska, traveling with S. Hall Young, and from his geological know-how suspected the possibility of gold in the area. This information was conveyed to Juneau and Harris and the hunt was on.

Joe Juneau's claims paid off handsomely; he sold them for so much he is said to have worried that he would never live to spend all the money, but he did. The gold content of most of the ore in Mount Roberts, however, proved to be too low grade to be profitable for prospectors. In 1897, the Alaska Juneau Company bought up the 23 lode claims that covered the most promising area and began an extensive low-grade mining operation that lasted until 1944. During that time, it reduced the cubic footage of Mount Roberts by an estimated 88.5 million tons of rock and netted about $77.6 million worth of gold. Some of the old AJ Company buildings still stand on the slopes above Juneau, but they are now unsafe. In 1861, another low-grade operation commenced on Douglas Island, directly across the channel from Juneau; in 36 years, John

Treadwell, a San Franciscan, is said to have taken out $66 million in gold. In 1917, a major cave-in and subsequent flooding by seawater of the Treadwell mine closed down the operation.

As the town of Juneau took shape, the first obvious place to go was up. The early builders fitted their homes, stores, hotels, and saloons into and onto the lower slopes of Mount Roberts, taking advantage of every small natural shelf. Much of their work still stands, and older Juneau is as colorful as many small European cities. The best way to see this part of Juneau or, indeed, all of Juneau is on foot: the Juneau Visitors Bureau, located in the Log Cabin at 3rd and Seward Streets, will provide you with maps and a suggested self-guided walking tour. You'll find the narrow streets that wind up and downhill past the well-kept Victorian houses don't always have sidewalks, but the traffic is usually light—Juneau has all of three traffic lights, which is more than the total in the rest of the Southeast. When the slopes get too steep, there are long wooden stairways built more than half a century ago for substitute thoroughfares, and these will take you to some of the best view points in town.

Juneau's suburbs reach north and south for many miles and include Auke Bay and the Mendenhall Valley. Territorially, Greater Juneau is, in fact, the largest city in the United States. Its 3,100 square miles stretch from the grand ice field above the town to the west side of Douglas Island and encompass several mountains and glaciers as well as the city of Douglas, itself, which is linked to Juneau by a bridge across the Gastineau Channel.

Juneau has been enlarged considerably through the years by fill, much of it supplied by the Mount Roberts AJ Mining Company tailings. This has expanded the waterfront area and provided for more building space. Today, you'll find that many important Juneau buildings stand on filled land: for instance, the Federal Building and the excellent Alaska State Museum. The principal food and service shopping mall, with its Foodland and Colonel Sanders, is also in this part of town.

Spanning the two main levels of the city vertically and being fitted into the hillside in the process is Juneau's largest structure, the State Office Building (sometimes referred to as the SOB). This building has its main entrance on Fourth Street up the hill, and its basement entrance eight floors below on Willoughby Street. (The main floor is numbered the eighth, and the basement is the first. There are actually eleven stories in this building.) If you stay around Juneau any length of time, you'll find it convenient, especially on rainy weekdays, to use its elevator to get yourself from "uptown" to "downtown" or vice versa. The state library, an excellent one, is located in the State Office Building on the main (eighth) floor; it has a great deal of Alaskana on its shelves, should you feel like browsing on a rainy day.

Although Juneau has been the official state capital since 1900 (the actual move from Sitka was not completed until 1906), it had few official buildings until 1912. That year, Congress made Alaska a proper territory with its own, elected legislature. (Its executives were federal appointees.) The event was

Saint Nicholas' Church, Juneau. Source: Mike Miller.

celebrated by the construction of the Governor's Mansion up the hill on Calhoun Street. The mansion fronts so directly onto Calhoun Street that people sometimes walk the few steps from the sidewalk to peer through the curtained windows, ring the doorbell, or even open the big front door if someone has forgotten to lock it. If you become so tempted, please refrain. Although Alaska is probably the most informal of the 50 states, and the governor and his family are easy to see around town, they are entitled to a little privacy. Incidentally, to illustrate Alaska's small-town atmosphere, every Christmas the governor holds an open house to which the entire state is welcome, and up to 1978 the mansion's telephone number was listed in the Juneau phone book.

Not far from the Governor's Mansion on Fourth Street is the State Capitol Building, which was erected by the federal government in 1931 at a cost of $1 million. The building is a monument to the decade of the thirties. This massive period piece with its pillars is worth a visit, if only to see how lavishly marble was used in its construction. Brought in from Prince of Wales Island, marble covers many of the walls. As you walk through the halls of the capitol, keep in mind that Alaska was so small when it was constructed that this building housed the entire Alaskan governmental operation; within these six stories were the territorial legislature, the U.S. District Court, twenty-five federal and seven territorial departments as well as the Alaska Historical

Library and Museum. Now the capitol building is occupied only by the state legislature and executive branches. (Judicial is across the street.) If you are in Juneau during the legislative session, which starts in January and may continue into June, try to find time to sit in on the assembly or the senate when one or the other is in session. There are few better ways to get a feeling for what Alaska is all about. Unfortunately, there isn't much of a gallery for either house of the legislature, but you may get a seat if you're lucky. (If you know anyone in the legislature, don't be surprised if you get introduced to everyone present.)

Up the hill from the capitol at 326 Fifth Street is Juneau's small and charming Russian Orthodox Church, Saint Nicholas's. Farther up the same hill is a fine totem erected by the Juneau Rotary Club and sometimes called the Rotary totem. Unfortunately for photographers, neither of these unique city ornaments can be photographed easily because of interfering telephone wires or poles.

If you plan any outdoor adventuring on your own starting from Juneau, you'll want to talk to the National Park Service and/or the U.S. Forest Service people in the Centennial Hall Information Center, 101 Egan Drive 1.5 miles from the downtown ferry. This is where you get firsthand information and printed material about the camps, trails, Southeast birdlife, and so on, within their bailiwicks—Glacier Bay, Admiralty Island, etc. You'll find a Post Office on the first floor of the Federal Building, too, in case you need stamps.

Not far from the Federal Building on Whittier Street is the Alaska State Museum. (Hours 9 A.M. to 5 P.M. Monday through Friday; 1 P.M. to 4 P.M. Saturday and Sunday.) This is one of Alaska's most interesting and comprehensive museums, so allow plenty of time to visit it. You'll find historical exhibits, including the replica of a gold assay office, Russian memorabilia, and good collections of Native artifacts—Eskimo, Athabascan, and Tlingit-Haida. (Unfortunately, so much of the Aleut culture was lost early on that this Native group is not well represented here or anywhere else in Alaska's museums.) There are some excellent wildlife dioramas that will give you an idea of what Alaska's animals look like. (The animals in the dioramas and elsewhere in the Alaska State Museum have been provided by the Alaska Department of Fish and Game, and most of them were killed accidentally: ADFG has a policy not to kill specimens for display only.) Works by contemporary Alaskan artists are on exhibition in the Governor's Collection. A number of these artists live in Juneau, and if you're interested in them and think you might like to meet one of them, you can contact Suzanne Janson at her shop, Faces, Places, and Things, on Seward Street.

Since Juneau is a waterfront city with an active harbor, you'll want to spend some time in the new marine park and along the wharf. You'll find boardwalks for strolling and watching the traffic in the channel. In summer, there will probably be a big white tour ship in dock or one of the smart-looking blue and gold state ferry liners. Small boats, including sailboats and fishing boats with their big cerise-colored halibut buoys, come and go, and you'll see small planes taking off or landing. Incidentally, the waters of the channel can be more dangerous on absolutely calm days, especially when the sun is very low, than when they're ruffed up by a light wind: the smooth luminous surface requires exceptionally good depth perception on the part of pilots. Be sure to look for whales and porpoises and a variety of waterfowl; in winter, a pair of old squaw ducks can provide hours of good watching. Don't forget to look up, down, around, and everywhere for bald eagles, particularly when you first get to Juneau. Later on, the bald eagles will be a familiar, always welcome part of the Southeastern scene, especially when you get farther away from built-up areas. The other big bird to become acquainted with is the raven, so much a part of the Indian cultures. The raven thrives not only in the Southeast but all over Alaska.

There are a number of restaurants, as well as gift shops in the wharf-side Merchant's Mall. (Two fine bookstores are nearby on Franklin Street, the Baranoff and the Hearthside, and both of them have good selections of Alaskana and selected local art work. They are also somewhat removed from the tourist

Raven (*Corvus corax principalis*). ***Range: throughout Alaska.***

crowds along the wharf.) You'll find a wide variety of places to eat and shop in other parts of the town, as well.

AVERAGE TEMPERATURE: JUNEAU

	F° daytime high	F° nighttime low	F° monthly average
Jan.	28.3	17.2	22.8
Feb.	33.5	21.9	27.7
March	37.6	25.2	31.4
April	46.1	31.3	38.7
May	54.9	38.0	46.5
June	61.4	44.2	52.8
July	63.7	47.2	55.5
August	62.4	46.3	54.4
Sept.	55.9	42.4	49.2
Oct.	46.8	36.4	41.6
Nov.	37.0	27.3	32.2
Dec.	31.6	22.2	26.9

Day-Hikes You Can Take From Downtown Juneau

There are 27 trails described in the U.S. Forest Service brochure, *Juneau Trails*. Four of these can be reached on foot from downtown Juneau. For Mount Roberts (a nearly 4,000 foot climb), you take the wooden stairway at the end of Sixth Street and continue upward. For the other three—Perseverance, Mount Juneau, and Granite Creek trails—you follow Gold Street up the hill to Basin Road and cross Gold Creek to commence your climb. In good summer weather, you may encounter Juneau people on the Perseverance Trail during lunch hour. The other trails make for more strenuous outings. Any of these trails will quickly acquaint you with typical Southeast hiking conditions.

Because of the great diversity in natural habitats these trails travel through, there are many different birds along them, and, in June and July, the birdsong is a delight. Listen particularly for the fox sparrow that introduces its song with a liquid whistle and then warbles its melody. At twilight, you may hear the gray-cheeked thrush alone or in charming duet with a Swainson's thrush.

At least six other interesting trails can be reached from downtown Juneau by bus. These include the Mendenhall Glacier trails, which range from a one and one half mile loop to longer trails which offer a chance to view mountain goats as well as ice fields. The U.S. Forest Service Visitor Center at Mendenhall Glacier has information on these. (Phone 907-789-0097.)

Other trails are the Lemon Creek Trail, which is fairly easy, but a scramble in places, and runs through lovely forest; the Salmon Creek Trail, a scramble,

Mountain goat (Oreamnos americanus). **Range: the alpine zone in Southeast and Southcentral Alaska.**

but with fine berry-picking in season; the Spaulding, which is easy and leads to good muskegs as well as the John Muir Cabin, built by the local Sierra Club group; the Mount Bradley (Mount Jumbo) Trail, which is difficult but has magnificent views and wildflowers in season; and the Dan Moller or Kowee Creek Trail, which is a former ski trail and is described by a Juneau friend like this: "The loveliest, readily accessible subalpine forest and meadow around Juneau are up Kowee Creek. The trail has a boardwalk through its lower muskegs and ends up, unlike other local trails, in an exquisite subalpine bowl. It can be hiked after supper on long summer evenings, but it is good at all seasons, although you do cross, briefly, several avalanche tracks. There are wonderful wildflowers in summer and birdsong in June and July."

Ask for a copy of the Forest Service trail guide, *Juneau Trails*, at the information center at 101 Egan Drive.

Some Useful Information About Juneau

Ferry

The state ferry liner runs daily during summer. Note that it has two slips, one downtown and the other at Auke Bay. Between these terminals, the Mendenhall and Lemon Glaciers pour out so much silt and sediment that the Gastineau Channel is too shallow to accommodate the big boats. Hence, Auke Bay is used primarily for travel to and from the north, avoiding the shallow areas. Ships docking at the downtown terminal travel out around Douglas Island to reach the deeper waters. The larger ferries serve the larger communities and carry the most tourists. Smaller ferries, the *LeConte* and the *Aurora,* serve the smaller villages, and, primarily, the local people.

Air Service

There is daily interstate scheduled service by **Alaska Airlines** and **Western Airlines**. Your agent can give you the latest schedules and tariffs. Intrastate scheduled flights to Haines, Skagway, and so on are provided by **L.A.B. Flying Service, Channel,** and **Wings of Alaska.** (See below for addresses and phones.)

Air Charter Service

Channel Flying, Inc.: Write Box 3577, RR3, Juneau, AK 99801; phone 907-586-3331. Amphibious or wheels. Air-taxi service, flightseeing. **L.A.B. Flying Service**: Write Box 2201, Juneau, AK 99801; phone: 907-789-9160. Amphibious or wheels. Air-taxi service. Flightseeing over Juneau Icecap and Glacier Bay National Monument a specialty. Scheduled flights to Haines and Skagway. **Wings of Alaska**: Write 1873 Shell Simmons Drive, Juneau, AK 99801; phone 907-789-0790. Flight-seeing. Air-taxi service. Scheduled flights to Haines, Skagway, Hoonah, Gustavus. The following are located in the Terminal Building Juneau Airport: **Ward Air**; phone 907-789-9150; service to Southeast Alaska and West Canada; **Glacier Bay Airways**; phone 907-789-9009; **Skagway Air Service**; phone 907-789-2006 (in Skagway, 983-2218).

If the weather is good when you are in or around Juneau and you can afford a flightsee over the Juneau Icecap, I recommend it highly; it will give you views unparalleled in the world.

Bus Service

Capital Transit System serves downtown Juneau, the airport, and the Auke Bay Ferry, traveling as far as DeHart's Grocery at Auke Bay. The bus also makes a loop run up the Mendenhall Valley to within a half mile of the Mendenhall Glacier and the Mendenhall Lake Campgrounds, and certain buses travel to Douglas Island across the Gastineau Channel. Runs hourly from 6 A.M. to 10 P.M., Monday through Saturday. Bus schedules are available at the Visitor Center on 3rd and Steward.

If the municipal bus is not around when you get into either the Auke Bay Ferry Terminal or the ferry terminal in downtown Juneau, you can usually find a limousine or privately operated bus available. Haida Airport Bus serves downtown hotels, the airport and the Auke Bay Ferry Terminal. See Haida Taxi, below.

Car Rental

Available at the Juneau Airport: **Hertz**, phone 907-789-9494; **Avis**, 907-789-9450. **Dawson's Automotive**, Box 675, Juneau, AK 99802; phone 907-586-2367 (handles Payless Rent-a-Car).

Taxi Service

Haida Taxi: phone 907-586-6660. **Taku Taxi**: phone 907-586-2121.

Boat Charter

Alaska Travel Adventures: Second and Franklin Streets, Juneau, AK 99801; phone 907-586-6245. Many local outings by boat as well as other means. **Omorka Charters**: Write Box 203, Auke Bay, AK 99821. Offers diving charters as well as local service. **M. V. Heron**: Write Box 295, Juneau, AK 99802; phone 907-586-3822. Good for wildlife photographers. **M. V. Westy**: 419 Twelfth Street, Juneau, AK 99801; phone 907-586-1107. King and silver salmon a specialty. **Alaska Discovery**: 418 South Franklin (water side), Juneau, AK 99801; phone 907-586-1911. Canoe and kayak tours in Southeast; also backcountry tours with experienced guides, and classes in outdoor (Alaskan) skills. **Charter Pacifica**: 328 Coleman Drive, Juneau, AK 99801; phone 907-586-3126. Very comfortable boat, with experienced guide who knows her way around Southeast waters.

Hotels

For bed and breakfast information write P. Denny, 526 Seward, 99801; phone 907-586-2959 or C. and C. Kelly, 7850 Glacier Highway, 99801; phone 907-789-0539. Juneau has nine hotels. **The Alaskan Hotel** (167 South Franklin Street) and **The Bergman** (434 Third Street) are both old enough to be classified as historical monuments, which gives them a certain charm. The tariff in these hotels, as well as the **Summit** (455 South Franklin) is reasonable, and you can experience some of the old Alaska atmosphere in any of these three. **The Alaskan**, the **Driftwood Lodge** (435 Willoughby Street), and the **Prospector** (320 Whittier Street) have housekeeping units. The **Baranof Hotel** (127 North Franklin Street), right downtown, is the center of many local activities, and local people as well as tourists come and go in it a great deal. The food and the rooms, however, are expensive. The same is true for the **Cape Fox Sheffield House** at 51 West Egan Drive. The **Breakwater Inn**, 1711 Glacier Avenue, is moderately expensive but has a good view. The **Tides Motel** (5000 Glacier Highway) is on the outskirts of things on the bus line. It is reasonable. You can write any of these hotels in Juneau, AK 99801.

There is a **Youth Hostel** run by American Youth Hostels (AYH) in the Northern Lights (Presbyterian) Church at 400 West Eleventh Street that is open during the summer months. Hours for registering here are from 7 to 11 P.M. only. There are no showers, and the maximum stay is three nights. If you roll out your sleeping bag here, it will cost you two dollars per night, or one dollar if you are an AYH member.

Campgrounds

There are two Forest Service campgrounds near Juneau, one at Mendenhall Lake, thirteen miles from downtown, and one at Auke Bay, eighteen miles from downtown. These facilities are five dollars per day if you have a vehicle. You can take the Glacier Transit Company bus from downtown to within walking distance of Mendenhall Lake, but the Auke Bay Campground is about four miles from the end of the bus line at DeHart's store at Auke Bay. Incidentally, if you plan to hitch with your backpack, don't despair if several cars pass you by; some Alaskans are still quite conservative about hitchhikers. On the other hand, you will find most Alaskans to be the friendliest people in the world, and sooner or later you will get a ride.

Storage

Limited locker storage is available at the Juneau Airport. Most hotels will keep your gear for short periods of time, especially on your day of departure. **Alaska Discovery**–Juneau Outdoor Center, 418 South Franklin will safekeep your backpack (free) while you explore the city.

Showers

Available at the **Harbor Wash Board**, see below, and at **Augustus Brown Swimming Pool**, 1619 Glacier Avenue.

Laundromats

Harbor Wash Board, 1111 F Street, off Glacier Avenue, behind the Alaska Laundry; also **Marine View Apartments**, South Franklin Street (ground floor, 10 A.M. to 10 P.M., near the downtown ferry. Near the airport, behind Madsen's Hardware Store on the Old Glacier Highway, is another laundry facility. The **Dungeon Launderette** at Franklin and 4th is open daily 8 A.M. to 8 P.M. Local trailer courts on the Mendenhall Loop Road have laundromats and showers, and one has a sauna. Inquire at **Visitor's Information Center**.

Special Events

The Salmon Bake is a traditional all-you-can-eat Juneau fish feed that is held nightly from June 1 to September 7 at the end of Basin Road in Last Chance

Basin. Hours are 6 to 9 P.M. Prices are reasonable and it's an easy walk from downtown, or you can catch a lift in the courtesy bus that makes pickups at the hotels. Ask about it at the Baranof Hotel. You'll find lots of local people eating at this open air—under a roof—special dining event, which says something about how good the good is. If you decide to go, you might want to arrive early and visit the Mining Museum on Basin Road nearby, which is open during the summer.

Local Outings
The Juneau City and Borough Park and Recreation Department (490 West Franklin) sponsors weekly outings every week of the year. These are open to everyone and include local hikes, cross-country ski trips in the winter, and visits to the excellent swimming pool in the Juneau High School. Inquire at the Park and Recreation Department for information or telephone 907-586-5226. These outings give you a good chance to meet local people.

For Further Information
Check with the cruise ship information kiosk on the dock next to Merchant's Mall on The Wharf (open in summer), or with the **Visitor's Information Center** on Seward and Third Streets. **The Foggy Mountain Shop** in the Mother Earth Mall on South Franklin Street across from the Red Dog Saloon may also be able to give you up-to-the-minute tips on local hiking and kayaking out of Juneau.

Some Useful Names and Addresses
Juneau Information Center: Free brochures and ready advice about what to do and see in the greater Juneau area. In **Chamber of Commerce** office. Write at Third and Seward, Juneau, AK 99801; phone 907-586-2201. **Alaska State Division of Tourism:** Write Pouch E, Juneau, AK 98111; phone 907-465-2010. You can get your free copy of *Worlds of Alaska,* a remarkable source of information for travelers in Alaska, by writing this agency. **Centennial Hall Information Center:** 101 Egan Drive, Juneau, AK 99803; phone 907-586-7151. This is a joint operation of the U.S. Forest Service and the National Park Service. You can make U.S. Forest Service cabin reservations here. **National Park Service:** Write Box 1089, Juneau, AK 99802; phone 907-586-7137. **Alaska Travel Adventures:** 200 North Franklin, Juneau, AK 99801; phone 907-586-6245. This outfit conducts daily outings (as well as longer ones), with everything taken care of, to such places as the Mendenhall Glacier. It's worth investigating, particularly if you have only a short time in Juneau. **Alaska Discovery:** Write 418 South Franklin Street, Juneau, AK 99801; phone 907-586-1911. Canoe and kayak rental by hour, day, or week.

Environmental Organizations
Southeast Alaska Conservation Council (SEACC): Write Box 1692, Juneau,
AK 99802. This group is concerned with protection of sensitive environmental
areas in the Southeast.

USGS *Topo Maps* Juneau Quadrangles A-1,2,3.

ADMIRALTY ISLAND .

Over a million beautiful acres in size—the island is nearly one hundred miles
long and close to thirty wide—Admiralty Island is a wonderfully representative
and relatively untouched sample of Southeast Alaska. Surrounded by saltwater, it has nearly seven hundred miles of coastline, which is intricately incised
with bays and inlets, aproned with tideflats, and ornamented with islands.
Admiralty rises high enough, over 4,500 feet, to cup snowfields as well as two
glaciers. It has idyllic lakes, white waterfalls, and lively streams, some of which
tumble directly into the sea. The tidal waters make for unique salt chucks,
and it is an extraordinary experience to watch an inland lake drop dramatically

Tidal flat in Admiralty Island National Monument. Source: U.S. Forest Service.

as the waters rush through its outlet at low tide. The land of Admiralty Island is densely clothed with a typical Southeast rainforest. Great old spruce and hemlock shadow a lush understory of devil's club, skunk cabbage, dwarf dogwood and ferns—all of which will delight the heart of a photographer.

The wildlife of Admiralty Island is rich and diverse. Humpback whales cavort in its coastal waters; sea lions use its islands for their rookeries. Fishing is good, a fact attested to by the prodigious number of bald eagles. In fact, according to the U.S. Forest Service, there are more bald eagles on Admiralty than there are crows, and in springtime, these birds congregate in the Seymour Canal, which cleaves Admiralty, in numbers unequalled anywhere on earth. Sitka black-tail deer use almost all of the island from the uplands to the tidelands, staying in front of the snowline as it inches down from the heights in autumn. Admiralty Island is also one of the last remaining large bastions of the great brown bear.

Tlingit Indians have lived on Admiralty Island and used its resources for their subsistence for many millennia. Sealaska, the Native Regional Corporation, has identified several historic sites and cemeteries on the island, and has selected and requested conveyance—under the terms of the Alaska Native Claims Settlement Act—of five locations, including the Chatham Strait pictographs. The village of Angoon, population about 500, the Native community on the island, has an interesting history. About a century ago, it was shelled by the revenue cutter *Corwin*—one of the few incidents where fire arms were used against Alaska's Native people by the United States. (The incident involved the killing of a Native by a whaler's gun, and the subsequent seizing of a white hostage by the Natives.) Angoon was a fishing center for many years and also the site of salmon canneries. The people were known as "Hootzenoowoos," a name that has become "Kootznoowoo" and has been taken by the Village Corporation.

Admiralty Island has been administered by the United States Forest Service since 1909. Under the aegis of this agency, the island has been managed for multiple use. There has been sporadic mining, and attempts to "harvest" the island's magnificent "mature" forests. In 1970 conservationists challenged the Forest Service on a logging contract which would have turned most of the island's trees into commercial timber. A landmark court decision resulted in the abandonment of the contract. This made possible the subsequent establishment of the 921,000 acre Admiralty National Monument by Congress in 1980. 23,000 acres of the monument were awarded the Native Corporation Shee-Atika as part of their entitlement under ANCSA, and are therefore not included in the wilderness status of the rest of the monument. The Forest Service is managing the rest of the monument as a roadless area, with emphasis on wilderness, cultural, educational, recreational, and scientific values.

Admiralty Island has some of the finest canoeing I have enjoyed in Alaska. A trans-island route takes you from Mole Harbor on the east to Angoon on the west. You paddle the length of one after another beautiful lake, portaging (alas) between them. (I remember only one portage, however, as being literally as well as figuratively, a drag.) Forest Service cabins en route provide restful layovers and welcome shelter from the frequently rainy weather. The tidal flats around Angoon are gorgeous and should, of course, be respected. The tidal phenomenon here is also noteworthy, and requires special caution of kayakers.

Some Useful Information About Admiralty Island

Scheduled air service goes only to Angoon, and then in the shape of the mail plane: inquire at the Juneau airport for the schedule. Other air access is by charter: see Juneau and Sitka information for the names of local air-taxi operators. Limited ferry service also serves Angoon.

Where to Stay

Thayer Lake Lodge on Thayer Lake is a beautiful, small, privately owned and reasonably priced wilderness lodge. If you can afford this kind of accommodation, a stay here will offer you a wonderful (and very comfortable) way to experience some of the magical qualities of the Southeast. Write Bob Nelson, Thayer Lake Lodge, Box 5416, Ketchikan, AK 99901; phone 907-225-3343—except from June 1 through September 14. During this period he can be reached by Radio KWA 78 via Alascom, Juneau, AK.

The U.S. Forest Service has several recreation cabins (including some of its most beautiful) on Admiralty Island. These are on a first-come-first-served basis, and reservations are essential. See section on United States Forest Service for further details. The Forest Service has an Admiralty Monument office in Angoon: write Box 181, Angoon, AK 99820. You can also get further information at the information center in Juneau at Seward and Third: or, write Admiralty Island NM Manager, Box 2097, Juneau, AK 99803; phone 907-789-3111.

There are two motels in Angoon: the **Kootznahoo Inlet Lodge,** write Box 134, Angoon, AK; phone 907-788-3501. The **Raven-Beaver Lodge,** write George B. Johnson, Jr., Angoon, AK 99820; phone 907-788-3601.

Consult the **Alaska Association of Mountain and Wilderness Guides,** Box 3685-DT, Anchorage, AK 99510 or **Alaska Travel Adventures,** 200 North Franklin Street, Juneau, AK 99501 or **Alaska Discovery,** 418 South Franklin Street, Juneau, AK 99501, for information about trips across Admiralty.

The village of Angoon is interested in quality tourism. Write Kootznoowoo, Box 116, Angoon, AK 99820 for information. The original native beadwork of the village women is beautiful; ask about its availability at the community building.

SITKA

Sitka (*Sheetkah*) was named by the Tlingit Indians for the tribe that lived here for many centuries before the Europeans found it. Some claim that this was the spot where Alexei Chirikof arrived in the *Saint Paul* on July 15, 1741 (the day before Bering landed on Kayak Island) and so is the site of the Russian discovery of America. Others, however, give this honor to Bering. In any event, there is no disagreement that this is the place where Alexander Baranof, head of Russia's early, most successful operations in Alaska, established his second Southeastern capital in 1804, calling it Novarkhangelsk, or New Archangel.

New Archangel began life as an interesting place, indeed. It was more important than San Francisco and boasted flour mills, tanneries, and sawmills, as well as being a major trading center, port, and ship-building center. By 1860, twenty-five seagoing vessels had been put together there, including the first steam-powered ship to be constructed on the Pacific Coast. Church bells were said to have been crafted here (a myth) but steam-engine parts were cast here by the Aleuts whom the Russians brought with them. In 1842, Father Ivan Popos Veriaminov (a great friend of the Aleuts) established an observatory here to study the earth's magnetic field. (Although now considered to be not ideally located, it is still a key magnetic observatory in the worldwide network of stations; Sitka is now also the site of a seismic station.) By 1861, New Archangel had two important institutes going: one zoological, the other devoted to the study of terrestrial magnetic phenomena. (This latter was supported by the British as well as the Russians.) Small wonder that it was known as the Paris of the Pacific.

When the United States purchased Alaska from Russia in 1867, the ceremonies sealing the exchange of the territory took place on an October day in front of the governor's house in New Archangel. (The wife of Prince Maksoutof, who was governor at that time, could be heard sobbing from the second-story window of the house.) The United States rechristened the place Sitka, a Tlingit name that means "by the sea." Within a week, two saloons, a restaurant, and two ten-pin bowling alleys were operating in the new American capital. The population of Sitka that year was about 3,500, but with the departure of the Russians, it dwindled rapidly, and a dozen years later it was less than 1,000. The saloons, restaurants, and ten-pin alleys were gone, along with most of the town's erstwhile glory. However, Sitka was the operating capital of Alaska until 1906. (See section on Juneau.)

Today, most of the original Russian buildings, including the Governor's House, have long since decayed or burned. But the beautiful old Saint Michael's Cathedral, which burned to the ground in 1966, has been lovingly restored, and the doors, icons, and many other items are from the original building. (Saint Michael's is open daily, in the summer, noon to 4 P.M.; a small donation is requested from visitors.) The Russian presence in Sitka also persists strongly in other ways. There is the old cemetery with its elegant Russian Orthodox crosses, the Russian Bishop's House—the second oldest building in Alaska (the oldest, built in 1832, has been added to over the years and now forms the heart of the Colonial liquor store)—and the street plan of the older part of town, which remains today so much the way it was laid out that Russian maps can still help you find your way. Another aspect of Sitka's Russian heritage is preserved by the New Archangel Dancers, who perform Russian folk dances regularly in the Centennial Building downtown. You can find out their schedule at this building.

Baranof showed good taste when he chose the site of Sitka for his capital. The small city sits behind a chain of picturesque tree-tufted islands that hold the Pacific surf away from a snug harbor. A sensational backdrop of mountains encircles the area to the east, some rising as high as 3,350 feet. On the west on Kruzof Island, the classically shaped volcano, Mount Edgecombe, stands watch with its cape of glittering white snow. This extinct volcano is often compared to Mount Fuji for the perfection of its silhouette. It was christened *Montana de Jacinto* by the Spaniards and, later, *Gora Sviataga Lazar'a*, or Mount Saint Lazarus, by the Russians. Captain Cook gave it its present name, which is believed either to honor the earl of Edgecumbe or to commemorate a mountain with the same name at the entrance to Plymouth Sound.

In this lovely setting, Sitka has attracted many artists, and it is the home of cultural activities that are unique in Alaska. In June, a festival of chamber music attracts people from Outside as well as many Alaskans. Art classes are frequently conducted here. There is an excellent workshop that teaches Indian arts at the Sitka National Historical Park.

Sitka is situated on Baranof Island (which memorializes the shrewd old Russian governor-trader) and is a natural gateway for anyone wanting to canoe or kayak along the shores of Chichagof Island (named after another Russian gentleman, Vasilii Yakov Chichagof, who explored the Arctic in the mid 1760s). These waters offer some of the finest small-boat recreation in Alaska, and the bays and coves of West Chichagof Island offer some beautiful snug harbors. The extraordinary wilderness of West Chichagof and its beauty have prompted major efforts to give the area wilderness protection under the Forest Service, which administers it. The Congress recognized these wilderness values in part by designating the Pacific side of West Chichagof as a wilderness area in 1980.

If you plan to do some small-boating in this area, you can make good use of the ferry. From Sitka, you can schedule your boating trip to meet the ferry

Sitka black-tailed deer (Odocoileus hemionus sitkensis). **Range: Southeast Alaska and, through transplanting, Kodiak Island.**

at, say, Pelican, where it makes monthly stops, or you can go farther to meet it in Angoon on Admiralty Island and continue on board to Juneau. If you're even more ambitious and have more time, you can travel to Juneau all the way in your small craft or continue to Glacier Bay. If you want to make a place like Elfin Cove your goal, you may be able to "hitch a ride" out of it on a fishing boat; ask around at the docks. Or you can, of course, charter a boat or a plane to pick you up. Larry Edwards in Sitka (see below for address and telephone) can give you good advice on planning any small-boat outing in this area.

Expert kayakers will find the most exciting part of a trip along Chichagof Island when they feel the force of the Pacific Ocean from Salisbury Sound around the Khaz Peninsula. Remember, this part of Southeast Alaska is not a place to learn to kayak or to canoe by yourself. If you plan any boating on your own, you must know what you're doing. (See section on Traveling in Small Boats.)

There are several lovely hikes that you can take directly from Sitka or from close by. If you like to stroll, it's a pleasant ¾ mile or so from town to the Sitka National Historical Park, which marks the site of the Tlingit Fort where the Russians asserted their superior strength through the use of gunpowder. There's a trail through the park that takes you into open forest and then along the beach, and there's also a picnic area if you want to take your lunch. You'll see many totems, and you can also visit the Native Arts Workshop. Along the way from town, you'll pass Sheldon Jackson College, once a school for Native Alaskans and now looking Outside for students. This is the legacy of an early missionary who had great influence in Alaska's preterritorial days. The college has a museum of Native artifacts that is worth visiting. Winter hours are 1 to 4 P.M. except Tuesday and Saturday; summer hours are 8 A.M. to 5 P.M. daily mid-May to mid-September.

If you want a little more strenuous activity, you can climb Gavan Hill (Harbor Mountain) directly north of Sitka, starting from downtown. This is a round trip of about six miles with an elevation gain of close to 2,700 feet, so you should allow the better part of a day for it. Although there are no particular difficulties on this trail, like many in the Southeast, it requires you to be a good hiker. This climb gives some superb views, and it has enough good camping places along it to offer backpacking opportunities, but you'll need to carry a stove.

Two other interesting trails are easily reached from Sitka. One will take you to the top of Mount Verstovia, which is named not for a person but for a Russian unit of measure—a *verst*, which equals 3,500 feet. This is about the height you will gain on this trail, and you will get some even more wonderful views than from Gavan Hill, but this trail requires even more stamina and hiking expertise as well. Take care when you reach the final summit of Mount Verstovia. As Margaret Piggott warns, a false step could land you in the pulp mill over 3,000 feet below. Don't attempt the summit if snow lingers on it.

The other interesting trail will take you along nearby Indian River—a less difficult outing, although it's a good ten-mile round trip and will be even longer if you walk the two and a half miles from town to the trailhead. This is a charming hike with an elevation gain of about 1,300 feet. You will see Southeastern forest, muskeg, a beautiful river, and lots of wildlife. The trail also opens up in places to splendid views of the Sisters and of Gavan Hill.

The Sitka Parks and Recreation Department has prepared a folder on local hikes. Ask for it at the city offices on Lake Street; any resident can tell you where the city hall is. Visit the U.S. Forest Service for further information about these trails and/or other local hiking opportunities (see below for address).

While you're in Sitka, you might want to visit the Alaska Pioneer Home, a stop on locally operated bus tours. This is the large building downtown that occupies part of what was once the parade ground of both the Russians and the early American garrisons which were stationed in Sitka. The old-timers in Sitka's Pioneer Home are full of Alaskan history, and if you have a chance to talk with any of them, you will probably find yourself enchanted by some of their tales. Most of them brought dreams to Alaska that never came true, but they like to talk about all the reasons they didn't. The state of Alaska is unusually kind to its older citizens, giving anyone who has resided in Alaska since before statehood, January 1959, and who has reached the age of 65 a tidy pension ($250/month), and the state also provides housing and medical care for older residents who have not provided for themselves.

The National Park Service is in charge of the Russian Bishop's House, located one block from downtown. The house was first occupied by Father Veniaminoff.

The pulp mill in Sitka is the Japanese-owned Alaska Lumber and Pulp Company. Unfortunately, the Sawmill Creek Campground is unavoidably close to it on Blue Lake Road, and Mount Verstovia is directly above it, so it's hard to stay away from its "perfume." It is even harder not to notice the clear-cut areas of timber that have fed this mill over the years it has been operating. Many of them are all too obvious on the ferry approaches to Sitka.

Some Useful Information About Sitka

Ferry
There are three northbound and three southbound ships per week in summer. The ferry terminal is about seven miles north of town, and there is a bus service into town. (If you have a bike, this is a good place to use it.)

Air Service
By **Alaska Airlines** to Anchorage, Juneau, Petersburg, Ketchikan, and Seattle; phone 907-966-2266.

Air Charters
Bellair Inc.: Write Box 371, Sitka, AK 99835; phone 907-747-8636. **Ravencopters**: Flightseeing. Write Box 2242, Sitka, AK 99835; phone 907-966-2275. Native operated. **Mountain Aviation**: Sitka Airport; phone 907-966-2288. **Livingston Helicopters**: Sitka Airport; phone 907-747-5533.

Bus
Sitka Bus Lines, phone 907-747-8443.

Taxis
Island Cab, phone 907-747-8657. **Haida Cab**, phone 907-747-6621.

Car Rentals
At the airport: **Avis**, phone 907-966-2404; **Hertz**, phone 907-747-8900; and **Rent-a-Dent**, phone 907-966-2552.

Boat Charters

Nature Cruise: Write Charles Johnstone, 1408 Sawmill Creek, Star Route, Sitka, AK 99835; phone 907-747-6881. Custom trips in forty-five foot diesel. Fine guide. **Allen Marine Tours**: Write Robert Allen, Box 1049, Sitka, AK 99835; phone 907-747-8941. Two-and-a-half hour tours daily on the sixty-five foot *Saint Aquilina*. **Sutter Fishing Charters**: Write Box 533, Sitka, AK 99835; phone 907-747-3628. Two twenty-one foot boats. Specializes in salmon sport-fishing.

Small Boat Advice and Occasional Guiding

Larry Edwards, Box 2158, Sitka, AK 99835, phone 907-747-8996. Edwards also handles folding boats for a good price and can arrange for delivery anywhere in the United States.

Hotels

Potlatch House (motel), between ferry and town. Write Box 58, Sitka, AK 99835; phone 907-747-8611. Restaurant, view, reasonable. **Shee Atika Lodge**, in town. Write Box 78, Sitka, AK 99835; phone 907-747-6241. Native owned. **Sheffield House**, in town. Restaurant, expensive. Write Box 318, Sitka, AK 99835; phone 907-747-6616. **Sitka Hotel**, in town. Write Box 679, Sitka, AK 99835; phone 907-747-3288. Older, reasonable. **Youth Hostel**, in United Presbyterian Church; phone 907-747-3356.

Campgrounds

Starrigavan Campground (Old Harbor): North of ferry terminal .7 miles. Water from creek only. This is the site of the first Russian settlement, Mikhailovskii Redut, and the terrible defeat of the Tlingits. **Sawmill Creek**: On Blue Lake Road past the ALP mill. Fourteen miles from ferry terminal.

Useful Names and Addresses

Chamber of Commerce: Write Box 638, Sitka, AK 99835; phone 907-747-8604. Publishes good street map and guide. **Sitka Convention and Visitors Bureau**: Write Box 1226, Sitka, AK 99835. **National Park Service**: Write Sitka National Historical Park, Box 738, Sitka, AK 99835; phone 907-747-6281. **U.S. Forest Service**: Write c/o Federal Building, Harbor Drive, Sitka, AK 99835; phone 907-747-6671. **Sitka Conservation Society**: Write Box 316, Sitka, AK 99835; phone 907-747-6980 for current officers.

USGS Topo Maps Sitka quadrangles A-2, B-1&2, C-1&2, D-1&2

HOONAH

The village of Hoonah lies a little off the beaten track, which adds to its charms. While it is not served by the large ferries, the smaller ships provide a pleasant short voyage from Juneau several times a week. (Check your ferry schedule.) It is also possible to reach Hoonah by air: there are several scheduled flights daily, but a trip on the mail plane is the most reasonable way to fly. (Check at the Juneau airport for Southeast Skyways, Inc. and L.A.B. schedules as well as the schedule of mail deliveries.) Once in Hoonah, you will find comfortable Native-operated accommodations, and it is possible to make a tour to Glacier Bay from this lovely spot. The Native people at Hoonah are very interested in tourism, and you will find a warm welcome. For further details, write: Huna Totem Corp., Box 290, Hoonah, AK 99829; phone 907-945-3330. For boat charter, write Double Eagle Charters, Box 94, Hoonah, AK 99829; phone 907-945-3253.

HAINES

When you travel up the Lynn Canal, you traverse part of the Chatham Strait–Lynn Canal Fault that delineates a major separation in the earth's crust and is considered one of the world's most spectacular fault systems. Movement along this fault through the millennia has shattered the rocks in the region. The great glaciers of the various Ice Ages quarried out the rock debris along the fault lines and flooded the deep cleft that remained in the landscape with their icy meltwater. This country is still restless, with major tectonic activity possible at any time. The snowy descendants of those earlier glaciers—vast ice fields and new glaciers—lie glittering and waiting on the mountain peaks as well, their meltwater pouring out in turbulent streams and rivers, which still nourish this part of the Inside Passage.

You will notice a change in both the landscape and the climate in this northern part of the passage, which makes for pleasant variety as you travel on the ferry. The island-studded channels of the southern reaches of the passage give way to a cleaner sweep of water that gradually narrows between rising peaks. The influence of the immediate ocean diminishes, although storms can and frequently do barrel in from the south.

The dark spruce and hemlock forests are softened here by deciduous trees that change with the seasons. In winter the bare branches of the birches and cottonwoods are a delicate smoky brown; in spring and summer their light green leaves tuft the landscape; in autumn their leaves blaze a tawny gold that illuminates the dark stands of conifers, as though by sunlight, and the leaves of small maples flame a brilliant red, a particular delight on gray days. But as you approach the Interior of the continent, the gray days are fewer; the winds, however, are more frequent and stronger, flowing in torrents through the high passes of the Coast Mountains that rise above the canal.

The Lynn Canal has historically served as a major passageway into the Interior of the continent from the coastal waters of the Southeast. At its northern end, it divides into two fingers. One, the Chilkoot Inlet, leads due north into the famous Chilkoot Pass, gateway to the Yukon. (It also provides access to White Pass.) This was the exclusive pathway of the Chilkoot Indians who guarded the pass zealously, using it for trade with the Tagish Indians of the Interior. (See section on Skagway.) The other finger of the Lynn Canal leads northwest, opening a way up the Chilkat Valley to Chilkat Pass. This was once the route of the old Dalton Trail, now largely gone back to wilderness. It is more or less the present route of the Haines Highway, which provides access to Whitehorse, Yukon, and Fairbanks, Alaska. The town of Haines, located on the Chilkat Peninsula, guards the terminus of both these well-traveled routes.

As you approach Haines on the ferry, you may leave some of the whales behind you but not the bald eagles. In fact in the fall and early winter, the eagles congregate in great number in the valley of the Chilkat River near Haines. Warm springs beneath the gravel outwash of this riverbed keep the water relatively ice free well into the colder months, and the chum salmon continue their run. Eagles by the thousands, literally, crowd after them to feed. More than 3,000 birds have been counted in a single day along the Chilkat. Once on a November morning, when the sun stained the snowy mountains of the Chilkat Range a deep orange pink, and snow outlined each bare branch of the cottonwood trees along the river, I heard the early morning conversation of a great gathering of these birds and watched them as they fished in the blue black waters. It was an unforgettable experience. Unfortunately, the Chilkat River is underlain in places with low-grade iron, and Japanese interests have investigated, and may pursue, mining possibilities there. There is also talk of logging the cottonwoods as part of a highly controversial Alaska State sale of timber in this region. It is both sad and incredible that the extraordinary wildlife values of this place should not take precedence, and be protected and preserved.

The town of Haines has a recorded history that dates back to 1878, a year before John Muir and his friend, the Reverend S. Hall Young, made their

Bald Eagle (Haliaeetus leucocephalus). **Range: Alaska's forested shores.**

first visit there. (The man who preceded them was George Dickinson, an agent of the Northwest Trading Company, who was scouting out fur-trading possibilities with the Chilkats.) Muir and Young were traveling in a large canoe manned by Indians from the Wrangell area, and Young was bent on converting the Chilkats. As they approached what was known as the village of Chilkat, they came into sight of the Davidson Glacier, which Muir described as "a broad white flood reaching out two or three miles into the canal with wonderful effect." Muir wanted to camp beside it, but a strong headwind held them back. (To Muir's annoyance, Young had refused to travel the previous day, when the wind was perfect, because it was Sunday.) The next morning, however, Muir wrote with typical exuberance: "The wind was fair and joyful . . . and away we glided to the famous glacier. In an hour or so we were directly in front of it and beheld it in all its crystal glory descending from its white mountain fountains and spreading out in an immense fan three or four miles wide against its tree-fringed terminal moraine." You can still visit the Davidson Glacier, which has retreated considerably, by taking the Mud Bay Road out of Haines.

Muir and Young found the Chilkats an independent but friendly people, and Young preached to them valiantly. They preferred, however, to listen to the more charming John Muir and required that he be given equal time. If taken aback, Young was not defeated; to carry on his efforts a couple of years later, he sent the Reverend and Mrs. Eugene Willard back to the village. They managed to establish a mission (although it took quite a while to convert the Chilkats), and it was the Willards who named the town Haines, in honor of Mrs. Francina Electra Haines of the Presbyterian Board of Home Missions.

Haines took its place in gold-rush history as the starting point of the Dalton Trail, which was much safer than the Chilkoot Trail, but it led in too long and circuitous a manner to the Yukon country, which was the pressing goal of the sourdoughs. The Dalton Trail was used largely for animals. More attention was paid to Haines in 1903, when the U.S. Army located there and built Fort William H. Seward, which still stands.

Although Haines is visited by many tourists who travel the Haines Highway and the ferries and it is also the site of an annual Alaska State Fair, the town is enough off the beaten track to have retained much of its particular Southeast flavor. It has had its share of salmon canneries, local mining efforts, and logging operations. It has also, since 1953, been the southern terminus of a six-inch gas pipeline that links it to Fairbanks; the pipeline is marked by a large tank near the ferry terminal.

In the opinion of many visitors Haines vies with Homer and Valdez for being the most beautifully situated community in Alaska today. The Chilkat Mountains form a dazzling and constantly changing display on the horizons around the town, and the mostly good (though windy) weather lets you enjoy the view. On quiet blue days, the water of the Lynn Canal reflects back the fishing boats floating in its small harbor as though they were painted on it.

There is good day-hiking around Haines, and the Chamber of Commerce puts out a pamphlet called *Haines Is For Hiking*, which you can write for. You can also climb from downtown Haines to the top of nearby Mount Ripinski and gain some stunning views of the snow and ice peaks that line the Lynn Canal and separate the Chilkat Valley from Glacier Bay National Monument. (Above treeline, the Mount Ripinski trail is a wonderful place to watch the storms sweep in from the south.) This is at least a day's hike, with an elevation gain of 3,563 feet, but the trail is good and is well maintained by local people. If you're interested in seeing more of the country around Haines with natives who know the area well, you can contact the Swift family, which has five members, any of whom can guide you on everything from a three-hour to a three-day trip. Write the Swift Family, c/o Haines Home Building Supply, ¾ Mile Haines Cut-Off Highway, Haines, AK 99827, or stop by when you're in town. Their telephone number is 907-766-2595 or 766-2576.

Haines is also the place you'll use as a takeoff point for one of Alaska's finest river experiences, the run of the Tatsenshini and Alsek rivers. When I first made this river trip, it was relatively unknown, but in the past several years it has been publicized and much advertised by commercial river-runners. If you would like to go with a guide, I would recommend one of Alaska's wilderness guides who meets the set of self-imposed standards a group of them has developed, that is, one who is a member of the Alaska Association of Mountain and Wilderness Guides. (Members of this group are also used by Alaska Travel Adventures.)

If you decide to make this river trip on your own, plan to arrange for wheeled transportation from Haines to the put-in point below Mile 107 on the Haines Highway: contact the Swift family (see above). You will also need for stupendous views of the north side of the Fairweather Range (which you see from the south in Glacier Bay)—if the weather is good, that is. Do not, under any circumstances, follow the Alsek River when you see it is going to swing toward the Alsek Glacier on the back of the range: it could cost you your raft or kayak and possibly your life, if you did, for the glacier engulfs the river during most of the year. As you approach the Alsek Glacier, stay along the right bank of the river and take your boat out as you reach the base of a large nunatak that looms directly ahead of you. You may have to make a short portage then to the lagoon that leads eventually back into the Alsek after it has emerged from the glacier, but this is a short haul at most and poses no problems. When we ran this section of the Alsek, it seemed to me that the wild joyous character of the upper Alsek vanished into the glacier, as though it had been captured; a broad, more dignified river emerges from under the ice and moves rather sedately—though still at a good rate of speed—carrying flotillas of icebergs downstream for many miles.

The Alsek is heavily fished in its lower portion, being a particularly fine salmon stream, and you can expect to encounter motorboats from the Alsek Glacier on. You will also probably see fish-processing scows at work, parked in sloughs along the way.

If you decide to make this river trip on your own, plan to arrange for wheeled transportation from Haines to the put-in point below Mile 104 on the Haines Highway: contact the Swift family (see above). You will also need an air-taxi pickup at the end of your trip at Dry Bay. (See Air Charters, Yakutat or Haines.) From Yakutat, you can fly on a scheduled airline either north or south.

Some Useful Information About Haines

Ferry
Runs daily in summer. Inquire about a Haines layover if you're going from Skagway to the south and want only a few hours in Haines; there is often a couple of hours' wait on the regular southbound run. There is baggage storage at the ferry terminal (about four miles north of town on Lutak Inlet) and bus service into town. For local ferry information, phone 907-766-2111.

Air Charters

L.A.B. Flying Service: Write Box 272, Haines, AK 99827; phone (Haines) 907-766-2222. **Wings of Alaska**: Write Box 574, Haines, AK 99827; phone 907-766-2468.

Bus Service

Available from both the ferry terminal and the airport (for scheduled flights, that is), and the bus stop at all downtown hotels; phone 907-766-2640.

Car Rentals

National, Eagle's Nest Motel; phone 907-766-2131. **Hertz**, Thunderbird Motel; phone 907-766-2131.

Taxi Service

Phone **Eagle Taxi**, 907-766-2171 or **Travelot Taxi**, 907-766-2040.

Hotels

Captain's Choice Motel, on the corner of Second and Dalton, has seven units on one level and courtesy coffee. Write Box 392, Haines, AK 99827; phone 907-766-2461. Interesting accommodations are available in buildings once used to quarter officers in the historic Fort William H. Seward in Port Chilkoot just south of town. **Hotel Halsingland,** a National Historic Landmark, has 60 rooms with bath; restaurant facilities. Family rates available. **Hotel Halsingland** also has showers and a laundromat. Reasonable. Write Box 158, Haines, AK 99827; phone 907-766-2641. **Fort Seward Condos** are converted officers' quarters in the same complex. Some have fireplaces; all have kitchens and good views. Three-day minimum stay; daily and weekly rates; fairly reasonable. Write Gregg Enterprises, Box 75, Haines, AK 99827; phone 907-766-2425. **Eagle's Nest Motel and Campground:** Mile 1, Haines Highway. Within walking distance of downtown; six miles from ferry (free transportation provided). Write Box 267, Haines, AK 99827; phone 907-766-2352. Ten-room motel, twenty-space campground (six with water and electric hookups), showers and laundry. **Mountain View Motel:** 151 Mud Bay Road, Port Chilkoot. Close to town, five and a half miles from ferry terminal. Write Box 526, Haines, AK 99827; phone 907-766-2542. Nine units: seven have housekeeping facilities. Reasonable. **Thunderbird Motel:** Dalton and Second Street, five miles from ferry. Write Box 159, Haines, AK 99827; phone 907-766-2131. Twenty units, six with kitchenettes. Downtown. Fairly reasonable. Small pets allowed. **Town House Motel:** Third and Main Street, five miles from ferry. Write Box 66, Haines, AK 99827; phone 907-766-2353. 24 units. Reasonable. Eighteen trailer units open May through September.

There is a Youth Hostel, **Bear Creek Camp and Hostel**, about a mile from downtown; phone 907-766-2259.

Campgrounds

Chilkoot Lake: Five miles from ferry terminal, ten from town. Public. **Portage Cove:** Two miles from town on Beach Road. Seven miles from ferry. Attractive but small. Public. **Mosquito Lake Campground:** Mile 27, Haines Highway. Thirty-two miles from ferry. **Chilkat State Park**, Mile 7, Mud Bay Road. Large facility of Alaska State Parks; phone 907-766-2293. Private facilities at **Hotel Halsingland** and **Eagle's Nest Motel and Campground**, see above.

Laundromats

Polyclean downtown and **Hotel Halsingland** at Port Chilkoot (see above). Both open 10 A.M. to 10 P.M. Laundry and dry cleaning center at 5th and Union.

Showers

Hotel Halsingland. Coin operated. Phone 907-766-2755.

Useful Names and Addresses

Haines Visitor Center at western edge of town at Mile 1, Haines Highway, next to Customs Service. Haines, AK 99827; phone 907-766-2202. **Chamber of Commerce**: Write Box 262, Haines, AK 99827; phone 907-766-2202. **Parks and Forests Information Center**: Staffed by U.S. Forest Service and Alaska State Parks. For information on resources, attractions, facilities, and services in Haines, the Tongass National Forest, and the Chilkat State Park, write Box 5, Haines, AK 99827; phone 907-766-2292.

SKAGWAY

You can step back into history when you walk up Broadway from the ferry in Skagway. This was the gateway to the Yukon in 1897 and the staging point of the great Klondike gold rush. If you listen carefully, you can almost hear the frantic, hurrying footsteps of thousands of men and women echoing on the boardwalks that border the street. Theirs was a poignant story: teachers, lawyers, conmen, farmers, bank clerks, prostitutes—they were infected with that fever for gold which spread like the plague once it became known that the precious metal was there for the taking in the Yukon. Seeking their fortunes, many of them found instead defeat, disaster, and often death. Almost none found gold, for by the time they learned of the strike on Rabbit Creek (gold was "caught between the rocks like cheese in a sandwich"), the best claims had all been staked.

Now, in the Klondike Gold Rush National Historical Park, the National Park Service has memorialized the thousands of "cheechakos" who poured through Skagway bent on reaching the Yukon. The town of Skagway has cooperated enthusiastically with recreating the scene much as it was some eight decades ago. The NPS has set up its headquarters and information center in the Arctic Brotherhood Hall, a gem of an old building, and such places as the Red Onion—now a saloon and gift shop but once the small city's "house"—have been carefully restored to give you an interesting look into Skagway's bawdy past. The Chilkoot Trail (out of Dyea, a few miles to the south) has also been revived with the cooperation of the Canadian Government and is part of a unique international park. This trail beckons any backpacker who has a sense of history and adventure—and a strong pair of legs and a good heart, for the Chilkoot is a tough pull; it is a testament to the courage, determination, and perhaps the foolhardiness of the "ninety-eighters," who would lock arms to pull one another over the summit.

The name *Skagway* probably comes from the Tlingit word *sch-kawai*, which means "end of the salt water," although it is also close to *skagua*, another Indian word, meaning "home of the north wind." Both names are appropriate to the place, which marks the northernmost arm of the salt water Lynn Canal and is also frequently buffeted by gales. The first white settler, who named the community, was a seventy-four-year-old former steamboat captain, William Moore, who surveyed for Canada and found a route across the Coast Range through White Pass. He figured that a port would thrive at the tidewater terminus of his route where the Skagway River poured its water into Lynn

Canal. Moore homesteaded there in 1888 and, with his son, constructed a wharf, and settled in to wait for the railroad to be built over White Pass.

The Moores had in mind that Skagway would become a gateway to the Yukon, for as early as the 1870s, hopeful miners had been prospecting in the streams along the great river to the north. When the great rush did come—it took almost a year after the initial strike on August 16, 1896, for the stampeders to reach Skagway—the Moores found themselves completely overwhelmed. The sourdoughs simply took over, threw up their shacks, and rigged their tents wherever they could find a spot of vacant ground. From a handful of people, the population of Skagway briefly burgeoned to 15,000 unruly souls. John Muir, who visited the place with the 1899 Harriman Expedition, called it "a nest of ants taken into a strange country and stirred by a stick."

Steamer followed steamer up the Lynn Canal the autumn and winter of 1897, hauling people, their tools, food, horses, and cattle into the rough new town. Among those who came was Jefferson (Soapy) Smith who brought his gang along with him and bullied his way into the control of Skagway to turn it into what was called "the roughest place on earth." When the town grew tired of his ruthless despotism, more sober citizens called a meeting of vigilantes to oust him. Smith confronted the group and in an ensuing duel mortally wounded the town's surveyor, Frank Reid, who died a couple of days later. Reid, however, had killed Soapy instantly with a single shot from his pistol. Now the two rest not far from one another in the Gold Rush Cemetery. Soapy left a legend, but Reid—the real hero of the incident—only left his name on a charming waterfall not far from his grave and the legacy of a neatly laid out town.

On July 10, 1900, William Moore's dream was fulfilled and a 110-mile-long railroad linking Skagway to Whitehorse was completed. By then, however, the gold fever had waned, and Skagway was on its way to becoming a more respectable little ghost town.

The construction of the White Pass & Yukon Railroad was a saga in itself. Although it was backed by a British financier and a Canadian railroad builder, when the Alaska-Canada border was finally established, the railroad turned out to be the first in Alaska. It was also an American, George Brackett, who had blasted out a toll road over White Pass during the gold rush and had unwittingly laid the bed for the narrow-gauge tracks.

For decades, the White Pass and Yukon Railroad and the ferry were Skagway's lifelines, but in the late 1970s a road from Carcross to Skagway was completed and in 1983 the railroad stopped running, thus ending a wonderful train ride. Busses now travel the new highway and the trip is not the same, but the route traverses some breathtakingly beautiful country, traveling from the rain forest zone with its thick stands of spruce and hemlock through mixed stands of birch, cottonwood, and alder (all second growth here, since the hillsides were stripped during the gold rush); it continues to the subarctic alpine tundra zone above the 3,000 foot level, where lichens, low-growing willow, dwarf birch, mosses, and heathers grow. On the Canadian side, you will move into a drier climate, since the Coast Range catches most of the rain. There, the sparser boreal forest takes over with its alpine fir, lodgepole pine, spruce, cottonwood, and aspen.

You can drive to Carcross on the lamentable (but beautiful) new road (open May to September 15); at Carcross you can pick up the Alaska Highway and continue on to Interior Alaska (or head back south). A ride on the bus, however, will let you relax and enjoy the fabulous scenery. There is regular motorcoach service from Carcross to Fairbanks from whence you can take off on many Interior adventures.

If you want to explore the area around Skagway on foot, there's a choice of interesting and beautiful trails. Once again, you can walk from downtown directly into wilderness, and there are opportunities for a short stroll or a major outing, depending on how much time you have. If you only have a few hours, go to the National Park Service Visitor Center on Broadway (only a short walk from the ferry dock) and ask about the trail to Lower Dewey Lake. You can make a two and a half mile circuit with an elevation gain of six hundred feet (time, about an hour and a half) to a lovely lake that is fine for swimming in the summer. (If you're there in the winter, it's also a good place to go ice skating.) There are good views along the way.

If you want a longer more strenuous outing, you can continue from Lower Dewey Lake to Upper Dewey Lake. You can make this a day's outing or an overnight trip, since there is good camping as well as a cabin at the Upper Lake. It is a round trip of seven miles from town, and you'll have to climb over 3,000 feet before you're through, but there are views along the way, and Margaret Piggott describes the lake as "a gem captured in a bowl of 5,000 to 6,000 foot peaks which back onto the Skagway Icecaps; its overflow spills almost directly into the beautiful fjords below, by a series of cascades."

If you visit Upper Dewey Lake, you'll probably want to go on another three quarters of a mile or so to the Devil's Punchbowl, which is 700 feet higher up. There are incredible views of Skagway on the way, as well as of Taiya Inlet and the spectacular peaks that surround it.

Another short hike will take you from downtown to the Gold Rush Cemetery, a view of the graves of Soapy Smith and Frank Reid, and then you can stroll to Lower Reid Falls, which are highly photogenic, especially when they are frozen in the winter. This is an easy five-mile round trip walk that will make up a pleasant afternoon. If you have a car, you can visit the area in an hour or so.

On the way from Skagway to Dyea, there is another area that is lovely for hiking: the Skyline and AB Mountain. To reach the trail, you can take the bus to Dyea and get off at Mile 3. Again, you have a choice of a short stroll with a good viewpoint, or you can climb 5,000 feet to the top of AB Mountain. This is not a trail for tenderfeet. (The name, AB, refers to the rough outline of the letters "A" and "B" which late snow forms on the face of the mountain.)

The U.S. Forest Service maintains trails to Denver Glacier and to Laughton Glacier. The Forest Service cabin, which sleeps six, on the way to Laughton Glacier is recommended. Contact the U.S. Forest Service, Chatham Ranger District, Box 1049, Juneau, AK 99801, for information about these glacier trails and the use of the cabin. Of course, the trail with the greatest challenge of all is the Chilkoot.

Hiking the Chilkoot Trail

The National Park Service advises you to allow at least four days to hike the Chilkoot Trail. It is 33 miles from its takeoff point at Dyea to its terminus at Bennett, British Columbia. You will gain 4,700 feet if you take the trail from Skagway to Bennett, 2,500 feet if you travel it north to south. If you are going to end your hike at Bennett and return to Skagway via one of the available motorcoaches, you will not have to check into Canadian Customs; but if you proceed on to Carcross or Whitehorse, it will be necessary to do so. Whether or not you check into customs, remember that the use of hand guns is prohibited in Canada, and you are not permitted to carry assembled firearms on the United States portion of the Chilkoot Trail. (You can check your guns at the Skagway Police Department, or, if you're hiking from Canada south, at the Royal Canadian Mounted Police at Carcross or Whitehorse.) On your return to Skagway, you must check into the U.S. Customs and U.S. Immigration in Skagway.

If you plan to return from Bennett via the WP&Y Railroad, it is necessary to buy your ticket in Skagway before you leave; this also entitles you to a huge lunch before you board the train. The WP&YR does not have facilities for hikers in Bennett and there is no campground there.

Before you make the Chilkoot Trail hike, you should check into the National Park Service Visitor Center at Skagway for latest information about the trail and to leave your schedule. You will find park service rangers at Sheep Camp and Lindeman along the way who can provide you with further information or assistance if you need it.

Equipment for this long hike requires a camp stove and fuel (there's no wood in places), warm clothing (wool, please) and good rain gear, good hiking boots, a freestanding lightweight tent with fly; a first aid kit, and plenty of food plus extras in case of emergency.

You will find historic remains all along the Chilkoot Trail. The park service requests that you not light fires near them and, of course, that you not disturb or remove them. Actually, the old wagon wheels and iron scraps and other bric-a-brac that you'll see beside the trail are mute testimony to the extraordinarily arduous trip the sourdoughs made getting to the gold country of Canada. There was a weigh scale at the summit of the pass, manned by the Royal Canadian Mounties, and every person entering Canada was stopped and required to produce fifteen hundred pounds of food supplies and equipment adequate to last a year. This near ton of necessary supplies had, of course, to be transported up and over the pass. Enterprising operators built tramlines up the steep slopes, but those who couldn't afford to pay the going rate had to relay their gear, piece by piece—and many did just that during the coldest parts of the bitter winter of 1897–98. (It is 16.5 miles from Dyea to the summit. Carrying sixty pounds on a single haul, it would have taken thirty-three round trips—about an even 1,000 miles—to get the required food and equipment to the weigh station.) It is estimated that, one way or another, over thirty thousand rugged souls managed to get across Chilkoot Pass and to the Yukon River headwaters between the winter of 1897 and the fall of 1898.

Although four days is the recommended minimum for hiking the Chilkoot Trail, if you are in top shape and enjoy backpacking, you can do it in three—provided you get a really early start on the first day. But this allows for no lingering along the way, no unexpected delays, and a hard push to connect with the bus in Bennett, if you plan to ride back to Skagway. Seasoned Alaska hikers point out that the Chilkoot Trail is subject to all the vagaries of any Southeastern Alaska trail. Stretches of it can be boggy; there are avalanche hazards in winter and spring in the upper elevations; and snow rests in the summit area for much of the year and can make for slow, soggy, and difficult travel. And the weather is unpredictable; many people have crossed the summit in fog, rain, or snow, grateful for rock cairns and the old tramway cable to guide them. Winters (when a snowshoe trip can be beautiful, especially from the Canadian side to the south) often bring thirty feet of snow to pile up on the summit. Almost any time of year, storms can come barreling in from the south to smash against the summit area. In the words of an Alaskan friend, "When the weather's good, you can plan on making three miles in an hour; but when it's bad it may take you three hours to make a mile." (If this prospect sounds exhausting, take note that rufous hummingbirds fly all the way from Mexico to cross the summit of the Chilkoot Trail. If you carry a red pack, one may even accompany you on your way.)

Furthermore, there's a lot to see along the 33 miles of this historic route, and you're bound to miss some of it if you hurry your trip too much. Not only does this trail have unique historic value (remember, it was used by the Indians in their time), but it also rises from sea level to cross a major divide. Here you have the opportunity to experience the full spectrum of zones in the Southeast, from sea level through the lush rain forest to the open subalpine, then the more forbidding alpine. To top it off, when you gain the rugged summit, you move into a wholly different ecological community. The Canadian side of the pass is much drier, being in the rain shadow of the coastal mountains. The country is softer, smoother, and more open, and there are lovely lakes and streams. Forests of lodgepole pine and subalpine fir greet you with their wonderful fragrance. One hiker stepping into the forest one day, took a deep breath of the perfumed air and exclaimed: "Ah, Wyoming!" (The stampeders used trees like these to build boats for the lake and river portion of their journey northward.)

For all these reasons, I recommend allowing plenty of time for this trek—at least five or six days, if you can. And remember not to box yourself in too tightly with commitments on the other end. You can get an excellent publication, *The Historic Chilkoot Trail* trail guide (put out by the Park Services of the United States, Canada, Alaska, Yukon, and British Columbia), from the NPS in Skagway or by writing them at Box 517, Skagway, Ak 99804.

You can get from Skagway to the trailhead for the Chilkoot Pass in Dyea by car, taxi, or bus. While you're in Dyea, you will probably want to visit the Slide Cemetery where rest sixty men and women who were killed on an upper slope of the Chilkoot Trail in the Palm Sunday avalanche of April 3, 1898—the worst of many disasters the stampeders encountered.

Some Useful Information About Skagway

Ferry
The year round ferry runs daily during the summer and docks almost downtown at the south end of Broadway. Phone 907-983-2229.

Air Service
LAB Flying Service and **Wings of Alaska** (see Juneau). **Skagway Air Service**: Write Box 357, Skagway, AK 99840; phone 907-983-2218.

Bus Service
There is no public transportation. **Alaska Yukon Motorcoaches** offers a scenic two-day drive from Skagway to Fairbanks; located in Golden North Hotel; phone 907-983-2828. **Atlas Motorcoach** is based in the same hotel; phone 907-983-2402. **Westours** is headquartered in the Klondike Hotel; phone 907-983-2241.

Taxi
Goldies; phone 907-983-2321. **Golden North**; phone 907-983-2451. **Koster's Cab**; phone 907-983-2636. **Skagway Inn**; phone 907-983-2289. **Skagway Travel**; phone 907-983-2500.

Car Rental
Skagway Car Rental; phone 907-983-2500. **Avis**; phone 907-983-2247.

Note: The passing of the White Pass and Yukon Railroad left empty one of Skagway's most interesting old buildings—the Depot. Now the National Park Service has taken it over and restored it. Their Visitor Center is a good place to start in Skagway to get any information you might need. The National Park Service also conducts interesting walking tours.

Hotels

The five hotels listed in Skagway are within a half mile plus or minus of the ferry depot, and all are on or just off Broadway. The **Golden North** at Third and Broadway has 34 rooms, gold rush decor, a restaurant, and so on (plush). Write to above address, Skagway, AK 99840; phone 907-983-2451. The **Klondike** is on Third between Broadway and Spring; it has 170 rooms and a large restaurant (plush). Write Box 515, Skagway, AK 99840; phone 907-983-2291. The **Skagway Inn,** on Broadway between Sixth and Seventh, was built in 1897. Write Box 483, Skagway, AK 99840; phone 907-983-2289. Gold rush atmosphere, reasonable, winter and weekly rates. The **Bunkhouse,** on Fifth between Broadway and State, provides dormitory bed, shower, towels. Bring your own sleeping bag. Very reasonable. Write box 1898, Skagway, AK 99840; phone 907-983-2468. **Taiya Lodge** is on 6th Avenue between Broadway and State; phone 907-983-2414.

Campgrounds

There is primitive and limited camping at Dyea, eight miles from Skagway. **Liarsville State Campground**, three miles off the Dyea Road, has six spaces. **Hanousek Park,** at Broadway and Fourteenth Avenue, has eleven spaces and modern facilities.

Trailer Parks

Karkross Kamper Kourt, on Fourth Avenue between Main and State Streets, has seven spaces and hookups.

Laundromat

Clothes Rush Laundry, Broadway and Fifth Avenue. Also showers. Hours 8 A.M. to 9 P.M. daily.

Baggage Storage

Atlas Travel (Broadway between Second and Third): small charge.

Guide Service for Chilkoot Trail

Alaska Travel Adventures: Write 200 Franklin Street, Juneau, AK 99801. **Klondike Safaris:** Write Box 1898, Skagway, AK 99840, or inquire at the **Bunkhouse** (see above).

Useful Names and Addresses

Visitor Information: **National Park Service Visitor Center** in the old Railroad Depot, Broadway and Second Avenue. Write Box 517, Skagway, AK 99840; phone 907-983-2400. **Chamber of Commerce:** Write Box 194, Skagway, AK 99840; phone: 907-983-2496. For information regarding the **Klon-**

dike Gold Rush National Historical Park, write Box 517, Skagway, AK 99840; phone 907-983-2299.

USGS *Topo Maps* Skagway Quadrangles B-1 and C-1.

GLACIER BAY

In Alaska, as in few places on our planet, you can observe great earth forces actively at work and see their effects directly on the landscape. Volcanism, mountain building, frost action, avalanches, erosion, and deep-seated earth movements along with glaciers, floods, and mighty and swift-flowing rivers—all constantly change the face of Alaska's land, frequently before your eyes. More subtle but just as exciting, the rapid evolution of the living landscape can be witnessed throughout Alaska. Nowhere in Alaska can you see both earth and life forces in action more easily and dramatically than at Glacier Bay National Park.

Glacier Bay is across Icy Strait from Chichagof Island, about 60 miles north and west of Juneau. Its icy waters are fed by 16 dazzling tidewater glaciers that surge from the precipitous high mountains rising from its shores. The bay is a recent feature of the landscape: only a little over 200 years ago, when Captain James Cook sailed through Icy Strait past what is now the mouth of Glacier Bay, it was little more than a slight indentation in the shore choked with the towering blue walls of a great glacier. (This explains why Glacier Bay is one of the few places in Southeast that was not named by Captain George Vancouver—it wasn't there when he traveled by. Glacier Bay was named in 1880 by Captain Lester Beardslee of the United States Navy, and the Beardslee Islands in Glacier Bay were, in turn, named for the good captain.) When John Muir visited the area a little over a century after Cook, however, Glacier Bay had not only come into being but had already grown to be some 48 miles long. Thus in little more than a dozen decades, the warming period that began around 1750 had caused a spectacular retreat of glaciers in this region—the most rapid ever recorded, in fact—and the consequent birth of a respectable body of water. Meltwater has continued to feed Glacier Bay during the past century, and the bay has now reached nearly 70 miles in length. Should the warming period hold and the glaciers on Mount Hay continue to thaw, this could pose an interesting international situation: the shores of Tarr Inlet at the northwest point of Glacier Bay Park are already close to the Alaska-Canada border, and they could end up in British Columbia, which would be happy to have this extra land. As it happens, however, the Grand Pacific Glacier at the head of Tarr Inlet (already in Canada) has—for reasons not understood—recently begun a slow advance.

As the earth around Glacier Bay emerged from beneath the ice, life pressed forward onto it. A fascinating process of plant colonization has occurred, with a sequence of ever-more-complex plant communities taking over. You can see this evolution of the living landscape—as though in some huge scientific laboratory—at Glacier Bay National Park. Starting at the head of the bay, you can observe how lichens take hold in the bare rocks: these primitive plants help fragment the rocks into soil. Then notice the soft tinge of green color made by the tough but inconspicuous mosses and primitive plants like the *Equisetum*, or horsetail. Then you can see how the first pioneer flowering plants, the magenta-stained dwarf epilobium and the creamy-blossomed dryas, push up bravely from the harsh, newly exposed, and rocky terrain. These modest plants will bloom intensely through their brief summer, their root systems helping to stabilize the raw land.

When cold weather comes, the decaying bodies of these plants will provide nutrients to the soil so that other plants can follow. As you proceed down the bay, you can see these other plants growing in orderly succession. The various species—the willow, the alder, the cottonwood—indicate the length of time the land has been available for plant life to succeed upon it. At the mouth of the bay to Bartlett Cove, you can go on to experience the beauty of the vigorous spruce-hemlock forest, with its lush understory and groundcover. This rep-

Yellow dryas *(Dryas drummondi).*

resents the climax community of this particular succession. (If it remains ice free long enough, the moister parts of this forest may give way to muskeg, and, indeed, Deer Island—never glaciated—near Gustavus is clothed in muskeg.) Then you can appreciate that, although it may only take you a few hours to travel the length of Glacier Bay, you have in effect moved in time through thousands of years of plant evolution—from a living Ice Age world into the present.

As the current warm period persists—though no one knows for how long—forests like those in Bartlett Cove are slowly taking over the areas where you now see the willows, alders, and cottonwoods, and even the dryas and epilobium. Forests have, in fact, grown the length of Glacier Bay many times in the past and then been engulfed in ice and stream-carried sand and gravel; this is evidenced by the ancient tree trunks and branches—known as interstadial wood—that are found here and there along the shores. These are thousands of years old. You can see many specimens of interstadial wood around Morse and Forest creeks and just north of Fingers Bay. (Interstadial wood burns easily, and the NPS asks that you stay well away from it should you build a fire during your travels. Of course, you should also not take or use it for your own purposes—leave it where it is.)

As the plant communities came to provide livable habitats, birds and animals in prodigious numbers also came to live in and around Glacier Bay. At any season you visit the monument, you can expect to see a spectacular panorama of life. This is the way the NPS overviews it:

> Spring and early summer: Snow persists, especially in the high country, and ice fills the inlets in the upper part of the bay. Mountain goats are down low, birds are returning north, and the plants are beginning to turn green again.
>
> Midsummer: Whales are gorging on krill in the bay, and the birds are raising their fledglings. The sea birds can be seen in variety and abundance. Wildflowers in vast array color the landscape. It is also time for insects to prosper.
>
> Late summer and early fall: Snow is all gone from the ridges and low peaks, but the rain and winds increase. Berries are abundant and the salmon migrate into the rivers. Vegetation shows off its splendor of fall colors. Whales and summer birds begin to leave. The aurora borealis appears during starry nights.

If this sounds inviting, here is a glimpse of some of the other wildlife you can expect to encounter on a visit to Glacier Bay Park during the months of May through September. From Bartlett Cove, in the evenings or in early morning, your chances are good of hearing the song of coyotes (and just possibly of wolves) on the nearby isolated Beardslee Islands. Black bear and brown bear roam the wilderness throughout the park. As snow and ice melt under the summer sun, the mountain goats clamber ever higher among the cliffs and mountainsides. The birds are everywhere—especially from May through July—sea birds, shorebirds, and land birds. There are at least 200 species that frequent the park. Many are particularly easy to see and identify when you travel by boat.

On the steep rocks that rise above the fjords and inlets and on the remote islands, you can sometimes observe the pigeon guillemot, tufted and horned puffins, glaucous-winged and herring gulls where they have tucked their nests and eggs onto the narrow ledges. A puffin is a particular delight to watch in the water. One always wonders if it will fly; the answer is, of course. Although its short whirring wings seem barely adequate to get its fat little body airborne, they actually work very well. Kittiwakes, among the loveliest and most prolific of Alaska's winged coastal residents, lift in moving clouds from their nests when disturbed. So do the terns. Dark little marbled murrelets fly vigorously above the water, racing to keep up with the traveler who shares their territory. Parasitic jaegers like to chase the fleet but vulnerable terns, while the beautiful pelagic cormorants wing their arrow-straight way above the water.

May, June, and July are crucial months for hatching and rearing young birds in Glacier Bay. If you visit the park during this period, be careful not to disturb the nesting bird colonies on the islands and along the shores. The National Park Service also warns kayakers not to approach icebergs with female seals and pups on them in May and June lest the family become separated. Best to watch and photograph quietly from the water.

On the land, you may find ptarmigan (the official Alaska State bird), com-

Horned puffin (Fratercula corniculata). Source: U.S. Fish and Wildlife Service.

mon redpolls, and snow buntings near the retreating glaciers. Yellow warblers and gray-cheeked thrushes wing among the alder thickets and the cotton-woods. And everywhere there are the barn swallows, ravens, and bald eagles which are not above taking on the terns, and vice versa. Young eagles can cavort in aerial battles that put the most skillful stunt fliers to shame.

You may not see the halibut that live in the cold bottom waters, but perhaps you can sample some of this delicious fish at the Glacier Bay Lodge at Bartlett Cove or at the Gustavus Inn. Commercial fishing is allowed in Glacier Bay, which accounts for the presence of the picturesque, red-bouyed halibut boats you'll notice here and there. You can also hope to see humpback whales, and you will certainly see harbor seals.

Glacier Bay is obviously a paradise for naturalists or would-be naturalists, which is reason enough for wanting to visit it. It is also a place of exceptional beauty. On a blue day, the waters may be as still and shining as a polished mirror; a motorboat leaves a wake that fans out into a wide ruffle which seems to float on the glossy motionless surface. Against the north and westward sky, a panorama of snow-shining mountains, the Fairweather Range, rises to over 15,000 feet. (If you should raft the Tatsenshini and Alsek rivers, you will see the other face of these tall mountains filling the sky to your south.) Around your boat, icebergs looking like small floating castles drift by, catching the sunlight and shattering it into a thousand flashing crystals. The intricately crevassed faces of the tidewater glaciers glow blue. On clear evenings at sunset, soft shades of rose and tangerine flood every white gleaming surface in this world of ice; and, on gray days, there is a special sense of mystery and wonder.

The beauty of Glacier Bay is best experienced from the water, whether you're on the deck of a large ship, a smaller tour boat, or better yet, in a canoe or a kayak, or even camped close to the shore. (After you have rigged your tent, you can sit for a moment to let the silence—broken, perhaps, by the thunder of the moving glaciers or the crash of ice into the water—seep into you.) Except around Bartlett Cove, this is not ideal hiking country, and the Park Service has not developed a trail system through it. Backpacking is made difficult and sometimes chancy by the unstable and slippery terrain, rockfalls, the heavy thickets of alder that must be beaten through, and the glaciers, which may require ice work. If you do decide to hike, be prepared for major scrambling. Unless you're a very surefooted and experienced hiker, keep in mind that your own discomfort (especially when bushwhacking) and the noise of rocks set rolling by your boots can be real distractions to your own full enjoyment of this very special place. (Margaret Piggott, who is both experi-enced and surefooted, has done a superb job of describing routes on land as well as on water in the monument. See Bibliography.)

One of the unique features of Glacier Bay National Park is the tour boat service. On its daily trip up the bay, the tour boat will drop you, and your kayak and/or your camping equipment, at the destination of your choice and pick you up when and where you wish. (The cost is minimal—the regular boat fare plus small drop-off and pickup fees; there is no charge for kayaks.) Friends of mine once spent a wonderful two weeks in Glacier Bay camping along the shores, being picked up and dropped by the tour boat. They moved three or four times—always further up the bay—until they had experienced the full spectrum of its wonders. Decades later, they are still talking about this trip. If you want to venture on a kayak outing (please, not alone, unless you really know your way around in Southeastern waters), you can likewise be picked up where you wish, on the date you decide on.

Whether camping or kayaking, be sure to check with the NPS at Bartlett Cove before taking off. The park service people can give you pertinent information about current conditions and help you plan your trip. They can also cue you in on what to look for and where to look for it, providing in-depth information that can add immeasurably to your experience. Leave your proposed schedule with them; then, should you get yourself lost or into any other trouble and not show up when expected, they will (sigh) come look for you. Be sure to check back when you return from your trip. Also, be sure to carry out your garbage.

A Few Final Tips

Guns are not allowed in the park; if you're carrying one, you can check it with the Park Service. State fishing licenses are required if you want to supplement your food with Glacier Bay fish: you can get a license at the Glacier Bay Lodge.

If you decide not to hassle with bringing your own kayak, you can join a kayak trip run by a local guide (see following) or you can ask the NPS about the possibility of renting one locally.

Remember that cruise ships have the right of way, and that there are a lot of them that travel Glacier Bay; check with the NPS for their anticipated schedules. (NPS biologists suspect that heavy boat travel may be causing an impact on the local marine life: The number of humpback whales in the park has dwindled alarmingly. Attempts to limit the number of cruise ships, however, have not been welcomed.)

There are no storage facilities for gear at Bartlett Cove. If you want to camp at Bartlett Cove, there is a good campground there and a spiffy bear food cache. If you decide to venture farther afield, consult Piggott's book, which has excellent suggestions, or write the NPS. Also check with the NPS regarding camping regulations.

Keep in mind that the tides in Glacier Bay can fluctuate as much as 25 feet, and it goes without saying that you should be prepared for rain and that you should have both sunglasses and bug juice along, although the colder areas are more likely to be insect free.

Hikes You Can Take From Bartlett Cove

There are two lovely and easy hikes you can take if you're staying at Bartlett Cove; even a nonhiker might enjoy them. Neither involves any major elevation gain, and both can be extended if you want a longer, more strenuous hike. You can do the Beach and Nature Trail in a half hour or so, but allow a couple of hours for a Bartlett River outing.

Beach and Nature Trail

The Park Service conducts a one mile round-trip walk daily along the beach and through the forest along the shore. If you are able to join a group with the ranger, it's worthwhile. However, it is easy enough to take this short, charming walk yourself. You can inquire at the lodge or at Park Headquarters for directions and/or information regarding the self-guided tour.

If you're a good hiker and enjoy making your way along a sometimes muddy, sometimes slippery, but always beautiful beach, you can continue on the beach southward to Point Gustavus (seven miles). Check the tide before you start out; a high tide may force you into a forest scramble.

Bartlett River

You can make this a morning's or an afternoon's stroll or a whole day of wandering beside a beautiful river. However you take it, the trail will offer you many joyful sights and sounds. You will pass through mossy forests along the shore, and, of course, alongside the river itself. Expect to hear birdsong and the scolding of red squirrels. When you reach the river (less than a mile and a half from the Gustavus Road), look for bald eagles, great blue herons, waterfowl and beaver, too. In season, the wildflowers should be lovely, with mimulus studding the grassy and wet places you pass through. Check with the National Park Service people for further details.

Note: Although Glacier Bay National Monument was enlarged by the Congress in 1980 and redesignated Glacier Bay National Park and Glacier Bay National Preserve, old and valid mining claims still exist within its boundaries. These pose periodic—and long-range—threats to the integrity of this national treasure.

Some Useful Information About Glacier Bay

There is scheduled air service out of Juneau to Gustavus, and bus service to Bartlett Cove, which is about ten miles distant. Air taxi service is available in Juneau, Haines, Sitka, and Skagway. (If you can afford a flight-see over Glacier Bay on a blue day, don't miss it. It could give you one of your greatest travel memories.) Many tour ships include the bay on their Southeastern itineraries, but the ferry liners do not. (Sometimes, in Juneau, you may be lucky enough to get aboard a chartered ferry, usually the small ferry liner

Aurora, if a group renting her has extra space. It's worth a call to the **Marine Highway System,** 907-272-7116.)

Where to Stay

The **Glacier Bay Lodge** at Bartlett Cove is beautiful, but heavily used by tourists. Reservations are required. Write Box 108, Gustavus, AK 99826. May through September; October through April, write 312 Park Place Building, Seattle, WA 98101; phone (toll free) 800-426-0600. I try to stay at the **Gustavus Inn** in Gustavus. This is also too often booked full, but you can try writing ahead. Although it's ten miles from Bartlett Cove, you can get a ride of one kind or another, or you can pedal one of the bicycles provided by the inn or hike the level (and lovely) road and get a ride back. The Gustavus Inn is a family operation that uses a big old and comfortable Quonset hut for sleeping accommodations as well as a big old and comfortable farmhouse for sleeping accommodations and dining facilities. The food is legendary. Write Box 31, Gustavus, AK 99826; phone 907-697-3311. Reservations required.

Some Useful Names and Addresses

There are numerous package tours available from Juneau to Glacier Bay. For starters, you might try one of the following. **Alaska Travel Adventures:** write 200 North Franklin Street, Juneau, AK 99801; phone 907-586-6245. **Glacier Bay Yacht/Seaplane Tours:** write Box 424, Juneau, AK 99802; phone 907-586-6835. **Alaska Airlines** also runs a short see-it-all tour. **Huna-Totem** operates tours as well; see Hoonah.

Boat charters and tours are also operated out of Gustavus. Write **Alaska Discovery Wilderness Adventures,** Box 26, Gustavus, AK 99826; phone 907-697-3162.

There are two daily tour boats. The *M. V. Glacier Bay Explorer*, which has 32 staterooms, sails daily on an overnight trip from Glacier Bay Lodge, leaving at 1:30 P.M. and returning at 10 A.M. the next morning. Park Service naturalists accompany this cruise. The *M. V. Thunder Bay* departs at 7 A.M. daily for a seven or eight hour cruise (120 mile round trip) up and back the bay. For further information about both of these tour ships, write Suite 312, Park Place Building, Seattle, WA 98101; phone (toll free) 800-426-0600.

The **Glacier Bay National Park and Preserve** is headquartered in Juneau (write Box 1089, Juneau, AK 99802; phone 907-586-7137), and in Gustavus (write c/o Bartlett Cove, Gustavus, AK 9986; phone 907-697-3341).

USGS Topo Maps Juneau quadrangles B-6, C-6, and D-6; Mount Fairweather quadrangles C-2, D-1, D-2; Skagway quadrangle A-4. These are available from the **Alaska Natural History Association,** Glacier Bay National Monument, Gustavus, AK 99826. Also write this association for an excellent bibliography for Glacier Bay.

YAKUTAT

The village of Yakutat is midway between Southcentral and Southeastern Alaska and is one of the only sizable coastal villages that cannot be reached by ferry. There are good reasons, of course, why this is so—the turbulent open waters of the Gulf of Alaska through which the ship would have to pass, for instance, and the fierce storms that batter this unprotected portion of the coast. Winds here can be even worse than at Valdez, where children have been tied together for safety to get them home from school. Yakutat is also the longtime site of violent tectonic activity, with a history of quakes that's enough to shake anybody up. Perhaps the worst seismic events occurred in 1899, when on September 3, the village was wracked by a quake measuring 8.3 on the Richter Scale and just a week later was slammed by one measuring 8.6.

Nearby Lituya Bay to the south has also been the center of some spectacular joltings. On July 10, 1958, one of the worst generated a wave 1,740 feet high—the biggest splash wave ever observed anywhere. It scoured the hillside above the bay bare. This same temblor hit Yakutat as well and caused spectacular "sandblows" on the Yakutat Forelands, which lie between Yakutat and Lituya Bay. The sand below the surface of the forelands was shaken down and consolidated, which caused it to fissure and erupt loose sand and water in spouts that rose several feet high in volcanolike fashion. In this same shake, a piece of Khantaak Island (about half a million cubic yards in size) in Monti Bay near Yakutat was swallowed by the bottom of the bay in a great dark boil of water. Three unfortunate people who were on the island were never seen again.

If you can manage a trip to Yakutat on a clear day, however, you will find it to be another seemingly serene place of beauty. Backdropped by snowy peaks, it has two wonderful accessible ocean beaches that you can walk along for miles. It also has comely forests of mossy trees and, in the Yakutat Forelands as well as other areas, some of the most beautiful flower gardens in all Alaska. (I have been on Dry Bay on a cloudy July day when a mass planting of blooming paintbrush seemed to light up the world as though with sunshine.)

The country around Yakutat is the primary home of the blue bear—or glacier bear. This magnificent animal is a rare color phase of the black bear, and has a surmised evolutionary history that is intriguing. Blue bears are believed to have been isolated from the rest of the local black bear population during the Ice Ages and to have adapted to a treeless situation where their pale bluish color gave them protection. Their heads are also shaped differently from those of black bears, and their teeth are not as differentiated; but, now

Lituya Bay. Source: National Park Service.

reunited with their fellow black bears, they interbreed with them readily. Scarce even around Yakutat, the blue bears are threatened by increased logging, possible oil development, and habitat destruction of their relatively small primary range.

There are many pleasant things you can see and do around Yakutat. You can reach Harlequin Lake by road. This is a large, spectacular glacial lake which is rimmed with flower-filled meadows. You can charter a skiff to wind your way among islands and then past a beach (where you may see a blue bear) on into a wide bowl-shaped bay surrounded by 12,000 to 18,000 foot peaks. Some people who know Alaska well call this the most impressive glacier-viewing spot they have seen. Or you can charter a wheel plane to fly you above the nearby Malaspina Glacier, which is certainly one of the great sights of the earth. Other, very short charter flights can take you to remote beaches which are ideal for camping. The beach to the north is part of the Wrangell-Saint Elias National Park and Preserve. Behind this beach, you can walk to ponds overlooking the Malaspina Glacier, or you can wander through half-mile-long meadows that, in early summer, are full of wildflowers "not excelled in Alaska," according to a friend. Also accessible is the Situk River, a short, intimate, gentle stream, with excellent fishing. This offers an ideal one day (or overnight) paddle down to a saltwater lagoon.

The bird life around Yakutat is fabulous. Another friend once saw 150 trumpeter swans on a pond in April when the snow was still on the ground. This is also the southernmost nesting area of the Aleutian tern, which can sometimes hold its own very well against the predatory bald eagles that find it here. (It is wonderful to see how the small birds gang up to chase the marauders away from their nesting grounds.) This is a favored area of snow geese as well, which can congregate here by the tens of thousands.

Alaska Airlines makes regular scheduled trips to Yakutat, weather permitting. There are several places to stay, including the Glacier Bear Lodge (write Box 303, Yakutat, AK 99689; phone 907-784-3202) and the Yakutat Airport Lodge (write Box 287, Yakutat, AK 99689; phone 907-784-3232). Air taxi service is available from Gulf Air Taxi, Box 367, Yakutat, AK 99689; phone 907-784-3240. (You can contact this service for pickup if you run the Tatsenshini and Alsek rivers: see section on Haines.)

U.S. FOREST SERVICE

For many decades, virtually all of Southeast Alaska was the exclusive domain of the United States Forest Service, the Tongass National Forest comprising some 16 million acres of land, an area larger than West Virginia. (Alaska's other National Forest, the Chugach, is discussed in the section on Southcentral Alaska.) Under the terms of statehood, however, the state was given 400,000 acres to be selected out of this forest, and under the terms of ANCSA, the Southeast Natives were granted five hundred thousand more acres of Forest Service land in settlement of their aboriginal claims. Not surprisingly, the areas selected for state and private property have included some of the most valuable commercial timber stands. Since the U. S. Forest Service (USFS) unfortunately overcommitted the commercial timber of the Tongass Forest in long-term contracts let during the 1950s, the state and Native selections have had a major impact on its resource management program.

Added to this, the 1980 Alaska Lands Act mandated a total cut of at least 450 million board feet every decade in the Tongass Forest and authorized major appropriations ($40 million per year) to help guarantee this cut. A program to encourage the increase of private logging enterprises in the Tongass was also mandated. Conservationists fear that this will lead to further destructive pressures on this magnificent forest.

At the same time, the new Alaska Land Law also increased the size of the Tongass Forest by some 1,450,000 acres—largely of ice and snow and including the Juneau Ice Field. It further established two national monuments—

Admiralty Island and Misty Fjords—in the Tongass Forest and designated a dozen new wilderness areas.

NEW TONGASS FOREST UNITS

National Monuments	Acreage
Misty Fjords	2,285,000
Admiralty Island	921,000

Wilderness Areas	Acreage
Endicott River	94,000
Warren–Coronation–Maurelle Islands	35,000
Petersburg Creek—Duncan Salt Chuck	50,000
Russell Fjord	307,000
South Baranof Island	314,000
South Prince of Wales Island	87,000
Stikine–LeConte	443,000
Tebenkof Bay	65,000
Tracy Arm–Ford's Terror	656,000
West Chichagof Island	265,000

The USFS maintains a unique system of wilderness cabins that are located principally on wilderness lakes or along wilderness shores. These cabins—some 130 in the Tongass Forest, and quite a few in the two national monuments—can be rented for a few dollars per day, a remarkable buy. Most have eight bunks and many are charming A-frames with good wood stoves and other amenities of comfortable wilderness homes. (No electricity or running water, of course!) Those located on lakes generally have their own skiffs, thanks to local sportsmen's clubs. (These clubs also help maintain the cabins.) You will have to fly into most of these cabins (notable exceptions are those on Prince of Wales Island, which are accessible by road), but they still provide wonderful places for a family or a group of friends to enjoy an Alaskan adventure for a minimum cost. They must be reserved in advance (see below).

When traveling in Southeast, keep in mind that the USFS is still the principal land administrator and is pledged to serve the needs of the public, including the recreationist. Do not hesitate to call upon the service to provide you with information or to help you plan an outing in this part of Alaska. It has some excellent (free) material, including maps, interpretive brochures, and a good checklist of Southeastern birds. For this material, and for information about the cabins and making reservations, write: Forest Supervisor, Tongass National Forest, U. S. Forest Service, Box 1628, Juneau, AK 99802.

Part III

SOUTHCENTRAL AND SOUTHWEST

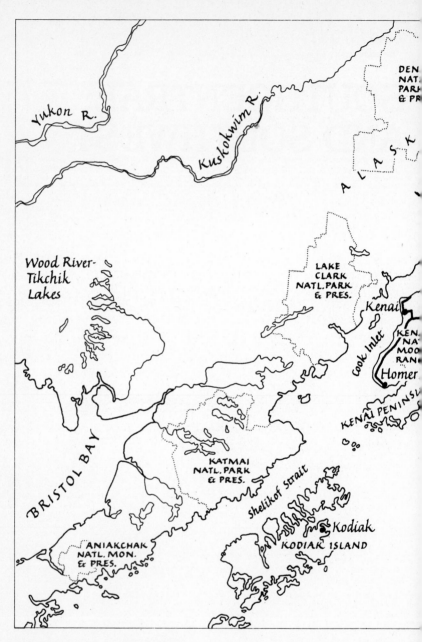

Southcentral and Southwest Alaska

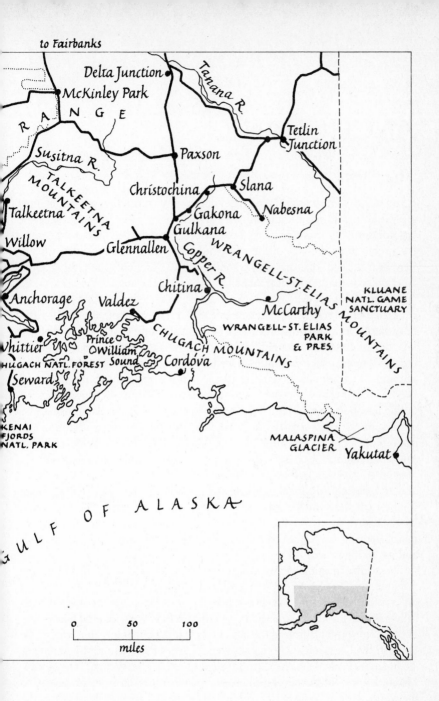

to Fairbanks

Delta Junction

McKinley Park

R A N G E

Tanana R.

Tetlin Junction

Susitna R.

Paxson

TALKEETNA
MOUNTAINS

Christochina

Slana

Talkeetna

Gakona

Nabesna

Willow

Gulkana

Glennallen

Copper R.

WRANGELL-ST.-ELIAS MOUNTAINS

KLUANE
NATL. GAME
SANCTUARY

Chitina

Anchorage

Valdez

McCarthy

CHUGACH MOUNTAINS

WRANGELL-ST. ELIAS
PARK
& PRES.

Whittier

Prince
William
Sound

Cordova

CHUGACH NATL. FOREST

Seward

KENAI
FJORDS
NATL. PARK

MALASPINA
GLACIER

Yakutat

GULF OF ALASKA

0   50   100
miles

ANCHORAGE

The City

If you talk to almost any Alaskan who doesn't live in Anchorage, the chances are you'll be told what a terrible place the city is. It's the Los Angeles of the last frontier, your friend may say—overpriced, overcrowded, and overbearing. It's a scourge on the face of the wilderness, a disgrace and a disaster. Or you may hear the old joke that goes something like: "The only good thing about Anchorage is that it's so near Alaska."

Talk to somebody who lives in Anchorage, on the other hand, and you may get a different story. True, Anchorage does have its share of problems—rush-hour traffic jams, urban sprawl, lack of adequate zoning, flag-flying used-car lots, too much plastic, too many fast food depots, and tourist-jammed hotels—but it has many urban amenities as well. Its bike paths, for example, although primarily recreational total more than 70 miles throughout the city, and they're well kept, well located, and quite beautiful in many places. It has a public transportation system, the People Mover, that does a remarkably good job despite the city's sprawl. Anchorage has its own symphony orchestra and a community chorus that ranks high nationwide. It has opera, dance, chamber music, and theater, two university campuses, a community college, a number of good art galleries and restaurants, well-stocked sporting goods stores, a zoo, and an excellent historical and fine arts museum (with, incidentally, one of the best gift shops in the state for Native artwork). Although it is not served by state ferry or cruise ships, Anchorage is Alaska's principal commercial marine port (second only to Kenai), and it is readily accessible by air, rail, and paved highway.

The scenic location of Anchorage, moreover, is one that almost any city might envy. The great tides that wash it on the northwest and southwest put on constantly changing and spectacular shows, at one time revealing beautifully patterned wetland, and then providing exciting views of tidal bores. And everywhere you look around the city, you see those encircling mountains. To the east, the Chugach—with names like Williwaw Peak, Mount Magnificent, Temptation Peak, Wolverine and Suicide Peaks, The Wedge, The Ramp, Mount Muir—lift upward as much as 7,800 feet directly from sea level. To the north rise the Talkeetnas, which can be viewed from high points in the city. To the west and south as far as the eye can see are the great peaks of the Aleutian Range—Spurr (11,670 feet and Anchorage's resident active volcano), Redoubt (10,197 feet), and—visible from the south of the city on clear days—

Iliamna (10,016 feet). Little Susitna (only 4,366 feet) seems almost an insignificant nubbin directly across the inlet. Clear weather also reveals the dreamlike shape of McKinley with Foraker on its shoulder—the high points of the Alaska Range—shimmering against the pale sky to the north. In good summer weather, you'll be struck by the brilliant greens of the nearby mountain swards, the dark, deep-colored rock, and the dazzle of white snow against blue sky. On rainy or hazy days, the mountains blur into soft gray, silver, and black like a fine photograph.

Along with its spectacular setting, Anchorage enjoys one of Alaska's more moderate climates, although it has its share of cloudy days and somewhat unpredictable seasons. Some winters, the temperature can plummet, and it will seem and be even colder when the wind blows. In frigid weather every branch of every tree can be etched with rime ice and the city will look like it's decorated for Christmas whether or not the month is December. (On December 21, Anchorage has just five hours and twenty-nine minutes of sunlight.) On the other hand, winter temperatures can be remarkably mild: One notable year, the coldest day's minimum in Anchorage through the end of February was identical to the coldest day's minimum in Dade County, Florida—17 degrees above zero. Another year, a used-car dealer kept a palm tree alive and happy outside all winter long. In the summer, the weather can vary equally; you should be prepared for temperatures in the 50's and gentle drizzles, as well as for pleasantly warm and sunny days.

Anchorage has another unique advantage; it lies in the heart of country that is not only magnificent but wonderfully hospitable to all sorts of outdoor recreation. As in Juneau, you can start your adventuring almost downtown; you cannot climb a mountain from a street corner, but you can run quite a respectable stream (Campbell Creek) right through the city. As noted above, you can also bike through some very pleasant urban terrain, and you can bird-

AVERAGE TEMPERATURE: ANCHORAGE

	F° daytime high	F° nighttime low	F° monthly average
Jan.	20.0	3.5	11.8
Feb.	26.6	8.9	17.8
March	32.8	14.6	23.7
April	43.8	26.8	35.3
May	55.2	37.2	46.2
June	62.9	46.2	54.6
July	65.6	50.1	57.9
August	63.8	48.0	55.9
Sept.	55.7	40.4	48.1
Oct.	41.8	27.8	34.8
Nov.	28.3	13.9	21.1
Dec.	20.6	5.3	13.0

watch on urban lakes and in publicly protected marshlands in and on the edge of town. What's more, it is only a few miles from downtown to the Chugach Mountains, and a gorgeous nearly half-million-acre state park where hiking, backpacking, rock climbing, and cross-country skiing are par excellence. Travel just a few hours to the south, and you can be in superb canoeing and kayaking country in the Kenai Moose Range. Take a slightly different direction, and you will reach the waters of Prince William Sound, which are ideal for sailing as well as kayaking. In winter, there is fine downhill skiing near the city at Alyeska, more skiing to the north on Hatcher Pass, and even good cross-country skiing, night and day, in Anchorage's municipal parks. (See Skiing, below.)

All of this outdoor pleasuring is readily available, of course, to visitors as well as residents, and since you don't have to leave the ground to reach these outdoor playgrounds, it is relatively inexpensive to enjoy them. But bear in mind that Anchorage is the population center of Alaska, and most Alaskans love the great out-of-doors. If you do your Alaskan adventuring in places readily accessible to Anchorage, you should be prepared to share your experience with a few, or many, people. The more popular recreation spots around Anchorage can be crowded, just as similar areas are Outside.

There is one more important plus for Anchorage: It is the gateway and point of departure for more distant wilderness and wildlife areas, including some of Alaska's most superlative wild places.

When you visit Anchorage, you may have to look for its Alaskan flavor, but it is there—in old clapboard cottages, and in a few log cabins still standing and occupied downtown, and in certain events like the Fur Rendezvous ("Rondy") and the Iditarod Race, which take place annually in the city. Anchorage is a young city which is still making its history.

Among the first people who used the Anchorage area were the Chugachimiut Eskimos and Tanaina Indians, and archeological digs at such places as Beluga Point on Turnagain Arm, reveal that there were settlements here at least 6,000 years ago. Captain James Cook was the first European to immortalize the region. He charted the waters here in 1778 and named Turnagain Arm, for obvious reasons. (Cook Inlet was named for him posthumously by his patron, John Montagu, First Lord of the British Admiralty.) The Russians left little evidence of passing this way, although there is an interesting Russian Church not far from Anchorage in Eklutna. Sourdoughs, however, crisscrossed the Anchorage bowl extensively around the turn of the century, looking for gold. They left a few old mining towns like Hope, which was once a bustling place of 5,000 souls, but is now gone ghost with only 25 names listed in the phone book. In 1907, the United States government moved in and established a Forest Reserve, the Chugach, with somewhat vague boundaries which included the Anchorage bowl within its 11 million acres (today, the Chugach Forest is closer to 5 million acres in size). A decade later, the government entered the scene again and sited a construction camp for the building of the Alaska Railroad on one of the bowl's better drainages, Ship Creek, so named because ships found good harbor at its mouth. At that point and in that place, Anchorage was rooted, albeit inadvertently, an offshoot of one of the first major federal projects in Alaska.

Like many Alaskan towns, Anchorage had an early series of booms and busts, but it ended up as the repair center and headquarters for the Alaska Railroad. By the mid-thirties, it had settled down into a small town with a population of just over 2,000 people, while Fairbanks (the northern terminus of the railroad) had about 2,100, and Juneau had over 4,000. But the advent of World War II brought major changes to Anchorage. The military moved in in force, building two major bases, Fort Richardson and Elmendorf Air Force Base, nearby. (Military personnel still constitutes a healthy percentage of the city's population.) Anchorage became linked directly to the world Outside with the construction of what would become the Alaska Highway. By the end of the war, the city had emerged as the state's principal transportation center, and it had been discovered by thousands of people. In the 1950 census, Anchorage had a population of 40,000, and the discovery and development of oil on the nearby Kenai Peninsula and in the Cook Inlet during the late fifties and early sixties clinched a pattern of continuing growth and expansion.

Good Friday in 1964 fell on March 27, a day that was to become the most memorable—and certainly the most dramatic—in the history of Anchorage to that date. That afternoon at 5:36 P.M., an earthquake measuring between

Fourth Avenue after the 1964 Good Friday earthquake. *Source: Bob Olendorff.*

8.4 and 8.6 on the Richter Scale—the strongest quake ever measured on the North American continent and one of the strongest ever recorded in the world—devastated large areas of Anchorage, including the residential area of Turnagain Heights. The earthquake left nine dead in the city. Statewide damage was estimated overall at between $300 and $400 million, with much of it centered in Anchorage. Within months, the federal government had funneled $406 million in disaster aid to the stricken areas, and Anchorage was on its way to a massive rebuilding effort.

The discovery of oil at Prudhoe Bay in 1968 and the subsequent construction of the oil pipeline in 1974 flooded Anchorage with more people and brought a renewed transportation, construction, and business boom. Most of the oil companies and unions involved in the Prudhoe Bay development chose Anchorage for their headquarters. Then banks, savings and loan companies, and other businesses moved in to service them. After the passage of the 1971 Alaska Native Claims Settlement Act and the establishment of Native regional corporations, more Alaskan Native activity came to be centered in Anchorage. And in the late 1970s, a local Native regional corporation, Cook Inlet Region, Inc., erected a glass-walled headquarters building that has already become one of the city's major landmarks.

By the time of the 1980 Census, the greater Anchorage area could count a population of over 200,000 people, some fifty percent of the state's population, and the city and the metropolitan area are still growing.

What to See and Do in the City

If you enjoy strolling along city streets, you can explore Anchorage and its somewhat meager but always charming history quite pleasantly on foot. Downtown Anchorage is generally level, and it's easy to find your way around. Running east-west are the avenues, which are numbered, with First Avenue being the nearest to and paralleling Ship Creek on the north. The north-south trending streets are arranged alphabetically on either side of A Street; those to the west are lettered B, C, D, and so on through W Street, while those to the east are named Barrow, Cordova, Denali, etc., until the pattern is interrupted at Orca by Merrill Field, the airstrip used by small aircraft.

A good place to start exploring Anchorage is at the Railroad Depot that is so much a part of the city's beginnings. Walk north on E Street until it dead-ends at First Avenue to reach the terminal. The railroad was almost completely rebuilt in the late 1940s, and this building survived the 1964 quake, although it was severely damaged. Inside, you can get information for the state ferry, which leaves from Whittier, as well as the railroad schedule. You'll also find a rather unique gift shop where railroad buffs can discover antique (if expensive) treasures. Across from the terminal stands old Engine Number I of the Alaska Railroad flanked by two handsome totems. (This engine is not, in fact, Engine Number I; that piece of equipment got scrapped along the way. But it is one of the railroad's original switch engines, a hand-me-down from the Panama Canal construction endeavor, and it did yeoman service in its time and makes an appropriate monument.)

You can walk from the depot across Ship Creek and upstream to a small dam where, during the summer, you may see salmon thrashing their way upstream to spawn. During the winter, the water impounded by this dam steams like a fumarole, being warmed by the discharge water from a nearby power plant. Many birds use this open water which makes it a fine place for hibernal bird-watchers. Two blocks north of the Railroad Depot, the C Street Overpass crosses Ship Creek and leads westward to the Port of Anchorage.

From roughly E Street to A Street and from Fourth Avenue north to Ship Creek, there is a region of highly unstable ground that turned to jelly during the Good Friday earthquake, sinking eight to ten feet in places and devastating many of the buildings then standing there. Major efforts have gone into attempts to stabilize this section of the city, known as the buttress area, and to make it safe for the reconstruction of buildings. Notice what look like smokestacks along the sides of the streets in part of this area; these are ventilating devices designed to help the moisture escape from the water-retentive ground. Also note that many new buildings have gone up, most of them since 1969. Among them is the Sunshine Mall on Fourth Avenue, an enterprise that is owned jointly by the Chugach Natives, Inc. (Prince William Sound, Copper River Delta, and lower Kenai Peninsula Natives) and Kotzebue's Native Kikiktagruk Inupiat Corporation. Next to it is the Post Office Mall. There are several good eating spots here.

On returning to the downtown area, you can enjoy the summertime flower beds that ring the block around City Hall, located between E and F streets and Fourth and Fifth avenues. If you stop in the Anchorage Convention and Visitor's Bureau office in the log cabin on the corner of Fourth and E, you'll find an abundance of literature and information concerning almost all aspects of Anchorage and its recreational opportunities. In the summer, you'll find a list of local Sierra Club outings, some of which may tempt you.

Then look for Club 25 on the southeast corner of Fourth Avenue and I Street. A restaurant for many years, this is the Wendler Building, the oldest building in Anchorage; it was constructed in 1915.

If you follow I Street on to the south, you'll come to Delaney Park and more summertime flowers. The park runs all the way from A Street to P Street and from Ninth to Tenth Avenue and is Anchorage's in-city playground. It began life as Anchorage's first airstrip and was used by early bush pilots until Merrill Field went into operation in 1930. The strip served as a firebreak as well, protecting the town from what was then the wilderness to the south of it. In a remarkable burst of community effort, the strip was constructed in a single weekend in 1923. (That was the year President Warren Harding visited Alaska to drive the spike completing the Alaska Railroad.)

At the west end of Delaney Park, on the corner of Ninth and P—a charming residential area of the city—there is a picturesque house with a lovely garden, fortunately largely visible from the sidewalk, which contains a fine sampling of Alaska's indigenous wildflowers. If you keep walking at the other end of the park, you'll come to the local cemetery, which is worth at least a few moments of your time. There you'll find the tombstones of people from many denominations, including Russian Orthodox. Many of the inscriptions sum up with wonderful conciseness the history or character of the person resting below. See if you can find my favorite marker which reads simply: Here Lies Lucky And Always Will Lie.

Not far from the cemetery is the Anchorage Historical and Fine Arts Museum, located on the corner of A Street and Sixth Avenue. There are interesting permanent Native and historical exhibits here as well as rotating art exhibits that sometimes feature the work of contemporary Alaskan artists. The Museum Gift Shop is a good place to look for Native craft.

Across from the museum to the south is the Federal Building, which has a good scientifically oriented reference library as well as a reasonable cafeteria that is open to the public. There is an excellent reference library for facts about Alaska at the Arctic Environmental Information and Data Center at 707 A Street (99501).

Unfortunately, there is no continuous public park strip along the downtown Anchorage waterfront. There are a few small city parks, however, including Resolution Park at the foot of Third Street where you can reach the high tide line. Resolution Park commands a good view of the Knik Arm and the grand mountains across the Cook Inlet; it also has a statue of Captain James Cook that is identical to the one in Whitby, Yorkshire, England, one of Anchorage's sister cities. You can also walk to the shore and along the high tide line in several other places where the avenues dead-end. From close up you can get a good look at the marshes with their beautifully sculptured wetlands and their extraordinary tidal range; tides in the Cook Inlet can go well over 30 feet and are exceeded world-wide only by those in the Bay of Fundy. When the going gets difficult along the shore, you can use the railroad right-of-way. Note: these inviting tidelands can be treacherous because of the swift onrush of the tidal waters, and hikers should be wary.

Annual Events

Every February, the Fur Rendezvous helps speed the long wintertime along in the city. Begun as an annual celebration after trappers had finished auctioning off their furs, the "Rondy" still has a fur auction but many other events as well. These include the world championship sled dog races and the world championship dog weight pull; a Saint Bernard set the record in 1976 by pulling 5,220 pounds of weight. There are also balloon races, snowshoe events, and the Miners and Trappers Ball.

March is the month for the Iditarod Race, which sees dog teams start from

Anchorage on a 1,000-mile pull to Iditarod. They follow the historic trail that originally started on the Kenai Peninsula (see Chugach Mountains, below) and then went over mountains, rivers, and tundra to reach the mining area around the Iditarod River, which flows into the Innoko and thence into the Yukon. (The Iditarod is a National Historic Trail and is administered, and is being enthusiastically developed, by the BLM.)

In June, the city puts on a Renaissance Faire. This is a weekend long celebration that features medieval costumes, Shakespeare, music, and feasting.

Some Useful Information About Anchorage

Air Service

Since it is one of the major refueling stops on the polar air route, Anchorage International Airport is served by numerous international air carriers including **Air France, British Airways, Japan Air Lines, KLM Royal Dutch Airlines, Korean Airlines, Lufthansa German Airlines, Northwest Orient Airlines, Sabena Belgian World Airlines,** and **Scandinavian Airlines.** Interstate passenger service to Anchorage is provided by four United States airlines: **Alaska, Northwest Orient, Western,** and **Wien Air Alaska** all fly out of Seattle, the principal air gateway to Alaska. Within the state, **Alaska Airlines** and **Wien Air Alaska** between them serve the principal cities and bush communities, with **Reeve Aleutian Airways** linking Anchorage to the Alaska Peninsula, the Aleutian Chain,and the Pribilof Islands. There are five other smaller carriers that serve various parts of the state from Anchorage as well. Air charters are too numerous to list. Inquire at Anchorage International Airport or write Chamber of Commerce (see below).

If you fly into Anchorage during the tourist season, you'll find the airport the scene of considerable commotion. The several money exchanges take care of a growing number of foreign tourists who are visiting Alaska, and the **Fred Harvey Restaurant** (a cut above many airport restaurants) is apt to be crowded around mealtimes. While you're waiting for your baggage, you might want to stroll along the lower level to see the display of mounted animals there; this will give you a chance to get an idea of the size and beauty of a variety of Alaska fauna: polar bear, brown bear, glacier (blue) bear, musk-ox, wolf (shown snarling, alas, thus embodying the obsolete idea that this animal is a varmint), moose, trumpeter swan, and bald eagle. There is good locker service in the airport, and you can store large items. They're used to taking care of the equipment of miners, geologists, and engineers. The price is not cheap, but you can leave your belongings for up to 30 days.

There is limousine and cab service from the airport into Anchorage. The cab costs approximately twice what the limousine does, and if you can share your ride into town with another person, it will be worth the extra you'll pay for a tip. The People Mover also runs to the airport about once an hour: it stops on the lower level.

INTRASTATE CARRIERS SERVING ANCHORAGE

To: Community and/or Area	Alaska Aeronautical Industries	Alaska Airlines	Galena Air Service	Great Northern Airlines	Kennedy Air Service	Polar Airlines	Reeve Aleutian Airways	Seair	Wien Air Alaska
Alaska Peninsula							X		
Aleutian Chain							X		
Aniak and area								X	X
Barrow									X
*Bethel and area								X	X
Cordova	X	X							X
Dillingham									X
*Fairbanks		X				X			X
*Galena			X						X
Gulkana						X			X
Homer	X								X
Iliamna									X
*Juneau		X							
Kenai	X								X
*Ketchikan		X							
King Salmon									X
*Kodiak		Inquire at Anchorage International Airport							X
Kotzebue				X					X
McGrath						X			
McKinley Park				X					
*Nenana		Inquire at Anchorage International Airport							
*Nome				X					X
Northway						X			
*Petersburg		X							
Pribilof Islands							X		
*Sitka		X							
Soldotna	X								
Talkeetna				X					
Tok						X			
Unalakleet				X					X
Valdez	X				X	X			
Wrangell		X							
Yakutat		X							

Starred communities have scheduled carriers serving other bush areas.

Bus Service

Scheduled bus service to Anchorage is offered by: (1) **Alaska-Yukon Motorcoaches** (Fourth and Battery Building, Suite 555, Seattle, Washington 98121), which travels between Haines, Skagway, Fairbanks, Denali Park, and Anchorage from mid-April to mid-November (this company also connects with service to Dawson City and Whitehorse: Write for schedule to the above address); and (2) **Transportation Services** (1041 East First Avenue, Anchorage, Alaska 99501), which runs between Denali Park to the north of Anchorage and Seward to the south.

It is also possible to visit Anchorage by bus from Seattle, Portland, and other points south. If you are interested, ask your travel agent to check the services offered by **Greyhound World Tours, Kneisel Green Carpet Escorted Tours** (operated by Kneisel Travel, Inc., Portland, Oregon) and **Westours Motorcoaches.**

Highway System

The Alaska highway system ties Anchorage directly to Seward, Kenai, and Homer to the south and to Fairbanks and the haul road to the north. It also links Anchorage with the Richardson Highway to Valdez and the Alaska Highway to Canada at Tok Junction. A good highway guide is *The Milepost*, published annually by the Alaska Northwest Publishing Co. (See Bibliography.)

Railroad

The Alaska Railroad (Pouch 7-2111, Anchorage, AK 99510; phone 907-265-2683) runs daily between Anchorage and Fairbanks, with stops at Denali Park and for locals along the way. It runs between Anchorage and Whittier from mid-May to mid-September. For the rest of the year, passenger service between Anchorage and Fairbanks operates twice a week. If you visit Anchorage during the daylight months, try to ride the Alaska Railroad. It will give you a feeling for Alaska that you can't get any other way, and, if the weather is clear, you'll get matchless views of Mount McKinley (Denali). Highly recommended. Note: it is a long ride from Anchorage to Fairbanks on the regular run, ten and a half hours in summer and twelve hours off-season. During the dark months, you lose much of the view, and it can seem like an endless trip; the cost, however, is about half the price of flying. A summer-only express stops once at Denali National Park, and takes only eight hours.

Public Transportation

Public Transit. The main Bus Accommodation Station is at Sixth Avenue and G Street, and you can get information about schedules there; phone 907-264-6543.

Taxis

Checker Cab, phone 907-276-1234. **Yellow Cab**, phone 907-272-2422. **Alaska Cab**, phone 907-563-5353.

Car Rentals

The Anchorage phone book lists about three dozen car rental outfits, including all the well-known companies. Check with your travel agent or try **Rent-A-Wreck** (utilizing older but serviceable vehicles), as I like to do, at 907-276-8459 (downtown) or 907-561-2218 (Anchorage International Airport). You can't beat the rates they offer.

Hotels

Anchorage has more than its share of hotels. Your travel agent—or the Anchorage Visitor's Bureau—can give you detailed information. Most are typical tourist accommodations, comfortable and more or less expensive—usually more—and there's not much choice. Among the higher-priced, you might consider the **Sheraton** (907-276-8700), the **Westward Hilton** (907-272-7411), or the **Captain Cook** (907-276-6000). I stay at the **Voyager** (501 K Street, 99501), which is relatively reasonable, quiet, and well-located downtown. Each room has a kitchenette equipped with utensils; phone 907-277-9501. (There is also a good gift shop—Alaska 49—in the lobby.)

The Anchorage **Youth Hostel** is located on the corner of Thirty-Second and Minnesota Drive, just south of Benson Boulevard, and can be reached by Bus Route 6 (People Mover) from the airport or from the Visitor's Center downtown on the corner of Fourth Avenue and F Street. Cost is $5 a night with hostel card and there is a three-night maximum stay; phone 907-243-3456. For bed and breakfast information, write Pat Denny, 526 Seward Street, 99801; phone 907-586-2959 or Charlie and Cameron Kelly, 7850 Glacier Highway, 99801; phone 907-789-0539.

Elderhostel is an international educational and hosteling program open to anyone who is 60 or older or whose spouse qualifies. It describes itself as being for those "on the move—not just in terms of travel but in the sense of reaching out to new experiences." Under Elderhostel auspices, participating universities and colleges, both large and small, offer weekly summer classes in a variety of interesting subjects. The cost is remarkably low and includes both tuition and board.

In Alaska, the Sheldon Jackson College in Sitka and other institutions of higher learning offer Elderhostel classes. You can choose from such subjects as The Ecology of Alaska, Between Alaska Tides, A Festival of Alaska Films, and so forth. The campuses are lovely and provide a unique and inexpensive way for elder citizens to get to know Alaska.

For dates of courses and further details, write: Elderhostel, 100 Boylston Street, Suite 200, Boston, MA 02116. Note: Elderhostel does not make travel arrangements.

The **YMCA** offers bunks and lockers (very reasonable). Write 609 F Street, Anchorage, AK 99501; phone 907-277-8522.

Campgrounds

Campgrounds are located at two municipal parks: **Centennial**, at 8300 Glenn Highway and Muldoon, and **Russian Jack Springs** at De Barr and Boniface.

The Centennial Camper Park has hot showers and trees all around and is
serviced directly by the People Mover bus; it is highly recommended. Campgrounds are also located in Chugach State Park and the Chugach National
Forest, but they require wheels to reach them. Inquire at **Parks and Forests
Information Center**, 225 Gambell Street; 907-271-4243.

Municipal Swimming Pools
Pools are available for public use at the following locations: **Dimond Pool,**
2909 W. Eighty-eighth Avenue; **East High Pool,** 4025 E. Twenty-fourth
Avenue; and **West High Pool,** 1700 Hillcrest Drive. Contact Cultural and
Recreations Services, Division of Parks and Recreation, Pouch 6-650,
Anchorage, AK 99502 for further information. You can also get complete
details of the municipality's other recreational facilities from this source.
YMCA showers and pool are at 5454 Lake Otis Parkway (99507); phone
907-563-3211.

Canoe Rentals
Canoes are available for rent out of Soldotna from the **Alaska Pioneer Canoers
Association,** Soldotna, AK 99669 (Write P.O. Box 931 or phone 907-262-
4003 for information). The APCA also provides complete outfitting and guiding as well as car pickups for canoeing in the Kenai Moose Range. You should
also check with the **Parks and Forests Information Center** at 2525 Gambell
Street to see if other canoe rentals are available. They may be able to refer
you to the Knik Kayakers and Kanoers, the local small-boater's association
(whose address and telephone number changes with its current officers); these
people will have the most up-to-date information for you regarding the local
canoeing and kayaking scene. You can also check with the other federal and
state bureaus listed below.

Bike Rentals
See section on Biking Opportunities.

Some Useful Names and Addresses
Alaska State Auto Club. Tour and travel services for Alaska members and
for visiting members of other automobile clubs. 525 West 3rd Avenue,
Anchorage, AK 99501; phone 907-276-3236. **Anchorage Convention and
Visitors Bureau**, and **Airport Domestic Information Center** are located in
the baggage claim area of the main terminal building of Anchorage International Airport. **Airport International Visitor Information Center** is located
in the international terminal of Anchorage International Airport. **Log Cabin
Visitor Information Center** is located at Fourth Avenue, Anchorage, AK
99501; phone 907-274-3531. **Visitor Information Phone Line**, recorded mes-
sages of current visitor attractions and events in the Anchorage area; phone
907-276-3200. **Anchorage Municipal Division of Parks and Recreation**, 2525

Gambell. Write Pouch 6-650, Anchorage, AK 99502; phone 907-264-4474. **Alaska Visitors Association**, P.O. Box 10-2220, Anchorage, AK 99510; phone 907-276-6663. **Alaska Association of Mountain Wilderness Guides**: write Box 3685, Anchorage, AK 99510. Contact regarding local guiding opportunities for backpacking, river-running, and so on. **Alaska Travel Adventures**: c/o Sheraton Hotel, 401 East Sixth Avenue, AK 99501; phone 907-276-6645. Contact regarding day-long outings—such as local hikes and glacier walking—as well as more extended wilderness trips out of Anchorage. In lower 48 call toll-free 800-227-8480.

Air Charters

There are too many to list them all. I have had excellent—and reasonable—service from **Birchwood Air Service**, P.O. Box B, Chuqiak, AK 99567; phone 907-688-2824.

Environmental Organizations

Alaska Center for the Environment, 1069 West Sixth Avenue, Anchorage, AK 99501; phone 907-274-3621. This is worth a visit if you would like to learn some of the environmental issues Alaskans are grappling with. It also has a good and growing library. Sells tee shirts for fund-raising. Open daily during the week. **Friends of the Earth** shares the space; phone 907-272-7335. **Sierra Club**, 241 East Fourth Avenue, Suite Five, Anchorage, AK 99501; phone 907-276-4040. This organization has an active membership and many local outings. **Trustees for Alaska**, 833 Gambell, Anchorage, AK 99501; phone 907-276-4244. **National Audubon Society**, 308 G Street, Suite 219, Anchorage, AK 99501; phone 907-276-1917. **Mountaineering Club of Alaska**, P.O. Box 2037, Anchorage, AK 99510. **Greenpeace**, P.O. Box 10-4432, Anchorage, AK 99510; phone 907-277-8234.

USGS Topo Maps: Available over-the-counter only—no mail order—at USGS Office, 508 Second Avenue, Room 108, Anchorage, AK 99501. This is also the place to purchase *Dictionary of Alaska Place Names* and other government printed books.

ANCHORAGE AS A GATEWAY

Anchorage is the immediate gateway to the mountain worlds of the Chugach-Kenai Mountains and the Talkeetnas. It is the takeoff point for the wonderful waterways and shores of the Kenai Peninsula and, via the Alaska Railroad and the state ferry, for the beauties of Prince William Sound. It is also the jumping-off place to more distant and inaccessible places that beckon lovers of true wilderness—the Lake Clark region, Aniakchak Crater, the Wood River–Tikchik, Katmai National Park and Preserve, the Pribilof Islands, Kodiak, the Wrangell—Saint Elias Mountains, the Kenai Fjords and the wild rivers of Alaska's Southcentral and Southwestern regions.

Many of these areas are in public hands, state or federal, although the Pribilof Islands are a special situation (see below). The Alaska Division of Parks administers nearly three million acres of superb state parkland including the Wood–Tikchik Park and Chugach State Park (which is directly out of Anchorage.) The United States Forest Service is in charge of the almost five-million-acre Chugach National Forest, which embraces Prince William Sound and its islands as well as the northeastern portion of the Kenai Peninsula. The United States Fish and Wildlife Service administers wildlife refuges on the Kenai Peninsula, in Kodiak, and in areas to the west. The National Park Service looks after the Kenai Fjords, the Lake Clark region, Aniakchak Crater, Katmai and Wrangell Parks, and the rivers that flow through these units. What's left of federal public land is administered by the Bureau of Land Management (BLM). Use these agencies to help you in your travels.

Public Agencies Administering Recreational Land Around Anchorage

National Park Service: Write 2525 Gambell, Anchorage, AK 99503; phone 907-271-4243. **United States Forest Service**: Publication information office located at 2221 East Northern Lights Boulevard, and also at Parks and Forests Information Center (see below). To reserve cabins, write **U.S. Forest Service, Pouch 6606, Anchorage, AK 99507; phone 907-345-2519. United States Bureau of Land Management**: Write Anchorage District Office, 4700 E. Seventy-second Avenue, AK 99507; phone 907-267-1200 or 267-1285. **United States Fish and Wildlife Service**: Write 1011 E. Tudor Road, Anchorage, AK 99503; phone 907-786-3487. **Alaska State Division of Parks**: Write 619 Warehouse Avenue, Suite 210, Anchorage, AK 99501; phone 907-274-4676. The **Parks and Forests Information Center** at 2525 Gambell is a joint service of the National Park Service, U.S. Forest Service, and Alaska State Parks. A stop here, or a phone call (907-271-4243) can be helpful.

CANOEING AND/OR KAYAKING IN THE ANCHORAGE AREA

River	Length in Miles	Time	White-Water Class	Open Canoes	Hazards	Put-Ins, Take-Outs (PI, TO)
Campbell Creek	6-8	1–3 hrs.	I	Yes	Tight bends, sweepers	PI: Folker St. behind Spada's Feed. PI or TO: Old Seward Hwy. bridge, Dowling Road, Arctic Blvd., Dimond Blvd. bridges
Upper Eagle River	13	3–5 hrs.	I, last mile II–III	Yes	Sweepers, log jams; last mile rocky rapids, last rapid III; open canoes should line and/or portage	PI: Ten miles up Eagle River Rd. where tributary is along road. TO: State park campground just above Glenn Hwy. bridge.
Lower Eagle River	8	2–3 hrs.	III	No	Many rocky rapids	PI: State park campground above Glenn Hwy. bridge. TO: military road bridge on Eagle River flats—take Artillary Rd. off Glenn Hwy.
Upper Kenai River	8	2–3 hrs.	I-II	Yes	Swift water in places, some rocks; best in spring when low	PI: Sterling Hwy. bridge at Kenai Lake outlet. TO: Sterling Hwy. bridge at Resurrection Trailhead; can also go on down to Jean Creek campground.
Kenai River canyon	6	1–2 hrs.	III	No	Large standing waves	PI: Jean Creek campground on Skilak Lake Rd. TO: Hike out 1.5 mile Hidden Creek trail from mouth or go down Skilak Lake 7 miles to campground on road; danger of strong wind and large waves on lake.
Lyons Creek/East Fork Sixmile River	9	2–3 hrs.	II above first Hwy. bridge; then I	Yes	Swift water, sweepers, log jams in upper part	PI: In higher water, Lyons Creek bridge just south of Turnagain Pass; usually better at Bertha Creek campground off Seward Hwy. TO: Just below Silvertip Hwy. camp where river next to road; no canoes beyond here!
Portage Creek	6	2–3 hrs.	I	Yes	Brush, logs, possibly jams, some shallow water	PI: Outlet of Portage Lake near Forest Service Visitor Center. TO: Seward Hwy. Bridge near Portage Glacier Rd.
Glacier Creek	3	1–2 hrs.	I-II	Yes experienced only	Very swift glacial water; sweepers and log jams are common	PI: Bridge just before Alyeska ski lodge. TO: Seward Hwy. bridge just south Alyeska Rd.
Little Susitna	17	1 long day or 2 short	I	Yes	Log jams in upper part	PI: Bridge crossing off Shrock Rd. ten miles out of Wasilla. TO: Parks Hwy. bridge (Mile 58).
Fish Creek	13	4–5 hrs.	I; last mile II	Yes	Last mile swift, brushy, jams possible	PI: Big Lake Rd. bridge at Big Lake outlet. TO: Knik Rd. bridge, fourteen mi. south of Wasilla.

WARNING: Don't trust this guide. People have gotten into trouble on the "easiest" of rivers. Water levels can alter conditions radically seasonally and even daily. New "sweepers" and log jams can occur any time. Wear life preservers, scout unfamiliar water, and line or portage when in doubt—no one ever drowned on a portage! Constant cold water temperatures can make even a class I stream into Class II.

Compiled by Patrick Pourchot

The World of the Chugach and Kenai Mountains

If you fly between Juneau and Anchorage on a clear day, the snowy peaks you admire along the eastern horizon for most of your trip will belong to the Chugach, or more properly, the Chugach-Kenai-Kodiak Mountains. This flyby is a good way to get a slight overview of this extremely rugged and impressive mountain system that is an approximately 500-mile-long segment of the Coast Range which curves around the Gulf of Alaska. Varying in width from 30 to 110 miles, the Chugach Mountains sweep north and westward from Mount Saint Elias and then, where they reach their greatest height (over 13,000 feet), they bend abruptly to the southwest. Marching the length of the Kenai Peninsula, they are known as the Kenai Mountains. After they plunge beneath the waters of the Gulf of Alaska, they finally emerge as the mountains of Kodiak Island, which are only 4,000 to 2,000 feet high. This great feature of the Alaska landscape is the scene of major earth activity. The epicenter of the Good Friday earthquake of 1964 was in the heart of the Chugach Mountains where they embrace Prince William Sound; portions of the entire range were displaced by the tremor.

The Chugach and Kenai Mountains are notable for their immense relief: valleys may have almost mile-high walls; peaks can lift directly from the sea to soar thousands of feet. Another of their notable features is the great burden of glaciers they carry. The word *burden* is deliberately chosen; the immense weight of the snow and ice in large glaciers actually depresses the land, a fact that is graphically illustrated in areas that have recently become ice free and are now springing up as much as an inch a year—more than eight feet in a century. (See section on Glacier Bay.) Spectacular ice fields sprawl between the high spires and ridges of both the Chugach and Kenai ranges. The Bagley Ice Field in the eastern section of the Chugach is the largest ice field outside those of Antarctica and Greenland; the ice fields on Mount Witherspoon in the central Chugach and the Harding Ice Field on the Kenai Peninsula rank among the greatest on the North American continent. Radiating from these snow and ice masses are dozens of great glaciers, many of which flow directly into tidewater. One of these, the Columbia Glacier, provides a fine spectacle for travelers on the ferry from Whittier to Valdez. Many smaller and almost more beautiful tidewater glaciers make the Kenai Fjords a unique area where you can watch and hear the rivers of ice as they plunge into the sea.

Sealed into the rocks of the Chugach-Kenai-Kodiak Mountains is the record of a restless and sometimes violent history. There has been immense earth movement at the junction of tectonic plates in this region during the last 100 to 150 million years. This has resulted in intermittent volcanism, submersion of the land beneath the sea, great uplifts of the land, and long periods of

Autumn in the Chugach Mountains. *Source: Pete Martin.*

erosion. The geology of these mountains fits the theory of continental drift to a fine degree. Anyone with an interest in geology will find travel through these mountains interesting, especially if done on foot. Roads through both the Chugach and the Kenai Mountains also offer interesting geological observation points, and there are lots of places where you can park and get out to explore.

Rising as they do from tidewater to above 8,000 feet, the Chugach and Kenai Mountains offer an extraordinary variety of Alaskan landscape for anyone who travels through their different life zones. You can start in marshlands, pass through dense and fragrant forests, slosh across lush bogs, boulder hop over joyous white-water streams (or get your feet drenched wading through them), make your way up ridges into meadows of heather and dry alpine tundra, and finally enter a world of perpetual ice and snow—all within a few miles. If this is not enough, along the way you may pass a glacier, a dazzling waterfall, or find lakes as lovely as jewels.

Sweeping in from the southeast as these mountains do, they also carry with them a sampling of both flora and fauna that may reach the northernmost and westernmost limits of their ranges here. And because they come together with other major features of the Alaskan landscape—such as the Talkeetna Mountains—this range also shares in the flora and fauna of other regions as well.

Thus you will find in these mountains a rare overall sampling of Alaska's birds and beasts, as well as flowers, trees, and other plants.

As you hike through this terrain, you can hope to see the more common species of fauna—black bear, moose, ground squirrels, maybe a brown bear or wolverine—but you may also have the unique opportunity of seeing both Dall sheep (not found in Southeast) and the more elusive mountain goat (not found north and west of here). You will also see many different species of trees, and you may be able to identify all three varieties of spruce that grow in Alaska—the Sitka spruce (tree of the Southeast forests that approaches its northern and western limits here), the black spruce (not found in Southeast), and the white spruce (a tree of the Interior and the Alaska Peninsula); only in this general region do the ranges of all three of these trees overlap.

The wildflowers bloom in profusion in these mountains and in exceptional variety. You can look for and find everything from the ubiquitous, but always beautiful, fireweed to rare species of orchids. In between, you can enjoy the shy plants of wet forests as well as the lupine and potentilla and polemonium (Jacob's ladder) of more open places, and the anemone and wild geranium. Look where you least expect to find a show, and there one may be. One summer afternoon I found the most gorgeous mass planting of dwarf dogwood I have ever seen within easy strolling distance of an access road out of Anchorage. Also, keep your eye out for berries; there are all kinds here from wild raspberries, succulent high-bush cranberries, low-bush cranberries, currants, and in the hills, crowberries and blueberries. The last named can make even the roughest scramble worth it, for they can be as sweet and juicy (and seem as big) as grapes. Incidentally, it is the leaves of the alpine bearberries that color the landscape such a gorgeous crimson in the fall.

The Chugach Mountains form, of course, the splendid ridge over which the sun rises to shine upon Anchorage. They are close enough and accessible

Nootka Lupine (Lupinus nootkatensis).

enough to Anchorage for the people there to look upon them as their own private mountains. In fact, to the east and to the north of Anchorage over 300,000 acres of these mountains form the Chugach State Park, administered by the Alaska Division of Recreation and Parks. This parkland offers a wonderful spectrum of outdoor activity almost all year round.

Chugach State Park

Chugach State Park is well described by its administrators as being an accessible wilderness. From the city of Anchorage, there are five ready entrances you can drive to and leave your car at before taking off into the backcountry: Prospect Heights, Upper O'Malley (difficult in winter), Upper Huffman, Glen Alps (very steep and difficult in winter), and Rabbit Creek. Upper Huffman is the central point of access for a number of summer trails and the access for snow machines in winter. Unfortunately, as of this writing, there is no public transportation to these trailheads, but it is planned for, and you should check at the Parks and Forests Information Center for latest information about how to get to the park. North of Anchorage, there are also access roads and campgrounds at Peters Creek, Eagle River, and Eklutna Lake. South of Anchorage there are a number of trailheads, a picnic site, and a campground at Bird Creek. You can pick up a good map of the Chugach State Park at the Parks and Forests Information Center.

The best way to explore this accessible wilderness is, of course, on foot, and there are many hiking opportunities on developed trails and easily identifiable cross-country routes. There are also a number of mountains that are delightful to climb in the summer. Thus, you can suit your schedule and/or your mood and take anything from an afternoon stroll to an alpine scramble or a week-long backpack trip. A major bonus of any hike you take will be the magnificent views you'll get as you gain the heights of these mountains. You can choose your route to get a panorama of the Alaska Range, the spectacle of changing tides in Turnagain Arm (and maybe the sight of a beluga whale), or all of Anchorage at your feet; or you can simply find yourself a superb vista of snow-filled cirques and rugged spires. The subalpine birch woodlands here, incidentally, are probably unique in North America, a biologist friend of mine tells me, and, with their grassy floors and picturesquely shaped trees, are particularly charming.

Some of the trails through Chugach State Park were originally blazed by miners and other early settlers of the area. Since the mountains rise so precipitously from the water in places, most of these routes took the easiest passes through the peaks. Many were winter trails and were traveled by dog teams and rugged drivers carrying the mail or news to the Interior. The Crow Pass Trail (best entered at its southern terminus through the Chugach National

Forest), Johnson's Pass, Indian Pass, and the Iditarod Trail all are full of history. Other trails have been more recently developed for cross-country skiing in winter and hiking in summer and are pleasant and often easy pathways across the landscape.

A wilderness as accessible as Chugach State Park is bound to attract not only a lot of foot travel but also pressures for the use of off-road vehicles. Dedicated to meeting the wishes of the public, the Chugach State Park people have set aside one area for four-wheel-drive vehicles, and certain areas of the park are open to snowmobiles in the winter. There are, however, other areas that are closed to motorized use, and you can enjoy them with only the sounds of the mountains around you. Hunting and trapping in specific areas of the park are allowed, in season, between September 1 and April 30. If you're going to travel the park during this period, it's wise to wear a bright-colored cap or carry a bright-colored pack. Several species of animals are protected in the park, including grizzlies, mountain goats (the taking of Dall sheep is permitted under regulation), beaver, wolves and wolverines. You should report any poaching to the park headquarters. The use of firearms is limited to hunting in season; target practice and the use of guns for trapping are both prohibited. There is a fee for vehicle use and for camping. Open campfires are not allowed in the backcountry, and you should plan to carry your stove if you're staying overnight or want a spot of tea during your park outing.

During the summer months, the Chugach State Park has weekend programs: Saturday mornings there are lectures on the natural and human history of the park area; Sunday, there are hikes and other outings led by park rangers. Schedules are available at the Parks and Forests Information Center.

The northern portion of Chugach State Park is roughly delineated by Knik Arm. You can reach it via the Glenn Highway, and there are campgrounds at Peters Creek Wayside (thirty-two units), Eagle River Campground (thirty-six units), or Eklutna Campground (seventeen units). There's a good trail up Peters Creek that goes, among other places, to Thunderbird Falls; Mount Rumble lifts about 5,000 feet above the headwaters of Peters Creek and is a dazzling snowy sight to see. Lovely Eagle River Valley is in the geographic center of the park, and it has the park's major visitor center. The road here runs the deepest into the park of any at sea level. This is where you'll want to go if you plan to run the upper part of Eagle River—class I and II; consult state park people (phone 907-279-3413) or the Parks and Forests Information Center.

The Eklutna Lake basin, a little farther north, is less than an easy hour's drive from Anchorage (25 miles). There are a dozen trails out of this basin into backcountry that is described by one knowledgeable resident of Anchorage as being "among the most beautiful in all Alaska—you can walk five miles into it and be in superb wilderness." The lake itself is milky blue with glacial till, and very cold. The lower altitude countryside is heavily wooded, with white spruce and birch forests and cottonwoods that glow gold in autumn. The autumn coloring is spectacular, and the spring wildflowers equally so. The peaks of the high country are brilliant with snow, there are dazzling waterfalls, and there's even a glacier within walking distance. Some of the highest mountains in this part of the Chugach Range are here—mountains with names like Bold Peak (7,522 feet), Bashful Peak (8,005, the Park's tallest), and Baleful Peak (7,900 feet). In season, the berrying is excellent.

There is a natural mineral lick north of Eklutna Lake that is the only place in Chugach State Park officially designated for wildlife viewing. If you hike in the higher altitudes, you can also expect to see both Dall sheep and mountain goats. Expect lots of company, as well, in the Eklutna Lake and Eklutna River region; this is one of the most heavily used parts of the Chugach State Park.

There are several beautiful hikes which commence at Eklutna Lake, with such destinations as East Twin Peak, West Twin Peak, the East Fork of the Eklutna River, and Hunter Creek Pass. There is also a pleasant hike which starts at the Peters Creek Wayside and climbs up to the Peters Creek Valley. Another interesting, but strenuous, outing you might want to consider in this part of the country is a trek up Ship Creek through Arctic Valley and out at Indian Creek—this is an old winter trail used by dogsledders. Ask the state park people for more thorough details and descriptions of the many trails in this region of Chugach Park, and/or consult 55 Ways Into The Wilderness (see Bibliography).

Note: as of this writing, the road around Eklutna Lake, blocked by landslides several years ago, must be hiked, and this adds several miles to any journey starting from the lake: repairs are scheduled for some time in the future.

The only canoeing or kayaking opportunities in the Chugach State Park are on the Eagle River. (It is also possible to run this fine river through military lands, but permission must be granted; check with the Parks and Forests Information Center and/or Knik Kanoers for details.)

CHUGACH STATE PARK TRAILS: HILLSIDE AREA

Destination	Access	Distance in Miles	Elev.Gain	Rating	Comments
Flat Top Mt.	Glen Alps	3.5	1,550 ft.	Moderate	Some steep rock scrambles. Fine views Anchorage, Alaska Range, Kenai Peninsula. Classic alpine plant communities.
Little O'Malley Peak	Glen Alps	7.5	1,937 ft.	Fairly easy	Fine mountain scenery, wildflowers, berries.
*Wolverine Peak	Prospect Heights	10.5	3,380 ft.	Fairly easy	Good views Anchorage, Alaska Range, Cook Inlet. White spruce, birch, mountain hemlock.
The Ramp The Wedge	Glen Alps	11	Wedge: 2,602 ft. Ramp: 3,182 ft.	Fairly easy	Dall sheep in summer. Berries in fall.
Knoya and Tikishla Peaks	Prospect Heights	Kn. 13 Ti. 15	Kn. 3,525 Ti. 4,075	Moderate to difficult	Portions of route are cross-country; for experienced hikers.
McHugh Peak	Rabbit Creek, McHugh Creek Way	5.7 7	1,551 ft. 4,201 ft.	Fairly easy	Highly scenic. Cross-country travel above brushline.
Rabbit Lake McHugh Lake	Rabbit Creek Valley	5	300 ft.	Easy	Exquisite alpine lake, set in high tundra beneath scenic Suicide Peaks. Short hike to McHugh Lake.
Williwaw Lakes	Glen Alps	13	742 ft.	Fairly easy	Exquisite alpine lakes backdropped by Williwaw Mountain. (5,445 ft.). Most scenic hike in Campbell Creek drainage.
Iditarod Trail	Crow Creek Road: Chugach N.F.	25	2,500 ft.	Fairly easy	Backpack. Historic route. Fine sampling of Alaska countryside: glaciers, high tundra, mountain passes, spruce forests, bogs, open meadows, fields of wildflowers.

Good for winter use. There is also extensive cross-country skiing in the Chugach State Park: check with park information. There is hiking plus water-based activities in the Eklutna Lake region, and it is possible to run the Eagle River.

Chugach National Forest

The Chugach National Forest adjoins the Chugach State Park on its southeast corner and embraces more of the fine alpine terrain of the Chugach and Kenai Mountains. Along the length of the eastern Kenai Peninsula, however, the mountains lose elevation as they trend southward in their gentle descent to the sea. With close to five million acres, the Chugach National Forest is the next to the largest unit of the United States Forest Service, being second only to the Tongass National Forest that comprises so much of the Southeast. This is also one of the oldest units of the United States Forest Service. The precursor of the present service was established in 1891 and, in 1892, President Benjamin Harrison designated Afognak Island, just off Kodiak, as a Fish and Forest Reserve. Afognak was incorporated into the Chugach National Forest when it was more formally established under Teddy Roosevelt in 1907. (Under the terms of the Alaska Native Claims Settlement Act, Afognak has become Native property.) Originally, the Chugach Forest boundaries took in a much larger area and included both the Anchorage bowl and the Kenai Moose Range, which adjoins it on the west. The boundaries presently encompass the northeastern shoulder of the Kenai Peninsula, and the land bordering Prince William Sound as well as the islands in it all the way to Cape Suckling in the south. This amount of territory gives the national forest an extraordinary range of terrain that includes some of Alaska's loveliest coastal scenery, some of its most beautiful forests and forelands, mountains and glaciers as well as areas that are exceptionally rich in wildlife, like the Copper River Delta.

Recognizing recreation as a primary use of the forest, the U. S. Forest Service has developed and maintains more than 100 miles of backcountry trails in the Chugach Forest, most of which are in the Kenai Mountains and readily accessible from the Seward Highway. The Chugach National Forest also contains about three dozen (plus or minus) cabins for public use, about half of which are on the Kenai Peninsula. As in the Tongass Forest, these cabins are accessible largely by foot, small plane, or boat only. The hike-in cabins have a three-day limit from May 15 to September 1 (a seven-day limit is the general rule). The cost, as in Southeast, is only a few dollars per night, and the facilities are rustic and comfortable. Most of the cabins located on lakes have their own skiffs: U. S. Coast Guard regulations require that each person using such a small boat must have an approved flotation device (not provided by the U. S. Forest Service). Small outboard motors are permitted if you can haul them in. The cabins have bunks to accommodate from four to eight people and either a wood or oil stove. You should check ahead of time to see which; if it's the oil type, five gallons of auto diesel oil or stove oil will stoke it for about 48 hours of continuous summer use. Summer temperatures will range from 30 to 80 degrees in this region, and you should, as always, be prepared for rain. Reservations for these cabins can be made up to six months in advance, on a first-come, first-served basis. Since hunting and trapping are permitted throughout the national forest, and since snowmobiling and cross-country skiing are excellent in some of the areas around the cabins, they get well used year round, and you should get your name in early if you want to enjoy one. Write U.S. Forest Service, Pouch 6606, Anchorage, AK 99502.

The Chugach National Forest is managed overall for "multiple use," so mining is legitimate, and there is considerable recreational gold mining. There are also mining claims that have been established long since and patented: it is illegal to tamper with mining equipment or to disturb a mining operation

CHUGACH FOREST SERVICE TRAILS

Destination	Access	Distance in Miles	Elev. Gain	Rating	Comments
Lost Lake	Gravel pits at Mile 5, Seward Highway	7	1,820 ft.	Good family trail	Fine views. Access to high country and good cross-country hiking. Salmonberries near Miles 4 and 5 in August. Carry stove if camping.
Ptarmigan Lake via Ptarmigan Creek	Mile 23, Seward Highway	3.5	755 ft.	Easy	Good chance of seeing sheep and goats. Carry insect repellent. Avalanche hazard in winter.
Crescent Lake via Crescent Creek	Mile 3½ Quartz Creek Road	6.2	1,864 ft.	Easy	Good trail; cabin at Crescent Lake. Closed to motorized vehicles April 1 through November 30. Avalanche hazard in winter.
Carter Lake and Crescent Lake	Mile 32 Seward Highway (Gravel Pit)	2 3	986 ft. 954 ft.	Moderate	Primarily used by hunters; steep in places, not well defined. Makes possible loop with Crescent Creek Trail.
Russian Lakes and Cooper Lake	Mile 52 Sterling Highway (Russian Lake Campground)	Lower Lake: 2.6 Upper Lake: 12 Cooper Lake: 21	100 ft. 290 ft. 768 ft.	Easy to fairly easy	Cabin at Upper Lake. Good fishing. Brown bear country. Avalanche hazard in winter above Lower Lake.
Johnson Pass Trail	Mile 64 Seward Highway	Will be 22	Approx. 1,000 ft.	Easy to fairly easy	As of writing, trail under construction. Historic. Great views. Brown bear country. Good access to cross-country alpine hiking. Recommend further inquiry.
Resurrection Pass (and Trail System)	Hope	To Schooner Bend Mile 52.3 Sterling Highway: 37.5	2,400 ft.	Easy backpacking	
		To Mile 39 Seward Highway: 30	2,400 ft.	Easy backpacking	
	Mile 39: Seward Highway	To Mile 52.3 Sterling Highway: 27.5	1,900 ft.	Easy backpacking	

Comments: The Resurrection Pass Trail System is the John Muir Trail of the Kenai. It is very popular and heavily used, with numerous routes possible. (This is brown bear country.) There are six cabins en route. The system is closed to motorized vehicles unless the snow is deep enough for snowmobiles. Contact U.S. Forest Service, 2221 E. Northern Lights Blvd., Anchorage, AK, 99504, or the Parks and Forest Information Center, 2525 Gambell St., Anchorage, AK 99503. USGS maps: Seward D-7, D-8, C-8, B-8.

For information regarding above trails, contact U.S. Forest Service, Box 275, Seward, AK 99664; phone 907-224-3023. For cabin reservations, write U.S. Forest Service, Pouch 6606, Anchorage, AK 99502.

in any way and, of course, to jump a claim.

Campfires are permitted throughout the Chugach—unless otherwise posted—but only dead and down wood may be used. If you're going into the high country there, carry your own stove since you won't find much wood of any kind. Be careful with fire in this country. Although the trees and tundra may look too soggy to burn, they can be flammable, and a wildfire can spread with alarming speed.

Rivers

The Tazlina River system includes the (glacial) Little Nelchina, Nelchina, and Tazlina rivers and Tazlina Lake. You can explore 74 miles of these waterways in four to six days. The rivers include class II and III whitewater, and Tazlina Lake can be dangerous in high winds. A raft or kayak is best: an open canoe is not recommended. Access in is on the Glenn Highway and the take out is on the Richardson Highway. Aircraft pickup is possible about midway at Tazlina Lake. Watch for log jams and interesting geological formations along the Little Nelchina. There is a dangerous whirlpool at the outlet of Tazlina Lake. For further information, contact the Parks and Forests Information Center and/or the BLM in Anchorage.

The Upper Tangle Lakes, Middle Fork of the Gulkana River, and the Gulkana River are clear-water lakes and streams which offer several possibilities to a canoer, rafter, or kayaker. You can put in from the Denali Highway and run 76 miles to Sourdough on the Richardson Highway; this is a five to seven day trip, and includes lake travel, several portages, possible lining, and whitewater that varies from class I to, in a few places, class IV. As an alternative, you can put in in Paxson Lake and run the Gulkana River to Sourdough—a two to three day trip. From Sourdough, it is possible to travel 35 miles on the Gulkana River to Gulkana, a nice one to two day trip. The Gulkana River flows into the Copper here, should you want a really major outing. These are beautiful waterways but heavy use dilutes the wilderness experience. For further information, contact the Parks and Forests Information Center and/or the BLM.

The Delta River has both clear and glacial stretches. It is 35 miles (two to three days) to the first take out, and 17 miles farther to Black Rapids. Any river craft is suitable for the first 35 miles, but there is a ¼ mile portage across the Denali Fault in this stretch and a nice little rapid to the take out point. The glacial, seventeen-mile portion of the Delta has some class IV rapids and canoes are not advised. An easy put in on the Denali Highway and take out on the Richardson Highway make this a very popular short trip, and the very heavy use dilutes the wilderness experience. For further information, contact the Parks and Forests Information Center and/or the BLM.

Downhill Skiing

Alaska's biggest downhill skiing resort is Alyeska, just an hour down the Seward Highway from Anchorage. This operation recently changed hands and is expected to offer even better facilities than it now has. It is anticipated, among other things, that the parking lot will be leveled out so that cars do not slide sideways into one another as they sometimes do now when conditions are icy. You can ride the chair lift here in summer as well as in winter for a fine overview of the surrounding country.

The Alyeska Bake Shop, located here, is also, and happily, open year round. It is justly famous for its large and luscious cinnamon rolls, as well as for hearty soups and excellent sandwiches. Bikers and drivers traveling the Seward Highway, as well as skiers, might keep this in mind.

Biking

You can bring your own bicycle to Anchorage via ferry and bus (as described in the Southeast section), or you can rent a bike by Bicycle R & R (908 West Northern Lights). The shop is not far from the Anchorage Youth Hostel and close to the People Mover bus stops. Frances Morton, the owner, can also rent you an outfit for touring and can steer you to specific information about contemplating bike trips.

Among the places you can travel locally are, of course, the quite extensive bicycle trails of Anchorage that can make for a pleasant day's exercise. You might also enjoy finding your way out to Earthquake Park, among other nearby places. If you're an ambitious bicycle rider and have more time, there are at least three week-long trips you can make. Each offers excellent possibilities for seeing some of Alaska's best. Each offers, as well, good biking on paved roads and the opportunity for an exceptional adventure. All are highly recommended.

Trip One

You can take the Seward Highway south to its junction with the Sterling Highway and continue from there into Homer. This is a long trip, 227 miles, but there are many excellent campgrounds along the way, starting just south of Anchorage with the state park facilities. Check with the state park people about what is available at McHugh Creek, Beluga Point (a beautiful spot with offshore islands and interesting archeological work in process that places Chugach Eskimos here over six thousand years ago), Falls Creek and Bird Point, where you may see nesting bald eagles as well as other raptors and seabirds.

A stop at the Forest Service Visitor Center at Portage is worthwhile to admire the very photogenic Portage Glacier. Keep in mind that Portage Pass is one of those classic Alaska wind tunnels, and if it's a blowy day, strong gusts can knock you off your feet. (A U.S. Forest Service ranger working there once watched a six-foot, two-inch, two-hundred-pound man get out of his car and sail through the air into a nearby clump of alders; no real damage was done, but it was a highly spectacular, if short, journey.) There are numerous other very good Forest Service campgrounds farther south along your route, as well as many operated by the U.S. Fish and Wildlife Service in the Kenai Moose Range. Check the Parks and Forests Information Center for details.

Once in Homer, you can camp on the famous Homer spit if you can abide wall-to-wall trailers. Despite the crowd, it is a spectacular place. You will probably want to visit Kachemak Bay State Park (accessible by boat) while you're there, and you might also enjoy a trip to Diana Tillion's studio on Halibut Cove. Tillion is a well-known Alaskan artist who uses octopus ink— a soft sepia color—for her medium. The Kachemak Bay Ferry Tour (at the small boat harbor) operates regular boat trips to the Tillion's place, and the trip takes about four hours.

At Homer, you can put your bike onto the state ferry for as long or short a trip as you like. The sea-worthy *Tustamena* plies between Homer, Seldovia, Seward, and Kodiak year round. Twice a year—in May and late September— it braves the open ocean and travels to Sand Point and King Cove on the Alaska Peninsula. If you're a good sailor and interested in bird-watching, you might check the dates of these trips; they may coincide with outstanding shows of migrating birds. Under any circumstances, you should get a current ferry schedule before you plan your trip. Note, from Seward, it is just 129 miles to Anchorage.

Trip Two

You can either bike down the Seward Highway to Portage, load your bike onto the Alaska Railroad train there and travel on to Whittier, or, if you want to avoid what is a well-trafficked road by Alaska standards, you can put your bike on the train in Anchorage for the same destination. The Alaska Railroad charges an amazingly low fare for bicycles and is reasonable for people as well. If you do bike this stretch of the Seward Highway, plan to take time out at Potter Marsh, just south of Anchorage, to admire the birds. (You can, of course, also do this biking south.) In Whittier, you can take the ferry for a sightsee run past the Columbia Glacier and a stop at Valdez, where you can pick up the Richardson Highway for a return trip to Anchorage (304 miles) after viewing the pipeline terminus. Or you can continue on the ferry to Cordova, where there are excellent opportunities for bird-watching as well as places where you can roll out your sleeping bag. There are reasonably good gravel roads for biking, and you can travel to the "Million Dollar Bridge" across the Copper River. There are also good opportunities for hiking. Talk to the Forest Service people at the Parks and Forests Information Center for more information about this lovely area. From Cordova, you can, of course, take either the road to Anchorage from Valdez (reached by ferry) or the ferry all the way to Whittier, retracing your original route. This ferry does not serve the Kenai Peninsula south of Whittier, or Kodiak regularly.

Trip Three

You can bike a paved road to Denali Park (formerly Mount McKinley Park) or carry your bike on the Alaska Railroad, if you prefer, and then explore Denali Park on your own wheels. This is a popular outing; Ms. Morton at the Bicycle R & R recommends it highly. The park service people can give you details of biking possibilities. Remember that there is a Youth Hostel in Denali Park if you don't want to hassle with camping equipment. The camps in this park, however, offer fine wilderness experiences if you want to do a little hiking out of them.

From Denali Park, it is possible to bike the Denali Highway into some very different and interesting country, if you have the time. BLM people can give you suggestions about camping facilities on this highway, which goes through extensive country above timberline, provides access to lovely mountain lakes, and has excellent birding.

Talkeetna Mountains

The Talkeetna Mountains are an hour or so drive north of Anchorage via the Glenn Highway. A discrete range of their own, they stand between the Alaska Range and the Chugach Mountains, guarding the wonderful lake systems of the Copper River Basin to the east. These beautiful rugged mountains reach heights of well over 8,500 feet and, with their granite outcrops, recall the Sierra Nevada to many visitors from the Outside.

The Talkeetnas are heavily used year round by Anchorage residents. They offer superb hiking as well as cross-country skiing, and their wildflowers are renowned throughout Southcentral Alaska. Most of the land in the Talkeetnas is private property or is in the hands of the state or BLM, and has long been prospected and, in places, mined. Roads run through the high country, and the superbly scenic ridges are readily accessible. You can also drive considerable distances through this lovely alpine country; the road to Willow runs through the Talkeetnas, and, while narrow and winding, it makes for a spectacular ride.

A favorite takeoff place into the Talkeetnas is the Independence Mine on Hatcher Pass, about 75 miles from Anchorage. You can park there to start your hiking, and there is a privately owned A-frame lodge with accommodations for 50 to 60 (and the "best sauna in Alaska") that can be rented reasonably for group outings winter or summer. (Ask at Alaska State Department of Parks for further information; the owner of the lodge is Hal Wurlitzer.) *55 Ways Into the Wilderness* (see Bibliography) gives the specifics of several hikes in the Talkeetnas. A friend of mine who knows the area well suggests that you use this book for starters and then just "keep on going." The upper Caribou Creek drainage, in particular, offers exceptional hiking opportunities through alpine tundra valleys which are connected by low and lovely passes.

Prince William Sound

Named by Captain James Cook in 1778, Prince William Sound shares many of the characteristics of Southeast Alaska, although it is a smaller, more compact area. It has lovely fjords and inlets, islands, and lush rain-forested shores. It has stunning tidewater glaciers, and spectacular mountains delineate its horizons. The area also has many lakes and streams and cascading ribbons of white water and lots of rain and unpredictable weather (more, in fact, than Southeast). It has a fabulous variety and plenitude of marine wildlife—mammals, fish, and birds. This is a world best explored from the water, and there's a state ferry plying through it from Whittier to Valdez and Cordova and back if you don't want to travel in a small boat. As in Southeast, most of the land in the region is administered by the U.S. Forest Service, being a part of the nearly five million acre Chugach National Forest, which is headquartered in Anchorage.

Unlike Southeast, however, Prince William Sound is readily accessible by highway as well as by train and ferry, and from a nearby metropolis. It is a pleasant 304-mile drive from Anchorage to Valdez, and Whittier is a pleasant hour or so train ride from Anchorage. Obviously there are both pluses and minuses to this fact. Being so easily reached from Anchorage makes it a relatively inexpensive area to visit. Using a bus or the ferry to get to it and around it, you can explore farther on your bike, or on your own two feet, or in a small boat at a minimum cost. You can also try for one of the U.S. Forest Service cabins in the area—say, one on Hinchinbrook Island—which can be quite reasonable to reach and, as noted, a real bargain for a family or small group. (Hinchinbrook Island is around ten minutes from Cordova in a small float plane.)

Furthermore, if you want to confine your exploration of Alaska to a relatively small and manageable area, Prince William Sound can add a major dimension to your experience. Use Anchorage as your gateway; the sound lets you sample the environment of the Southeast, and then you can go on to enjoy that of Southcentral and possibly the Interior—all within a fairly short time and at a relatively low cost. For example, you can make an interesting triangular trip using public transportation entirely: go from Anchorage to Fairbanks by train, from Fairbanks to Valdez by bus, and from Valdez back to Anchorage via Whittier by ferry and by train. Or, if you have more time and like to bicycle, you can put your bike on the train at Anchorage, get off at Denali National Park, travel the park, then bike the Denali Highway (which has good BLM camps along the way) to the Richardson Highway, thence south to Valdez and back to Anchorage via the ferry, train, and the Seward Highway.

The minus side of the accessibility of Prince William Sound is that a place so beautiful and easily reached is bound to have heavier use than more remote areas. The sound is a principal water playground for Anchorage folks, and many of the city's residents keep small boats (motor-powered or sailboats) available at Whittier or Seward for weekend or week-long use. This means that you may encounter a good number of people if you decide to travel by small boat yourself. If you're seeking the solitude of the wilderness, you may have to travel farther afield. Add to this the fact that in the very heart of the sound is the busy port of Valdez, which was once a small, quiet, idyllic Alaska town. This is, of course, now the southern terminus of the trans-Alaska oil pipeline, and it presently has a battery of eighteen enormous holding tanks, each with a capacity of 510,000 barrels (one barrel equals forty gallons). Eleven more such tanks are planned. There is also much coming and going of numerous oil tankers. This might not be the kind of thing you would travel all the way to Alaska to see.

However, these drawbacks are minor compared to the wonders of Prince William Sound, and they should in no way discourage you from making a visit to this part of Alaska. In fact, the ferry ride from Whittier to Valdez-Cordova and back is one of the more special short trips you can take in the state. The ferry takes the same route through the sound as the cruise ships do. Near Whittier, there is a spectacular colony of black-legged kittiwakes that decorates the cliffs and the sky above the harbor; they will give you an unforgettable send-off. Once on your way, you can look for sea otters, sea lions, and harbor seals. Your chances of seeing one or more species of whales are good; killer whales and minke whales travel the waters of the sound in goodly numbers, and there may be more humpbacks here than in Glacier Bay. You can also expect to see many different sea birds. There is a U.S. Forest Service naturalist on board the ferry to help you look in the right places for the marine wildlife and to give you interesting highlights of the places you pass. (The M. S. *Bartlett* makes this particular run.) Incidentally, you may find several Anchorage residents on this trip, showing off the scenery to visitors from Outside. The loop through Valdez and back to the city along the Glenn Highway is a favorite local sightseeing trip.

Shortly before you reach Valdez, you will pass the Columbia Glacier, and the ferry captain pays appropriate attention to this extraordinary tidewater monster, slowing down and lingering to give you a good chance to look, as well as blasting the ship's whistle to set off the calving of an iceberg or two. Even in poor weather it is a memorable sight, this white and deep aquamarine facade of ice that is visible for more than two miles and is actually five miles wide in all. It seems to jam the whole horizon. The Columbia is so large that 2,300 feet of it are underwater here.

Alone of Alaska's tidewater glaciers, the Columbia is in much the same position it was 200 or more years ago; the others have moved, and some have retreated dramatically. (See section on Glacier Bay.) The retreat of this glacier is anticipated in the immediate future, however, and glaciologists expect that it will gallop backward at the rate of a mile a year for the next 40 or so years. If it does, it will launch whole armadas of icebergs into Prince William Sound, thus posing major traffic hazards for the tankers serving Valdez. A $3 million boom has been proposed to handle this situation, although it is a moot point whether or not such a boom could hold back the anticipated onslaught.

It takes about seven hours on the ferry from Whittier to Valdez and another six hours—plus or minus—to Cordova. (The fare is the same whether you go to Valdez or Cordova.) Cordova is enough off the beaten track that it gets a minimum of recreational use. It is, however, situated very beautifully, with the backdrop of Mount Eccles rising behind it. It has tourist accommodations, but if you prefer to go it on your own, you should check with the Forest Service about the status of campsites. If you do visit Cordova, try to get up to Miles Lake and the Copper River Delta; the latter is one of Alaska's greatest wildlife areas. During the migratory seasons, this region is marvelous for bird-watching. (See section on Biking Opportunities.)

If you want to spend some time enjoying Prince William Sound for itself alone, you will want to explore it in a small boat. Again, you have several options as to how you do it. One of Alaska's few commercial sailboat operations is located in Prince William Sound, and it is possible to take one- or two-week sailing excursions on a twenty-five-foot sailboat that accommodates up to four people. (You will be expected to help sail the boat, and if you don't know how, you will be instructed in the art.) According to all reports, this can be a unique and marvelous experience and a wonderful way to see the wildlife of the area.

It is also possible to take kayak excursions with a local guide, and these, too, are reported to be a good introduction to the area. If you prefer, of course, you can always do it on your own.

If you do go on your own, the following advice from a local kayaker may be helpful to you: *There is food everywhere:* pink salmon, clams, mussels, rockfish, flounder, Dungeness and tanner crabs. You can fish from the shore with a line; look for a salmon stream. Or you can bring your own collapsible crab pot. Use herring, sculpin, or other fish for bait, set your pot close to shore (out to a depth of 60 feet), and wait six to eight hours for a feast. (Author's note: best not to count on this wholly on your first trip here.)

Camping is a challenge. What looks like a meadow may be a soggy marsh. (Snow melt is much later here than in the Southeast.) Look for a small tundra-covered knoll. Carry nails with you in case you come across an old platform to which you can fasten down your tent. While much of the coastline is not good for camping, some tidal meadows do have dry areas in their upper portions, and you can usually find a place. Be sure your tent has a dry bottom and a fly because it rains a lot. Also have good stakes.

(Note: commercial boat guides have fixed campsites of their own that save a lot of time and trouble for people traveling with them. Also, if you travel on your own, keep in mind that you should have at least two boats in your party.)

Kayak trips can be made any time between May and September, but, in general, early summer is the best time. Late summer is windier and better for sailing. There are four U.S. Forest Service cabins you can tie into when kayaking out of Whittier: (1) Schrode Lake has a nice A-frame and sleeps eight to ten; this requires a two-mile hike from the shore. (2) Pigot Bay, another spacious A-frame; this one requires a boat to reach it. (3) Coghill Lake has great fishing for red salmon; it also requires a short hike from the shore. (4) Harrison Lake is not as attractive as the others but is a good haven in a storm. (There is a U.S. Forest Service Office in Cordova: write Box 280, Cordova, AK 99574.)

Paddle as close to shore as possible, and always be prepared for storms. Prince William Sound can have four or five days straight of terrible weather. Then again, it may be so beautiful you'll find it hard to bear. Plan to stay from 2 days to 2 months.

How to Get There
Whittier is accessible by train with or without your car or bike or kayak. You can also bike first to Portage and then hop on the train. From Whittier on, you're on the water—ferry or cruise ship (see *Worlds of Alaska*) or sailboat or kayak.

Sailing and Kayaking Outfits
Alaska Wilderness Sailing Safaris: Write Jim and Nancy Lethcoe, Box 701, Whittier, AK 99502 for information. For bookings, write Dan Riker, P.O. Box 4-275, Anchorage, AK 99509. Jim and Nancy Lethcoe offer one and two week trips. They are deeply interested in the natural history of Prince William Sound and in preserving the special qualities of this beautiful area. **Bear Brothers:** Write Eric Singer, 1640 East 27th Avenue, Box 42084, Anchorage, AK 99509; phone 907-272-8820. The emphasis of this outfit's well organized kayaking outings (four to fourteen day fully outfitted expeditions in the Sound) is on environmental awareness. Bear Brothers also runs winter dogmushing and cross-country ski trips. **National Outdoor Leadership School:** Write Box AA, Landor, Wyoming 82520. As part of its Alaska program, this school conducts a climb of Mount McKinley and a kayaking class in Prince William Sound. This is serious business and turns out accredited outdoor leaders.

Where to Stay
There are facilities at Whittier, Valdez, and Cordova. Contact **Chambers of Commerce** for information: Whittier, Box 608, Whittier, AK 99502, phone 907-472-2337; Cordova, Box 99, Cordova, AK 99574, phone 907-424-7260; Valdez, Box 512, Valdez 99686, phone 907-835-2330.

Air Charters
Chisum Flying Service, Box 1288, Cordova, AK 99574; phone 907-424-7671/ 424-7672. **Chitina Air Service:** See Wrangell-Saint Elias Information.

The Kenai Peninsula

The Kenai Peninsula is not the place to look for a lonely wilderness experience, although all the warnings about being careful as you venture into the Alaskan wilderness still hold there. (Especially in the winter, you can get into major difficulties on the Kenai if you forget to be prudent.) This region has a remarkable diversity of landscapes and life zones. It is also a place to look for almost any variety of outdoor recreation that you enjoy, for it seems to have something for just about everyone. It offers fishing, cross-country skiing, hunting, canoeing, day-hiking, backpacking, biking, snowmobiling, bird-watching, glacier watching, horseback travel, sailing, kayaking, or simply looking and enjoying. There's even downhill skiing on the way from Anchorage. Being readily accessible (by ground and water transportation as well as air), this unique part of Alaska is not only Anchorage's playground, but also probably the most heavily used part of the state when it comes to recreation.

Providing all these opportunities is the wonderfully varied terrain. Having been shaped and formed by glacial action, the Kenai Peninsula's landscape has a glacial outwash plain filled with lakes and rivers (a paradise for canoers), those splendid Chugach-Kenai Mountains, some very large and beautiful glacial lakes, including Skilak and Tustumena, and even a magnificent ice field (the Harding) from which hang a whole series of active glaciers. Add to this a lovely coastline and relatively livable climate, particularly for the Southwest. (Backed by the high ridge of the Chugach-Kenai Mountains, the eastern side of the Kenai enjoys all the pluses and minuses of the Gulf of Alaska. Thus Seward gets 67.35 inches of precipitation a year including 80.6 feet of snowfall in the mountains behind it; Soldotna, on the west, gets a total of about 18 inches.) Homer, at the southern end of the peninsula, has some of the best weather in Alaska: I once sat for five days in Anchorage in a chilly unpleasant summer rain and, in desperation, drove to Homer and found it warm and sunny.

The Kenai Peninsula was home to Tanaina Indians when the Russians first began to settle on it in the late eighteenth century. The first Russian shipbuilding operation was in what is now known as Resurrection Bay, on which the town of Seward fronts. There are several Russian churches on the Kenai; as much as any part of the state, it bears the imprint of these first Europeans. (It is interesting to note that in the one and a quarter centuries the Russians claimed Alaska, there were rarely more than a total of six hundred Russians living there, and their explorations were limited largely to the coasts.) The Russian Orthodox churches in Kenai and Ninilchik are both interesting, and the one in Ninilchik is easily visited from the Sterling Highway. The church is in the middle of a lupine-filled meadow on a bluff above the Cook Inlet. If you're there on a clear day, you'll have a fine view of the snowy volcanoes across the water.

After the United States acquired Alaska, first Seward and later Whittier became important ports and points of access to the Cook Inlet region and the Interior. Seward enjoyed its heyday as the southern terminus of the Alaska Railroad during the earlier years the trains were running. During World War II, Whittier took over and enjoyed its brief boom when the railroad was tunneled through the Chugach Mountains to reach a saltwater port with fewer problems. During the war, an eleven-story office building—now called the Begich Towers in honor of Congressman Nick Begich, who was killed in a small plane while campaigning for reelection—was constructed by the United States Army. This incongruous structure sticks up like the proverbial sore thumb and is presently used for apartments and condominiums; there are plans to develop it for tourist accommodations in the future.

Homer, which has become an artists' colony and is sometimes called the "Carmel of the North," is one of Alaska's most charming towns. Not only is its climate relatively benign (although it does, of course, get its share of storms and winds), but the scenery around it is wonderful. It also has some great tides, superb fishing (its shellfish are legendary), and crowds of people descending upon it during the fishing season.

Almost all of the Kenai Peninsula has at one time or another been in the hands of the U.S. Forest Service or the U.S. Fish and Wildlife Service, and most of it still is. Additionally, the National Park Service now has its new Kenai Fjords National Park (see below). The land in private ownership has skyrocketed in value since the building of the pipeline when many Outsiders discovered the charms of the Homer area. Now most of the older homesteads—many staked out in the wake of World War II—are being subdivided at prices that might make you gasp.

The Kenai National Wildlife Refuge, administered by the U.S. Fish and Wildlife Service, comprises close to two million acres. It takes in the lush wetlands of the northwestern section of the peninsula as well as a section to the south and east that includes most of the Harding Ice Field and Skilak and Tustumena lakes. The original Refuge was designated in the early 1940s by President Franklin Roosevelt when the U.S. Fish and Wildlife Service was first established. (This essentially involved the transfer of federal land from the Department of Agriculture—U.S. Forest Service—to the Department of the Interior.)

The northwestern section of the range is some of the best moose habitat in the region. During the fifties and sixties, however, it also proved to be an area with great oil potential. A great deal of seismic exploration went on and now, when you fly over the area in a small plane, it looks as though some strange prehistoric people had inscribed huge hieroglyphics all over the ground. (If you're lucky, you'll see a moose on such an overflight or a pair of trumpeter swans housekeeping their own small lake.) Oil was brought in during the fifties, and presently there are active oil wells, an oil refinery and pipelines, roads, and much activity—with which the moose must coexist. A major fire in 1968 served to refurbish the area with willow and gave the animals a boost.

The Fish and Wildlife Service does its best to protect the range for its natural values, to cooperate with oil development while minimizing its impact (there are no more disfiguring seismic explorations going on), and to encourage recreation that is not disruptive. In fact, the wildlife range offers some of the most rewarding recreational opportunities on the peninsula. The Swan Lake and Swanson River canoe trails are beautiful; there is hiking in the lake regions; there are numerous U.S. Fish and Wildlife Service campgrounds and camping spots, as well as four cabins, or shelters, which are free.

Where the Fish and Wildlife Service leaves off, in the northern part of the peninsula, the Chugach National Forest picks up. It is responsible for a large chunk of the Chugach-Kenai Mountains and maintains a number of campsites, cabins, and more than one hundred miles of trails.

How to Get There

You reach the Kenai Peninsula by railroad (to Whittier only, unfortunately, since passenger service to Seward has been discontinued except for a ski train or two during the winter), by road or, of course, by air. You can also use the ferry to explore the coast of much (but not all) of the peninsula: the Cook Inlet presents some formidable obstacles to passenger ships, including turbulent waters, tides, and storms. The road system is conducive to biking; the Sterling Highway goes all the way to Homer, branching off the Seward Highway a short distance down the peninsula. (See section on Anchorage: Bicycling Opportunities.) The **Kenai Peninsula Bus Line** provides regular bus service for the peninsula; for time-table, phone 907-283-3028. The scheduled air service to Homer uses small aircraft and, on a clear day, offers some dramatic views, including a fine vista of the Harding Ice Field and the Aleutian Range across Cook Inlet. (Note how evenly spaced Spurr, Redoubt, and Iliamna are. They are actually about 40 miles apart; the volcanoes to the south on down the Alaska Peninsula are also nearly equidistant from one another, being roughly 30 miles apart.)

Air Charters: **Cook Inlet Aviation, Inc.**, Box 175, Homer, AK 99603; phone 907-235-8164/234-7655. **Kenai Air Alaska**, P.O. Box 1921, Kenai, AK 99611; phone 907-283-7561.

Where to Stay

Consult the **Chambers of Commerce** in Seward and Homer (and Kenai and Soldotna if interested) for names of hotels, or see *Worlds of Alaska*. (**Land's End** in Homer is a delightful hotel to stay in, being right on the water.) Write: Box 756, Seward, AK 99644; phone 907-224-3046. Box 541, Homer, AK 99603; no phone. Box 497, Kenai, AK 99611; phone 907-283-7989. Box 236, Soldotna, AK 99669; no phone.

The Kenai Peninsula is full of places to camp, especially along the northern part of the Sterling Highway. For information, contact: **Parks and Forests Information Center**, 2525 Gambell Street, Anchorage, AK 99503; phone 907-271-4234. (Note: there are twelve state park units with camping facilities that include 230 campsites on the peninsula.) **U.S. Forest Service**, Box 275, Seward, AK 99664. **U.S. Fish and Wildlife Service**, Refuge Manager, Kenai National Wildlife Refuge, Box 2139, Soldotna, AK 99669; phone 907-283-4877.

The four free-cabin-shelters maintained by the U.S. Fish and Wildlife Service are located at: *Emma Lake*—a nice one-and-a-half-hour hike in from the upper end of Tustumena Lake; also accessible by boat, has four bunks. *Finger Lake*—in canoe system; can also be reached by a one-and-a-half-hour hike from Soldotna, on Swanson River Road. *Vogel Lake*—reached by float plane; north end of refuge. *Trapper Joe*—another fly-in on the northeast side of the refuge. Cabins are on raffle during peak seasons, otherwise on a first-come, first-served basis: contact Refuge Manager at above address.

Kenai Wildlife Refuge offers some of the best—and most popular—canoeing and kayaking in Alaska. You can take almost any length trip you want—for a minimum of expense—in the canoe system. For information regarding small boating (including the rental of canoes in Soldotna) and other recreational opportunities in the Kenai Wildlife Refuge, contact the Refuge Manager at the above address, or the Parks and Forests Information Center in Anchorage. Also contact Alaska Travel Adventures: see Anchorage Information.

KODIAK

Although Alaska has such an impressive coastline—nearly 40,000 miles of it—much of it delineates fjords, bays, and channels or more or less enclosed seas, and it is not easy to find ready access to the wild and wave-washed ocean shore. One of the few places in the state where you can find this, and right from a road, too, is on Kodiak Island, which is also a place of many other unique and interesting features. Located southwest of the Kenai Peninsula, Kodiak and its adjacent islands, including Afognak, are an extension of the Chugach-Kenai Mountains, chunks of the earth already detached from the mainland and partially drowned. The area is still sinking slowly beneath the ocean. During the 1964 earthquake, for example, the town of Kodiak subsided over five feet. (Following this great shake, the ocean side of Kodiak was also bludgeoned by a huge tsunami, only one in a succession of destructive waves that have historically battered this island.) Although an apron of continental shelf extends from Kodiak beneath the Pacific Ocean, this sea bottom is edged abruptly by the Aleutian Trench; thus Kodiak is immediately adjacent to a region of intense seismic activity.

Kodiak's rugged mountains rise from 2,000 to as much as 4,000 feet above the sea. Totaling about 3,670 square miles of land, the island is so deeply incised by beautiful fjords that there is no point on it more than fifteen miles from seawater. Much of the coastline is precipitous, but there are narrow beaches and picturesque stretches of open rocky shore.

Kodiak shows much evidence of massive glacial action as well as the effects of the earth's convulsive movements. During the Ice Ages, the whole region was buried under ice and snow with only a small area on the island—known as the Kodiak refugium—remaining uncovered. Now lakes lie in ice-rounded basins in the glacially sculptured high country. The rivers are short, and clear swift streams tumble down steep slopes. There is also evidence of nearby volcanism: Kodiak has been repeatedly smothered with ash from the volcanoes of the Aleutian Range from which it is separated by the narrow waters of Shelikof Strait. In the road cuts, you can examine the most recent layering of ash sandwiched between glacial till.

The flora of Kodiak is gorgeous. Although much of the island is exposed bedrock, you will probably remember the place as being a glowing green—I do. Alaska's lovely Sitka spruce forest reaches its western limits here and on Afognak Island. It is noteworthy that this forest is very young—from four to eight hundred or so years—and that it is still pressing its way westward. You can see its vanguard of young trees invading the lush meadowland west of Cape Chiniak. This interesting community of grasses, leafy woody plants, and thorny salmonberry is classified as tundra. It may be beautiful, but it is almost impossible to hike through. The wildflowers on the island are spectacular; cinquefoil, wild iris, wild geranium, and other bright blooming plants color the landscape. The alpine tundra has yellow heather, among other unique flowering plants.

Kodiak's fauna is equally outstanding. This is the place where Alaska's great brown bear has reached its maximum size—or so claim the residents of the island—and there is a big statue of the animal in downtown Kodiak. (Sadly, the big brownies here are being pressured by the increasing development that is occurring, with a subsequent loss of wild habitat. Fish and Wildlife biologists note that the largest of these impressive bears have already been hunted out.) This is also the westernmost range of the Sitka black-tailed deer, one of the species that has been introduced successfully. Another is the mountain goat. (On Afognak, there is the only population of elk in Alaska, again a successful transplant.) Kodiak is a wonderful place to see and hear red foxes, which are abundant, and the shores are home for many sea mammals. The bird life is beautiful and varied, and the ease of seeing the avian population here makes this an unusually fine area for bird watchers to visit. Almost any time of year, for example, you can be quite sure of having what an Alaskan birder describes as "fabulous views" of seabirds along the northeastern shoreline—and these from the road. During migration (and in the winter), you are likely to see emperor geese and/or the elegant harlequin duck or Steller's eiders. The latter provide a special show as they cavort about in the water as charmingly as buffleheads.

Kodiak was the site of the first Russian headquarters in North America. In 1784, Grigori Ivanovich Shelikof, founder of the Russian American Company, chose to settle the shores of an inlet he named Three Saints Bay (after his flagship). Eight years later, Alexander Baranof, who had assumed charge of the Russian operation, moved everything to Pavlovsk Gavan or Paul's Bay—later Kodiak Bay—because, a historian notes, it was "higher and drier and . . . was surrounded by the timber to build boats, buildings and better fortifications." Actually, and far more dramatically, Baranof moved because of a particularly severe earthquake and a resultant tsunami that proved disastrous to his group because there was no high ground for refuge. Baranof's new settlement eventually became the town of Kodiak. Although Baranof uprooted a second time in a matter of a few years and sailed off to Sitka (in 1800, having nearly exhausted the sea otter populations nearby), the early Russian influence has persisted in Kodiak. There are place names like Shelikof Strait, Kupreanof Strait, Mount Glotoff, and Olga Bay, and Russian crosses stand in the cemeteries. There is a Russian church in the town of Kodiak, flanked, unfortunately, by a huge gas storage tank. This was the first Russian Orthodox church in the New World, although the original building, like many other Alaskan churches, burned, and the one you see today is a restoration.

The Russians undoubtedly brought Aleuts with them when they came to Kodiak and a few names—like Ayakulik—attest to their presence here. The people who met these invaders of the island, however, were Pacific Eskimos, the Koniags, who were longtime residents. Theirs was a highly successful indigenous culture, and it is estimated that their population totaled at least 8,000 when the Europeans found them. Disease and the sometimes cruel domination of the Russians, especially the promyshleniki, took a high toll of the Koniags. Most of the place names on the island, however, derive from their language.

After Baranof's departure, Kodiak continued as a center for tanneries and for salteries (cod was the first fish to be utilized here). During the 1830s, there were also some minor whaling activities in the waters around the island, but most captains took their ships north to the Arctic to hunt the bowheads. The American acquisition of Alaska had little effect on Kodiak until 1882, when the first salmon cannery in the Southcentral region was built at Karluk; at that time the Karluk River was one of the most productive salmon streams in Alaska. This marked the beginning of Kodiak as a major fishery. Today it is one of the state's major fishing and canning centers, although in recent years shellfish have mostly taken the place of salmon, whose numbers have declined. The waters of the continental shelf area around Kodiak are exceptionally rich in king crab, tanner crab, and shrimp—it is hard to say which is the most delicious. The town of Kodiak holds a Crab Festival (usually in May), and its harbor is one of the busiest fishing ports in the area, with canneries lining its shore.

During World War II, the military went into operation on Kodiak, and one of its relics is Fort Abercrombie, now owned by the state. (This is one of the places you can camp on the island; there is a developed campground with fourteen campsites here.) A major U.S. Coast Guard station remains on Kodiak (the largest in area of any in the United States) and is the center for patrol operations to control illegal fishing, as well as for search and rescue missions. A substantial part of Kodiak is now protected in the Kodiak National Wildlife Refuge.

Placement of a DEW-line site (now a communications saucer) on top of 1,270-foot Mount Pillar, just above Kodiak, has resulted in a good road that can take you to fine overviews of the surrounding countryside. There are, in fact, several stretches of road that you can travel—by car, bicycle, or on foot— around the northeastern lobe of the island.

It can be a fine adventure to take the ferry to Kodiak from Homer (thirteen hours) or from Seward (fifteen hours). Along the way, you can enjoy fine vistas of spectacular scenery, if the weather cooperates. Sometimes the ferry from Homer passes among immense gatherings of sea lions and seabirds that congregate on the Barren Islands, one of the newly established wildlife refuges. You might also be able to see many species of seabirds resting on the water. Windy days seem to bring out more birds, and there are many windy days in this part of the world. (Although the wind averages only 8.7 knots, it often blows nonstop, and it has been known to reach a speed of over 100 knots.)

In the summer, Kodiak is apt to have many mild and cloudy days, enjoying as it does a maritime climate. As in so many parts of Alaska, however, there are miniclimates around the island, and the ranges of temperature and precipitation changes are sizable. Rainfall, for example, varies by as much as 70 inches. A frequent visitor to Kodiak comments that in some places on the island it's wet, foggy, and windy; in other places it's wetter, foggier, and windier—this in spite of the fact that Kodiak residents sometimes refer to their home as the "Sunshine Isle of Alaska." The town of Kodiak, where the ferry docks, has temperatures between 45 and 60 degrees during the summer (with a record high of 86) and, typically, only five days will see the thermometer top 70. Winters are moderate as well, with the temperatures sliding between 19 and 45 degrees and a record low of minus 5. Precipitation, including 72 inches of snow, is right about 60 inches a year. The last two weeks of May are probably the best bet for good weather in Kodiak, but stay away in September when the storms begin to roar in.

There are three motels in Kodiak as well as the state-owned campground at Fort Abercrombie and many good camping spots along the road system. In the summer, however, keep in mind that all the facilities can be crowded by the influx of fishermen and cannery workers. You can bicycle or hike many of the roads, or you might want to rent a car for longer trips.

The road south of town to Cape Chiniak and Sequel Point is spectacular. It runs along an area of ocean coast with sea stacks and islets offshore that is evocative of Oregon's shore. The surf here can be memorably beautiful. Look for sea lions along this road—there's a good colony of them just off Cape Chiniak. Also keep your eyes out for shorebirds, including the black oyster-catcher, and watch for puffins, cormorants, glaucous-winged gulls, and kittiwakes, which are easy to see on the small islands near the shore. In the winter, there can be thousands of Steller's eiders here, and in the summer this is a nesting area for Pacific common eiders. This is also the most accessible place in Alaska where you might be able to encounter nesting Aleutian terns. These lovely birds make their homes in grasslands.

If you'd like a most pleasant and reasonably strenuous hike, there is a trail up Barometer Mountain near the U.S. Coast Guard station. This is roughly a 3,000-foot climb with a good trail all the way. There are splendid views and a chance to see the alpine tundra. It is also possible to hike, bike, or drive the gravel road over the mountains from Kodiak to Anton Larson Bay. (This is about a two-hour trip by bike.) This part of the island has its own different charm. Sheltered from the ocean, it has quiet coves and beaches, and the deep red of its rock is set off by the green trees and the dark blue water. If you want to visit Afognak Island, you can get there by ferry. Or you can charter a boat or a small plane.

Some Useful Information About Kodiak

Ferry
The state ferry serves Kodiak year-round. Write **Alaska Marine Highway System**, Pouch R, Juneau, AK 99811, for a schedule.

Air Service
Scheduled commercial air service is available from Anchorage (see chart of airlines serving bush communities) and from Seattle (check with your travel agent).

Hotels
Kodiak Star Motel (26 room, kitchenettes, laundry facilities), 119 Brooklyn Terrace. Write Joe Carbin, Mgr., Box 553, Kodiak, AK 99615; phone 907-486-5657. **Sheffield Kodiak** (47 rooms, restaurant), on South Benson, adja-

cent small-boat harbor. Write Manager, above address, Kodiak, AK 99615; phone (collect in Alaska) 907-274-6631; in lower 48, phone 800-544-0970. **Shelikof Lodge** (40 rooms, restaurant), 211 Thorsheim Ave. Write to Shelikof Lodge, Box 774, Kodiak, AK 99615; phone 907-486-4141. Reservations advisable, if not essential, during the fishing season at all of these hotels.

Camping facilities

You can write the **Kodiak Area Chamber of Commerce** (see below) for further information—or just play your luck. The *Milepost* (see Bibliography) notes several undeveloped campsites along creeks in its auto logs of roads out of Kodiak, but there are others as well. For information regarding camping at Fort Abercrombie, write **Alaska Division of Parks,** 619 Warehouse Ave., Suite 210, Anchorage, AK 99501. The **U.S. Fish and Wildlife Service** has several shelter-type cabins in the Kodiak Wildlife Refuge. These are available on a first-come, first-served basis, are free, and can be used by one party for as long as seven days. Write Refuge Manager, **Kodiak National Wildlife Refuge**, P.O. Box 825, Kodiak, AK 99615. The **U.S. Forest Service** has had cabins on Afognak Island, which may possibly be maintained after the island passes into Native ownership. Write Regional Supervisor, **Chugach National Forest**, Box 1456, Post Office Building, Kodiak, AK 99615; phone 907-486-3320. These cabins are accessible by air charter from Kodiak.

General Information

In downtown Kodiak, be sure to visit the **Baranof Museum**. This is the oldest Russian building in Alaska and was erected by Alexander Baranof as a warehouse for sea otter pelts in 1793. It is open to visitors during the summer, and a one-dollar donation per adult is requested. If you would like to visit the **Russian Orthodox Church,** phone 907-486-3854 for an appointment. Visitors are welcome. Annual events include the **Kodiak Crab Festival,** mentioned above, and the pageant, Cry of the Wild Ram, which tells of the arrival of the Russians and the trials and tribulations of Alexander Baranof. This is performed during the first and second weeks of August. For further information, write the Chamber of Commerce.

Taxi, car rental, air taxi, and charter boats are available. Write the **Chamber of Commerce** if you need information on these facilities before you get to town. **Kodiak Area Chamber of Commerce,** Box 1485, Kodiak, AK 99615; phone 907-486-5557.

WRANGELL–SAINT ELIAS NATIONAL PARK AND PRESERVE

Ask anyone who has traveled widely in Alaska to name the most beautiful part of the state and you're apt to get several answers—or none at all—because the choice is so difficult to make. One well-known Alaskan, however, Ernest Gruening, had no problem making up his mind. As long ago as 1938 he singled out the Wrangell Mountains. "It is my personal view that from the standpoint of scenic beauty, it is the finest region in Alaska." Gruening wrote the Secretary of the Interior that year, "I will go further and state my belief that nowhere on the North American continent is such striking scenery to be seen. It is . . . greatly superior to McKinley National Park . . . this is the finest scenery that I have ever been privileged to see." Other Alaskans are content to call the Wrangells simply the "jewels" of their state.

The Wrangells are an extraordinary group of massive volcanoes that rise to over 16,500 feet. Located in the southeastern portion of the main body of Alaska, this compact immense cluster of mountains measures about 100 by 70 miles, and it rears up to a stunning 14,000 feet above the Copper River plateau. The snowy summits of Drum, Sanford, Blackburn, Wrangell, and Jarvis can be seen from the roads and highways that skirt the periphery of the Wrangells and from great distances across the surrounding countryside as well. High palisades of dark rose-colored basalt vividly give evidence of past volcanic activity. At least one of them—Mount Wrangell—is still active, breathing out sulfurous steam and occasionally belching ash from its snowy crater.

The Wrangells are at the heart of the recently established Wrangell–Saint Elias National Park (8,147,000 acres) and Preserve (4,171,000 acres). South and east of these magnificent giants, the park boundary embraces other towering icy spires including Mount Saint Elias (at 18,008 feet, the third highest mountain on the North American continent and the zenith of the highest coastal range on earth). At its feet is the great apron of the Malaspina Glacier, half again as large as Luxembourg, which has a population of about half a million people. (Malaspina has none.) To the south and southwest, the parklands include a portion of the Chugach Mountains, taking in the Bagley Ice Field and lakes like Tebay and Rock, which are unmatched for their beauty. Within the park complex, there are a grand total of eight peaks over 14,500 feet high. As Alaskan author Chip Brown puts it, no other area of Alaska surpasses it for "sheer mountainousness."

Sheer mountainousness, however, is only one feature of this unit of the National Park System. The geology of the Wrangell Mountains is both complex and interesting; few places show so clearly such a rich diversity of rocks—and such a clear record of uplift, volcanism, glaciation, and other earth processes. (Trips across Skolai Pass have been described as travels "through a geology text.") Furthermore, the flora is extraordinary. With plant communities ranging from those of the moist warm coast to the high frigid alpine tundra, almost all of Alaska's vegetation types are represented. The list of animals found here reads like a catalog of Alaska's species (see below); this is one of Alaska's principal wildlife areas. Among these animals are the caribou—three of Alaska's eleven herds use the area—which wander freely through the great sweep of country that is their ancestral territory, unmindful that the Canadian border cuts through it.

Russell Glacier, Wrangell-Saint Elias National Park. Source: *National Park Service.*

Recognizing the significance of this and other wildlife resources and shared scenery as well, Canada established the Kluane National Park in 1972, which transferred upland areas to the already established Kluane Game Sanctuary. The sanctuary, incidentally, permits mining and prospecting but prohibits hunting. These two Canadian preserves together comprise some 6,625,000 acres. They are contiguous to the 12,318,000 acres of the Wrangell–Saint Elias parklands; this means there are nearly 19 million acres of relatively protected land—a true international treasure.

Almost five million acres of the Wrangell–Saint Elias complex is ice and snow, making this parkland a glaciologist's paradise, probably the best place on the North American continent to get an idea, on a broad scale, of what the Pleistocene landscape was like. More than one hundred major glaciers radiate from the massive ice fields on the Wrangells, Chugach, and Saint Elias Mountains. Some of them are so immense that, along the coast, where they meet the sea, they flow underwater. (See Prince William Sound.) Inland, they pour their meltwaters into powerful, milky, braided rivers like the Chisana and the Nabesna, which eventually drain into the Yukon; and the Tana, Bremner, and the Chitina, which empty into the Copper, one of the great rivers of this continent. Blue-watered lakes rest in basins scooped out by the ice, adding to the enormous volume of water that already flows through this region. The amount of raw energy concentrated and circulated through this glacial ecosystem is almost incalculable.

The weather is obviously favorable to glacier making, which means that summer days are frequently cool and cloudy, and winters can be very cold, especially in the higher places. It should also be noted that this region is renowned for its great winds at higher elevations and where the Copper River cuts through the mountains near Chitina.

Responsive to the dynamic ebb and flow of glaciers, wild rivers, and a climate that can be cruel, a remarkable spectrum of living communities has evolved here. Creeping from the edges of the ice in high places, the plants of the alpine tundra cling to the raw land—lichens and mosses, saxifrages, louseworts, mountain avens (or dryas), and moss campion. Fingering this fragile tundra world and clothing the lower mountain slopes are dense brush communities with alder and willow, dwarf birch, blueberries, other berries, and shrubs; these are broken up here and there by meadows of bright flowering annuals. Black spruce and white spruce stud the valleys, bearing prodigious crops of cones in the summer to ensure their survival in this rugged country. In wet places, masses of cotton grass edge the lakes and ponds like circles of white clouds; cinquefoil gleams like scraps of sunlight, and the leaves of alpine bearberries splash the autumn landscape with crimson. In places, bogs and tussocky tundra make the going rough for two-legged animals. (To say nothing of the streams and rivers that can suddenly turn to torrents when the sun does shine in the summer; these are actually the greatest barriers to foot travel.)

Four-legged animals have no such troubles with the terrain. Along with caribou, you may encounter moose and bear (the smaller black bear stay out of the way of the great grizzlies; you will want to also). Dall sheep dance over the high crags inland, and mountain goats are frequently seen in places like the south side of the Chitina Valley. Wolves, wolverines, foxes, marten, ermine, river otter, ground squirrels, snowshoe hare, muskrat, beaver, porcupines, voles are all here. Trumpeter swans nest in the riverine lowlands, loons call from the lakes, and bald eagles soar silently above. If you enter the Saint Elias section of the park from Yakutat, its gateway, you can expect to see many seabirds and sea mammals such as harbor seals, sea lions, and whales. (You will also find Southeastern type coastal forests around Yakutat.)

Until recently, humans did not succeed so well as other creatures in colonizing this demanding region. The ruggedness of the terrain and the scale of the landscape are almost overwhelming to people. Mile-high cliffs hulking above wild-rushing glacial streams make awesome scenery but hardly a place for settling in. As a consequence, aboriginal people used much of this area lightly. Although a few Eyak Indians and Ugalakmiut Eskimos occupied the nearby Copper River delta where the climate is wet and mild and the wildlife is especially abundant, the population of Native people inland was confined to the lowlands. Small groups of Nabesna Indians (closely related to the Tanainas) subsisted on the flora and fauna of the valleys of the Nabesna and Chisana rivers. Along the upper Copper River and its tributaries lived small groups of the Ahtna tribe of Indians, and some 500 of these people still live in this area. (All of these Native groups have selected lands in this region under terms of ANSCA.)

Although the Russians made their first landfall in Alaska in 1741 not far down the coast from the parklands and gave Mount Saint Elias its name, major explorations of the Wrangell area by white men were delayed for more than another century. In the last decades of the nineteenth century, the search for minerals—and, after 1867, Army explorations—got under way and brought adventurous souls into and through some of the most difficult terrain in Alaska. (Rusty stoves are still occasionally found on ice caps where prospectors hauled them and had to abandon them.)

Men swarmed through the Copper River Valley, lured by the size of the great copper "shields" that the local Indians had been using in trade. By 1901, when Captain W.R. Abercrombie of the United States Army made one of his several reconnaissances through the area, he found that "the entire valley, embracing the main and subdrainage of the Copper River, was as well known as that of most any mining district in Montana." The miners' search paid off with the location of an exceptionally rich vein of copper in the Chitina Valley above the moraine of the Kennicott Glacier, named for Robert Kennicott, a pioneer Alaska explorer.

Fired by the reports of the lode and the preliminary surveys, financiers Guggenheim and Morgan formed the famous Alaska Syndicate to get at the copper (as well as coal in other parts of Alaska). At a cost of $23,500,000, they managed—after some bad weather, bad luck and bungling—to build a 196-mile railroad from Cordova on the coast up the Copper River to Chitina and thence to Kennicott, the site of what would be the Kennecott Copper Mine. (The misspelling of Kennicott, it is said, was done deliberately to legally avoid the notion that the new community was a "company town," although it was run much like one.) When things went wrong with the locating of the railroad, J.P. Morgan is reported to have banged the table with his fist and bellowed to his colleagues: "Whatever the route, we've got to get that copper out of there."

The railroad was completed in 1911, and mining operations began in 1913. Before the mine shut down in 1938, it had paid its owners $300 million. Many of the colorful old mine buildings still stand, testament to a 25-year operation that left the boom towns of Kennicott, McCarthy, Strelna, Chitina, and Cordova nearly ghost towns.

It was the idea of getting another economic base for the stricken region that prompted Ernest Gruening to propose the Wrangell area as a national park. (He was a man ahead of his time.) While Washington did give consideration to the proposal, nothing came of it. Cordova slowly recovered, but in much of the rest of the region the wilderness began to creep back. With the copper gone, the railroad stopped running, and the last of the wooden bridges that had spanned the Copper River at Chitina went out during spring breakup in 1939. (Inexpensive bridges had been built year after year, only to be swept away by ice and high water.)

Not until the late 1960s did attention focus again on the area; then both the National Park Service and the BLM made studies for possible park and/or recreational use. The passage of ANCSA brought new explorers into the region, including people who were seeking a better ecological understanding and possible protection for the extraordinary scenic and wildlife resource here. In 1978, President Jimmy Carter recognized the area by establishing the Wrangell–Saint Elias National Monument, and, in 1980, Congress finally decided the long-range fate of the Wrangell–Saint Elias area by establishing the present park-preserve complex.

Rivers

The glacial Chitina River is cold, silty, and heavily braided. You can put into the Kennicott River at McCarthy, float into the Nizina, and thence into the Chitina to continue to the town of Chitina, where the river joins the Copper. This 62 mile trip usually takes about two or three days, being mostly class II with stretches of class III water. A raft or a kayak is suitable. The upper end of the Kennicott River is shallow and you'll have to line. The lower end of the Nizina flows through a narrow canyon with turbulence and tight turns. Caution is required crossing the Copper River at the town of Chitina. This river trip takes you through gorgeous and historic country. The upper Chitina is also accessible by wheeled aircraft. For further information, consult the National Park Service in Glenallen and/or the BLM in Anchorage.

The Copper River is one of the continent's great waterways. It is accessible by car at Slana, Chistochina, Gakona, Copper Center, and Chitina. You can continue from Chitina on to a final take out at Cordova. This section of the river from Slana to Cordova is 244 miles long, and will take from seven to twelve days. Canoes, kayaks, and rafts are all suitable, although there are stretches of class III and class IV water. You will pass from Interior to Southeast climate on this run, so be sure you have adequate rain gear. The scenery en route is magnificent and includes glaciers. There is also fabulous bird life. The Copper is not for novices on their own, but it can be run by almost anyone if there are experienced boaters in the party. For further information, contact the National Park Service or the BLM in Anchorage.

How to Enjoy

Since this is a new unit of the National Park Service, planning for the Wrangell–Saint Elias parklands is still in process. There is no developed trail system. Hiking routes are demanding, following old prospectors' routes and game trails. They will take you into Chitistone Canyon (which could hold several Yosemites) with its fabulous cascade of a hanging river and into the drainages of Beaver Creek, Jacksina Creek, and the Kuskulan and Kotsina rivers. You can also hike over Nikolai and Skolai passes. Be aware that the river crossings will be the major limiting factor to your adventure; they can be lethal. Write the National Park Service Area in Glenallen for details, or plan a trip with a local guide (see below).

Many high mountains in this area offer challenges to mountaineers. Drum, Sanford, Wrangell, Blackburn, Bona, and Saint Elias are among the major magnets, and there are also numerous unnamed and unclimbed peaks. (Saint Elias, incidentally, was first climbed in 1891 by Italy's Duke of Abruzzi. It took over a month just to travel to the base of the mountain.) Most of these are expedition-type peaks, and again you should write the National Park Service for further information about them or go with a local guide. If you are interested in a first ascent, this is a prime area for it.

River-running by raft is excellent, and you can find any class of white water that you would like. The Chitina River drains all three of the mountain ranges in the parkland, and you can put in upstream via air-taxi. The Bremner rises in the Chugach Mountains and is also reached by small plane. The Copper River is accessible by car; and you can drive to Chitina to put in and arrange for a pickup out of Cordova. You can also drive to the headwaters of the Kennicott and float the Kennicott-Nizina-Chitina-Copper rivers.

July is probably the best month to visit the Wrangell–Saint Elias park, but you can't count on good weather even then. In August and September, the mosquitoes are gone and the river crossings are easier. This is fall in this

The University Range, seen from Chitistone Canyon. Source: *National Park Service.*

country. It is gorgeous, but it comes and goes at unpredictable times and is all too brief. The first few days of September, give or take a week, usually offer the peak of color.

Some Useful Information About Wrangell–Saint Elias

It is possible to drive to McCarthy usually from early June through September with a truck or a four-wheel-drive vehicle. You can reach Chitina (last gas stop) without difficulty. From there you cross the Copper River on the Copper River Bridge, which was built largely with federal funds, to finally replace the succession of old railroad bridges. You continue on a 60-mile "jeep road," which is the old railroad bed. There is a final cable-tram crossing (foot traffic only) of the Kennicott River and a few minutes walk to McCarthy. It is wise to inquire about road conditions before attempting this trip: contact the Alaska State Department of Transportation or inquire at the Chitina Bar. (A rental car is not advisable because of occasional washouts and the chance of getting stuck.) Allow three to four hours driving time from Chitina to McCarthy. McCarthy, by the way, is one of the most scenically situated little towns anywhere—when you can see the scenery around it. If you make it your takeoff point for any expedition, remember that supplies in such a remote place are limited. You should bring your own. Another jeep road, passable during the summer, goes from Slana on the Tok cutoff into the ghost town of Nabesna on the north side of the park. (The first half of this road is pretty good, but then you need a four-wheel drive.)

If you prefer to fly in, a good takeoff point is Gulkana Airport in Glennallen, which is served regularly by air from Anchorage and has several air-taxi services of its own. An alternative is to drive to Glennallen or Chitina (or take the ferry to Cordova) and take the mail plane, which flies weekly into McCarthy, stopping also at the above-mentioned towns.

Air-taxi Services

Ellis Air Service (formerly Wildon Air Service), Mile 118, Richardson Highway. Write Box 105, Glennallen, AK 99588; phone 907-822-3368 or 3062. Operates Tuesday mail plane out of Gulkana Airport, Glennallen. Make reservations for passenger service at least 24 hours in advance. Also has charter service (more expensive than just mail plane). **Alaskan Adventures Air Taxi,** Dan and Patti Billman, float and ski plane. Mile 148, Glenn Highway, AK 99588; phone 907-822-3905. **Gulf Coast Air Taxi Service:** Write Box 167, Yakutat, AK 99574; phone 907-784-3534. Also check with the National Park Service (see below).

Where to Stay

As of this writing, there are no developed campgrounds in the Wrangell-Saint Elias park. There are, however, BLM campgrounds at Liberty Falls near Chitina, and at Sourdough, north of Gulkana. These are described by the BLM as being "rustic," which simply means there is neither electricity nor running water. There is also a private campground, the Sourdough, at Tok (phone 907-883-4271).

There are several privately owned and operated wilderness lodges within the area, and you'll also find comfortable facilities at towns on the highways that skirt the park. If you want a real Alaska experience, you may want to stay in McCarthy at Sally's Place, whose owner describes it as a hostel (not affiliated with American Youth Hostels) "because that implies friendly, inexpensive, and informal accommodations," which is what to expect. This is the former McCarthy General Store, built in 1911, now listed on the National Register of Historic Places. Its owner, Sally Gilbert, has restored the building and equipped it to sleep fifteen (bring your own sleeping bag). You can write Sally c/o McCarthy via Glennallen, AK 99588; she has no phone.

If you're traveling on your own, it's a good idea to check with the National Park Service for latest information on this changeable region. You should also leave your itinerary with them whether you're hiking, climbing, spot camping, or river running. No need to do this, of course, if you're staying at a lodge or are with a registered guide. Write Superintendent, Wrangell-Saint Elias National Park/Preserve, Box 29, Glennallen, AK 99588; phone 907-822-5234.

Mount Sanford, Wrangell-Saint Elias National Park. *Source: National Park Service.*

The Alaska National Interest Lands Conservation Act of 1984 called for the establishment of three major information centers in Alaska, to serve the various new parks, refuges, and wilderness areas. There is one center in Juneau (at the Centennial Hall), one in Anchorage (at 2525 Gambell Street) and, the most recently opened, one in Tok. You can write for advice if you are passing through. This center, as well as the National Park Service in Glenn-allen can give you the names of current guides for the Wrangell country, and the locations of wilderness lodges. There is also a National Park Service Ranger Station in Chitina (very useful if you need help or advice when running the Copper River). You can write Box 39, Chitina, AK 99566, or phone 907-823-2205.

KENAI FJORDS

The Alaska coast is to become the showplace of the earth, and pilgrims, not only
from the United States but from far beyond the seas, will throng in endless proces-
sions to see it. Its grandeur is more valuable than the gold or the fish or the timber,
for it will never be exhausted.   *Henry Gannett, 1901*

You will find some of Alaska's most beautiful coastline along the southeast
shores of the Kenai Peninsula in the Kenai Fjords. Here, dark slate gray cliffs
soar abruptly from the water's edge, sculpted by ancient glaciers, storms, and
the sea. Blue-iced tidewater glaciers chill the air in deeply incised bays,
announcing their presence by magnificent cannonades of sound when they
drop ice into the deep waters. Higher hanging ribbons of ice release their
meltwaters, which plunge like silvery meteors into the sea or cascade intricately over the dark rock. Wherever there is a toehold on the steep slopes, a
dusky green spruce tree clings; where the land is gentler, whole forests stand
with mists swirling and smoking among the tall trees. Kittiwakes nest by the
thousands on the high cliffs and fall into the air like clusters of white flowers
at the noise of a boat. In places, the rocks are tilted to form broad shelves at
the water's edge, and here Steller sea lions crowd to bask in the sun—the great
bulls surrounded by their obedient harems bellowing their alarm at a visitor's
approach. Overhead, bald eagles ride the thermals, observing the colonies of
seabirds which come here by the tens of thousands to nest and rear their
young. On the jewellike ice floes that surround your boat, harbor seals watch
you with their great brown eyes. A porpoise might escort you; if you drift
quietly, you might, as I once did, come upon a sea otter sleeping peacefully
in the water on its back.

The glaciers that ornament this landscape so gorgeously depend from the
Harding Ice Field, a mile-high, one-thousand-square-mile catchment basin
that collects the near 400 inches of snow that can fall here in a winter and
compacts it into ice. As in Southeastern Alaska, such prodigious snowfall is
caused by the warm ocean currents that send mild moist air up to condense
at higher altitudes into snow. This same current is also part of the process of
upwelling that occurs here in the deep waters, which brings an abundance of
nutrients to the surface and accounts for the rich communities of living creatures.

The geological forces that formed the Kenai Fjords are unique and fascinating; the southern portion of the Kenai Peninsula is actively subsiding and
diving beneath the sea. In the 1964 Good Friday quake, as an instance, the

Kenai Fjords National Park. Source: National Park Service.

land here sank as much as seven feet in a matter of minutes. Should you visit the Harding Ice Field, you will be able to see graphically how the high terrain slopes off gradually to the south. From the air, you can also observe how the tops of the already drowned mountains still show evidence of ancient glaciation. Where old cirques lay, there are now deep-scalloped bays; where ridges once protruded above the ice, long fingers of land now protrude above the water. The farther out to sea you look, the lower the islands and sea stacks.

The Russians were the first Europeans to explore the region of the Kenai Fjords, but they were looking more for furbearing sea mammals than for lovely scenery and interesting geological formations. They found prodigious populations of sea otter and, with their Aleut slaves, they went to work systematically hunting them out of the deep blue waters. There were enough to prompt Alexander Baranof in 1795 to construct a shipyard in the largest of the fjords, Resurrection Bay. There the *Phoenix*, the first sailing ship built in northwest America, was launched to carry the beautiful pelts to Russia. When the sea otters were gone, the Russians moved on too.

Not until 1909 was the coastline to be more systematically explored. That year, U. S. Grant and D. F. Higgins of the U.S. Geological Survey traveled the length of the fjords, carefully mapping the geological formations and searching for minerals, of which they found very few. They photographed the tidewater glaciers, produced the first topographical map of the region (published in 1915), and voiced the hope that their report on the Kenai Fjords might gain recognition for "some of the most magnificent scenery . . . accessible to the tourist and nature lover."

It took six decades for that recognition to come nationally. In 1978, President Jimmy Carter established the Kenai Fjords National Monument, and, in 1980, Congress established the 567,000-acre Kenai Fjords National Park. The following is borrowed from National Park Service descriptions.

What to do and see: Entering the Kenai Fjords by boat is a popular and rewarding experience. Seabirds, sea lions, seals, porpoise, and whales are frequently sighted along the rugged coastline. Tidewater glaciers in Aialik Bay, Northwestern Lagoon, and Nuka Bay actively calve huge blocks of ice. Fishing for salmon and bottom fish is usually productive. The terrain is so steep throughout most of the Kenai Fjords that camping and hiking opportunities are extremely limited.

The Harding Ice Field is an awesome and beautiful phenomenon. Air charters out of Seward, Homer, and Anchorage can provide spectacular views of the ice field, glaciers, and the coastline. Crossing the ice field on foot or skis or travel on glaciers is recommended to only experienced and well-equipped mountaineers.

Weather: A maritime climate prevails in the area, bringing abundant rain and snow. The driest month is May; successive months receive increasing amounts of precipitation. Mid-June is the normal beginning of the visitor season, for spring storms have generally passed, and temperatures reach into the 50s and 60s (degrees F). June, July, and August are the best months for boat travel. Warm, sunny days are welcome exceptions. September initiates the usual wet and stormy fall. Snow can occur on the Harding Ice Field during any month.

Clothing: Comfortable wool clothing and rain gear are essential.

Precautions: The Kenai Fjords are rugged, remote, and exposed to the tempestuous Gulf of Alaska. Strong currents flow past them and few landing sites exist. Visitors are strongly advised to employ an experienced guide and seaworthy craft. Those entering the fjords without a guide should be very experienced and should seek information on landing sites, weather conditions, and navigational hazards from the National Park Service, U.S. Coast Guard, and other knowledgeable parties and sources.

Crevasses and foul weather pose dangers on the Harding Ice Field and its glaciers. Experience, skill, good equipment, and stamina are required for successful ice field and glacial travel. For your further safety, it is wise to leave your itinerary with family or friends.

For more information contact Kanai Fjords National Park, P.O. Box 1727, Seward, AK 99664; phone 907-224-3874.

The picturesque town of Seward, nestled against the mountains at the head of Resurrection Bay, is the gateway to the Kenai Fjords. There is bus service to Seward from Anchorage, and the drive is highly scenic; or you can reach Seward by ferry from Homer or Whittier, another scenic adventure. Scheduled air service is also available. For where to stay and boat charters, contact the Seward Chamber of Commerce, Box 756, Seward, AK 99644; phone 907-224-3046.

LAKE CLARK NATIONAL PARK AND PRESERVE

Towering snowy volcanoes, legions of finely sculpted gray granite peaks, beautifully striated sedimentary formations colored with yellows, grays, and deep browns, and metamorphosed mountains as if painted from an artist's palette with ochre, umber, rose madder, and dark alizarin crimson—these are the Chigmit Mountains. Although they are of modest height by Alaskan standards—most are around 8,000 feet in altitude—they are aptly called the Alps of Alaska. They mark the junction of the Alaska Range with the Aleutian Chain in a most dramatic manner.

Once heavily glaciated, many of these mountains still wear living glaciers. The milky meltwaters from these tongues of ice pour into troughs and basins scoured out during the Ice Ages, thus forming some of Alaska's loveliest lakes. A series of these lakes ornaments the western slopes of the Chigmits like great gems—Lake Chakachamna, Two Lakes, Telaquana, Twin Lakes, Turquoise, Kontrashibuna, and, the most magnificent of all, Lake Clark. When Stephen R. Capps of the U.S. Geological Survey came upon Lake Clark early in this century, he called it one of the most beautiful bodies of water in the world.

Among the exceptional things about this lake are its color—deep true turquoise—the thick, deep green forests along its shores, and the breathtaking splendor of the snow-streaked, colorful mountains around it. Add a feeling of intimacy that is not a usual feature in Alaskan landscapes as large as this; Lake Clark is 75 miles long. Because it is only one to four miles wide, however, you can nearly always see across the water to the tree-lined shores. If you go ashore, you will likely walk through a garden of cerise fireweed or perhaps a beautiful tangle of wild roses.

Park-minded people have been trying to gain protection for Lake Clark and the superb country around it for the past two decades. In 1978, President Jimmy Carter proclaimed the Lake Clark National Monument; in 1980, Congress redesignated the area into a 2,439,000-acre national park and a 1,214,000-acre national preserve. Boundaries of the park-preserve, which is located about one hundred miles southwest of Anchorage, take in all of Lake Clark and the country lying largely north and east of it. (Certain land around the lower end of the lake is private property, much of it Native owned.) National Park Service headquarters are at Port Alsworth, halfway down the lake.

Almost as much as the Chugach Mountains, this wilderness parkland contains a nearly comprehensive sampling of Alaskan terrain and life zones. It goes from coastlands to the steamwreathed summits of two high volcanoes—Mount Iliamna and Mount Redoubt; both tower above 10,000 feet. In between there are crowds of peaks, glaciers, lakes, and countless rushing streams and waterfalls. There are silty rivers that braid over the land, and there are rivers so clear that flowering plants grow in them underwater. Forests contain good-smelling white spruce and delicate-looking birches and handsome balsam poplars. There are mountain meadows embroidered with wildflowers, and high open tundra ridges that accommodate to boots as well as to the hooves of Dall sheep and caribou.

Along the shores of Cook Inlet, the seals and otter play, and you might be able to see a white whale traveling by while a bald eagle watches you from above. The bird life is rich from coast to mountain crest, and most of Alaska's great mammals abound in this wild and beautiful country. (A notable exception is the mountain goat, which is not found west of Kodiak, where it was introduced.) Added to this, Lake Clark is part of the drainage system of Bristol Bay and thus helps support the greatest sockeye salmon fishery in the world.

In good weather, the Lake Clark parklands provide for some of the finest outdoor recreation in Alaska. (But note that Anchorage recreationists and hunters are aware of this.) Many of the lakes are not only lovely to look at but are also gateways to excellent alpine hiking and backpacking. There are challenges galore for mountaineers in unclimbed peaks. Ski-touring can be superb in March and early April, though mid-April through late May thaws can make travel difficult. River-runners will find some of the world's most beautiful wild rivers in this region.

However, and alas, weather must again be a subject of major consideration. As on the adjacent Alaska Peninsula, it varies on either side of the high mountain barrier, and within the mountains themselves. On the Cook Inlet side, the maritime influence brings average summer temperatures of 50 to 65 degrees F, lots of rain, and low-lying clouds that can limit small-plane travel. The interior and western regions are more apt to be pleasantly dry and warm, though often overcast. (I once rafted the Chilikadrotna and Mulchatna rivers in western Lake Clark country during weather so hot and sunny we could have traveled happily in bathing suits that nobody, of course, had considered bringing. We did, however, enjoy a swim in the warm river water. Another time I ran the same rivers and never saw the sun.) The biggest adverse factor in the weather, however, is the classic problem of the Alaska Peninsula winds; they can come roaring in at any time of year and in any part of the Lake Clark area, and they can turn the lakes into small stormy seas. Since they can also reach hurricane speed through the mountain passes, they add another uncertainty to air-taxi pickups and deliveries. In short, the Lake Clark weather, while milder than in many regions, is totally undependable and unpredictable;

you should be well prepared for storm as well as shine. You should also be prepared to wait on your bush pilot at either end of your journey.

Mosquitoes, by the way, can be particularly ferocious in June and early July. If you visit this area then, be sure to take good insect repellent, a secure tent, and a head net; rig your tent high above—and as far away from—swampy areas as you can.

The Lake Clark region lies enough off the beaten track and is well enough guarded by the rigorous terrain of its mountain passes to have remained relatively lightly used until recent times. Native people fished its rivers for salmon and took grayling and trout through the ice of its lakes. They also pursued the abundant moose, bear, and caribou. (The present Mulchatna caribou herd numbers between 12,000 and 14,000 animals and was probably larger in times past.) The only known traces Native peoples left, however, are recent ones. Archeologists digging on the Stony River, Telequana Lake, and at the site of the former village of Kijik on Kijik Lake have found artifacts of Tanaina (Athabascan) Indians. But mixed with the Indian artifacts were Russian and English goods, indicating that these camps or settlements date back less than two centuries. Kijik village itself was abandoned in 1902 after a devastating measles epidemic; the Kijik people moved first to Old Nondalton and then, in 1940, to the present town of Nondalton on lower Lake Clark.

The Tanainas did not welcome the Russians, and they are known to have destroyed a Russian trading post on nearby Iliamna Lake and to have martyred a well-known Russian missionary, Father Yakove Federovich Juvenal, in a village near Lake Clark (probably Kijik). Despite all this, many Tanainas adopted Father Juvenal's religion and ended up with Russian names.

The Americans fared better with the Native people. In 1897, when the Eleventh Census was under way in Alaska, Alfred B. Shanz (an extraordinary census taker who had led an expedition to Alaska for the *Frank Leslie Illustrated Newspaper*) was much impressed by the hospitality of the people at Kijik as well as by the cleanliness of the village. He, too, noted that the Indians had many Russian trade items. It was Shanz, incidentally, who gave Lake Clark its name, in honor of John W. Clark, head of the Nushagak Trading Post on an arm of Bristol Bay. Clark was supposedly the first white man to discover the beautiful lake.

Around the turn of the century the lure of gold brought prospectors into the Lake Clark country. They struggled across rough passes, over glaciers, and through the impossible alder thickets to stake their claims early on at places like the upper Mulchatna River basin. In 1908, there was even a small gold rush in this area, but little came of it. About this time, claims were also staked around the head of Lake Clark. Then in 1911 and 1914, the USGS entered the scene and did extensive exploration and mapping in the area. Today, there are still sporadic mining efforts going on (hope never dies in a miner's heart). And in the impossible terrain of the Lake Clark Pass, where the rambunctious glaciers meet and part like agile boxers, there are minerals of dubious value that have prompted serious proposals for a road from the Cook Inlet to the summit of the pass.

Although there was some homesteading around Lake Clark before World War II, it was during the years after that war that a modest influx of people arrived to stake out claims along the lakeshore. Some farmed, some built hunting lodges, and some just enjoyed the scenery. Among them were two people who would make Alaskan history. One was Jay Hammond, the Alaska governor who built his beautiful log cabin on Lake Clark in the 1950s and was for many years a big-game guide in this region as well as a well-known bush pilot, poet, and state legislator. The other was Babe Alsworth, who chose a cove on the south side of the lake, married a Tanaina girl, and founded the small settlement of Port Alsworth and something of a dynasty. The best landing strip on the lake belongs to the Alsworths, and Babe's son, Glen, is an air-taxi operator who knows the country as well as anyone and can spot you into and off a river or suggest a special place for you to adventure. (See below.) Babe and his wife Mary, incidentally, have retired to Hawaii.

If the Tanainas found the hunting good in the Lake Clark region, so did the sportsmen after World War II. This has been an increasingly popular place for hunting since the fifties. During the hunting season, the buzz of small planes fills the air over outlying lakes near the park boundary. If you don't hunt, take this into account if you plan a trip into the area. Hunting season starts on September 1.

Rivers

You have a choice of marvelous waterways in the Lake Clark country, both inside and close to the national parklands. Here, for starters, are brief descriptions of seven such rivers (the park service can give you further information on these and others). All require air-taxi service for access.

Crystal-clear, swift-flowing, the beautiful Chilikadrotna River offers an excellent white-water experience for the intermediate floatboater.

The Mulchatna is shallow, rocky, and single channelled above Bonanza Hills (the first 22 miles). Downstream, it becomes an easy, leisurely float, wandering through a forest. A most pleasant river in its lower stretches. The Chilikadrotna flows into the Mulchatna.

The Copper (Iliamna) River is a fast, clear-water river flowing through a forest with lovely scenery and seasonally good fishing. Wildlife viewing is good. This makes for a nice, relatively short raft trip.

The Stony River is a swift (average five miles per hour) silty river flowing through a forest. It offers good mountain scenery upstream from the Necons River and good camping on its gravel bars.

The Telaquana and Necons rivers are relatively short, moderately swift, semiclear streams which are tributaries to the siltladen Stony. They are scenic, and offer good hiking and seasonally good viewing opportunities for moose, caribou, bear, furbearers, and waterfowl.

The Tlikakila is an extremely fast, small glacial river flowing through a narrow, deep valley. (It has been described as "one long rapid.") You can run it from Summit Lake to Lake Clark in three days. From start to finish, there is a continual array of jagged ice and snow-capped peaks, glaciers, waterfalls, caves, perpendicular rock cliffs, and glacial cirques to be seen from the river. The view at the river's end of Lake Clark and the surrounding mountains is a fine climax to the already enjoyed scenery. The valley floor is covered by alpine tundra around Summit Lake but is heavily forested with white spruce and paper birch along the river. The river offers an enjoyable float experience suitable for an entire family.

Some Useful Information About Lake Clark

There is scheduled air service to Iliamna, the nearest commercial airfield, and from there you can air charter into your destination in the Lake Clark country. You can also charter from either Homer or Kenai for a direct flight across the Cook Inlet; this will mean flying through one or another of the passes into the region. (Note that there is limited bus service to Kenai or Homer, but you can take the train to Whittier and from there the ferry into Homer.) Or, if it fits your wallet and schedule, you can air taxi from Anchorage; it takes an hour to an hour and a half to get almost anywhere you want inside the park boundaries from this metropolis.

I highly recommend a flight in a small plane from Anchorage to Lake Clark. (Since you will have to pay for round-trip time anyway, you might consider originating your flight from Lake Clark with a pilot like Glen Alsworth; that way you'll get a fine overview with someone who knows the country well.) If you do make this flight, you will fly above the waters of Cook Inlet and can see the oil platforms flaring gas like strange flaming nautical candles. You will pass over the wetlands on the west where the drainage patterns twist and branch in intricate and seemingly infinite designs. To the south, snow-clad Mount Redoubt (10,197 feet) will loom larger and larger against the horizon; a wisp of steam may be visible from its summit area. Then, at Trading Bay, you will head west through one of the most scenic and geologically fascinating passes in Alaska, Lake Clark Pass. Here the mountains, chiseled and molded by past glaciers, are festooned with blue-crevassed hanging glaciers that overflow the high cirques. Avalanche tracks streak down the rock slopes with waterfall after waterfall plummeting between them. Above, the dark peaks brood, made darker and more brooding by the dazzling whiteness of snow and ice around them.

On top of Lake Clark Pass rests small, shallow Summit Lake whose existence is subject to the whims of the glaciers that feed it. In colder periods, when the ice surges forward (as it has in very recent times), the eastern outlet of the lake gets dammed up, and the lake enlarges and deepens. Then its waters flow westward into the Tlikakila River, thence into Lake Clark and eventually into Bristol Bay and the Bering Sea. When the glaciers are in retreat, as they are at present, the dam disappears and Summit Lake gets little meltwater. What it does get drains both east (into Cook Inlet and the Pacific Ocean) and west. Because of its "unique display of numerous hanging and valley glacial features," Lake Clark Pass has been proposed for a National Landmark.

There are as yet no developed national park service campgrounds, but camping is permitted throughout the park-preserve.

Lodges

Koksetna Camp: Write Sara Hornberger, Box 69, Iliamna, AK 99606; no phone. Chuck and Sara Hornberger have built from scratch a beautiful and comfortable place which has outstanding gardens. Sara is renowned for her cooking. This is one of the few wilderness lodges that gets its electricity from a wind generator, installed by Chuck in 1975, hence the wonderful sounds of the wilderness here are not disturbed by a diesel or gasoline generator. The wilderness photographer, Boyd Norton, conducts summer workshops here. Sara Hornberger can provide information. **Van Valin's Island Lodge:** Write Glen Van Valin, Port Alsworth, AK 99653; phone (via radio, WHM 26) 907-345-1160. Glen Van Valin has his own aircraft and provides air taxi service as well as flightseeing. He also conducts river, backpacking, and camping photography trips. The food is fine and abundant and the accommodations very comfortable. Open year round.

Air Charters

Lake Clark Air Service: Write Glen Alsworth, Port Alsworth, AK 99653; phone 907-781-8001. **Glen Van Valin** (see above). **Iliaska Lodge:** Write Box 28, Iliamna, AK 99606; phone 907-571-1221. **Talarik Creek Lodge:** Write Box 68, Iliamna, AK 99606.

If you simply want to relax and enjoy an Alaskan vacation, you can spend a weekend or a week at one of the lodges on Lake Clark and have a wonderful time. (Try late June, July, or early September.) Boating and viewing from the lake can usually be arranged from the lodge you choose, and if you're at one of the more plush accommodations, you can get airlifted to one of the various lakes nearby to fish, photograph, or hike. Lodge owners can give you a good steer for the kind of outdoor recreation you're interested in.

If you want to explore the backcountry, the hiking and backpacking are outstanding, and there are opportunities of many kinds. Although there is no developed trail system, there are many summer and winter routes that are fine traveling. (**Kijik Treks**, write in Port Alsworth, AK 99653—offers great trips.) Game trails (made by moose and bear) abound, and the alpine tundra is a pleasure to hike on. Check with the **National Park Service** in Anchorage (phone 907-271-3751) to get an idea about itineraries for backpacking and/ or skiing. Mountaineers can also get information from this source.

KATMAI NATIONAL PARK AND PRESERVE

Katmai is a wild, elemental place where great earth forces are obviously, and gorgeously, at work. You can sense there the overwhelming power of these forces, which we like to theorize about but do not yet fully understand. From Katmai's pure and primitive landscape you can conjure up an image of how the world might have looked when land first poured from the depths of the earth to rise above the sea.

The best known and one of the most stunning parts of Katmai is the Valley of Ten Thousand Smokes, which was formed as recently as 1912, the result of one of the greatest volcanic eruptions of all time. Fragmentary accounts tell of this sudden, awful event. Early in June that year, increasingly severe earthquakes shook Mount Katmai and the land around it, and the Native residents of Savonoski on the north and Katmai village on the south had the good sense to leave. On the evening of June 5, when the skies were clear and cool, they could look back and see an ominous black storm lowering over the three-peaked, nearly 9,000-foot-high summit of the mountain. The earth continued to shudder, and the next afternoon, the mountain exploded in a series of thunderous blasts, one so colossal that it was heard in Juneau, 750 miles away. The terrible shaking continued until the night of June 7, when another major convulsion seized the mountain, and a blaze of light over the Katmai area was said to have lit up the peaks "like sunshine." (So reported geologist George C. Martin who was sent to the scene later that summer by the National Geographic Society.) This violent illumination apparently marked a prodigious outpouring of incandescent ash that roared at fantastic speed from Novarupta, a vent that opened near Mount Katmai. As the chief of Savonoski village put it with Biblical succinctness: ". . . fire come down trail from Katmai." A towering funnel of ash and steam soon rose skyward for several miles and spread an enveloping canopy of darkness. Ash rained from the sky, and fumes heavy with sulfuric acid spewed out with such force that they traveled as far away as Vancouver, British Columbia, where they ate

Ash flow strata, Valley of Ten Thousand Smokes, Katmai National Park. Source: National Park Service.

away linens hung out to dry. Across Shelikof Strait, amid thunder, lightning, and storms of ash, the people of Kodiak thought the end of the world had come and, mindful of Pompeii, took to the sea to escape. Ivan Orloff, a Russian on a fishing expedition at nearby Kaflia Bay wrote his wife, Tania, on June 9: "A mountain has burst near here so that we are covered with ashes, in some places ten feet . . . deep . . . We cannot see in the daylight. In a word, it is terrible, and we are expecting death at any moment, and we have no water. All the rivers are covered with ashes. Here are darkness and hell, thunder and noise. . . . Pray for us." Before it was all over, the skies of virtually the entire North American continent were dimmed by a haze of ash, and the summer of 1912 was notably cool.

When the molten outpour from Novarupta finally did stop, Mount Katmai had collapsed into itself and was 2,000 feet lower than it had been. What had been a high snowy summit became a broad crater filled with milky blue green water. At the foot of the mountain, a valley area of forty square miles was engulfed with searing ash and pumice to a depth of from 300 to 700 feet. The blast of intense heat from the torrent of ash devastated the landscape in every direction; the villages of Katmai and Savonoski had been desolated by what Martin called simply "a breath of hell." In the valley, an eerie scene even more evocative of Hades was in the process of evolving: the streams and waters beneath the fiercely hot ash and pumice had started to shoot out sulfurous steam in thousands of fumaroles. But no one was to see this staggering sight until July 31, 1916.

On that date, Robert Fiske Griggs, a botanist on his second exploratory expedition for the National Geographic Society, labored to the top of Katmai Pass and was about to turn back when he saw a whiff of steam that pulled him a few steps farther, and there he stopped, stunned. Later he reported, "The sight that flashed into view . . . was one of the most amazing visions ever beheld by mortal eye. The whole valley as far as the eye could reach was full of hundreds, no thousands—literally tens of thousands—of smokes curling up from its fissured floor." The air reeked of sulfur. The sound was "as though all the steam engines in the world, assembled together, had opened the safety valve at once." D. B. Church, the photographer on two of Griggs's expeditions stated, "It seemed to me . . . that this was the Devil's own private corner in hell itself." Griggs named the place the Valley of Ten Thousand Smokes. (After further explorations in the area, he said he should have called it the Valley of a Million Smokes.)

By 1917, Griggs had led three expeditions to Katmai. The information he brought back and the photographs taken by Church and others that had been published in the National Geographic Magazine fired the imagination of the world. Influenced by Griggs's enthusiastic reports and by the prestigious National Geographic Society, President Woodrow Wilson on September 24, 1918, established Katmai National Monument. Seventeen hundred square miles—more than one million acres—in size, the monument encompassed only the volcanic area around Mount Katmai, including, of course, the by-now-famous Valley of Ten Thousand Smokes. (Griggs, incidentally, returned one more time in 1919 for a last look at the extraordinary scene and, in 1922, published his book, *The Valley of Ten Thousand Smokes*; highly recommended reading.)

Perhaps it is as well that the place which Church described in 1917 as being so awesome that it "was not for human eyes to see nor human ears to hear" was destined to change both rapidly and completely. Although Griggs was unaware of it, the process of cooling was under way during the years he explored the valley, and today the valley is long since quiet but for wisps of sulfurous smoke at its upper end. The thick blanket of ash that was laid down in three outpourings has compacted into mesas of gray and beige tuff, a type of volcanic rock. Rivers have cut through the tuff like a knife through cake. (One of the valley's major streams is Knife Creek, which seems most colorfully named until you note Knife Peak, from whose glacier it flows, on older maps

. . . the name has recently been changed to honor Griggs.) The mists creep quietly over the eerie buff-colored expanses, and the loudest sound is the rush of the rivers and the roar of the winds. But life is slowly and surely beginning to creep back, and one day the valley may once again be green.

While Mount Katmai appears to slumber, not so nearby mountains Mageik, Martin, and Trident, which are smoldering and sending up plumes of smoke and have steam hissing from the rusty and evil looking yellow throats of fumaroles in many of their high places. (Griggs was struck by the colors of the Katmai landscape and wrote of the "gaudy muds"—gray, yellow, chocolate, red, black, blue—from which "very creditable pictures could be painted.") The Katmai region seems to be just waiting, the cauldron of molten rock deep beneath its surface ready to bubble up again at any time. Geologists have found evidence of at least ten violent eruptions in the vicinity of Katmai during the last 7,000 years, and who knows when another will occur.

Volcanism, however, is only one of the major earth forces displayed in Katmai National Monument. The land here rises to over 7,600 feet from the deep blue waters of Shelikof Strait, high enough to hold a small but active glacial system. Snowfields sprawl among the peaks, and glaciers hang down from them: Serpent Tongue Glacier, Knife Creek Glacier, Fourpeaked Glacier, Hallo Glacier, and others. Steam rises from the snowfields draping Mount Mageik. Ice as well as fire has formed, and is still forming, this terrain. Evidence of past much more extensive and massive glaciation shows in the long lakes that finger the land on the west side of the park; one of these lakes, Naknek, is large enough to be referred to as an inland sea. (It is the fourth largest lake in Alaska.) To the east, where the mountains rise from the sea, the coast has been sculpted into deep fjords where cascades of water fall over steep slopes above the beaches.

In this awesome primeval place it is somehow reassuring to find that a lovely and varied flora has successfully evolved. Along the coasts glow the deep green of alder and willow. Forests rim the low-lying lakes with tall white spruce, and the balsam poplars—a species of cottonwood—have gained immense girth over the years, sometimes as much as four feet in diameter. Birch trees grow with the balsam poplars, coloring the landscape with shimmering soft greens in the summer and warm golds in the crisp air of autumn. The low-rolling hills are tapestries of berries and dwarf birch. Higher, the sturdy, tenacious primitive plants of the alpine tundra take over, pushing to the frigid edge of the ice. It is interesting to see how closely the flora here is related to that of Siberia. I once walked up the gentle slopes of Mount Dumpling from Brooks Camp with a Norwegian botanist who was delighted, but not surprised, to find species after species that confirmed this fact. (Katmai, of course, is only one of many places where the close similarities of the living communities on the two sides of the Bering Strait can be observed.)

Except for the enclaves where people come together in Katmai, notably on the shores of Naknek Lake and at the tourist facilities at Brooks Camp, this

Arctic tern (Sterna paradisaea). **The world traveler which may challenge your presence on many Alaskan rivers.**

park is still marvelously wild, and the animals and birds go their ways generally unmolested. The trails you will follow if you hike or backpack off the beaten track here will probably have been made by the bears, a point to keep in mind, for Katmai is one of the last relatively undisturbed homes of the brown bear, and the great animals flourish here. In the wet places and around the lakes and rivers, you may see moose or river otter, mink and beaver, or a beautiful brown weasel, with its cream-colored belly, dashing out of sight. Along the little-visited coasts, there are sea lions, hair seals, and the charming sea otters sporting in the deep waters. Throughout, there are the predators—shy foxes (both red fox and arctic fox are here), wolves, lynx, and wolverines, and, in the skies, hawks and falcons, owls, and bald eagles.

Katmai is a place that is indeed rich in a variety of birds. Dozens of species of songbirds—as many as forty—gather here in the summer to pour out their melodies, mate, and nest. Whistling swans find the lakes here to their liking; if you are lucky, you may see and hear them in flight. (One of Griggs's parties surprised 500 of them resting on a sandbar.) Arctic terns nest and rear their young on the gravel bars of Katmai's wild rivers and, if you're a river-runner, you may choose—as I once did on a Katmai river—to retire from a choice camping spot because a pair of terns had gotten there first and had started a family. It should be noted that leaving such an avian family alone is not only required wilderness manners, but these birds can also hold their own. A furious dive-bombing tern has been known to connect with a human head on occasion, and the hysterical screams of a couple of outraged tern parents can send almost anybody hurrying down a river to get out of earshot.

Among the most prodigious wildlife of Katmai are the fish. Each summer, the Naknek Lake and river system (which empty into Bristol Bay, the world's greatest sockeye fishery) is invaded by nearly a million salmon. The spawning fish jam the waters in dense rosy crowds; each fish, its life nearly done, is stubbornly bent on finding its place of birth to help start a new generation of its species. The lakes and streams are thick, too, with char, grayling, northern pike, and whitefish. If you cast out your line at a place like, say, Brooks River, you will almost certainly get yourself a fish. At the same time you will be carrying on a tradition that is thousands of years old, for parts of the Katmai area have been inhabited by fishermen and hunters for millennia.

The first people to settle here were undoubtedly drawn by the richness of the fishing and hunting resources. Later, they also came in search of a way across the Alaska Peninsula from Bristol Bay to Shelikof Strait, for such a route would save them from a long and dangerous trip by sea around the tip of this tumultuous jut of land. From Katmai Bay, they found three such routes—one was the 125-mile drag across Katmai Pass. They must have been a hardy lot; the trails they left demand extraordinary toughness and stamina of anyone who tries to follow them. Their iglus, built largely underground, testify to the fact that Katmai's weather was not any more hospitable in the past than it is now. (There are interesting archeological digs at Brooks River where 800-year-old Eskimo buildings have been restored.)

Katmai's weather, in fact, is modified on the south by the warmer waters of the Pacific Ocean, but it is also in the pathway of storms generated in the Gulf of Alaska. On its northern side, the cold air of the Arctic comes down to pile up against the mountain barrier of the Aleutian Chain, of which the Katmai mountains are such a spectacular part. Winters can be cruel and summers cool. Eighty percent of the summer days are overcast, and furious wind-blown rain can sweep in at any time during the warmer months. Throughout the year there is the wind, forever the wind. Frequently it comes from the south and is funneled through the mountain passes in gales. (Griggs described Katmai Pass as being a two-ended funnel for the winds. He had four different camps blown down in the area.) The wind gusts across the lakes, plowing the waters into high surf. It blows night and day without stopping and can be canoe-capsizing as well as tent-transporting, so if you visit this area, be prepared. Experienced canoers and kayakers have enormous respect for the wind on the lakes, particularly Naknek Lake; the word is to travel close to shore. Katmai's wind is an earth force of its own.

Records of explorations in the Katmai region are meager, but the Russians obviously found this area long before Alaska became a territory of the United States. They left their religion and their names among the people, and place names like Shelikof, Becharof, and Savonoski on the maps. (The name of Savonoski was given not only to a village but to a short splendid river that gathers the meltwaters of several ice fields in Katmai and carries them into Naknek Lake.) The few Americans to report on the region before the turn of the century nearly all traveled across Katmai Pass to the east from Bristol Bay to Katmai Bay, battling the blizzards or bending into the torrents of wind that so frequently pour through the pass. One of them, Josiah Edward Spurr of the U.S. Geological Survey, crossed Katmai Pass on an expedition in mid-October of 1898 and noted that it was "extremely wild and rugged . . . the most difficult mountain pass we crossed during the journey."

By the turn of the century, the trail—such as it was—over Katmai Pass was feeling the boots of untold numbers of stampeders. They likely had the wind at their backs, however, for they were headed for Nome. They may have been, as Griggs once was, lifted off the ground by the wind and sent flying down the pass, feet barely touching the ground, but they did not bother to record their adventures in this part of the world. It remained for Robert Griggs to put the Valley of Ten Thousand Smokes and the area around it on the map and to help bring about the establishment of Katmai National Monument.

The original Monument fortunately proved to be only the beginning for Katmai. The valley was recognized before long to be only one of many extraordinary features here and volcanism only one of the great natural phenomena of the area. Successive presidents—Herbert Hoover in 1931, Franklin Roosevelt in 1942, Lyndon Johnson in 1969, and Jimmy Carter in 1978—acknowledged the national significance of the region by enlarging the Monument; in 1980, Congress increased the size of the Monument by 1,037,000 acres, gave it National Park status, and added 308,000 acres of land in National Preserve status. This National Park Service unit now totals 4,137,000 acres.

Some Useful Information About Katmai

How to Get There

Times have changed considerably since the Federal Writers' Project volume on Alaska, produced during the 1930s, stated simply that Katmai National Monument was "inaccessible to tourists." But access to Katmai is still limited—as it should be. Road proposals for the area—there have been serious suggestions for a road over Katmai Pass and/or through the Valley of Ten Thousand Smokes, (Griggs, himself, having made the first one)—cause the eyebrows of geologists to twitch; the life expectancy of any road in this geologically active area would be dubious. (Taxpayers should note that Alaska's roads have traditionally been funded almost entirely with federal money.) But far more important, roads would destroy the invaluable wilderness values of the Katmai region.

To reach Katmai, you can fly commercial aircraft to King Salmon and from there take an amphibious air taxi (operated by **Peninsula Airways**) to Brooks River where there is a National Park Service ranger station and campground and a Wien-operated concession. Or you can travel up Naknek Lake into the park by chartered boat.

If you can afford it, you can of course charter your own amphibious bush plane into Katmai or avail yourself of an air overlook of the region. A flight over Katmai can be one of the finest ways to see many of the wonders in this parkland. I have been lucky enough to see Katmai many times from above and will keep forever memories of evening mists lit by the slanting summer sun, smoking over the pale landscape while the mountains gathered their own golden clouds.

The **National Park Service** has headquarters in King Salmon within easy walking distance of the airport, and you can get up-to-the-minute information there about conditions in the park and access into it. You can also write: National Park Service, P.O. Box 7, King Salmon, AK 99613.

Where to Stay

In King Salmon, **The King Cove Inn** is near the airport, and, as of this writing, has good homemade pie and coffee. Write King Cove Inn, King Salmon, AK; phone 907-246-3377.

The only developed campground in Katmai is at Brooks River. It has tables, fireplaces, wood, water, shelters, and a food cache. Space, however, is limited. Consult the Park Service in advance if you plan to use this camp.

An attractive, though expensive, facility that includes cabins with modern plumbing and a lodge serving good food is operated by **Wien Air Alaska** at Brooks River. Another smaller more primitive camp at Grosvenor Lake is also run by Wien. Package tours to these concessions are available out of Anchorage. Write Wien Air Alaska, 4100 International Airport, Anchorage, AK 99502; phone 907-243-2400 for information. Camping equipment including tents and stoves, fishing equipment, and canoes can all be rented at Brooks River from the Wien concession. You can also take your meals in the **Brooks River Lodge** if you want to camp out. Otherwise, bring your own supplies.

Camping for backpackers, canoers, and river-runners is permitted anywhere in the park. A fire permit is required and can be obtained at the NPS Ranger Station in King Salmon or at Brooks River. Note to fishermen: a state fishing license is required in the park and regulations regarding limits, possession, and types of lures must be observed.

How to Enjoy Katmai

National Park Service ranger-naturalists present evening programs at the Brooks River Lodge throughout the summer and lead hikes and nature walks during the day. They also accompany bus tours (tickets available at the lodge) to the Valley of Ten Thousand Smokes where there are foot trails for further explorations. There is no developed trail system in Katmai; consult the NPS in King Salmon or at Brooks River for specific information about backpacking and/or backcountry day-hiking. Note to hikers and backpackers: extensive hiking on volcanic material can be very hard on footwear, and it is easy to wear out a pair of boots in a short time in Katmai.

There has been a great deal of pressure from certain quarters to "open up" and "develop" Katmai, so that more people can get into it and see it (and local business can thereby profit as well). This would, of course, mean the end of Katmai's special wild qualities, qualities that have survived in so few places on earth and are, even in Alaska, becoming increasingly rare. To date, the cost and logistics of road-building in the area have protected Katmai; and the National Park Service, due both to sensitivity and lack of funds, has been unable to do much in the way of development. I hope the National Park Service and an enlightened people everywhere will continue the protection afforded so far to this remarkable national treasure.

Think twice before undertaking an extensive visit to Katmai—beyond a stay at Brooks River or an outing on one of its lakes or rivers. And before you plan any kind of outing into the backcountry of Katmai, read Dave Bohn's book: *Rambles Through an Alaskan Wild: Katmai and the Valley of the Smokes.* (Read the book, anyway, if you love the wilderness.) As Bohn puts it,

> There are hundreds of places where you can stay in posh surroundings and watch thousands of other tourists. Don't ask for that here. Katmai is wild country, not a spa. You come to Katmai because it is something else. That something else will be destroyed for *everyone* (that especially includes the bears) if too many of you come . . . If you are a backpacker with a good pair of legs and can go into Katmai by yourself [author's note: not recommended] or with one or two others, your gain is on behalf of all of us. When you can no longer do it on your own, however, don't ask for a road across the Valley of Ten Thousand Smokes or a chair lift to the top of Mount Katolinat. Instead, pass on the philosophical space to someone else, and in this way the whole of it is not lost.

Katmai is wild country all right, and for the sake of all of us and our children, let it remain so. If you can visit it on its terms, it can give you an unforgettable wilderness experience (that may include some of the most arduous hiking you have ever achieved and some of the worst weather). But consider your priorities—as well as your condition—before you plan a visit to the backcountry of Katmai National Park.

If you do decide to visit Katmai, you might want to consider the possibility of a side trip to the McNeil River Bear Sanctuary to the north of the park.

This is one of the best places in Alaska to see and photograph bears. The sanctuary is administered by the state of Alaska Department of Fish and Game, and visitation is strictly limited, as again it should be. A letter to the Alaska Department of Fish and Game, P.O. Box 37, King Salmon, AK 99613, will get you the information you will need.

The waterways on the west side of Katmai National Park make for wonderfully adventuresome kayaking and canoeing. They include Naknek Lake with its lovely Bay of Islands (tree-covered islands stud the upper end of the lake) and the Alagnak and King Salmon Rivers. The latter is especially suited to a family outing. For information, contact the National Park Service, Box 7, King Salmon, AK 99613; phone 907-246-3305.

ANIAKCHAK

One of the strangest, most impressive features of the Alaskan landscape is a remote volcano located about halfway down the Alaska Peninsula. What makes it supremely unique is its caldera, which is one of the largest in the world, with an average diameter of six miles. (By comparison, the caldera cupping Oregon's Crater Lake is closer to five miles in diameter and is, of course, filled with water, the lake surface having an area of over twenty square miles.) Along with this extraordinary geological phenomenon, Aniakchak also has a rich and varied floral and faunal community. Because it is relatively inaccessible, its ecosystem has survived as one of the least disturbed in Alaska. In recognition of the many exceptional values of this volcanic area, Congress in 1980 established a 138,000-acre national monument there, with a contiguous 376,000-acre national preserve.

There are good reasons why Aniakchak has been left alone. It is a long way off, some 400 miles from Anchorage, and the only community anywhere near it, Meshik–Port Heiden, has only a handful of people. But more than distance and few people nearby isolate this new parkland; there is also the weather. Rain and fog smother the mountain most of the time. In 1973, an intrepid freelance writer spent six weeks in the crater and only eight days of his sojourn were sunny. In an average year, the Pacific side of Aniakchak gets soaked with 126 inches of rain, while the Bering Sea side is almost continuously fogged in. Along with this, a microclimate within the caldera brews winds of hurricane force. The visitor just mentioned had his camp blown down twice, watched Niagaras of fog pour over the crater's rim, and, during one storm, had his wind gauge carried off by a gale. During this episode, he was forced to take shelter in a depression in the crater wall to save his life. Aniakchak's temperatures, it should be noted, go to 30 degrees below freezing in the winter; in summer, they gyrate between the upper 40s and a possible but unusual 70 degrees.

On top of all this, Aniakchak is still alive, being one of the 47 active volcanoes in the 1,600 mile Aleutian Range that has erupted since 1760. Aniakchak went off as recently as 1931, but the great explosion that formed its caldera occurred long before there was any written history. That eruption left a high rim (some 2,000 feet above the caldera floor), which is crenellated into mountains. On early topographic maps, these were shown as a peculiar ring of low peaks. When viewed from the sea (on those rare days when they could be seen), they gave no hint of the extraordinary crater they embraced. For this reason and the weather conditions of the region, the Aniakchak caldera was not officially discovered until 1922 when an exploratory team of USGS scientists noted interesting pockets of ash some thirty miles northeast of Aniakchak on the Alaska Peninsula. Following their lead to the southwest, they came upon a whole valley buried in ash at Cinder Creek. With growing excitement, they climbed the slopes above and reached the crater's rim to look down, in amazed delight, upon the extraordinary sight below them. With the discovery of the immense caldera, the curious circle of mountains on their maps was graphically explained.

The Aniakchak River flowing through "The Gates" in the Aniakchak Crater wall.
Source: National Park Service.

To conjure a picture of Aniakchak, imagine if you can Crater Lake without its lake but with a small turquoise-colored body of water, named Surprise Lake, tucked into one side of it. Imagine the terrain stained mahogany brown and black, deep maroon with darkly smudged yellows, and over it all an openwork pattern of white snow looking like some huge dazzling piece of lace had been dropped onto it. Off center in the bizarre landscape is a small secondary crater, Vent Mountain, which has its own snow-filled caldera. Nearby there is a smaller, perfectly round formation, aptly named Doughnut Cone.

Adding to this whole strange scene is an abrupt gash in the crater's rim called "The Gates," which drains Surprise Lake and lets the white-foaming, boisterous Aniakchak River (floatable) race to the flatland below where it gentles out and flows into Aniakchak Bay. Without this drainage system, the caldera, like that of Crater Lake, would be filled with water, and Vent Mountain would make a creditable second Wizard Island.

Just when Aniakchak blew its top is not known, but since there is no evidence of glaciation in the drifts of ash it left, it must have been after the most recent Ice Age. Geologists estimate the height of the original mountain to have been above 6,000 feet; Aniakchak Mountain at 4,400 feet is now the highest point that remains. Before it exploded, Aniakchak was a mass of sedimentary rock of Jurassic age, which rested at a slight angle on its huge base. When the eruption occurred, it threw more than fifteen cubic miles of volcanic material over the landscape for twenty miles in every direction. This was three times as much ejecta as Krakatoa spewed out in 1883. Thus Aniakchak's big blowout was truly a monumental geological event.

Aniakchak's more recent activity has been mild in comparison; although in May 1931, it belched flames 7,000 feet into the sky and sent up a plume of ash that reached 30,000 feet and rained down over an area 1,200 miles in diameter. (At the village of Chignik, 60 miles away, ash poured from the air at the rate of a pound per square foot per hour.) A year later, Father Bernard R. Hubbard, the "Glacier Priest," on his third visit to Aniakchak, found a scene that he described as "a prelude to Hell: black floor, black walls, black water, deep black holes, and black vents." Even then, the mountain had not fully quieted, and every morning Father Hubbard donned his robes and held Mass, using the immense columns of steam that ascended thousands of feet into the sky as altar candles. Living creatures were already returning to the scene of devastation, and Hubbard shared his caldera altar with brown bear and ptarmigan.

The great brown bear continues to be one of the foremost members of the caldera's wildlife population. The bears have been known to seek out the steaming mud ponds where they wallowed as though, in Hubbard's words, in "a Turkish Bath." They also leave their immense tracks deeply imprinted in the volcanic ash, and Hubbard noted that they stepped carefully in the same footprints over and over again. Caribou use the caldera too. They are members of the 12,000 to 15,000 head Alaska Peninsula herd, and they wander through low passes into the crater to seek snow patches, where they stand in striking silhouette, trying to avoid the torment of mosquitoes. Moose and other mammals large and small use other areas of the new parklands, including the outer slopes of the mountain and its lowlands.

Flower lovers will find a beautiful sampling of Alaska Peninsula plants inside the park's boundaries. When Father Hubbard first visited the caldera before the 1931 eruption (which, incidentally, he predicted), he found a variety of plants growing there including the ladyslipper orchid and luxuriant ferns that flourished in the moist warm places.

Some Useful Information About Aniakchak

How to Get There
Access to the Aniakchak caldera is not cheap and is difficult and uncertain. Scheduled airlines serve King Salmon (150 miles distant) and Meshik–Port Heiden (10 miles away), and it is possible to charter a small plane to Aniakchak from either place. Service to Port Heiden, however, is on a three-day-a-week schedule. People have been known to walk the ten miles from Port Heiden to the parkland, but it's a rough scramble, with uneven tundra and heavy thickets of brush. You also have to climb at least 2,000 feet to get into the caldera. It is possible to follow the Aniakchak River and enter the crater floor through the Gates. (This hike is not recommended.)

Far easier and more spectacular is an air flight over the caldera, weather permitting. I have lucked out twice in viewing the caldera from the air, and it is an unforgettable sight. If you are very tough and adventurous, you can, of course, be deposited in the crater; it is possible to land a floatplane on Surprise Lake, and wheeled planes can usually find a level stretch to set down.

Where to Stay
There are no visitor facilities at Meshik–Port Heiden. Camping is allowed anywhere inside the park boundaries.

How to Enjoy
As noted, a flightsee trip over the Aniakchak Crater is highly recommended. It is also possible to raft the Aniakchak River, which is designated a wild river. It is 27 miles in length, and its upper stretch is white water. However, it ends up meandering comfortably into Aniakchak Bay. The National Park Service in King Salmon can give you further information regarding air charters and the possibility of a commercially run river trip. Write Box 7, King Salmon, AK 99613; phone 907-246-3305.

Aniakchak is a magnificent geologically and ecologically important unit of the national park system. It is a fascinating natural wonder to view from the sky. But, except for the Aniakchak River, this is not recreational country. If you decide to visit it, be prepared for a rough outing, miserable weather, and maybe even another display of volcanism. Aniakchak is still very much alive.

ALASKA'S STATE PARKS

Alaska's state park system, while still relatively young, could well be the envy of almost any state. It contains around three million acres of superlative terrain. (This is considerably less than 1 percent of the acreage in Alaska!) Development of the system has largely been devoted to readily accessible areas and especially to waysides along the state's more heavily traveled highways. Of 82 units, 52 are designated waysides. These provide welcome places for bikers as well as drivers to stop, stretch, picnic, or perhaps to camp. Some of the waysides are quite large—several hundred acres in size—and can include such amenities as toilets, drinking water, shelters, camping units. Several have boat launching into lakes or rivers; others serve as trailheads.

The state park people also maintain designated campgrounds and recreation areas. The latter can be several thousand acres in size and have extensive campgrounds, canoe trail systems, snowmobile areas, cross-country ski trails, or other developed recreational facilities. The state historic parks, another unit classification, primarily help preserve some of Alaska's rich history, but in Kodiak (Fort Abercrombie) the historic park also has camping facilities.

The largest units of the state park system are the state parks themselves. Most of these are undeveloped or in the process of development, including Wood–Tikchik (1,428,349 acres), Kachemak Bay State Park (118,970 acres), Wilderness Park (206,320 acres), and Denali State Park (336,489 acres). Denali was the first major unit in the state park system (1969) and is scheduled to be a focal point of visitor services for the new Denali National Park. Although facilities here are still limited, there are interesting backpacking opportunities, and you can get to the takeoff point on the Alaska Railroad. (Check with the state park people in Anchorage for details.) The most highly developed is the Chugach State Park, just outside of Anchorage, which is discussed in some detail in this book.

The Alaska Division of Parks puts out a useful folder that gives an inventory of its various units, their locations, and the facilities they include. (Pamphlets giving details of some specific areas are also available.) If you're planning an auto or bicycle excursion into Alaska, this information can be very valuable to you. To obtain the _State Park Recreation Guide_, write to Alaska Division of Parks, 619 Warehouse Avenue, Suite 210, Anchorage, AK 99501; phone

907-274-4676. A ten dollar per year fee is charged for use of state park facilities—and is well worth it.

The Wood-Tikchik State Park is located about three hundred air miles west of Anchorage and it is one of the loveliest regions in all of Alaska. There are two sets of lakes adjacent here, each with six gorgeous bodies of water. Each set gathers its waters from a different watershed, and each drains into a different river, although the waters of all end up in Nushagak Bay.

The higher lakes are tucked between soaring peaks where the snow gleams against swathes of emerald green heath tundra. The lower lakes are fringed by dark spruce forests with birches scattered here and there. When the salmon are running, they are so thick in the "river bays" between the lower lakes that it is hard to see the bottom, although the water is as clear as glass.

Under the terms of statehood, Alaska was able to select a large part of this magnificent area and did so in the early 1960s. Almost immediately, there were strong pressures on the state to subdivide the lakeshores into five-acre "wilderness estates"—one of its land-disposal classifications. Fortunately, there were even stronger pressures to preserve this region more or less intact,

King salmon (Oncorhynchus tshawytscha), **Alaska's state fish. Range: southeast Alaskan waters to Chukchi Sea.**

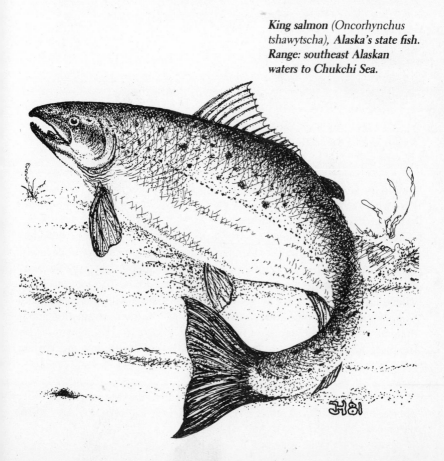

Pacific walrus *(Odobenus rosmarus divergens).*
Range: Bristol Bay to Point Barrow.

and, in the late 1970s, the state legislature established the Wood-Tikchik State Park which everyone can enjoy. With its 1,428,000 acres, this is by far the largest unit in the state park system.

The Wood-Tikchik State Park is still undeveloped. It offers superb wilderness experiences, primarily water based, during the summer. (The usual caveats about rain, mist, coolness, and wind all apply.) You can fly commercial to Dillingham, where there are tourist facilities. You can reach the wilderness part of the park by small floatplane. Check with the Alaska state park people in Anchorage; they can help you with further information about the park and with the names of facilities in Dillingham. Dillingham is also the place from which you travel—by boat or by air—to Round and Walrus Islands.

Air Charters: Armstrong Air Service, Box 204, Dillingham, AK 99576; phone 907-842-5940. Yute Air Alaska, Box 180, Dillingham, AK 99576; phone 907-842-5333.

PRIBILOF ISLANDS

The only way you can reach the Pribilof Islands is to fly there via Reeve Aleutian Airlines—unless you're lucky enough to somehow find transportation by boat. Once there, the only lodging is the Native-operated hotel on the largest island, Saint Paul. (There is one other sizable island, Saint George, and three little ones—Otter, Walrus, and Sea Lion.) The islands lie in the Bering Sea just about due west of Naknek, and if the weather is good when you visit them, you will have some fine aerial views of the Alaska Peninsula en route to or from Anchorage.

The great attractions of the Pribilofs are their Russian history (dating back to 1786 and memorialized by, among other things, a wonderful Russian Orthodox Church), their colonies of northern fur seals, their fabulous bird life (176 species have been recorded on the islands), and their uniquely accessible sea bird nesting cliffs.

The Aleuts who inhabit the islands harvest the fur seals as part of their economic subsistence, with the operation monitored by the Department of Commerce under whose aegis the hunting of sea mammals is managed. Tourism is another major source of local income. (Make your travel arrangements through your travel agent or Reeve Aleutian. Write 4700 West International Airport Road, Anchorage, AK 99502; phone 907-243-1112.)

The accommodations on Saint Paul are clean, informal, and more or less of the bedrock type. (The bathroom is down the hall.) The opportunities to photograph the wildlife are fantastic—if the weather is good. Unfortunately, most of the time it isn't, so be prepared accordingly. Rain, mist, winds, or a combination thereof, are usually the order of the day.

Part IV

INTERIOR AND ARCTIC

INTRODUCTION

Once you leave the tumultuous mountains of the Alaska Range and head northward, you encounter the Interior, a country with a very different kind of magic. If Southcentral (and Southeast) Alaska can be described as vertical terrain, the Interior can be described as horizontal. There is a softer feel to this gently tilted landscape, termed the Intermontane Plateau by geologists. Your eyes can reach across vast stretches of space to what seems to be an infinitely distant horizon. True, that horizon may be delineated by high shining mountains, but more often there is a lower uplift of the land, a bank of hills whose outlines are superimposed and marked by different shades of blue—deep, deeper, deepest—in a curiously two-dimensional effect. The dark spiky shapes of spruce trees punctuate the grand vistas and fringe the lakes and oxbow sloughs and ponds that gleam like polished black mirrors in the still summer air. Lush green gold mosses weave themselves together in the muskegs. Gardens of fireweed splash cerise all over the ground as though huge buckets of rich rose-colored paint had spilled here and there.

This is the region in Alaska where in hot summer days thunderstorms move their dark blue black shadows over the land, trailing sunlit shafts of rain and rainbows. Birches and aspens shake out their soft green leaves that turn silver in the wind. The sun can be so hot and the air so warm that you are tempted to snooze away an afternoon in a proper siesta, but afternoon, evening, night, and morning blend almost imperceptibly into one light-filled day. The light itself has wonderful qualities, flooding golden during the day and often becoming rose or orange as the sun dips lower on the horizon.

Autumn comes to the Interior like a visiting artist for a few brief weeks. The broadleaf trees glow like bright torches; spruce cones turn royal purple; delicate-looking larches pale to a smoky yellow before their needles fall to the ground. The plumes of horsetails float in a soft creamy haze above the forest floor; cranberries turn a brilliant red and so do the leaves of the bearberries.

Then as the earth moves more deeply into the dark months of shadow, colors fade to muted browns, tans, and grays. The first chilly rains can freeze and cover the world with a brief shine of ice. The heat of the land—gathered during those sunlit near-twenty-four-hour summer days—begins to drain inexorably into the infinite depths of space. Day after still, clear day sees the temperature slide lower until the snows come whirling and whispering down to color the land white. Great masses of polar air slide in from the west to be held fast by the high walls of the Brooks and Alaska ranges, and the cold deepens. During the brief daylight hours of winter, the sun rolls along the

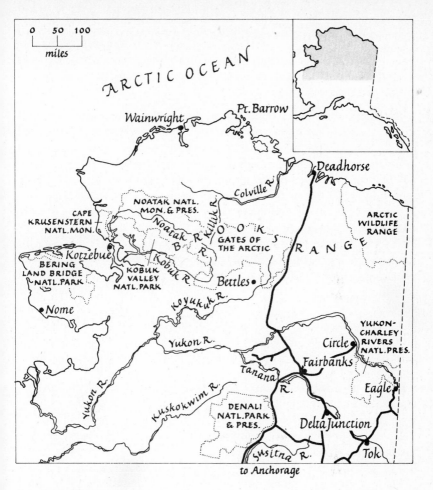

Interior and Arctic Alaska

horizon like a brass disk and gradually tips out of sight. In this pale slant of sunlight, the soft dry snow glitters, and floating ice crystals sparkle in the calm air. A small cloud of ice fog forms when you breathe, and when darkness grips the world, auroras come to flame the sky.

Like Alaska itself, the aurora is difficult to describe. Here is one attempt, written nearly a century ago by Fridtjof Nansen, the Norwegian explorer who spent three years in the Arctic. Two of those years were spent in his ice-bound ship, the *Fram*. His classic book is called *In Northern Mists*.

> Nothing more wonderfully beautiful can exist than the Arctic night . . . the aurora borealis shakes over the vault of heaven its veil of glittering silver—changing now to yellow, now to green, now to red. It spreads, it contracts again, in restless change, next it breaks into waving many-folded bands of shining silver, over which shoot billows of glittering rays . . . an endless phantasmagoria of sparkling colour,

surpassing anything that one can dream. Sometimes the spectacle reached such a climax that one's breath was taken away; one felt that now something extraordinary must happen—at the very least the sky must fall. But as one stands in breathless expectation, down the whole thing trips, as if in a few quick light scale-runs, into bare nothingness.

It is small wonder that some Eskimos believed the aurora was a heaven where it was always warm and wonderful and life was eternally easy and beautiful.

But the lengthening days of spring dim the northern lights and, as the skies stay brighter, the fronds of the spruce trees start to drop their loads of fluffy snow until the forests are filled with glittering cascades. Meltwater begins first to ooze and then to stream from the snowbanks, and the first flowers come to star the brown wet ground. The ice-bound rivers creak and heave until huge blocks of ice break loose and start their ponderous journeys downstream, sometimes piling up on one another and jamming the rivers until they flood their banks and drown the land. When the ice slabs collide, the air is filled with the deep, primeval sounds of irresistible forces meeting an immovable object.

There is a feeling of timelessness about this elemental land. Although its great rivers have changed their courses, and the land itself—much of it underlain by permafrost—has been patterned and repatterned by the earth-shaping forces of freezing and thawing, and buried and reburied by loess and sediments from the mountains that embrace it, the basic landscape has remained essentially unaltered for the hundreds of thousands of years it has been above the sea. When the great Pleistocene glaciers covered the Brooks Range to the north and the Alaska Range to the south, they stopped short of this immense plateau. This was the place of refuge for countless living things that could not breach the world of ice and snow surrounding them.

Many of those living things still flourish here, having survived from those times, though, strangely, many great mammals, herbivores and carnivores alike, have disappeared within the ken of prehistoric people. This is the land of muskegs and tundra, tangles of low-growing berries and, in places, of devilish tussocks, sedges, or cotton grass. It is the land of the taiga, the boreal forest community of white spruce, black spruce, alder and willow, larch, birch, and aspen. This is the land of moose, caribou, and wolves, of lynx and snowshoe hares, of the grizzly bear and red fox, the vole and the red squirrel, which is the alarm sounder of the forest. It is also the land of raptors, and on its tundras and in the wetlands of its great rivers, it is the land of migratory birds, hundreds of thousands of winged creatures that follow an undeniable pull to what has been one of earth's stable ecological communities. They come to the Yukon and Tanana wetlands, their wingbeats filling the skies, waterfowl in overwhelming numbers.

Millions more birds—waterfowl and seabirds, many species of shorebirds and songbirds—prolong their migratory flights northward, some finding their

Caribou (Rangifer tarandus). **Range: once throughout most of Alaska but for Southeast and Aleutian Islands, now the largest herds are in the northern portions of the state.**

way through the passes of the Brooks Range or over these beautiful mountains, others arriving via the Pacific flyway. Their goal is the Arctic Slope with its braided rivers, thousands and thousands of thaw lakes, marshes, and coastal plains—all so rich in insect life during the summer months. As with the Interior, the Arctic Slope escaped glaciation during the Pleistocene Ice Ages (above ground, that is; below the surface, the ground froze nearly solid and has remained so). As a consequence, the Arctic Slope, too, was a refugium for certain plants and animals and a haven for certain migratory birds like the eiders, Canada geese, and old squaws, which still feel the pull that returns their species to this place summer after summer.

The Arctic Slope is the part of Alaska believed to have been formed by the breaking off and rotation of a piece of the Canadian shield around a pivotal point in what is now the Mackenzie River delta. As this huge block of rock swung round through a shallow sea, the theory goes, it helped push up the Brooks Range that, in turn, contributed an immense quantity of outwash and sediments through the millennia to help build up the surface of a new land-mass. (In this millions-of-years-long process, geologists explain, oil was trap-ped between the basement rock and the surface layers; hence Prudhoe Bay.)

Arctic Slope

Although separated from the Interior by the Brooks Range and essentially sharing these mountains with it, the Arctic Slope is very different from Alaska's central plateau. This relatively flat and thoroughly frozen slab of land is gripped by continuous permafrost, which may extend as much as 2,000 feet below the surface. Everywhere in the Arctic there is evidence of this phenom-enon, but perhaps the best way to get a perspective of what permafrost can do to the land—as well as to enjoy some of its especially picturesque aspects—is to fly over the Arctic Slope in a small plane on a clear summer day. Below you this vast segment of gently tilted earth—snow free under the summer sun—will be cracked into a network of giant polygons, many of which will be outlined by thin shining ribbons of water in the troughs that separate them.

You will also see beaded streams wandering across the landscape. These are small ponds formed at the intersection of ice wedges and connected by short threads of water running between the polygons. You will see literally thou-sands upon thousands of thaw lakes shimmering in the sunlight, for in the summer, the Arctic Slope is more water than land in places. A few thaw lakes are round, but many are oval or almost rectangular; and while some are tiny,

Aufeis, Artic Slope. Source: U.S. Fish and Wildlife Service.

no more than a few feet long, others are twenty miles or so in length. In many areas their long axis is oriented just west of north, reflecting the general direction of the prevailing winds, which are southeasterly. Contrary to what might be expected, the winds spread the water at right angles to their impact and build up wave-generated shelves on the shores in front of them, hence the long narrow shapes.

Another Arctic phenomenon that makes interesting viewing from the air is the *aufeis* which forms in north-flowing rivers. It may look as though there were snowfields on the waterways in midsummer, but, in fact, *aufeis* is something like a riverine glacier. Each season, a layer of ice is formed when overflow water freezes. This can build up into a sizable striated platform of ice, which is as blue as the best of glaciers when seen from the river itself. (Note to river-runners: avoid collisions with *aufeis* and, above all, avoid going under it.)

If you fly far enough north, you will leave behind the patterns of the Arctic land and will see, instead, the extraordinary patterns of the Arctic ice pack. Summer usually breaks the frozen Arctic Ocean up into millions of chunks of ice that, seen from the air, form an incredible silver white jigsaw puzzle in the dark blue waters. Land and linger, if you can, along the Arctic coast. To stand on the shore of the Arctic Ocean or clamber onto a chunk of its ice is quite an experience; should you visit this region on a clear midnight when the Arctic sun rolls along the ice-roughed horizon, flooding the world with a cold golden light, you will enjoy one of Alaska's truly great sights.

From the ground, you may also have a chance to see a pingo, or ice blister. A pingo can result from the draining of a lake. The permafrosted land encroaches into the empty lake basin from all sides until it finally approaches the center, where the icy ground has no place to go but up; hence, a low frozen hill results. A pingo makes a valuable reference point as you travel across what seems to be a flat and featureless landscape.

Although soggy in the summer, (not recommended for cross-country hiking), the Arctic Slope can be described accurately as a frozen desert. Precipitation here is the lowest in Alaska and ranges between five and eight inches a year across the sweep of this region. (This includes both rain and snow.) Cold is a fact of life year round, and spits of snow can sting your face here in July and August. Because the winds sweep constantly over these vast reaches of open land (Barrow for example, reports calm conditions only one percent of the time), what snow there is seems more often to travel horizontally than vertically, and it piles up only where it meets an obstruction. Windblown snow can cause a whiteout that competes with summer fogs in making ground travel a challenge and flying an uncertainty in this part of the state.

While the climate of the Arctic Slope can be especially bitter, particularly in light of the wind-chill factor, weather is only one aspect of the unique character of this place. The other is the presence or the absence of sunlight and/or twilight. Barrow is not completely dark for nearly 119 straight days during the year. (This counts some 67 days when the sun is above the horizon and another nearly 52 days when bright twilight illuminates the world even when the sun is below the horizon. Because of the latitude and the cold, refraction maximizes this twilight period.) On the other end of the scale, Barrow residents go for nearly 67 days without ever seeing the sun, although more or less brief periods of twilight lighten the sky during this long period of darkness. (Interestingly, though, Barrow still receives an overall total of solar energy greater than that received by Palmer, which is just north of Anchorage.)

The flora that lives in this world of ice and night has adapted to it in interesting ways. The tundra plants of the North Slope grow on the polygons there much as they would on small soggy islands, hanging on for dear life with their shallow roots in the thin "active layer" of soil that covers the forever frozen ground beneath. Many of the plants mat themselves together thickly to conserve what heat they can, protect themselves from the blasts of wind, and preserve the little snow that falls on them for moisture. They may also form cushions or tussocks so that dead leaves are caught around their roots and protect them. Leathery leaves, which help avoid the desiccation inflicted by the cold dry winds, are commonplace, just as they are in warmer deserts. And the ability to photosynthesize even in very low temperatures keeps many of these sturdy Arctic dwellers alive.

Few of the tundra plants are annuals, for they would be too hard pressed to mature and seed in the brief six weeks that is the growing season of the Arctic summer. The perennials that succeed often reproduce vegetatively, even though they may also be capable of producing seed as a backup means of perpetuating their species. Some of the plants, such as the willows, are able to hybridize readily; this is another mechanism for survival. Others, like the various species of lichens that grow on higher ground have the advantages of being two plants at once, fungi and algae.

Even as the flowering plants cram a lifetime into the few relatively warm days of summer, some members of this tundra community manage to prepare themselves for what lies ahead. For example, the willows put on their buds for flowers and leaves in early autumn in anticipation of the first sunny day to come the following spring; then they are ready to pop open and take advantage of every moment of sunshine. In such a rigorous regime for growing things, it comes as a beautiful surprise to find crowds of yellow poppies dancing in the Arctic wind, in seeming bright defiance of all the rules.

The Arctic fauna also use interesting mechanisms to succeed in these northerly latitudes. For example, mammals of all sizes and shapes may not only wear a white fur coat at least part of the year, but they will also have good insulating layers of fat. Some of the birds are feathered in white during the winter; other species, of course, time their arrival and departure to the change of the seasons. Your chance of seeing some of the fabled Arctic beasts like the polar bear are slim, but not because of their protective coloration: hunting pressures and the impingement of civilization on this once wild habitat have reduced the numbers of these animals and made them very wary. You might, however, hope to repeat the experience of friends of mine who, one sunny summer day, stopped for lunch on a gravel bar in an Arctic river and whiled away a half hour or so with a charming fox, which posed amiably over and over again for photographs.

The Arctic has been inhabited by people for untold ages (at least 27,000 years, according to some anthropologists), and there are many important archeological sites hidden in its frozen ground. Along some of its beaches, the bones of woolly mammoths are embedded in permafrosted cliffs, reminders of animals struck down by the early hunters here who prized these creatures as game. Along other beaches, the artifacts of more recent cultures wash in and out with the storm-driven sea. (In contrast to other parts of Alaska, the tides in the Arctic Ocean can be measured in inches rather than feet.) The present people of the Arctic, the Inupiat, carry on their treasured traditional ways, often practicing the demanding skills that enabled their forefathers to survive in this vast and strangely beautiful frozen world.

Brooks Range

Separating the Interior plateau and the Arctic Slope—and contributing much to the character of both of these vast regions—is the Brooks Range. The range was named for the explorer and onetime head of the Alaskan Branch of the United States Geological Survey, Alfred Hulse Brooks. Stretching from the Canadian border to the Chukchi Sea, this Arctic alpine province is a mountain world of extraordinary beauty and variety. The early uplifting of these mountains, which at their highest rise just a little less than 10,000 feet, is pegged at somewhere around 150 million years ago (as compared to the Rockies, which were uplifted starting perhaps 70 million years ago). But the rocks of the Brooks Range also tell of many earlier earth processes. Regions of these mountains lay beneath ancient seas, as long as 360 million years ago, and gathered the grains of long lost continents that were washed into their waters. Sediments, built up slowly over time, were finally upthrust and metamorphosed so that now they are stained with lovely colors and form fascinating striated patterns. In their stacking, folding, and deformation, there is graphic evidence of the powerful forces that have shaped this part of the earth through many millennia. Evidence of more recent geological activity lies in the heart of the range, where fiercely sharp granitic peaks, young and untempered, have burst through the older formations in an upwelling of the earth's hot magmas.

So large is the sweep of the Brooks Range that it contains several mountain systems within it. The mountains closest to the Canadian border—the Davidson and Romanzof groups—rise higher and higher as they travel westward. Their foothills are clothed with pale green tundra, which may be powdered with snow off and on during the summer. (It is quite an experience to be caught in an early July storm, as I once was while traveling through these mountains, and watch the perfectly even snow line come lower and lower down the hillside until, only a few hundred feet above you, it gives way to frigid rain.) Through and over these foothills flow the crowds of the Porcupine Caribou Herd, animals that roam the lands of Canada and Alaska as they follow the instinctive patterns that pull them back and forth across the tundra.

To the west of the Romanzofs are the Franklin, Shublik, Sadlerochit, and Philip Smith mountains. Among their summits lie scraps of glaciers, reminders of the Pleistocene ice sheets that covered and sculpted this land. Beyond lie the Endicott and Schwatka ranges, and forming the westernmost end of the range are the pastel gray and beige De Long Mountains and the Bairds—only 3,000 to 4,000 feet high—which escaped later glaciation and have weathered into beautifully rounded shapes.

To the north, the Brooks Range is bordered by two sets of foothills whose ancient sediments have been tossed up here in tumultuous waves or stacked like shingles. Because it lies beyond the tree line, the bare structure of this fascinating piece of the earth can be clearly seen.

The Brooks Range has an interesting pattern to its drainage; waters flow north, south, and west from its peaks and ridges. North-trending streams, like the Kongakut, Hulahula (there were once more Hawaiians in Alaska than there were the Russians that claimed it, hence place names like this one), Canning, Sagavanirktok (for a while, you were supposed to qualify as an Alaskan if you could pronounce the name of this river, but then after the pipeline got going, everybody started calling it simply the Sag), and Colville, all rush from the high country to break into braids that intertwine their channels across the gently sloping apron of the northern province. One great river, the Noatak, rises from the granite heart of the range, flows due westward, and then makes a 90-degree angle south to empty into Kotzebue sound. Most of the south-flowing streams, lovely rivers like the Sheenjek, the Koyukuk, the Dietrich, the John, and the Alatna, contribute to the volume of the Yukon River. But whatever their directions are, the rivers of the Brooks Range, still wild and free, are among Alaska's most beautiful (and sometimes challenging) streams; they can carry you through some of Alaska's most interesting and unique scenery.

The Brooks Range is a redoubt for some of Alaska's finest wildlife. One of my greatest Alaska memories is of floating the Kongakut River on a cold misty afternoon and looking up to see two Dall sheep lying on the dark cliffs above, silently watching our slow progress downstream, and somehow embodying the pure spirit of this wilderness. Other wildlife is not so silent, and the thousands of shorebirds that nest along the Arctic rivers of the Brooks Range are not at all shy about announcing their presence—and trying to get rid of yours. Although there are still many grizzlies and wolves (as well as caribou and moose) in the Brooks Range, you may not be as fortunate as wildlife biologist Averill Thayer—who knows and loves this territory so well—who once spent several days on the Sheenjek River in the company of a family of

Lake Norvik, Brooks Range. Source: National Park Service.

forbearing wolves and a grizzly that was more frightened of him than he was of it.

Gardens of wildflowers brighten the tundra swards of the Brooks Range— marsh marigolds, mertensia, potentilla, anemones—and in the higher terrain, the hiking is good. In wet places, however, you can encounter the ubiquitous tussocks that force even the most nimble hiker into a careful balancing act.

Despite the tussocks, the Brooks Range offers splendid backpacking. It is also a wonderful place to be spot-packed into; you can stay awhile and absorb the beauty and the wildness of this part of Arctic Alaska. As always, of course, warnings about the weather apply, with the added one that, especially to the north, bone-chilling storms can sweep in any time of the year as can bitter winds, and the weather can change with speed remarkable even for Alaska.

Sometimes people fall in love with a particular part of Alaska, and this love affair changes their lives. Such was the case for Robert Marshall, who visited and lost his heart to the Brooks Range during the 1930s. He climbed and named Mount Doonerak (Spirit Mountain), which broods above all the other peaks in the Endicotts. He was stunned by the beauty and grandeur of Boreal Mountain and Frigid Crags, which he christened, and then aptly described as the "Gates of the Arctic." He spent happy months in the little mining town of Wiseman on the Middle Fork of the Koyukuk River, where he found in the simple and accepting community living a social model he would have liked to see emulated by the rest of the world. He wrote eloquently and delightfully of his time in this magnificent wilderness, which he was among the first to try to protect. His book, *Alaska Wilderness*, is required reading for anyone who visits the Brooks Range. (See Bibliography.)

Until recently, many of the extraordinary values of the Arctic—the cultural, ecological, and scenic among them—were given little attention by our government. The first major federal withdrawal of Arctic lands was for oil. Incidently, the Eskimo people had known about the presence of oil there since time immemorial. The 23 million-acre Naval Petroleum Reserve Number 4 was established in the 1930s. Subsequent oil exploration in the Preserve yielded no bonanza, but it did inflict major and perhaps irreparable damage on parts of this fragile terrain. The U.S. Navy has since turned this acreage over to the Department of the Interior, and former Secretary of the Interior James Watt opened up a 6 million-acre portion of it to renewed exploration. Limited but important scientific research came with the establishment of the Naval Arctic Research Laboratory in Point Barrow, an effort that has been discontinued. And in 1960, the Arctic National Wildlife Range was established in a first official nod to the importance of the Arctic wildlife resource.

Although the state of Alaska, also looking for oil, selected strategic lands in the Arctic under the statehood act early on, it took bringing in petroleum at Prudhoe Bay in 1968 to turn the national spotlight onto this part of Alaska. While the subsequent construction of the Trans-Alaska Pipeline, with its attendant haul road, forever ended the wild integrity of the region, the 1980 congressional dispositions of Arctic public lands within and south of the Brooks Range has, at last, acknowledged some of the major human and conservation values here. Sadly, the Arctic Slope itself, that vast, fragile, and magnificent area that is unique in the United States, fared less well. Only a small percentage of it was given adequate protection by the federal government; oil exploration was authorized in the Arctic Wildlife Range. The rest of this vulnerable and beautiful terrain faces an uncertain future, as does the wildlife it presently supports.

Rivers

Clear and cold, the Colville River offers a relatively easy (class I and II) fifteen-day run from the Kiligwa River to Umiat, with another five days from Umiat to Nuiqsut. You can get in by wheel plane from Bettles or Kotzebue to gravel bars upstream, out by wheel plane from Umiat or Nuiqsut, or you can continue to Deadhorse where there is commercial air service. Raft or kayak is preferred river craft. The Colville is Alaska's largest river north of the continental divide. It flows through rolling, treeless, Arctic terrain, with good views of wildlife possible, but poor fishing likely. For further information, contact the BLM and the Alaska State Division of Forest, Land and Water Management. Write Umiat and/or Nuiqsut if you plan to stop in one or both of these villages (see Appendices).

The Ivishak is a swift, flat-water, clear, Class II river. An 80-mile trip on it will take four to five days. Access in is by wheel or float plane from Bettles or Kotzebue. You can fly out by air taxi, or join the Sagavanirktok River and continue on to Deadhorse. Raft or kayak is preferred craft because of access. Extensive aufeis may close the river channels until middle to late June. The Ivishak flows through the Philip Smith Mountains where there is good hiking, and you may see fine wildflowers and many butterflies in season. For further information, contact the U.S. Fish and Wildlife Service.

The Killik River is a beautiful, clear, swift, Arctic stream. It will take about six days on it to reach its confluence with the Colville, then three more days to Umiat. The river is generally class I and II with possible III rapids. Rafts or kayaks are preferred. Access is by float plane from Bettles or Kotzebue to lakes upstream. You can be picked up by a wheel plane from a gravel bar at the Colville River, or continue down the Colville to Umiat. There is good hiking in the upper reaches of the river and you will pass within sight of large sand dunes. For further information, contact the NPS and BLM. Write the Arctic Slope Regional Corporation, as well, since this river flows through their land (see Appendices).

The Sagavanirktok River is another clear, swift, north-flowing Arctic stream. You can spend about six days on it from Galbraith Lake to Franklin

Junction of the Kokrine River with the Yukon. Kokrine Hills in background.
Source: Alaska Environmental Information and Data Center, University of Alaska.

Bluffs, and add another two days to reach Deadhorse. This is an excellent white water river for experienced floatboaters; you may encounter class IV rapids in Atigun Canyon, otherwise it is class II and III. The Sag flows through some very lovely country, and parallels the pipeline and Haul Road for two-thirds of its length. Access in and out may be possible from the Haul Road, which will allow the use of canoes. Otherwise, you will need an air taxi and may prefer a folding raft or kayak. For further information, contact the BLM.

The Middle Fork of the Koyukuk River is a relatively easy, clear stream which passes through historic country, has good fishing, and is suitable for a family outing. It can provide a pleasant five day trip from its headwaters to Bettles, weather cooperating. Access in is by haul road and out by scheduled air service out of Bettles. Canoe, raft, or kayak is suitable. The river passes through mining properties in Wiseman, Nolan, Coldfoot, and Tramway Bar: these should be respected. For further information, contact the BLM. Write Tanana Chiefs regarding Native properties along the Koyukuk.

The Porcupine River is large and generally slow-moving, and poses few challenges to a small boater. However, it is an historic waterway which flows from Canada into Alaska and it offers a wonderful eight to ten day river experience from Old Crow, Yukon Territory to Fort Yukon, Alaska (if you don't mind mosquitoes). There are numerous places to put in in Canada: write to Printing and Publishing, Supply and Services Canada, Ottawa, Canada, KIA 059 for the Parks Canada Booklet, *Wild Rivers: Yukon Territory* (modest price). You can take out at Fort Yukon, or continue down the Yukon River. There is commercial air service out of Fort Yukon, or you might want to investigate putting your raft, canoe, or kayak onto a barge at Fort Yukon and returning to Old Crow. The Porcupine passes several Native villages and through a good deal of Native-owned territory: write Tanana Chiefs if you wish to stop along the way. For further information, contact the U.S. Fish and Wildlife Service.

Other interesting river and small boating opportunities in the Interior and Arctic include: Nigu-Etivluk Rivers (NPS); Black River (USF&W); Kasegaluk Lagoon (BLM and village of Wainwright); Yukon (USF&W, NPS, BLM); Alatna (NPS). Write for information to the agency or village indicated (see Appendices).

FAIRBANKS

In a gentle valley cradled on three sides by subdued rolling hills and within sight of some of the most spectacular peaks of the Alaska Range lies Fairbanks, the city of the Interior. Less than 150 miles south of the Arctic Circle, its location happens to be very nearly in the geographical center—or what is referred to as the "golden heart"—of Alaska. Like Juneau, this is a town that came into being because there was gold nearby; and like Anchorage, it has strong "ties" to the Alaska Railroad, being its northern terminus. But there the resemblance to Alaska's two other principal cities stops. Fairbanks has a distinctive character all its own. While Juneau has early history, charm, and bearable—if soggy—weather, and Anchorage has size, lots of business activity, and a spectacular setting, Fairbanks has the feel of a frontier town, with moose in its gardens, magnificent auroras, the University of Alaska (intellectual center of Alaska) in its backyard, and a climate that demands obeisance of anybody who lives in it. Those who do live here include some of the most independent, colorful, and individualistic people in the state—true Alaskans to the core.

The stories about the uniqueness of Fairbanks folks are legion and apocryphal. For example, some time ago the community hospital became so run down that it was clear that it would have to be replaced. For three years in a row the people of Fairbanks voted down a proper bond issue to fund a new medical facility. Conditions worsened and serious medical cases had to be sent to Anchorage for treatment; still the voters said no. Then somebody decided to pass the hat to get the money for a new hospital—and, sure enough, the people of Fairbanks, on their own, came up with more money than was needed. (I asked the friend who told me this story why she enjoyed living in Fairbanks so much and she replied that its faults are its greatest charm.)

More recently, in the 1980 election, the Fairbanks people once again demonstrated the independence of their thinking. To speak for them in the state legislature in Juneau, they elected six representatives in the following order: two Libertarians (the only two in the United States to be elected to any state office that year), one conservative Republican, and three Democrats. Nosed out in this election was a man who is spoken of as a Socialist.

It might be argued that the environment of Fairbanks accounts for the uniqueness of some of its citizens. To survive in it one has to be tough and self-sufficient, know what one is doing, and know how to make the right decisions. People who live in lesser climates might find it hard to comprehend what a Fairbanks winter is like. One Fairbanks resident described it to me as not being so bad—there are only three or four weeks when it's below 35 or 40 degrees; he meant 35 or 40 degrees below zero. In that kind of weather, things that most of us take for granted simply won't work. Not only can automobile engines solidify overnight (sometimes even when plugged into a heating system, and many parking meters have plugs), but steering wheels can also lock, frozen stiff, while you're driving down the highway. When it drops down to 60 below zero—and it does—if you throw a glass of water out the window, it will freeze before it hits the ground. Soap bubbles become as rigid as glass and roll around on the snow. Ungloved fingers will freeze in a matter of minutes, and so will uncovered noses and cheeks. The smog you breathe (and Fairbanks has some of the world's worst smog) will be frozen. It's too cold to cross-country ski in such weather, but if you tried it you would find the snow so dry that it has the harsh consistency of sand. Unfortunately, if you plan to keep warm inside, you might find that the power has gone off and all of your pipes hold nothing but ice. In newer apartment buildings you may be requested not to open your windows from November 1 to May 1.

People who endure this kind of winter climate—which they like to describe as "dependable cold, none of that messy freezing and thawing"—share experiences that bond them together. Add to this another shared experience—that of the long, almost constantly dark winter—and the bond becomes stronger. Perhaps understandably, Fairbanks people tend to feel a little different, like members of an exclusive club to which you have to be initiated, a little stronger than people from Outside. You might encounter this attitude when you visit Fairbanks; you might, for example, hear the contiguous 48 states described as "the lesser states."

Along with this, you'll find that most Fairbanks residents are also hospitable and friendly people who are happy to share the loveliness of their summers with you. (Unless you like really cold weather, a winter visit just for the fun of it is not advised for a first Alaska experience.) Their summers can be wonderfully warm and full of sunshine and other attractions. (I have been in Fairbanks in July when the temperature was nearly 80 degrees F. at 7 P.M., but remember this is Alaska, so don't count on finding it the same next July.) There are beautiful rivers that you can run from right downtown or from an easy bus ride away. There are pleasant walks to take inside the city limits and fine hiking not far away. There's an interesting museum and university campus to visit, and a good bus system to get you there. There's a lot of local history to explore from the ground, and a helpful Chamber of Commerce to give you a hand in exploring it. There are also a couple of excellent sporting goods stores with cooperative people who will help you plan a canoe or kayaking trip with Fairbanks as your base.

Fairbanks ties into a network of roads that can lead you to the Yukon—and beyond, with the opening of the Haul Road—and to other interesting and historical places. Along the way, you will find outstanding parks and recreational areas to visit, as well as some good camping. And, of course, Fairbanks is the gateway to some of Alaska's most magnificent and remote wilderness,

Fairbanks home. Source: Yvonne Mozée.

in both the Interior and in the Arctic. From here, you can fly to takeoff points for the Brooks Range, the Arctic Wildlife Range, and—to the west—Nome and Kotzebue and some unique and interesting units of the National Park Service.

Many visitors to Alaska see the state almost entirely from the air, with twelve- to twenty-four-hour layovers arranged by tour operators in particular places selected for their tourist attractions—whether they be picturesque qualities, good accommodations, or something sensational like the oil pipeline. Fairbanks is a principal depot for this kind of Alaska sightseeing, and during the summer you will find it full of tourists. There isn't a great deal in the way of tourist hot spots here, so the usual routine is to haul busloads of people out to Fox to see the pipeline firsthand or take them to Alaskaland or to the university museum (see below). Then the next day, the air tour begins, most likely to Nome, Kotzebue, Point Barrow, Deadhorse (where the pipeline operation is shown off), and back. If your time is limited, and you want this kind of overview, you might want to take advantage of one of the tour packages that will give you such a bird's-eye view (weather permitting) of the Interior and the Arctic. For this, see your travel agent.

Whatever brings you to Fairbanks, you can spend some enjoyable time in this small city. It can provide you with another dimension of experience in Alaska, one that you won't get anywhere else.

AVERAGE TEMPERATURE: FAIRBANKS

	F° daytime high	F° nighttime low	F° monthly average
Jan.	− 2.6	− 20.7	− 11.7
Feb.	7.7	− 14.9	− 3.6
March	22.2	− 5.0	8.6
April	41.0	18.6	29.8
May	58.6	36.3	47.5
June	70.2	47.5	58.9
July	71.6	50.0	60.8
August	65.7	45.2	55.5
Sept.	54.1	34.9	44.5
Oct.	33.3	18.1	25.7
Nov.	11.0	− 5.5	2.8
Dec.	− 1.0	− 17.5	− 9.3

History

The gently rolling hills that cup the Tanana Valley are clothed in places with aspen, birch, and spruce; in other places, lovely swards of tundra embroidered with tiny shrubs and flowering plants and berries cover the permafrosted ground. Caribou travel this country; wolves sing in the night. Bears, beaver, moose, muskrat, lynx, hares, and wolverines also inhabit this subarctic land. The rivers born in the nearby hills run clear, while those that reach from the Alaska Range may be thick with glacial silt; almost all of them carry fish. Along the rivers, shorebirds nest, and in the wetlands millions of wildfowl congregate.

While this land is far from the sea and its bounty—and the climate can be cruel—there is subsistence here for those ingenious and strong enough to take it, people such as the Athabascan Indians. Through many centuries, the Athabascans have hunted game, fished, and gathered the berries here, devising ways to survive in a demanding environment. Long ago they fashioned highly sophisticated traps and snares that enabled them to hunt "in absentia." They invented snowshoes to take them over the winter terrain and double parkas and jackets with separate hoods to protect them from the cold. They kept their history in elaborate songs and dances, and they explained the world about them and its mysteries in parables as well beloved and believed by them as those of the Bible. They exchanged stories (if not insults) with their different neighbors, the Eskimos. In their language, they spoke of themselves as *Dena* which means "the people" or "us." Where the town of Fairbanks now spreads out was once part of their unboundaried land.

Fairbanks had its beginnings when Elbridge Truman Barnette decided in 1901 to establish a trading post at Tanacross where the historic trail from Eagle to Valdez crossed the Tanana River. Barnette hoped to supply the sourdoughs who were flooding into the Interior in pursuit of gold. He ran into a series of accidents trying to get to Tanacross and ended up on the Chena River instead of the Tanana trying to take a shortcut. When the river grew too shallow, he landed on what was described as "a high, dry bank with good timber for a cache and cabins." (This "high, dry bank" has since been all but drowned by the flooding Chena.)

Barnette intended to move his goods on to Tanacross when Felix Pedro discovered gold just twelve miles north of his cache in July 1902. Meantime, Barnette had promised his friend "Sunny Jim" Wickersham, the first district court judge of Alaska, that he would name his new trading post for Wickersham's political backer, United States Senator Charles W. Fairbanks (later Theodore Roosevelt's vice-president). With gold at its doorsteps, Fairbanks came into being on the banks of the Chena. The next year, two more of Sunny Jim's political allies were immortalized in Fairbanks when two of the town's major streets were named for United States Representatives Lacey and Cushman. In 1904, Wickersham reciprocated in full; he officially moved his court from Eagle to Fairbanks, by then a booming mining town. (Barnette donated the land on which the new courthouse and jail were built.) This added stature and prestige to Fairbanks, recognizing not only that it was the major town in the Tanana Valley but that its founder, E. T. Barnette, had lots of political savvy. (Barnette, however, was forced to skip town only a few years later when the bank he founded went broke and the townspeople discovered he was an ex-convict and turned against him.)

Although Fairbanks all but burned to the ground on May 22, 1906, rebuilding started the next day, and the local newspaper ran a headline that stated simply: "Fire Cannot Stop Fairbanks." This proved, indeed, to be true over and again during the following decades; Fairbanks has had between twenty and thirty major fires during its lifetime.

Gold kept the town flourishing until the supply began to run out, and it was getting so low by the late teens that Fairbanks was on the verge of going ghost. (Nonetheless, more gold, over seven million troy ounces, was taken out of the Fairbanks area than out of the Yukon.) But just in time to save things, the northern terminus of the Alaska Railroad was relocated to Fairbanks (from Nenana) and what would become the University of Alaska was established in College, just outside the town's boundary. The construction of the Alaska

Railroad was completed in 1924, and Fairbanks became the major "port" serving the Interior. (Freight brought in by rail was shipped out on a network of rivers to nearby villages—and it still is.) However, by the time of World War II, Fairbanks still had only around 2,000 residents, and the community welcomed the input of money and people brought by the location of two military installations nearby. (Fort Wainwright and Eielson Air Force Base— formerly Ladd Field—are still active and important to the region's economy.)

The building of the Trans-Alaska Pipeline, however, was what brought Fairbanks the biggest infusion of people, money—and problems—that it has had in its history to date. Between 1973 and 1977, Fairbanks became a principal gateway to the North Slope, and a boom city to end all boom cities, as materials and pipeline workers flooded in and out, all but bursting the seams of the community. Every room in town (and every tentsite) was occupied; there were waiting lines in every supermarket; prices soared; and traffic became gelatinous in a town where traffic jams had once been laughed at. The smog, already a problem, grew worse and worse, especially on cold winter mornings when thousands of cars warmed up their motors and poured their carbon monoxide out into the dense heavy air. Some of the true Alaskans living in Fairbanks wondered what had become of their cherished way of life.

However, with the pipeline completed and in operation, Fairbanks has returned somewhat to its older ways, although the Yellow Pages of the phone book still carry ads for Las Vegas casinos. The city is larger now, older and perhaps wiser, as another boom may take shape ahead when and if a gas pipeline is built.

What to Do in Fairbanks

On a warm summer day it is most pleasant to stroll along the streets of Fairbanks. This is a compact low-rise small city with many of its older buildings still standing to tell of its history. If you start your walk at the log cabin Visitor Center on 1st Street on the banks of the Chena River, you can pick up a city map, bus schedules, and a copy of *Ghosts of the Gold Rush*. This excellent booklet tells you how to find the old sites and buildings and what their stories are. The First Street bridge across the Chena, by the way, marks the site of Barnette's first landing.

A walk across this bridge will take you the the *Fairbanks Daily News Miner* building; this newspaper is the oldest institution in Fairbanks, having been published continuously since 1903, when its founder, W. F. Thompson, arrived to "engage in the dissemination of well-known truth." Enjoy the flowers blooming in front of this building and elsewhere, and note the story-high delphiniums that grow around town.

Near the *News Miner* building is the Alaska Railroad station where you can pick up a schedule, if you need one. Directly across from the station is Northern Alaska Environmental Center (218 Driveway Street), housed in a small old-fashioned cottage; it is well worth a visit. (Outdoor travelers please take note, however: there are not facilities here, no place to pitch a tent, no showers, and so on.) Along with getting an update on current environmental endeavors in this part of Alaska, you can also buy birch baskets and tee shirts here (sold as fund raisers) and, sometimes, authentic Native smoked salmon or "squaw candy." You may also want to inquire about wilderness trips being run by the center or about local wilderness guides. (See below.)

Back across the bridge into downtown Fairbanks, you can take a look at Second Street—somewhat the town's skid row—the old post office building, and the new Federal Courthouse, built in 1932 after the original burnt down; this had the first elevator in town. It is worth noting that in 1967, all of Fairbanks, including this part of it, was several feet under water when the Chena River flooded.

A short bus trip (better check routes) will take you to what was once Creamer's Dairy and is now a migratory waterfowl refuge administered by the Alaska Department of Fish and Game. There is a nearly two-mile nature path there that can give you an excellent overview—in miniature—of the typical habitats of the Interior, from floodplain to woodland to bog, seasonal stream and pond to upland forest, thermokarst pond, and tussock meadow. You can even see ice-wedge polygons. The Alaska Fish and Game people have a good descriptive folder that serves as a guide keyed to the signposts along the trail. From late April through early to mid May, this is one of the best places around to bird-watch. You can expect to see sandhill cranes, Canada geese, white-fronted geese, many different ducks, and so on in some quite spectacular migratory shows. There may be as many as 1,000 birds here at a time. Well over a hundred different species have been recorded as visitors to or residents of this particular refuge. The Creamer Nature Path, incidentally, is used by cross-country skiers in winter as well as by joggers in the summer. Directly across the street from Creamer's Field, there is a borough park where you may be able to see beavers and/or muskrat—a good place to take a sandwich for lunch.

Continue out College Road (you can take the same bus) and you'll come to the University of Alaska (more colorful gardens to see). There is another opportunity here to take a short hike and/or do some more bird-watching at the right time of year. The Experimental Farm lands are heavily used by migratory birds, and there is also a loop trail system that can give you a look at the pleasant countryside surrounding the campus. You can inquire at the museum for directions (see below), and while you're there, pick up check lists of Alaska birds and mammals.

The university buildings are also interesting. The Alaska State Constitution—an important step toward statehood—was drafted and signed in 1956 in one of them, Constitution Hall, and the museum has some interesting displays, although you might have to share the space with busloads of tourists trying to see them. Note the huge copper nugget in the lobby, the good array of Alaska's large mammals, and the only confirmed meteorite in Alaska (which resembles a small ham in size and shape, weighs 58 pounds, and was found near Council on the Seward Peninsula). The university, described by one of its faculty as a "fantastic cultural small town," is the site of important wildlife and geophysical research.

If it's a clear day when you're at the university, be sure to look just to the west of south for Mount McKinley; it can be seen from the ridge at the west end of the campus. (McKinley, some 160 miles away, is actually below the horizon; however, because of the angle of refraction occasioned by the latitude, and sometimes intensified by the cold, the light rays bend in such a manner as to give you a splendid view of this magnificent mountain. Small wonder that the locals who made the first ascent of its north peak in 1910 waved a flag from the top to let their friends back home know where they were!) The mountains closer by to the south are Mount Hayes, Mount Deborah, and Mount Hess; all are over-12,000-foot giants of the Alaska Range. Mount Hayes is actually 13,700 feet high.

Starting from downtown, you can also travel by bus to Alaskaland, a sort of fairground of the state's centennial celebration (also flooded in 1967). This is a major tourist attraction these days, and from near here you can take a boat ride down the Chena River in a stern-wheeler.

If you're interested in a local excursion by bike or by canoe or kayak out of Fairbanks, there are two places you'll want to visit. One is Beaver Sports (Jim Whisenhart) at 2400 College, not far from Creamer's Field, and the other is Clem's Backpacking and Sporting Goods Store (Clem Rawert) at 315 Wendell, near the Chamber of Commerce. Between these two operations, you can get an excellent idea of local outdoor opportunities; you can also possibly rent or buy the equipment you will need. Jim Whisenhart can handle almost any kind of local canoe outing for you (best to write ahead if you have a long one in mind), including transportation, local camping accommodations, food, etc., and canoe rental (or sale—he will buy back from you). Jim also rents one-speed bikes for local touring. Clem Rawert is very experienced and knowledgeable about local backpacking and kayaking opportunities. (Incidentally, if you would like to travel down the Chena River and into the Tanana to take out at Nenana—about a twelve-hour trip on the water—and return to Fairbanks on the Alaska Railroad, you can put into the river right across the street from Clem's store, and he can tell you just what to expect.) Clem sells all kinds of backpacking equipment as well as kayaks, and while he won't buy back a kayak that he sells to you, he will help you resell it and says it is usually not too difficult to do. Some people sell their small boats downriver in the town or village where they take out.

Hiking

If the weather's nice when you're in Fairbanks and you have some time on your hands, you can find a number of pleasant local walks to take. Already mentioned are the Ghosts of the Gold Rush historical walk that will take you around the downtown area, the Creamer's Field Nature Path on College Road, and the loop walk on the university campus. It is also possible to take a dirt road to the top of nearby Ester Dome; ask at the Visitor Center or at the Department of Fish and Game for directions and other suggestions.

Farther afield, there is some excellent hiking. The Chena River Recreation Area has many miles of hiking opportunities and offers a good overview of the Interior countryside, from beaver-occupied sloughs to mature spruce forests. A trip up Granite Tor will give you a nice workout. Ask the state park people for details.

The BLM also administers some good hiking country in the area. Between Fairbanks and Livengood on the Elliott Highway (used as part of the haul road), there is a trail system that leads from the highway to a recreation cabin (the Borealis-LeFevre) at Beaver Creek, a wild river within the new one million acre White Mountain Recreation Area. The 21-mile summer trail starts at Mile 28 and heads eastward over Wickersham Dome. (A hike to the dome, itself, makes a pleasant four-hour round-trip circuit from the road.) The Winter Trail takes off at Mile 23.5 of the Elliott Highway but is too wet and boggy for summer use. There are a few good scrambles on the Summer Trail and switchbacks up the steeper slopes. Although water will probably be available, the BLM advises either carrying your own or boiling (or chemically treating) water from streams or lakes. Cost of the cabin is two dollars a night. Reservations can be made through the BLM people. If you want to camp farther up the Elliott Highway, you can stop at Tolovana Campground at Mile 57. On this and other hikes, remember to pack out what you pack in and treat the tundra gently.

The BLM also administers the Pinnell Mountain National Recreation Trail. (This is one of 22 trails so designated in the United States.) This is a 24-mile alpine trail that traverses ridge tops around the 3,500 foot level. It is rugged in places and steep, but it offers some fine views of the Alaska Range on the south and the Yukon Flats and Brooks Range to the north, and the hiking through the tundra country is excellent. From mid-June to mid-July, the wildflowers are gorgeous. This is also a good trail to take around midnight between June 18 and June 25; then the midnight sun is visible from many high points. During this week, you can also see the midnight sun from the Eagle Summit trailhead parking lot. There are trailheads for the Pinnell Mountain trail at Mile 85.6 and Mile 107.3 (Eagle Summit) on the Steese Highway. You may want to make a short hike from either trailhead, or both, and return to your car, or you could arrange a shuttle or a pickup. Water is scarce along the way, so be sure to carry a full canteen. Refer to the BLM office in Fairbanks for further information. (Note, alas, that the protozoan, *giardia*, is present in many Alaskan watersheds; do not drink stream water indiscriminately.)

Small-Boating

Fairbanks is the gateway to several accessible rivers that are excellent for river-running. You can check with Clem Rawert at Clem's Backpacking Shop or with Jim Whisenhart at Beaver Sports for good firsthand information about local small-boating opportunities. If you prefer to do your river-running on your own, talk to the BLM people in Fairbanks, or write them beforehand (see below for address). They can give you detailed information about the Tanana, Fortymile, Chena, and Chatanika rivers, and about Birch Creek and Beaver Creek—the most popular nearby streams.

Driving

Pay attention to any sign that says DIP. Because Interior roads are frequently constructed on permafrost, there may be massive cave-ins when ice lenses melt due to the fact that their cover has been removed. (See section on Permafrost.)

If you're traveling to Circle, you'll take the Steese Highway; to Livengood, you'll take the Elliott Highway; to Eagle, you'll pick up the Taylor Highway at Tetlin Junction (off the Alaska Highway). These three historic roads will be more interesting to you if you get one of the BLM folders, which give good background and describe points of interest along them. (They have many points of interest: for example, the Steese Highway has numerous historical sites as well as a NASA satellite tracking facility alongside it that is open to the public at selected hours—ask when at the Visitor Center; the Trans-Alaska Pipeline (TAPS) parallels the Elliott Highway; the Taylor Highway provides ready access to running the Fortymile River.) Write the BLM to obtain copies of "Alaska's Steese and Elliott Highways."

The 74-mile section of the Elliott Highway between Fairbanks and Livengood has been part of the TAPS haul road since the pipeline was constructed. As of this writing, you can continue on the haul road across the Yukon River to (and possibly beyond) Camp Dietrich in the Brooks Range. This opens some of Alaska's most vulnerable wilderness to many people. This part of the haul road also travels through regions of dramatic climate changes, when the weather can change so quickly it becomes dangerous if you're not prepared for it; the road also cuts through areas where the wildlife is still unaccustomed to heavy visitation. The Native people of the region have opposed the opening of the haul road, being fearful that the intrusion of many vehicles and people may threaten their subsistence hunting. Conservationists have also steadfastly opposed the opening of the haul road, which is subject to extremely heavy industrial use, to private cars. Think twice before you decide to drive it; it's heavily rutted and dusty.

Biking

The City of Fairbanks has extensive bicycle trails that you can find on the map you get at the Visitor Center. Of particular interest is the trip around Farmer's Loop, which is extensive enough to give you a good overview of the community and its surroundings. You can also take bike trips on the Steese and Elliott Highways, as well as on the Taylor (if you don't mind the traffic you'll encounter on the Alaska Highway getting to Tetlin Junction). Be advised that these roads are mostly dirt.

Miscellaneous

You can take a twenty-mile stern-wheeler trip with Captain Jim Binkley on the *Discovery II,* one of the last operative stern-wheelers in Alaska. The riverboat carries 335 people and travels the Chena River into the Tanana and back at least once a day from June 1 through September. Call 907-479-6673 for details about sailing.

The University of Alaska Museum is located on the upper campus and is open 9 A.M. to 5 P.M. May through September; otherwise 12 P.M. to 5 P.M. Take Bus Number 1 to Eielson Building and the shuttle (leaves twelve, thirty-two, and fifty-two minutes past the hour), or take the pleasant campus walk to the museum. You may see Mount McKinley en route.

Eskimo Olympics

This marvelous display of Native skills and games takes place each midsummer at the Patty Gymnasium on the University of Alaska campus. If you happen to be nearby around this time of year, don't miss it. You can get information as to exact dates by writing the University of Alaska, College, Alaska 99701.

Some Useful Information About Fairbanks

Hotels

Wedgewood Manor: 212 Wedgewood LDrive, Fairbanks, AK 99707; phone 907-452-1442. Not cheap but not expensive either, and you get a full-sized apartment with cooking facilities, swimming pool, sauna, jacuzzi, etc. Comfortable and quiet. Bus runs to the door. **Fairbanks Hotel:** 517 Third Ave., Fairbanks, AK 99707; phone 907-456-6440. Small and very reasonable, especially without bath. **Alaska Motel:** 1546 Cushman St., Fairbanks, AK 99707; phone 907-456-6393. Small and very reasonable. **Alaska Motor Inn:** Fourth and Lacey, Fairbanks, AK 99707; phone 907-456-5414. Kitchen units available. Pets allowed. **Cripple Creek Resort:** Ester, AK 99725; phone 907-470-2500. Good if you have a car and want an "Alaskan" atmosphere. Close to town and very reasonable, but *summers only.* **Golden North Motel:** 488 Airport Way, Fairbanks, AK 99707; phone 907-479-6201. Touristy, but they may be able to take you when other hotels are full. **Golden Nugget Motel:** 500 Noble St., Fairbanks, AK 99707; phone 907-452-5141. First class (expensive), with the usual trimmings but also touristy. **Tamarac Inn:** 252 Minnie St., Fairbanks, AK 99707; phone 907-456-6404. Reasonable. Laundry and cooking facilities. **Chena Hot Springs Resort:** If you're driving or biking and don't mind traveling about 60 miles out of town, this resort has a hot swimming pool, a lodge or cabin facilities and, in winter, excellent cross-country skiing. Open year round. Write Drawer 25, 1919 Lathrop Street, Fairbanks, AK 99701; phone 907-452-7867.

As of this writing, public campgrounds are meager. Consult the Visitor Center for other hotels.

Campgrounds

Although people do camp in various of the public parks in Fairbanks, the Chamber of Commerce does not list any public campgrounds in the city. The nearest free campground is run by the borough and is accessible by public bus: **North Pole Park**, Fifth Ave., North Pole. Telephone (in Fairbanks) 907-456-6683 (this is the number of the Borough Parks and Recreation Divison). Five-day limit, rest rooms, fire enclosures, small, no charge. Good idea to check by phone before going. Take bus Number 50 to North Pole.

There is also the **Harding Lake Recreation Area** out of North Pole at Mile 42 on the Richardson Highway. This has water and rest rooms (is heavily used locally) and is developed for car and trailer camping. Harding Lake, incidentally, poses a few problems because it has no outlet.

If you have wheels, there are three state park campgrounds within a reasonable distance: **Harding Lake** (see above). The **Chena River Recreation Area,** which takes in some 254,000 acres of land, lies between Mile 26 and Mile 52 of the Chena Hot Springs Road. There are many places to camp here on river bars and so forth. There are no facilities beyond pit toilets. Fine hiking and some river-running too. You can hike here to a tundra ridge exhibiting dozens of spike-like granite monoliths called tors. These make for a remarkable sight, especially in moonlight. The **Chatanika River Wayside** at Mile 39 on the Steese Highway has water, pit toilets, and 73 campsites.

You can pick up a list of private campgrounds at the Visitor Center in Fairbanks. Most of these are geared to take care of trailers and range in cost from $5 per space up.

Showers

Norlite Campground, Mile ¼ Peger Road (907-453-4206) has coin-operated showers. **Monson Motel Campground,** 1321 Karen Way (907-479-6670) charges $2.00 a shower. **Tanana Valley Campground,** Mile 2 College Road (accessible by bus; 907-452-3705) has showers for $1 (also welcomes tent campers; $6/night). Shower, sauna, and swim are available at the University of Alaska.

Car Rentals

Avis: International Airport; phone 907-456-7900. **Budget Rent-A-Car:** International Airport; phone 907-456-4281. **Payless:** International Airport. Free pickup and return; phone 907-452-2177 or toll-free (nationwide) 1-800-541-1566. **Hertz:** Airport Road and Stacia; phone 907-452-4444, Fourteenth and Stacia; phone 907-456-4004. **Miller Machinery** (used car rentals): 226 Illinois; phone 907-452-4243. **Rainbow** (used car rentals): phone 907-456-5900. **Rent-A-Wreck** (used car rentals), pickup and delivery, 2105 Cushman; phone 907-456-8459 or 452-1601. Recommended.

Motor Coach Service

Alaska-Yukon Motorcoaches: 900 Noble, Fairbanks; phone 907-452-8518. **Alaskan Coachways:** 208 Wendell, Fairbanks; phone 907-456-7072.

Youth Hotel and Bed and Breakfasts

Both are available. Check at **Log Cabin Visitor Center** for latest information.

Airlines to Lower 48 States

Alaska Airlines: International Airport; phone 907-452-1661. **Northwest Orient:** International Airport; phone 907-452-8700. **Wien Air Alaska:** International Airport; phone 907-452-8201.

Scheduled Airlines Flying Locally

Air North: P. O. Box 60054, Fairbanks, AK 99701; phone 907-456-5555. Services Fort Yukon and Bettles. (Note, near Bettles in the Kanuti National Wildlife Refuge is Sithylemenkat Lake, meaning, in Koyukon language, "Lake in the Hills." It has recently been strongly suspected to be a meteorite crater. 500 meters deep and 7.7 miles wide, it may have been formed bya 55 million-ton meteor perhaps 100,000 years ago. Look for it about 50 odd miles south of Bettles.) Also provides charter service for backpackers, float trips, etc. **Alaska Central Air:** International Airport; phone 907-452-4411. Serves Tanana-Yukon Valley regions. **Aurora:** International Airport; phone 907-452-5422. Serves local bush villages, the Brooks Range, Delta Junction, Northway, Tanacross, Tetlin, and Tok. **Frontier Flying Service:** 3820 University Ave., Fairbanks, AK 99701; phone 907-452-1014. Services Bettles, Anaktuvak Pass, and other points in the Brooks Range. Inquire at the Visitor Center for further air carriers.

Laundromats and Dry Cleaners

Busy Bee: 229 Third at Graehl (across from Gavora Mall); phone 907-452-1025. **Coin-King Laundromat:** 431 Gaffney; phone 907-452-6295. **Norge Village Laundry and Dry Cleaning:** 1255 Airport Way. Open 8:30 A.M. to

10 P.M. seven days a week; phone 907-456-4211. **Norlite Campgrounds:** 1660 Peger Road. Trailers, showers; phone 907-452-4206. **Royal Masters Cleaners:** 617 Gaffney; phone 907-452-2479.

Wilderness Guides

Arctic Treks: Write Carol Kasza and Jim Campbell, Box 73452, Fairbanks, AK 99707; phone 907-455-6502. Backpacking and rafting trips; also base camps. **Mountain Windflower:** Write Jim Kowalsky, SR Box 570704, Fairbanks, AK 99701; no phone. Personal guiding; backpacking; small groups. **Canoealaska:** Write 1738 Hilton, Fairbanks, AK 99701; phone 907-456-8198. River-running and small-boat outings. **Hal Dinkins:** Star Route Box 50584, Fairbanks, AK 99701; phone 907-488-2610. Canoe trips; flies his own aircraft; complete service. **Northern Alaska Environmental Center:** See below. **Jerry and Liz Stansel:** Backpacking in the Brooks Range. Write SR Box 20154-X, Fairbanks, AK 99701; phone 907-455-6012. **Dan L. Wetzel:** Natural history tours from Wiseman and Prudhoe Bay. Write Box 10224, Fairbanks, AK 99701. No phone. **Molly McCammon and Wilbur Mills:** Backpacking, river trips, and base camps in the Brooks Range, out of Ambler. Write Box 73534, Fairbanks, AK 99701. No phone. Write also: **Alaska Association of Mountaineering and Wilderness Guides,** Box 3685 DT, Anchorage, AK 99510; **Alaska Travel Adventures,** 499 Hamilton Avenue, Palo Alto, CA 94301. And *Worlds of Alaska* (see Bibliography). **Alaska Backcountry Guides Cooperative:** Write P.O. Box 81533, College, AK 99708; phone 907-456-8907. Independent Alaskan guides with "small is beautiful" philosophy; everything from easy hiking to ski trips to challenging mountaineering.

Some Useful Names and Addresses

Alaska State Department of Fish and Game, 1300 College Road, Fairbanks, AK 99701. **U.S. Fish and Wildlife,** 101 Twelfth Ave., Fairbanks; phone 907-452-1951 or 452-3234. **Alaska State Division of Parks,** 4420 Airport Way, Fairbanks, AK 99701; phone 907-479-4114. **BLM,** Box 1150, Fairbanks, AK 99701; phone 907-452-4725. (District Office is at 1028 Aurora Drive in Fort Wainwright.) **National Park Service,** 201 First Avenue, Fairbanks, AK 99701; phone 907-452-5241. Summer hours: 8 A.M. to 5 P.M. Monday through Friday, or write for information. **North Star Borough: Division of Parks and Recreation,** 520 Fifth Avenue, Fairbanks, AK 99701; phone 907-456-6683. **City of Fairbanks, Parks Office;** phone 907-456-2575; tourist information, 907-452-4529. **Visitor Center,** 550 First Avenue, Fairbanks, AK 99701. **Northern Alaska Environmental Center,** 218 Driveway, Fairbanks, AK 99701; phone 907-452-5021. Open 9 A.M. to 5 P.M. Monday through Friday. (Note: BLM is hard to get to. Phone for information before make the trip to Fort Wainwright.)

Alaska Topo Maps available over the counter only—no mail order—at 101 Twelfth Avenue, Room 26, Fairbanks, AK 99701.

DENALI NATIONAL PARK AND PRESERVE

In a land of superlatives, it is hard—especially for an observer who loves it all—to single out any one place or any one mountain as being "the very most." But anyone who has seen Mount McKinley in all its snow-shining glory—perhaps rose-colored in early dawn, or stained with blue evening shadows—will probably remember it forever as *The* Great One. Surely, any viewer will be grateful to see one of the grand sights of the planet, a mountain that rises higher than any other anywhere from the land at its feet to become the summit of a continent. As Charles Sheldon put it so simply after first seeing McKinley in July of 1906, "I can never forget my sensations at the sight. No description could convey any suggestion of it."

A few statistics, however, can help give a small idea of the impressiveness of this snowy mountain massif, which with its "foothills"—those over 10,000 feet, that is—occupies an area approximately seventy miles long and ten miles wide. Standing 20,320 feet above sea level, the peak of this massif is nearly four miles high. Since it rises from a fairly level elevation of a little over 2,000 feet, you see this magnificent mountain occupying some 18,000 feet—well over three miles—of sky. In contrast, Mount Everest, the tallest peak on earth, has its summit 29,028 feet above sea level, but it rises only 11,000 feet above the Tibetan Plateau.

What makes the McKinley group so high? Geologists explain that the rocks of the area are relatively lightweight (think of them as floating on the earth's mantle) and so are being shoved against one another and piled higher and higher as a result of the Pacific plate being pulled beneath the North American plate in this general region. Geologists add that there could also be another reason for this tremendous uplift: earthquakes and other evidence from local faulting suggest that the boundary of the Pacific plate, delineated by the Denali fault, makes an abrupt turn southward in the region of McKinley. This could serve to concentrate its thrust in a northwest direction. (A *Geologic Guide to Mount McKinley National Park* by Wyatt G. Gilbert is recommended reading. See Bibliography.)

The height of the mountain, however, is only one of a number of interesting geological features in Denali Park. The Denali fault system, which is in fact the largest crack in the crust of the North American continent, slices through the park, separating the oldest rocks in Alaska (roughly to the northwest) from

Mount McKinley: Denali National Park. *Source: Yvonne Mozée.*

the much younger rocks of the Alaska Range. Thus you can see there a great spectrum of Alaska's "recorded" geology.

The range, of course, acts as an enormous barrier between Southcentral and Interior Alaska, and while the Interior was largely ice free during the last periods of glaciation, a fine glacial system remains on the mountains around McKinley to remind you of how things once were over vast reaches of this countryside.

As though the sheer size and snowy splendor of the McKinley massif were not enough to bedazzle the viewer of this continental phenomenon, many of the older foothills that guard the giant are gorgeously colored. Some vistas look as though a great painter had created a giant mural using every shade of the rainbow—Polychrome Pass is aptly named. A flyover of the park reveals even more striking scenes, for glaciers make fascinating patterns as they actively sculpt this colorful land. Add to this a gentle looking green cloak of tundra above the tree line, which occurs here at about 2,700 feet. This high, dry tundra makes for delightful hiking, and you can find myriad flowering plants, including dwarf dogwood and tapestries of dryas stitching down the thin layer of soil. (In other parts of the park, the moist tundra has unfortunately clumped itself into the miserable kind of tussocky terrain that is very hard to hike over.)

This is taiga country, and the conifers—the ubiquitous white spruce and black spruce—grow most often in mixed stands with aspen, paper birch, and—in the wetter places—cottonwood. In the light summer breezes, the leaves of these deciduous trees turn and twinkle to catch the soft slanting light. Along the gravel streambeds cut by the fiercely flowing glacial rivers, the broadleaved trees can grow in pure stands, colonizing the new rough terrain and adding color to the autumn hues. Underfoot, the floors of the sparse forests are often tufted with mosses and lichens.

In this world of extraordinary terrain and frigid subarctic weather, some 37 species of mammals manage to survive, and the count of bird species that use Denali Park totals 130. As the National Park Service notes, cold-blooded reptiles and amphibians can hardly be expected to live happily here (or most other places in Alaska), but one—the wood frog—has succeeded in thriving despite the overwhelming odds against it.

The mountain we call McKinley was viewed in awe by untold generations of Athabascan Indians who named it Denali, the Great One, but it was first described to the Outside world by a prospector, William A. Dickey, in 1897. Dickey, who was a Princeton graduate, wrote an article for a New York newspaper describing what he correctly identified as the highest peak in North America: ". . . never before," he wrote, "had we seen anything to compare with this mountain." He christened it in honor of William McKinley, who would shortly be elected president of the United States. Five years later, Alfred Hulse Brooks helped survey and map Mount McKinley for the U. S. Geological Survey, and he is credited with being the first white man to venture onto its slopes. He didn't get too far, however, for he wrote that he was ". . . satisfied to have been able to traverse the great lowland to the base and to climb the foothills." It remained for four Fairbanks sourdoughs to make the first successful ascent of the mountain in 1910; two of their party reached the north (and, at 19,470 feet, the lower) summit, and there they planted the spruce flagpole they had hauled up with them. The flag fluttering from this pole was supposed to alert their friends in Fairbanks—120 miles away—that they had made it to the top. Three years later, the south summit was conquered and, since then, the mountain has been climbed perhaps too often if the litter left on its slopes is any indication. Early mountaineering parties often used dog teams to get their equipment partway up the giant mountain until the use of small ski-equipped aircraft became common. Now the parties that get routinely landed on the Ruth Glacier might consider what those first climbers went through; how they forded the glacial streams, which, in summer, can rise four or five feet in a matter of hours, made their way through thickets of brush, across tundra slopes, and onto the snow before they ever really started to climb. Tough folks, those early sourdoughs, who made it to the top in their old clothes, without oxygen, without freeze-dried food, without anything, really, but true grit.

Like many other Alaska places, Mount McKinley has had its special advocates, the first one being Charles Sheldon, who discovered this country soon after the turn of the century. An influential member of New York's Boone and Crockett Club, Sheldon spent several years studying the wildlife of the McKinley region and led in the effort to gain establishment of McKinley as a national park. The establishment of this park is one of the few in history that had the support of the mining community; since there was gold in the Kantishna Hills, to the northwest of the mountain, and a park road would provide ready access to the precious metal, the sourdoughs joined the ranks of park proponents and helped win the park. (In return, mining was permitted inside the park until only recently.) The 90 mile road remains—providing ready access to a key section of the park. In February 1917, President Woodrow Wilson signed the act establishing the original 1,989,493-acre McKinley National Park. That act left out half the mountain massif as well as important wildlife terrain; in 1980, Congress enlarged the park by 2,426,000 acres, rechristened it Denali National Park, and created an adjacent 1,330,000-acre Denali National Preserve. (The total acreage of the new Denali parklands comes to 5,695,000.) Thus the name *Denali* took the place, at long last, of William McKinley, a president from Ohio who never lived to see the mountain. (To date, the Congress has not changed the name of the mountain itself.)

Some Useful Information About Denali

How to Get to Denali National Park
This is the most accessible unit of the national parks and preserves in Alaska. In summer, you can drive or bike to the eastern entrance of the park. From Anchorage (to the south), it is 240 miles and takes about six hours to drive. Fairbanks, about 120 miles away to the north, takes closer to three. The **Alaska Yukon Motor Coaches** (327 F Street, Anchorage, AK 99501; phone 907-276-1305) runs regularly between Anchorage, Denali National Park, and Fairbanks. There is also scheduled air service by small plane. (See section on Anchorage.) **Avis Rent-A-Car** has an office at the Denali Station Hotel. Note: To protect the wildlife and other wilderness values of the park, private vehicles are not to be driven beyond Savage River (Mile 12) on the park road unless they are going—by reservation only—to campsites. (See below.) Year round, the **Alaska Railroad** runs to the eastern park entrance from Fairbanks and Anchorage.

Where to Stay
There is a large concessionaire-operated hotel and restaurant facility with grocery store, service station, and so on at the eastern entrance to the park. After the old hotel building burned in the early 1970s, railroad cars from the Alaska Railroad were pressed into service to provide sleeping quarters, and they remain in use. (One of these is a **Youth Hostel**.) There are also newer buildings with plusher accommodations. Write ahead for reservations, as this facility is heavily used by organized tour groups: **Mt. McKinley Park Company**, Denali National Park, AK 99755.

One of Alaska's unique wilderness camps, once outside the park boundaries, is now an inholding in the expanded parklands. This is Camp Denali. If you can afford a stay here, this is one of the finest places to go for your first (or fiftieth) visit to Alaska. You will find good food, and charming and comfortable accommodations, which are, however, "rustic" as the BLM says, meaning no electricity; there is running stream water for washing. The Camp Denali bus meets the train on Mondays, Wednesdays, and Fridays from early June to early September, so you have your own wildlife viewing tours en route to and from the facilities. Wally and Jerri Cole make a wonderful host and hostess; they stress the values of the wilderness and offer an interpretive visit that will, almost certainly, give you an unforgettable experience. When the mountain is "out," the view from Camp Denali is superb. Be sure to write ahead for reservations, as this is one of Alaska's most popular wilderness lodges. Address: Wally Cole, **Camp Denali**, P.O. Box 67, Denali National Park, AK 99755. Phone (winter) 907-683-2302; (summer) 683-2290.

There are also a half dozen National Park Service campgrounds located along the park road as follows: **Riley Creek:** at the eastern entrance to the park (large); **Savage River:** at Mile 12 on the Park Road (large); **Sanctuary River:** at Mile 22 (small); **Teklanika River:** at Mile 28 (large); **Igloo Creek:** at Mile 33 (small); **Wonder Lake:** at Mile 85, tent camping only. Inquire about fees.

The National Park Service runs a free, scheduled shuttle bus service to these campgrounds and to other points of interest along the park road. As stated, private vehicles may travel the park road beyond Savage River only for campground access to reserved campsites. Beyond reserved campsites, you must take the shuttle bus.

Backpackers will find many wonderful places to pitch their tents in the wilder regions of this great park. The shuttle bus will drop you at the place of your choice and stop to pick you up along the road when flagged. Discuss with park rangers the kind of itinerary you may want to follow.

What to Do in Mount Denali

Denali Park offers some of the finest—and most available—opportunities for wildlife viewing in Alaska. The concessionaire runs a tour bus that travels to Eielson Visitor Center (Mile 65 on the Park Road) every day, starting very early, from late spring to early fall. (You get a box lunch for the price of the tour.) The National Park Service shuttle (which is not so plush) regularly travels the Park Road all the way to Wonder Lake. (Bring your own lunch for this one.) Seated in either of these vehicles on a routine early morning foray, you can expect to see creatures such as Dall sheep, their delicate creamy silhouettes delineated clearly against the dark foothills of the Alaska Range. You may pass by a grizzly sow with her cub, munching away on berries and unmindful of your presence. Caribou may lift their elegant racks from the green brush or tundra or trot across the uneven ground for you with their heads held high. (I was once traveling in a shuttle bus along the park road when we overtook a caribou jogging down the middle of the road. The animal kept ahead of us for several minutes, and several hundred yards, with every-body aboard madly snapping pictures of its rear end, before he figured out what the monster was behind him. I have also seen a wolf race across the park road—dark, sleek, and strong—the epitome of wildness.) And, finally, the little ground squirrels will almost certainly charm you as they sit up perkily in front of their burrows, ready for their instant disappearing act.

If you stop to snack at Polychrome Pass or go on to Eielson Visitor Center to lunch, a mew gull may try for a share of your food. It could even be a bird that you've seen before, close to your home—if you live along the Pacific flyway, that is. You may also hope to see a long-tailed jaeger, which winters in Japan; a golden plover, which prefers Hawaii; an arctic tern, which may commute from Antarctica; or a wheatear or arctic warbler, which will take to the air for Asia when the weather begins to turn cold.

Keep in mind, however, that—as one longtime lover and frequent visitor to the park once told a disappointed tourist—"This ain't no zoo." You could be lucky and see just about all the birds and animals mentioned above, and more, on a single morning's outing, but you might only get a glimpse of one or two.

The same, of course, goes for the mountain. If it's "out" the day you set aside to view it, count yourself fortunate indeed; you will see an unforgettable sight. If it's cloud-shrouded, enjoy the rest of the scene (which is gorgeous, no matter what the weather) and try again some other time for your revelation of the Great One.

Denali National Park, Alaska 99755, or phone 907-248-2489, 683-2496, or 456-1851. Backcountry Guides Coop (see Fairbanks, Useful Information) offers a variety of trips in the park backcountry.

and find good going most of the way. You can also take day-hikes, utilizing the shuttle bus for your transportation. Park rangers can give you a good idea of how to work out the kind of foot travel you have in mind to your best advantage.

The rivers in Denali Park are frequently shallow, heavily braided, and very fast flowing glacial streams—not suitable for pleasant river-running. There is, however, a commercially operated raft trip that you can take down the Nenana River for a short run from the park. Write: **Alaska Raft Adventures,** Box 66, Denali National Park, Alaska 99755, or phone 907-248-2489, 683-2496, or 456-1851. **Alaska Backcountry Guides Coop,** Box 44, Denali National Park, AK 99755, offers a variety of trips in the park backcountry.

Comments

For many years, park lovers fought to keep the commercialism of this national park to a minimum: they managed to stop the building of a hotel on the fragile tundra near Wonder Lake (where sewage alone would have posed an unbelievably complex problem), and they managed to gain expansion of the park to preserve some of its principal wildlife and scenic values. As of this writing, however, the legislation that enlarged the park and added the Denali Preserve is subject to interpretation, which may mean far less protection for the terrain and the wildlife than was formerly in effect for the smaller original park. Snowmobiles and sports hunting both pose threats to wildlife, which is being increasingly pressured outside of this sanctuary. I once stayed at Camp Denali just outside the border of the then McKinley Park and heard the first shots of hunters as the hunting season opened. My hostesses swore that the animals knew where the boundary was and that they moved into the park at this announcement of impending doom.

For further information about Denali Park and/or to register for campsites, write: Superintendent, **Denali National Park**, P.O. Box 9, Denali Park, AK 99755; phone 907-443-2522. See also Parks and Forests Information Center in Anchorage.

The late Adolph Murie, another man who gave so much of his life, intellect, and devotion to the Denali wilderness and wildlife, summed up some of the essence of this area and its incalculable value.

> The grizzly has survived in only a few states, more by accident than by our planning for his future. In Alaska we have a great opportunity for giving the grizzly and the rest of the fauna ample room for carrying on their living in a natural, free manner. The grizzly needs extensive wilderness country for his way of life, and wild country is also vital for the highest development of human culture. If we provide for the future of the grizzly, we at the same time provide wilderness for our own needs.

YUKON-CHARLEY RIVERS NATIONAL PRESERVE

The Yukon is one of the great rivers of the North American continent. Gathering its waters all the way from Southeast Alaska to north of the Arctic Circle, it drains approximately 330,000 square miles, an area almost as large as France and Poland combined. It travels 2,300 miles from its headwaters in Canada to its rich delta on the Bering Sea. Only four rivers in the world have a greater capacity—the Amazon, Mississippi, Missouri, and Saint Lawrence. In some places it is almost twenty miles wide.

Far more than the Arctic Circle, which is, after all, a line on the map, the Yukon physically delineates the northern province of Alaska from the southern. While it has been a barrier in some respects (the only successful bridge to span it is the one built in the mid 1970s for the TAP haul road), the Yukon and its tributaries formed Alaska's earliest transportation network, providing access for people since they first came into this part of the world. From the sea to the Interior and beyond, the river led. In winter, frozen solid, it was easy to travel (and still is, especially by snowmobile); and in the summer, the river was a challenge to the boat builders of their time. (Although motorboats still chug their way up and down the Yukon, it seems a pity that the fine old fabled stern-wheelers no longer do.)

The Yukon is full of history, of course, and archeologists continue to find evidence of people who camped along its course or one of its tributaries many thousands of years ago. The trapping and trading of the late nineteenth century and the great gold rush at the turn of that century, however, probably brought the river its most colorful times. Then the shallow-draft stern-wheelers came more and more to crowd out the canoes and other small river craft, steaming up and down the silty waters that formed the principal highway system to the gold fields. (Among those who tried to make their way up the length of this broad brown powerful stream to its gold-filled tributaries was the mayor of Seattle, who, in 1898, organized a party of fellow citizens for a municipal gold hunt. Alas, they never made it and had to sail back home empty handed.) Before the rush was over, settlements of one kind or another dotted the riverbanks here and there from Whitehorse to Saint Michael. Roadhouses, trading posts (the Hudson's Bay Company and Alaska Commercial Company among them), and small towns burgeoned, boomed, and then most of them went ghost. Two in Alaska, Eagle and Circle, managed to survive, relics of those heady bawdy days when all in this northern land that mattered was gold—and the mood of the mighty river.

Between Eagle, the first incorporated city of the Interior, and Circle, once known as the "Paris of the North," roll some 160 miles of the Yukon. Here the river passes between colorful bluffs and palisades while dark blue cloud shadows move across the more distant mountains. (This is ancient land; in places, the rocks tell the story of the earth since pre-Cambrian times.) Now and then the waters part to embrace a forested island. Raptors ride the thermals above the tundra-clothed hills. In summer, thunderstorms can race up the river, whipping the waters into high waves and sending spindrift into the suddenly cool air. Midway in this particular section of the Yukon, the Charley River pours out its green crystalline waters to be lost in the muddy flow.

The watershed of the Charley drains portions of the Yukon-Tanana uplands that are too far inland to gather enough snow for glaciers to form: hence, the lovely clarity of the Charley's waters, which in early summer, dance into white rapids along their 88 mile course. The Charley watershed is a region that largely escaped the hordes of gold seekers, protected in part by those rapids and the mountains that cradle the river, but more by the fact that this area had little of the precious metal to offer. (One of its lower tributaries, Bonanza Creek, was obviously better endowed.) Thus this watershed has remained

Charley River, Yukon-Charley Rivers National Preserve. Source: National Park Service.

rarely undisturbed and pristine, with only a trapper's cabin here and there within its limits and a primitive landing strip at its headwaters. Caribou roam its hills, Dall sheep clamber up and down the precipitous cliffs through which the river cuts in places, and this is a place of refuge for the endangered peregrine falcon. The banks along its lower course also contain a fine show of ice lenses in the permafrost—which underlies this entire region.

The 1,713,000 acre Yukon-Charley Rivers National Preserve embraces the watershed of the Charley and takes in about 140 miles of the Yukon River and a portion of the land through which it flows. To the east, it is bounded by the Canadian border and has as its gateway the town of Eagle. Downstream, little Circle City, which once had a library, a hospital, and an opera house, lies a few miles outside the boundary of the preserve, making another point of entry or, if you will, a convenient point of exit.

This unusual unit of the National Park Service offers a variety of experiences to the Alaskan adventurer. Since both Eagle and Circle are accessible by road, it is possible to arrange a trip down (or up) the Yukon to enjoy its scenery, history, wildlife and wilderness qualities, and to get a feel for its incredible riverine power. Reached by the Taylor Highway (which ties into the AlCan Highway and thence into Fairbanks), Eagle is a fascinating historical town. Around the turn of the century, it was booming as the trading center for the mining area around it, and was as well the port of entry for Canada. It was here that Judge James Wickersham headquartered his first judicial system and had Alaska's first courthouse and jail constructed. The U. S. Army established Fort Egbert adjacent to Eagle in 1899 and for the next few years directed a major undertaking to tie it into the rest of the world via the WAMCATS (Washington Alaska Military Cable and Telegraph System). It took Lieutenant Billy Mitchell (later of World War I aviation fame) to get the line strung successfully from Valdez, but by the time WAMCATS was in good working order, the wireless was coming into increasing use, and the need for military maintenance of the old system diminished. Fort Egbert was closed down by the U. S. Army in 1911. Meantime, Wickersham had moved the seat of his judicial operations to Fairbanks. Eagle never recovered its former prestige.

Fortunately, in recent years Eagle has been given tender care by some of its citizens and the BLM (which has proposed it for historical landmark status). Restoration of historical sites and buildings has gotten under way, and residents of Eagle now conduct walking tours in the summer to show off interesting parts of the town and what remains of Fort Egbert. Nearby Eagle Village belongs to Han Indians, descendants of the earlier settlers on this picturesque bank of the river. There is good camping at Eagle, with pure spring water nearby (a point worth mentioning along the Yukon), and a place to bathe or swim in Mission Creek. And while, as the National Park Service people put it, facilites such as restaurants and lodges "open and close without ceremony," you can always get food at one of the stores.

In Circle, which is accessible by the Steese Highway, you'll find yourself on your own to explore the old buildings and relics of times gone by. There are, however, a restaurant, a lodge (with showers), a bar, and a camping and picnic ground on the banks of the Yukon. The Steese Highway, incidentally, offers a number of good hikes and/or small-boat trips along its length. (See section on Fairbanks.) And you can stop off for a good soak in the pool at Circle Hot Springs.

At Eagle, you can charter a powerboat, a guide, and camping gear for a trip on the Yukon. Circle has air charter service. Inquire at Beaver Sports in Fairbanks if you want to rent canoe service for a trip from Eagle to Circle.

The gentle, tundra-covered domes in the Yukon-Charley Preserve and along the Taylor Highway provide excellent cross-country hiking and, in early summer, fine birding. Around the first of September, the tundra plants begin to turn, and the bearberry, dwarf birch, and blueberry make a kaleidoscope of colors as brilliant as the broad-leafed trees of New England.

The Charley River offers a fine wilderness experience. It demands, in return, that you be well equipped, know what you're doing in a canoe or kayak, and that you respect its unusual wild values. Keep in mind that this river country is the home territory of an endangered species, the peregrine falcon, and, despite its almost gentle character in the summer, it is fragile terrain. Also note that fishing is undependable. For details about this river, write the National Park Service, Box 64, Eagle, Alaska 99738; no phone.

Air Charters: Tatonduk Flying Service, Box 55, Eagle, AK 99738.

ARCTIC NATIONAL WILDLIFE REFUGE

One of the best interpretive guides to any part of Alaska is the leaflet put out by the U.S. Fish and Wildlife Service on its Arctic National Wildlife Refuge. (You can write for this to the Refuge Manager, Arctic National Wildlife Refuge, 101 Twelfth Avenue, Fairbanks, AK 99701.) This leaflet will give you all the detailed, practical information you will need to visit this beautiful, fragile, significant piece of Arctic wilderness. More importantly, it will help you to understand, enjoy, and protect some of the Wildlife Refuge's extraordinary values. Here are a few of the things it says.

On Wildlife Viewing

On the south side of the Wildlife Refuge the warm summer days bring cumulus clouds, often followed by afternoon rain showers. Many species of wildlife are least active during this time of day when conditions may also be less favorable for pleasant hiking. Hiking conditions and opportunities for wildlife observation are usually best from evening until about noon the next day. The standard calendar day is an artificial designation unsuited to the north. Ignore it, live with the land, enjoy the spontaneity of the wilds.

To aid in seeing wildlife, route your hikes over low hills and other vantage points. Examine the land carefully with binoculars. Look around near you. Don't overlook small creatures such as shrews, voles, lemmings, and insects (other than mosquitoes). When looking for wildlife, wait quietly and move slowly. Animals watching you will be less alarmed. The quiet is important—your experience is more environmental than social, you can talk later.

On Camping

Camping is permitted throughout the Refuge. You will find no artificial trails, trail signs, or campgrounds. With foresight, knowledge, and self-reliance, you'll not need or want them. Camp where you will not disturb wildlife. Camp should be moved every day, at least a few hundred yards, to minimize trampling vegetation and soil. Leave your campsite in a natural condition; leave no trace of your presence. Pack out all containers, film wrappers, etc.—they cannot be disposed of properly in the Wildlife Range. Part of your experience is escaping a littered environment.

On Having a Total Experience

Be alert for signs of ancient camps and trees cut with stone axes. Leave them undisturbed for others to see. It does no harm to wonder: "Who camped here, what route did they travel, and what story of the trail did they tell?"

Hearing improves with practice. The distant call of the loon, the fall of a mountain stone, and the falcon's cry are the experiences of a silent background. Seek a place out of the wind and away from the stream's rush, and wait patiently. Let in the northern mystique.

Along with such sensitive advice, which can only come from one who loves and knows this country well, the leaflet also tells how to get to the Refuge and where to get proper USGS maps. It lists air charter services in the gateway areas, overviews canoeing and kayaking possibilities (see below also), gives tips on hiking, stream crossing, route planning, and what equipment and supplies you will need (including an alcohol or gas stove because "wood grows slowly in the north; the centuries' accumulation of dead wood will not last long"). There is also a charming description of the rhythms of the Arctic seasons.

But you should think twice before visiting the Arctic National Wildlife Refuge—and not only because this is Arctic country, which can give you a very cold if compelling experience to remember. This is also a fragile region and highly sensitive area for the Porcupine Caribou Herd that uses the north slope of the Range in its migratory travels for food. The future of these great animals—and the others protected in the range—depends upon how far the animals are pressed not only by the destruction and commercial development of their habitat, but also by the presence of people. The Refuge has been under increasing pressures from recreationalists as well as developers.

When I ran the Canning River—one of the range's loveliest streams—in July 1976, there were few days one or more helicopters did not beat through the skies en route to drill sites just outside the then-boundaries of the Refuge. Now that the entire (enlarged) area has been opened by Congress to exploration for its mineral potentials, developmental pressures are inevitably increasing.

When I ran the Kongakut River a year later, the U.S. Fish and Wildlife Service asked our party and all other parties visiting the area that summer— there were dozens of them—to fill out a questionaire about our reasons for visiting the Arctic Wildlife Refuge, our experiences, observations, and so on. This reflected an awareness on the part of the Fish and Wildlife Service that a great many people were beginning to use the area for recreational purposes, and it laid the groundwork for limiting the number of recreational users of the range. To date, such limitation has not been imposed, but it still may

Dall Sheep (Ovis dalli dalli).
Range: Alaska's high mountains, except in Southeast.

need to be. Should such be the case, you can understand that there are good reasons for limitations, accept them, and appreciate this agency's concern with protecting a magnificent wilderness and its wildlife.

If you do visit the Arctic Wildlife Refuge, there are a few more things to keep in mind. Running a river is a wonderful way to experience an area, and it can be the least damaging to the terrain and its wildlife. The north-flowing rivers of the range can give you a true Arctic experience—in every sense of the word, including an encounter with Arctic weather, which is temperamental and totally unpredictable. When I ran the Kongakut in early July, it had been so cold—and it continued to be—that the river was perilously low from lack of runoff. In fact, I have personally never been so cold in the wilderness as I was on one of those Arctic July days. The south-flowing rivers travel through country that will likely be warmer, and it is also gentled by trees, if not by its immense magnificent scenery. In June and July, however, the mosquitoes are out by the millions. "If you're going to enjoy the wilds,

don't let mosquitoes or anything else dictate [the] time [of your visit]," says
the Fish and Wildlife leaflet.

Entering the Arctic Wildlife Refuge from Barter Island (Kaktovik) may give
you an unexpected and memorable Alaska experience; you may have to wait
days to be flown to your destination because of the weather, and there may
be a dozen or more people waiting ahead of you. Kaktovik is small; there are
no tourist or camping facilities; there is no running water except in the school,
which will probably be locked, and in the DEW-line station, where they
probably won't let you in. After you've photographed the Arctic Ocean, the
whalebones left on the beach by the local hunters, and the polar bear skins
stretched to dry on racks here and there around the village, there isn't an
awful lot to do. Be sure to bring a couple of good paperbacks along.

Despite the fact that the wildlife range is a sensitively administered, protected wildlife area, there is no guarantee that you will see the wildlife you
set out to view. On our trip down the Kongakut we encountered members
of a film crew that had been waiting for weeks for the caribou to cross the
river. When we left, the caribou still had not budged from their place on the
North Slope. Neither the caribou, nor any wild animal, runs on strict schedule.

However, as the Fish and Wildlife leaflet points out, a visit to the Arctic
Wildlife Refuge can give you another kind of experience. It may help you
to " . . . be aware of self-change, maintain a high level of keenness, promote
spontaneity, be self-aware, have patience and make demands on yourself—
not on the land." It can also make you even more grateful that we as a people
have had the wisdom to set aside, and give at least some protection to, such
a priceless national wilderness treasure.

Air Charters: Audi Enterprises, Box 40, Kaktovik, AK 99747; Arctic Circle
Air Service, Box 109, Fort Yukon, AK 99740; phone 907-662-2320. See also
Fairbanks.

GATES OF THE ARCTIC

The 7,052,000-acre Gates of the Arctic National Park and the contiguous
900,000-acre Gates of the Arctic National Preserve embrace the heartland of
the Brooks Range, including the Endicott Mountains to the east and the
Schwatka Mountains to the southwest. Between these two ranges soar the

Chandler Lake Area, Gates of the Arctic National Park. Source: National Park Service.

Arregitch peaks, a fantastic array of fiercely steep, slick and smooth-faced granitic spires—an alpinist's dream. (*Arregitch* is an Eskimo word meaning "fingers of a hand outstretched," as though the earth here were literally reaching up to touch the skies.) To the north, the parklands also include a small portion of the strangely lovely Arctic foothills with their pale green tundra and layers of sediments stacked nearly on end. Within the parklands are some magical lakes—Chandler, Walker, and Takahula among them. And among the most outstanding features of this reserve, of course, are Mount Boreal and Frigid Crags, the two splendid alpine guards that flank the North Fork of the Koyukuk River. These landmark mountains were named "The Gates of the Arctic" by Robert Marshall because they open the way to a more or less unobstructed path northward to the polar region itself.

The Gates of the Arctic National Park and Preserve encompass territory that was used traditionally by Eskimos who have roamed the passes here in pursuit of caribou and other wildlife for untold centuries. (Among their legends are tales of their vanquishing another people, Kutchin Indians, from this same territory, and archeological explorations indicate human occupancy, of one kind or another, in parts of this region that may date back 16,000 years.) These national park units were established with a keen awareness of the cultural importance of these lands to the Eskimos and with their participation in many decisions. The Nunamiut village of Anaktuvuk Pass lies within the boundaries of the parkland as do certain lands selected by the Native corporation of this village and by the Arctic Slope Regional Corporation. (The Eskimo word *anaktuvuk* means "place of caribou droppings.") The park legislation allows for the continuance of traditional hunting practices and other subsistence uses of the land. With an area of this size under park protection, it may be that the animal and plant resources will continue to flourish and that the subsistence way of life may survive.

This is no easy environment for people or animals to live in—despite its overwhelming beauty. The climate is demanding, veering from continental zone extremes south of the continental divide, which snakes through the Brooks Range, to the fierce winds and icy temperatures of the Arctic zone to the north. The terrain is, in many places, difficult, and tussock tundra—often composed of big tufts of slippery cotton grass—makes hiking in poorly drained areas a drudgery. ("Tussock walking can be about the most difficult type of

Mount Igigpak. *Source: National Park Service.*

arctic hiking," Dr. James Greenough, an ardent Alaskan explorer and out-doorsman wrote. "For every step onto the top of a tussock—a spongy mass of organic matter too wobbly to stand on but too firm to ignore—there is another step down into the narrow, boot-clutching crevasse that surrounds it.") In the more alpine country, it should be added, the tundra is often matlike and makes for fine traveling. Tree line occurs almost precisely along the continental divide and, while on the south of the divide you may see stands of white spruce fingering the canyons and black spruce leaning tipsily in wet and lichen-tapestried meadows, to the north of the divide, the conifers disappear. Only cottonwoods, among the trees, can make it in any number in this inhospitable region, and then only in a few selected places. (It comes as a great surprise, traveling in this country, to find a forest of cottonwood as one does at places like the Shublik Hot Springs, or to find a lone and scraggly spruce prostrate in the tundra struggling to survive.) The willows, however, can attain heights of twenty to twenty-five feet and diameters of five or six inches.

Where there are willows in Alaska, there are likely to be moose—a truism that is proved again in the Gates of the Arctic parklands. (Moose, incidentally, comprise the largest percentage of biomass in Alaska.) You may encounter these great beasts along the waterways and marshes and around the lakes. And you may see other familiar Alaskan mammals in this parkland. One of the largest populations of Dall sheep in the state inhabits the high windy ridges of this region. (The wind, which can chill you to your very core, doesn't bother these hardy creatures, and it performs the important function of keeping the ground swept clean of snow, thus allowing year-round forage.) There are black bears here and grizzlies, although the number of grizzlies is kept in limits naturally by the eating requirement of these huge animals; a single grizzly must have as much as 100 square miles in this spare habitat to support itself. A community of wolves must have an equally large range to keep going here. Of course, a major portion of the wolves' subsistence—and that of the people here as well—is furnished by the crowds of caribou that mill through the mountain passes here following in the footsteps of their ancestors.

These Arctic parklands, the Gates of the Arctic Park and Preserve, offer beauty and wildness on, literally, an overwhelming scale. They offer the chance to observe the alpine Arctic wilderness in all its moods. They offer challenging mountaineering, excellent backpacking, and fine river-running. But in turn, they require good physical condition, a pair of sturdy legs (if you're traveling on foot), good protective equipment, a willingness to put up with insects (the worst mosquitoes I have ever encountered in Alaska were on the Alatna River following a rain), and the ability to get along reasonably happily in poor weather, perhaps while waiting an indeterminate length of time for your air taxi pickup. They also require a thoughtful approach on the part of the wilderness traveler: this Arctic wilderness, for all its ruggedness, is extraordinarily delicate. The nest you trample on so carelessly along the shore of Takahula Lake contains a new generation of yellow-legs; the tundra you

Arregitch Peaks, Gates of the Arctic National Park. Source: National Park Service.

trample or lay bare for your fire can take years to recover, if it ever does; the wood you scrounge could take decades to be replaced. The Arctic is an area to visit with wonder but also with special respect.

The immediate entryway to the Gates of the Arctic Park and Preserve is Bettles, a small settlement that has an FAA station and a well-developed airstrip just outside the southeast corner of the parkland. Bettles has two general stores with the basics, and a canoe rental. It also has a two-story lodge, which, when I first stayed in it, had a slightly drunken appearance and a wavy floor, both of which announced its location directly on the permafrost. A few years ago, however, the building was straightened up and face-lifted, and it now appears much more staid and solid. If you don't want to spend the night at the lodge, you can get a meal there and, when I last ate there, the portions were generous and the food was good, if simple.

You can buy freeze-dried food (and almost everything else) at the Bettles Trading Post. Canoe rentals and guided trips are run by Sourdough Outfitters, Bettles, AK 99726; phone 907-692-5252. There is also a National Park Service field office in Bettles: write c/o Bettles, AK 99726; phone 907-692-5494. Wien Air Alaska and Frontier Flying Service both provide scheduled air service to Bettles.

You can fly to Bettles commercially from Fairbanks. There is also commercial air service to the village of Anaktuvuk but, as of this writing, there are no accommodations. (You should write ahead if you wish to stay in Anaktuvuk.) Remember that the general stores in villages like Anaktuvuk are hard pressed to supply the local villagers; do not expect to pick up your supplies so far afield. And do not be surprised to find a high school with a swimming pool at Anaktuvuk: the Arctic Slope Regional Corporation is responsible for this educational amenity.

Although there are no developed National Park Service facilities in the Gates of the Arctic parklands, there are many fine places to camp. A good way to pay your first visit to these Arctic parklands is to be flown into a lake for a week or two and then picked up, or you may want to run one of the rivers. (The Alatna, John, and the North Fork of the Koyukuk all offer wonderful wilderness river experiences. All are accessible by air taxi from Bettles. All are administered by the NPS.) As noted, there are also superb rock-climbing and mountain-climbing challenges.

Many guide services are available for this region of Alaska and so are many outfitters. Refer to those listed under Fairbanks and, for further references and information, write the National Park Service, Box 74680, Fairbanks, AK 99707.

NOATAK NATIONAL PRESERVE

The Noatak River rises in the granite heart of the Brooks Range, its headwaters draining part of Mount Igikpak, which, at over 8,500 feet, towers above most of its neighboring mountains. (A flyby of Mount Igikpak can be a stunning experience; its upper slopes are breathtakingly perpendicular and sheathed with snow that has been pleated by avalanches into marvelous vertical patterns.) From this high dramatic mountain world, the Noatak travels more than 425 miles to empty into Kotzebue Sound. Most of its course is due westward, but the last 100 miles or so it bears abruptly to the south. For much of the way, the Noatak cleaves two beautiful mountain ranges, the Baird Mountains to the south and the De Longs to the north. These ranges swing close to form spectacular canyons above the river and then curve gracefully apart to cradle its huge river basin.

Although born of snowfields and glaciers, the Noatak gathers the clear waters of many rivers along its pathway and is itself generally clear, dark bottle green, and smooth flowing, a class II river. In good weather, its rapids froth with only medium-sized standing waves, and, when the weather is hot and dry, you may have to avoid rocks and very shallow places. But let a summer storm come up, and—as with all Arctic rivers—the character of the river can change radically. The clear waters can rise, and become thick with silt in a matter of hours. In the resultant flash flood, the rapids can well up to offer some challenging runs to a canoer or kayaker. In the lower reaches where the current slows down, upriver winds can be—and frequently are—quite literally a drag.

The Noatak is not all that large when compared to, say, the Yukon, but its substantial length makes it one of the most interesting of Alaska's Arctic rivers to run. From its source to its mouth, it travels through a fine spectrum of Arctic scenery, and if you do some exploring in the countryside along the way, you can become familiar with several different Arctic environments. The Noatak will also carry you—without too much effort on your part—through some of the magnificent wilderness regions of the north.

The great basin of the Noatak is particularly rich with wildlife and birds, as well as being almost overwhelming in its sense of size and space. This is the part of the river that has been set aside by Congress in a 6,460,000-acre National Preserve. If you float this part of the river, you may have an unforgettable avian show. Horned grebes, long-tailed and parasitic jaegers, arctic loons, common loons, arctic terns, a variety of ducks—these are only a few of the many species that come in from all over the world to breed here. High above you a gyrfalcon or an owl may circle, or you may see a rough-legged hawk or a golden eagle where the river enters its own "Grand Canyon." You will also have a good chance on this run to see the great mammals like the grizzly and the moose.

If you have the time to travel the entire length of the Noatak in a leisurely way, taking, say, a month or more—a fabulous experience according to those who have done it—you will have many unique opportunities. You will have a chance to climb a pingo (50 feet high), which will give you a fine view of Mount Igikpak. The forked summit of this mountain prompted its Eskimo name, which means "two great peaks." You can explore Portage Pass, used by prehistoric peoples as well as by early white explorers of this region. You may be piped along your way by lesser yellowlegs, see Dall sheep, red fox, wolves, and caribou as well as moose and grizzlies. As you drift below the

Grand Canyon of the Noatak, you can take a stroll through the Poktovik Mountains and/or the Igichuk Hills. And should you run this river late in August, you may have a memorable show of autumn colors, made especially intense by the backdrop of the pale Baird Mountains. You can, in fact, spend a summer on this river highway, or you can plan a put-in and a take-out for only a week. The National Park Service can give you further details. Consult them in Kotzebue, or in Anchorage.

Air Charters: Brooks Range Aviation, Inc., Bettles Field, AK 99726; phone 907-692-5444/5333.

KOTZEBUE

Since passage of the Alaska Native Claims Settlement Act (ANCSA), Kotzebue has been growing rapidly and is assuming its place as the business and tourist center of northwest Alaska. (Ten years ago, it was more properly a village than a town.) The Northwest Alaska Native Association (NANA), the local Native Regional Corporation, is interested in tourism and is behind the development of quite elaborate and interesting tourist attractions in Kotzebue. The Nuk-luk-vik Hotel, built by NANA, is the most comfortable, and the most expensive, hotel in town.

Kotzebue has no public campgrounds and there is no Youth Hostel as of this writing. It is also not very hospitable terrain when it comes to rolling out a bag; the beach is narrow and slanting, and there is private property to be respected. Plan accordingly—it's kind of all or nothing.

However, Kotzebue is worth spending some time in. Where else will you find a Dairy Queen north of the Arctic Circle? And where else can you watch the sun barely above the ocean, rolling along the horizon at midnight, pouring out a great flood of liquid red gold light across the water. The evening sea air becomes diffused with a luminescence that is almost tangible. The quality of this light earns a lot of money for film companies; photographers find it difficult to resist. One of Kotzebue's main streets, incidentally, runs right along the beach, and it seems as if everybody in town turns out along it on clear nights—and never goes to bed. You may do likewise.

Kotzebue also has a good natural history museum, in fact the most sophisticated in the state. This is another NANA enterprise. The museum has interesting dioramas, good specimens of large Arctic mammals, and descriptions of the Native subsistence uses of them. There are also a number of

Native artists in Kotzebue, and you might find prices for Native artwork lower here than in Anchorage.

Kotzebue is close—minutes by air—to several of the new units in the national park system. Here is where you make your charter arrangements to visit the Cape Krusenstern National Monument, Kobuk Valley National Park, and the Noatak National Preserve. You can also charter a floatplane here if you wish to run the Selawik River which is administered by the U.S. Fish and Wildlife Service. The Selawik is a long, low-lying, slow river, which winds through country that is rich in wildlife and birdlife (and mosquitoes). For information, contact the USF&W in Fairbanks. Write the village of Selawik, where you can use scheduled air service for your return, regarding your plans. You can also get information from the National Park Service, General Delivery, Kotzebue, AK 99752; phone 907-442-3890.

Air Charters: Aircraft Services, Box 741, Kotzebue, AK 99752; phone 907-442-3525. Baker Aviation, Box 116, Kotzebue, AK 99752; phone 907-442-3108/3209. Shellaberger Flying, Box 11, Kotzebue, AK 99752; phone 907-442-3281/3187. Walker Air Service, Box 57, Kotzebue, AK 99752; phone 907-442-3263.

KOBUK VALLEY NATIONAL PARK

When you hike the springy tundra of the hills above the Kobuk Valley or watch the pale green waters of the Kobuk River move sinuously westward, you can experience the same sense of timelessness that pervades the Bering Land Bridge Preserve. The Kobuk Valley, too, is an island of unglaciated Pleistocene landscape; and because of its particular soil, climatic, and geographic conditions, it remains remarkably like it was when wooly mammoths lumbered through it many millennia ago. Many of its present plants—grasses, sedges, and a single sagebrush, *Artemisia borealis*, are the same species as those that bent before icy Pleistocene winds. One charming legume, *Oxytropis kobukensis*, has survived from those long-ago times to grow only here in the world.

Although glacial barriers may once have encircled the ancient Kobuk Valley on three sides, the fourth side lay open periodically to the Bering Land Bridge (which, evidence indicates, was carpeted with the same forbs that still thrive in the valley). Thus, this was one of the gateways through which early people wandered, following the bison and mammoths and caribou, stepping unknowingly into what would one day be called the New World. There were many different early people who came this way, leaving the silent evidence of their presence in more than a dozen major archeological sites, including Onion Portage, which has been described as the most important "ever found in the Arctic." Along with Cape Krusenstern, Onion Portage (named for the wild chives that grow abundantly here) is used as a kind of archeological yardstick against which all other arctic sites are now measured; artifacts here have been dated as more than 10,000 years old.

The late J. Louis Giddings, the archeologist who discovered Onion Portage—and uncovered there some 30 layers of artifacts and evidence of at least seven different cultures—was responsible for a magnificent scientific contribution as well as a story that has become popular folklore. Giddings made his first visit to this region in the summer of 1940, rafting his way from the headwaters of the Kobuk toward Kotzebue Sound. As he proceeded downstream, his raft became waterlogged, and, by the time he encountered the first Eskimos along the riverbanks, the raft was barely clearing the surface of the water. As he stood waving his greetings, he appeared to the astonished eyes of the Eskimos to be walking down the river. When he proved, after all, to be only a mortal, he formed a fast friendship with the people of this region.

Along with being highly important in terms of its geological and cultural history, the Kobuk Valley is a region of great interest to botanists, and not only for its relict land bridge flora. Here the boreal forest reaches its most northwestern continental limit, but not in the abruptly drawn tree line that marks its boundary in the Brooks Range. Rather it intertwines delicately with the Arctic tundra; spruce and birch trees stand separately and alone in the lichen-carpeted meadows in a kind of lacy sparseness. This encounter between two major biomes—the tundra and the boreal forest—is one of precarious balance; responding to climatic changes, one or the other pushes forward. Thus in periods of warmth, the forest presses northward; when the climate is cold, the sturdy plants of the tundra invade the open forests and move to the south. This intermingling of forest and tundra is found more commonly in Siberia and Canada, but it is rare in Alaska.

Another interesting and unique feature of this region is the presence here of vast stretches of inland sand dunes. The Great Kobuk Sand Dunes and the Little Kobuk Sand Dunes each lie within hiking distance of the green Kobuk River, the former sprawling over 25 square miles of the land in a true and sizable desert. The temperatures here can crawl above 100 degrees in the summertime, and the air will bedazzle you with its heat. The great yellow dunes, some a hundred feet high, look as though they should be in the north of Africa rather than the northwest of Alaska. The result of wind-transported river sand, both sets of dunes have assumed the classical forms of waves and upended U shapes; they date back at least 33,000 years.

The wildlife in the Kobuk Valley is abundant and varied, and it includes a spectrum of mammals that ranges from the alpine Dall sheep, which skip along the ridges of the Baird Mountains, to migrating herds of caribou and riverine creatures like the beaver, muskrat, and moose, which occupy the watery lowlands. The rivers also carry abundant salmon and sheefish. The Asian flyway and the North American flyway conjoin in this valley so that dozens of birds—waterfowl, shorebirds, and songbirds—from many continents breed here too.

As it has for untold generations, the rich profusion of wildlife in the Kobuk Valley region provides subsistence for people today. The people of the Kobuk, Kuuvangmiit, have roots that go deep into prehistory, and they have adapted well to the demands of a north-of-the-Arctic-Circle climate, which can send the thermometer to 90 degrees in summer or to 60 degrees below zero in winter. As did their ancestors, the Kuuvangmiit hunt the caribou that follow their own ancient migratory patterns as they cross the Kobuk River at Onion Portage. And these people still travel the river to Kotzebue Sound and on to the Chukchi Sea to exchange their inland products—furs and the liver of mud sharks—for seal oil from the coastal dwellers.

Two principal villages of the Kuuvangmiit, Ambler and Kiana, lie outside the boundaries of the Kobuk National Park, and the parklands are open to these Natives and other Alaskans for subsistence use.

The Kobuk Valley National Park is 1,140,000 acres in size. Along with the diverse values outlined above, it contains in its northern section a sensitive region of the Baird Mountains where passes used historically by the caribou are now protected. It also contains several intact south-flowing Arctic watersheds as well as a beautiful section of the Kobuk River. One of its loveliest smaller rivers is the Salmon, which is a clear, brilliant aquamarine. Seen from the air, its waters make a stunning pattern as they braid through the pale landscape of the Baird Mountains. The Kobuk itself winds its serene way across the southern section of the park, which is bordered by the Waring Mountains.

The Kobuk Valley National Park, like other National Park Service units in the Arctic, is, and should remain, undeveloped wilderness. This means, of course, that there are no designated campsites, no trails, nor other facilities or services. The park offers fine spot-camping (you can be flown in from Kiana or Ambler), wonderful backpacking opportunities, and some excellent, if not challenging, river-running on the section of the Kobuk inside its borders. The Salmon is a joyous and fast-moving river in places and can be handled by any reasonably experienced kayaker. This is, of course, a place of great interest to archeologically or botanically minded people. June and July are likely to be the clearest months of the summer here; winter use is not advised.

Kotzebue, which lies about 75 miles to the west, is the principal gateway for the Kobuk Valley National Park and the location of the nearest National Park Service facilities. You can reach Kotzebue by daily scheduled air service out of Anchorage or Fairbanks. You can also fly commercially to Kiana and Ambler from Kotzebue, and you can charter from any of these three communities. You may also be able to charter boat service in Kiana and/or Ambler.

There is a lodge at Kiana and guide service available. If you wish to use the facilities of either village or to spend any time in them, you should write ahead and make arrangements. (See section on Visiting Native Villages.) You can backpack from either Ambler or Kiana into the park.

The subsistence use of the Kobuk Valley region is a vitally important part of the local life-style. It is wise to check with the National Park Service to avoid visiting this area when hunting and/or fishing use is at its height. You should check in with the NPS anyway, if you plan a trip here. Not only can they give you further information, but they would also like a copy of your proposed itinerary.

W. Mills and M. McCammon operate a guide service, Natmaktugaiq, out of Ambler. Write c/o Ambler, AK 99786. See also Fairbanks information.

Rivers

The Ambler is a small, very clear river which flows through spruce forest. It will take you from six to eight days to make an 80 mile run on it. Its upper section, the most scenic, has many small, class II rapids; the middle reach is braided; the lower is wide, single-channeled, shallow, and slow. The best hiking is in the upstream area. Access in is by wheel plane, and you can take out at Ambler, where there is a scheduled commercial air carrier, or you can continue on down the Kobuk River. For further information, contact the NPS. Also write the village of Ambler regarding your plans.

The Squirrel is a very small, extremely clear stream which tumbles slowly through the low, southwest foothills of the Baird Mountains. It makes for an excellent four or five day family float trip for relatively inexperienced small boaters. Fishing, particularly for grayling, is good. Access in is by wheel plane from Kotzebue or Kiana, and out from Kiana, which has scheduled commercial air service. Write NPS for further information. Write Kiana regarding air charter service and/or accommodations.

The small, brilliantly clear Salmon can be reached by wheel plane from Kotzebue or Kiana. You can spend from a few days to a week on this beautiful river which flows through alpine, tundra-covered country in the Baird Mountains. Its lower 25 miles cross the Kobuk lowlands. For further information, contact the NPS and the village of Kiana where you may wish to take out.

The Kobuk River can be run 125 miles from Walker Lake to the village of Kobuk. Rapids just below Walker Lake require a portage unless you're an expert small boater, and there are class II to IV rapids in the lower Kobuk Canyon. Otherwise, this is a class II river. Access in is by float plane to Walker Lake from Bettles or Kobuk. For further information, write the NPS and, if you plan to stop there, the village of Kobuk. It is possible to continue down the Kobuk to Kiana.

Air Charters: Ambler Air Service, Ambler, AK 99786; phone 907-445-2122.

CAPE KRUSENSTERN NATIONAL MONUMENT

The 560,000-acre Cape Krusenstern National Monument lies only ten miles northwest of Kotzebue at its closest point. This is an area that has been set aside for its cultural and archeological values more than for its stark but very real Arctic beauty. It is a coastal region where storm-shaped beach ridges have been building up the shoreline for close to 5,000 years. Each successive beach has left a ridge—there are 113 of them—and virtually every ridge contains relics of different human occupants. Thus, as you move inland, you travel neatly back in archeological time.

Archeologists digging in these ridges have identified artifacts from every known Eskimo culture in North America. The oldest (most inland) artifacts belonged to the Denbigh Flint people who lived around 2,300 years B.C. These first Eskimo hunters of seals and other sea mammals left few traces here beyond the beautiful and lethal microblades that they fashioned as arrowheads. Among those who followed the Denbigh hunters were the Old Whaling people (ridge 53) whose culture differed in many ways from their predecessors as well as their successors. Then there were the Choris (ridges 51–44) and Norton (ridges 44–36) cultures and, among the most intriguing of all, the Ipiutak people. The Ipiutaks left their tantalizing artifacts on beaches 35 through 29, and the period of their occupancy appears to have been from the time of Christ to 600 A.D. Skull figures with jet and ivory eyes, curiously fashioned ornaments, and elaborate etched pebbles all have intrigued and puzzled archeologists since their discovery (first, as it happens, at Point Hope not far to the north) in 1939. These artifacts suggest not only superb artisans but also a culture that included unusual burial practices and perhaps mystic rites of augury, as well as the skillful practice of seal hunting with finely made ivory harpoon points. Interestingly, the Ipiutaks left no shard of pottery; apparently that useful adjunct to living that was used in cultures before and after them was unknown to them.

The Eskimos who presently use the Cape Krusenstern coast in much the way their ancestors did are descendants of a people who first occupied this region 1,400 years ago. They followed the Western Thules, who dominated the entire Arctic coast for 800 years, moving across Alaska to settle as far away as Greenland. Today's Eskimos may see, in their own lifetimes, the beach they know and use overridden by wind-driven ice floes and the beginning of a new beach take shape.

The land of the Cape Krusenstern Monument includes low, rolling, and stark grayish-white hills that are fringed with yellow-green tundra. The slanting, changing light works magic on these hills, and you may find a rough-legged hawk perched on the crest of one, or a family of red foxes patrolling the slopes. In autumn, the skies here fill up with geese, and, if you're hiking inland, you may come upon musk oxen. There is also the flat coastal area in the monument where there are the many ponds and lagoons whose black waters may rest on some of the earlier beach ridges. All of this earth has been profoundly shaped by ice as well as by the sea, and the powerful winds that cut across it scythe it clean of most vegetation. (Any tent pitched here, by the way, is subject to a battering by those winds.) Still, the tundra plants—dwarf birch and willow, wild sour dock and many berries used by Eskimos today in their subsistence lifestyle—manage to cling to the soil and bind down the sea-transported sands and gravels.

If you have a grand scenic experience in mind, this is not an area to seek out, especially if your time in Alaska is limited. True, you can hike or backpack across the tundra-covered ridges, whale watch for the white belugas that shimmer by, or look at the myriad and interesting birds that summer here (the ponds and lagoons are among the most northern nesting sites of the Aleutian tern, and there are yellow wagtails that drop in from Siberia and jaegers here from Japan). If you're seriously interested in geology, you can also find in this new monument the only Illinoisian esker known to have survived in Alaska; it is an oblong mound some 225,000 years old.

This is country with other and profound values. It is still used by the Eskimo people for subsistence much as it was used by their ancestors. In summer, the big white canvas tents go up along the shore. Eskimo women skillfully make the sealskin pokes to be filled with the prized seal oil, so much a part of their traditional diet. Children run and laugh along the beaches. The spring hunt for seals on the frozen seas may be over, but the men have whales and fish to bring in. Later, the gathering of berries and herbs will get under way.

This is homeland to people who do not always welcome the small plane roaring over them and intruding on their beaches—with good reason. And there are as yet no guides to take you on a visit to this area where you will not intrude. (Your air charter pilot, however, might be able to help on this: see Kotzebue Air Charters.) If you decide you want to visit the Cape Krusenstern area, be sure to go over your plans at length with the National Park Service people. You can write ahead to Anchorage, or spend some time with the district ranger in Kotzebue before you venture into this very special place.

BERING LAND BRIDGE NATIONAL PRESERVE

Fire and ice together have helped to preserve some of the remarkable history of the 2,457,000 acres of the Bering Land Bridge National Preserve. This region was once a part of the wide pathway where the first hunters wandered to find, unknowingly, the North American continent. Now the permafrosted land holds intact the leaves and twigs of plants that grew those thousands of years ago; a beaver's dam constructed industriously in Pleistocene times, tiny insects, small mammals, and the remnants of larger mammals such as the woolly mammoth are here as well, preserved in near-perfect condition. Sealed beneath the outpourings of volcanic ash that have buried parts of this area, there are also samplings of whole vegetative systems that flourished millennia ago.

Those early people who came this way left few marks of themselves or clues to their cultures, although there are exciting traces of their presence sealed here into the ground, and there are well-based hopes that more will be found. Later peoples, however, left strange cairns, now thickly covered with moss and lichens, that stand against the pale northern sky. Why did they stack these flat slabs of volcanic rocks on the crests of low craters? Perhaps they were building beacons to give points of orientation in this relatively flat and seemingly featureless landscape; perhaps they were trying to funnel the many caribou that once filled this region (but do so no more) into traps where the animals could be easily taken; or perhaps these cairns had a deeper, religious significance. No one knows the answer, but these monuments are interesting reminders of people who knew this land long before we came to it.

There are significant volcanic features in several parts of the Bering Land Bridge National Preserve. The land bridge was still intact when volcanoes here last spewed out their lavas and ash to freeze in the near Arctic cold. (The Arctic Circle just tips the northern boundary of the preserve.) It must have been terrifying to the wanderers passing through to witness the massive flows of lava, one of which, the Imuruk, is the most northern flow of major scale in the United States. Even more frightening would have been the vast explosions that formed the beautiful clear maars—unusual volcanic lakes—which occur in pairs here, a great geological rarity.

There are many other lakes and lagoons and clear-water streams as well as low wet tundras, all prime avian habitat, which makes for spectacular bird life in the preserve. During the lengthening days of springtime, the skies fill up with birds coming in from all over the world—sandhill cranes, ducks, geese, swans, and shore birds by the thousands. In the brackish marshes, the air vibrates with the cries and movements of loons. Songbirds arrive as well, seeking the dry upper tundra for their homes. Of the 112 species of migratory birds that crowd the preserve each year, many come from Asia, Europe, and even Africa; thus it is possible to see here, routinely, numerous Old World birds. (A note of caution: Parts of the shores of many of the preserve's loveliest lakes are thick with the green droppings of geese.)

There are many mammals here as well, and you can hope to see grizzly, muskox, moose and, at certain times of the year, seals, walruses, and whales along the coast. You will also find a remarkably rich flora thriving in what might seem at first glance to be a barren land. There are almost 250 species of flowering plants that burst into bloom during the long summer days, splashing colors on the ground or hiding shyly for you to find them. In late August and early September, they paint the landscape in brilliant hues, just as they did when the first people came this way.

While this is obviously not a place to come for spectacular alpine or riverine

Muskox (Ovibus moschatus). Source: U.S. Fish and Wildlife Service.

scenery, there are several very special values here. In this gently rolling treeless land of lava and tundra, you can gain a true sense of timelessness. This terrain looks much as it did, it is believed, at the time those earliest people moved across it, perhaps in pursuit of one of the woolly mammoths whose ivory tusks lie frozen in the permafrost. If you are interested in birds and/or archeology and paleontology, this may be a part of Alaska that you will especially want to see.

A unique place, the Serpentine Hot Springs, lies on the southeast side of the preserve, and is accessible by air charter from either Nome or Kotzebue (it is about midway between the two towns). A friend of mine writes: "In addition to its body-soothing attractions, the hot spring has an unusually varied flora around it, and the area attracts distinctive birds. The surrounding hills look like castle battlements; gentle domes bristle with tall thin granite spires, or tors. At twilight, you may feel that you are in a haunted netherworld."

There are no accommodations in the Bering Land Bridge Preserve. Primitive campgrounds may be developed along some of the lakeshores in the future, but for now, if you come here, you will be on your own. You will need to be a good and well-equipped backpacker to enjoy this area, and there should be two or more in your party in what is a vast, remote part of the world. There is not much driftwood along the preserve's beaches and virtually none inland, so carry a stove. While Nome and Kotzebue (the gateways to the preserve) both have reasonably well-stocked stores, supplying backpackers is not a priority, and you should bring your own freeze-dried food and any other special items you'll need.

The climate of the preserve is generally maritime in summer, averaging in the mid-40s along the coast and the mid-60s inland between mid-June and mid-September. When the Chukchi Sea is ice free—from mid-June to late October—there is apt to be cloud cover and fog in the area since the humidity is relatively high. When freeze-up occurs, the climate becomes continental, and winters can be bitterly cold.

The Bering Land Bridge National Preserve can be reached by small plane from Kotzebue or Nome, and the bush pilots in both of these towns may be able to offer you good information about the area as well as expert air service. If you choose Nome as your point of entry (and the National Park Service would like to use Nome as the official gateway), you can also go by road to within hiking distance of the preserve. There are two Native villages very close to the preserve, Shishmaref and Deering, and if you would like to visit these villages, be sure to write ahead to make arrangements. The people living there, understandably, do not care to be just dropped in on. (There are some very fine carvers in Shishmaref, and you may be able to find their work in Nome or Kotzebue.)

Nome has a few heavily used tourist hotels which are bare boned and expensive. If you plan to use one, consult your travel agent and make reservations. There is a Youth Hostel in the Methodist Church.

The main street of Nome. *Source: Yvonne Mozée.*

For more details about the Bering Land Bridge National Monument, write the National Park Service, General Delivery, Nome, AK 99762; no phone. Plan to go over your itinerary with them and also let them know when you leave the preserve.

Note that Nome is a fascinating relic of gold rush times and is worth a visit on its own merits. It is a town joke that the churches outnumber the bars one year and vice versa the next. (There are, in fact, about a dozen of each in this community of 2,273 souls.) Nome is strung out along the coast of the Bering Sea and is periodically slammed into and flooded by intense storms that sweep in from the west. In 1974, there was a real holocaust, and Nome was declared a disaster area. The story goes that during this particular storm, one bartender nearly drowned while trying to sweep the flooding ocean waters out of his saloon. If you're interested in Native artwork, Nome is a good place to look for it; the prices are usually reasonable.

Air Charters: Bering Air, Box 1650, Nome, AK 99762; phone 907-443-5464/2696. Foster Aviation, Box 1028, Nome, AK 99762; phone 907-443-5292. Seward Peninsula Flying Service, Box 142, Nome, AK 99762; phone 907-443-2229.

BIBLIOGRAPHY

The following list only cracks the door on the wealth of fascinating literature which exists on Alaska. Readers are urged to explore further.

Alaska Northwest Publishing Company, publisher of ALASKA magazine, has produced numerous excellent books on Alaska including *Alaska-Yukon Wild Flowers Guide* and *The Milepost*—a must for motorists—and *A Guide to the Birds of Alaska* which includes an excellent bird list. These are widely available in Alaska, or write Box 4-EEE, Anchorage, AK 99509, for a complete list.

Arnold, Robert D. *Alaska Native Land Claims.* Anchorage: Alaska Native Foundation, 1976. Helps explain the Alaska Native Claims Settlement Act.

Berton, Pierre. *The Klondike Fever, The Life and Death of the Last Great Stampede.* New York: Alfred A. Knopf, 1958.

Alaska Regional Profiles. Sponsored by the State of Alaska in cooperation with the Joint Federal-State Land Use Planning Commission for Alaska. This six volume series gives unique and valuable information. Available at state libraries in Alaska and at the Arctic Environmental Information and Data Center in Anchorage.

Bohn, Dave. *Rambles Through An Alaskan Wild: Katmai and the Valley of the Smokes.* Santa Barbara: Capra Press, 1979. A perceptive and provocative book.

Brooks, Alfred H. *Blazing Alaska's Trails.* Fairbanks, Alaska: University of Alaska, 1953. This and any other writings of this early explorer are recommended.

Burroughs, John, et al. *Harriman Alaska Expedition. Volumes I and II.* New York, Doubleday Page Co., 1904. A marvelous series of essays.

Chrisler, Lois. *Arctic Wild.* New York: Harper and Brothers, 1958. A lovely book.

Colby, Merle. *A Guide to Alaska, Last American Frontier.* New York: The Macmillan Company, 1942. This Federal Writers' Project is full of anecdotes and historical tidbits that you won't find elsewhere.

Cooley, Richard A. *Alaska, A Challenge in Conservation.* Madison, Wisconsin: University of Wisconsin Press, 1966. This book is a gold mine of information.

De Armond, R. N. *The Founding of Juneau.* Seattle, Washington: Olney Printing Company, 1967. De Armond is one of Alaska's best historians.

Du Fresne, Frank. *No Room For Bears.* New York, Chicago, San Francisco: Holt, Rinehart and Winston, 1968. Required reading for travelers in bear country.

Fejes, Clare. *The Villagers.* New York: Random House, 1981.

Gilbert, Wyatt G. *A Geologic Guide to Mount McKinley National Park.* Anchorage: Alaska Natural History Association, 1979.

Griggs, Robert F. *The Valley of Ten Thousand Smokes.* Washington, D.C.: National Geographic Society, 1922. A wonderful story of discovery.

Gruening, Ernest. *The State of Alaska.* New York: Random House, 1968. Interesting history by one of the movers and shakers in Alaska's politics.

Hopkins, David M., Ed. *The Bering Land Bridge.* Stanford, California: Stanford University Press, 1967. Two dozen, provocative, often fascinating, essays.

Hultén, Eric. *Flora of Alaska and Neighboring Countries.* Stanford, California: Stanford University Press, 1974. The Alaskan botanist's Bible.

Johannsen, Neil and Elizabeth. *Exploring Alaska's Prince William Sound.* Anchorage: Alaska Travel Publications, Inc., 1975.

Marshall, Robert. *Alaska Wilderness.* Berkeley: University of California Press, 1970.

McPhee, John. *Coming Into The Country.* New York: Farrar, Straus and Giroux, 1977. Beautifully written, this catches much of the spirit of the place.

Miller, Mike, and Peggy Wayburn. *Alaska, The Great Land.* San Francisco, Sierra Club, 1974.

Muir, John. *Travels in Alaska.* Boston, Massachusetts: Houghton Mifflin & Co., 1979. Muir and Alaska at their best.

Murie, Adolph. *The Wolves of Mount McKinley.* Washington, D.C.: United States Government Printing Office, 1944.

Murie, Margaret E. *Two in the Far North.* New York: Alfred A. Knopf, 1962.

Murie, Olaus J. *Journeys to the Far North.* Palo Alto, California: American West Publishing Company, 1973. All three Muries offer fine Alaskan reading.

Naske, Claus-M., and Herman E. Slotnick. *Alaska, A History of the 49th State.* Grand Rapids, Michigan: Wm. B. Eerdmans, 1979. A good, standard overview.

Nelson, Richard K. *Hunters of the Northern Forest.* Chicago: The University of Chicago Press, 1973.

Nienhauser, Helen, and Nancy Simmerman. *55 Ways to the Wilderness in Southcentral Alaska.* Seattle: The Mountaineers, 1978. An invaluable guide.

Orth, Donald J. *Dictionary of Alaska Place Names.* Washington, D.C.: U.S. Government Printing Office, 1971. Geological Survey Professional Paper 567.

Pewe, Troy L. *Permafrost and Its Effect on Life in the North.* Corvallis, Oregon: Oregon State University Press, 1970.

Piggott, Margaret. *Discover Southeast Alaska with Pack and Paddle.* Seattle: The Mountaineers, 1974. An essential guide.

Pruitt, William O., Jr. *Animals of the North.* New York: Harper and Row, 1967.

Schwatka, Frederick. *A Summer in Alaska.* St. Louis: J. W. Henry, 1893.

Sheldon, Charles. *The Wilderness of Denali.* New York: Scribner's, 1930.

Sherwood, Morgan B. *Exploration of Alaska, 1865–1900.* New Haven, Connecticut: Yale University Press, 1965. Look for other Sherwood books.

Veirick, Leslie and Elbert L. Little, Jr. *Alaska Trees and Shrubs.* Washington, D.C.: U.S. Department of Agriculture Handbook #410. Essential for tree lovers.

Wahrhaftig, Clyde. *Physiographic Divisions of Alaska.* Washington, D.C. United States Government Printing Office, 1965. Professional Paper #482.

The publication, *Weatherwise,* devoted its October, 1980 issue to Alaska's weather and climate. Write 4,000 Albemarle Street N.W., Washington, D.C. 20016.

Worlds of Alaska. Published by the Alaska State Division of Tourism, this brochure contains a great deal of useful information for any traveler in Alaska and a good-sized, detachable map. Free. Write Pouch E, Juneau, AK 99811.

Pertinent Legislation: Public Law 96-487, December 2, 1980. The Alaska National Interest Lands Conservation Act (ANILCA). Public Law 92-203, December 18, 1971. Alaska Native Claims Settlement Act (ANCSA). Public Law 72-339, July 7, 1958. Alaska Statehood Act.

USGS Maps. Write U.S. Geological Survey Branch of Distribution, Box 25286, Federal Center, Denver, CO 80225. (You can request the index for Alaska if you don't have quad numbers.) The National Park Service can supply information for maps for the new park units; write Park Superintendent.

ALASKA NATIVE REGIONAL CORPORATIONS (Non-Profit)

Aleutian/Pribilof Islands Assoc., Inc
1689 C Street
Anchorage, Alaska 99501

Arctic Slope Native Corporation
Barrow, Alaska 99723

AVCP Calista
P.O. Box 219
Bethel, Alaska 99559

Bristol Bay Native Association
Dillingham, Alaska 99576

Cook Inlet Native Association
P.O. Box 515
Anchorage, Alaska 99510

Copper River Native Assoc., Inc.
Copper Center, Alaska 99573

Kawerak, Inc.
Nome, Alaska 99762

Kodiak Area Native Association
Kodiak, Alaska 99615

Mauneluk, Inc.
Kotzebue, Alaska 99752

North Pacific Rim Native Corporation
903 W. Northern Lights, Suite 203
Anchorage, Alaska 99503

Tanana Chiefs Conference
Doyon Bldg. 1st & Hall Street
Fairbanks, Alaska 99701

Tlingit/Haida Central Council
One Sealaska Plaza
Juneau, Alaska 99801

ALASKA NATIVE REGIONAL CORPORATIONS (Profit)

Ahtna, Incorporated
Drawer G
Copper Center, Alaska 99573

Aleut Corporation
725 Christensen Drive
Anchorage, Alaska 99501

Arctic Slope Regional Corporation
P.O. Box 129
Barrow, Alaska 99723

Bering Straits Native Corporation
P.O. Box 1008
Nome, Alaska 99762

Bristol Bay Native Corporation
P.O. Box 198
Dillingham, Alaska 99576

Calista Corporation
516 Denali Street
Anchorage, Alaska 99501

Chugach Natives, Incorporated
903 W. Northern Lights, Suite 201
Anchorage, Alaska 99503

Cook Inlet Region, Incorporated
P.O. Box Drawer 4-N
Anchorage, Alaska 99509

Doyon Limited
Doyon Bldg, 1st & Hall Streets
Fairbanks, Alaska 99701

Konaig, Incorporated
P.O. Box 746
Kodiak, Alaska 99615

NANA Regional Corporation
P.O. Box 49
Kotzebue, Alaska 99752

Sealaska Corporation
One Sealaska Plaza
Juneau, Alaska 99801

VILLAGES, ZIP CODES, AND PHONE NUMBERS

Community	Zip Code	Rural Phone Number	Community	Zip Code	Rural Phone Number
Adak	99695	*	Anvik	99558	907-462-8001
Afgonak	99550	*	Arctic Village	99722	907-587-8001
Akhiok	99615	907-299-8001	Atka	99695	907-767-8001
Akiachak	99551	907-543-2001	Atkasuk	99721	907-433-8001
Akiak	99552	907-543-2002	Attu	99695	*
Akutan	99553	907-698-8001	Auke Bay	99821	Via Juneau
Alakanuk	99554	907-685-8001			
Alatna	99790	*	Baranof	99822	*
Aleknagik	99555	*	Barrow	99723	*
Alexander Creek	99695	*	Barter Island	99790	*
Alitak	99615	*	Bear Cove	99695	*
Allakaket	99720	907-968-8001	Beaver	99724	907-628-8001
Ambler	99785	**	Belkofsky	99695	*
Anaktuvuk Pass	99721	907-668-8001	Bell Island	99950	*
Anchorage	99501	**	Berry	99725	*
Anchor Point	99556	*	Bethel	99559	**
Andreafski	99695	*	Bettles	99790	*
Angoon	99820	*	Bettles Field	99726	*
Aniak	99557	*	Big Delta	99790	*
Annette	99920	*	Big Fort Walter	99850	*

*No phone available as of this writing. Communication is by radio.
**Has local exchange service. For information, dial 907-555-1212.

Big Lake Lodge	99695	*		Clam Gulch	99568	*
Big Mountain	99695	*		Clark's Point	99569	907-842-5943
Biorka Island	99850	*		Clear	99704	*
Birch Creek	99790	907-662-2430		Coal Creek	99790	*
Border	99750	*		Coffman Cove	99950	*
Bornite	99789	*		Cohoe	99570	*
Boswell Bay	99695	*		Cold Bay	99571	*
Boundary	99790	*		College	99735	Via Fairbanks
Brevig Mission	99785	*		Colorado Creek	99695	*
Broad Pass	99695	*		Colville	99790	*
Buckland	99727	**		Copper Center	99573	**
				Copper Landing	99572	*
Campion AFB	99790	Military		Cordova	99574	**
Candle	99728	*		Crafton Island	99695	*
Cantwell	99729	*		Craig	99921	**
Canyon Village	99790	*		Cripple Landing	99695	*
Cape Lisburne	99790	*		Crooked Creek	99575	907-432-8001
Cape Newenham	99695	*		Crystal Falls	99695	*
Cape Pole	99950	907-879-8001		Curry	99695	*
Cape Romanoff	99695	*				
Cape Sarichef	99695	*		Dan Creek	99695	*
Cape Spencer	99850	*		Deering	99736	**
Cape Thompson	99790	*		Delta Junction	99739	**
Cape Yakataga	99560	*		Dillingham	99576	**
Caswell	99730	*		Diomede	99762	*
Central	99730	907-520-8001		Dot Lake	99737	*
Chalkyitsik	99790	907-848-8001		Douglas	99824	Via Juneau
Chandalar	99790	*		Driftwood Bay	99695	*
Chaneliak	99695	*		Duncan Canal	99850	*
Chatanika	99731	*		Dutch Harbor	99695	*
Chatham	99823	*				
Chauthbaluk	99557	907-675-4352		Eagle	99738	907-459-8001
Chefornak	99561	907-787-8001		Eagle River	99577	*
Chena Hot Springs	99790	Via Fairbanks		Edna Bay	99950	*
Chenega	99562	*		Eek	99578	907-543-2004
Chernofski	99695	*		Egegik	99578	907-246-3430
Chevak	99563	907-441-8001		Eielson AFB	99792	Military
Chicken	99732	*		Eklutna	99695	*
Chignik	99564	907-749-8001		Ekuk	99695	907-842-5937
Chignik Lagoon	99565	907-947-8001		Ekwok	99580	907-464-8001
Chignik Lake	99695	907-556-8001		Eldred Rock	99850	*
Chisana	99695	*		Elfin Cove	99825	907-697-3131
Chistochina	99695	*		Elim	99739	907-885-8001
Chitina	99566	907-496-8001		Ellamar	99695	*
Chowocotolik	99695	*		Emmonak	99581	907-687-8001
Chugiak	99567	*		English Bay	99965	907-235-8292
Circle	99733	**		Entrance Island	99850	*
Circle Springs	99734	**		Eshamy Bay	99695	*

Eska	99582	*	Hooper Bay	99604	**
Ester	99790	Via Fairbanks	Hope	99605	Via Anchorage
Excursion Inlet	99850	*	Hughes	99745	907-889-8001
			Huslia	99746	907-829-8001
Fairbanks	99701	**	Hydaburg	99922	*
Fairmont Island	99695	*	Hyder	99923	*
False Pass	99583	907-548-8001			
Farewell	99695	*	Icy Bay	99850	*
Farragut Bay	99850	*	Idago Inlet	99850	*
Ferry	99790	*	Igiugig	99695	907-533-8001
Fire Island	99695	*	Ikatan	99695	*
Five Fingers	99850	*	Iliamna	99606	**
Flat	99584	*	Indian	99540	Via Anchorage
Folger	99695	*	Ivanof Bay	99695	907-669-8001
Fort Greeley	99790	Military			
Fort Richardson	99505	Military	Jonesville	99695	*
Fort Wainwright	99703	Military	Juneau	99301	**
Fort Yukon	99740	**			
Fortuna Ledge	99585	*	Kaguyag	99697	*
Fox	99790	Via Fairbanks	Kake	99830	**
Funter	99850	*	Kaktovik	99747	Call LD Op
			Kalakaket Creek	99790	*
Ganes Creek	99695	*	Kalskag	99607	907-675-4352
Gakona	99586	**	Kaltag	99748	907-534-8001
Galena	99741	**	Karluck Lake	99697	
Gambell	99742	907-746-8001	Karluk	99608	907-458-8001
Girdwood	99587	**	Kasaan	99924	907-542-8001
Glennallen	99588	**	Kasigluk	99609	907-543-2032
Golovin	99762	907-775-8001	Kasilof	99610	*
Goodnews Bay	99589	907-382-8001	Katalla	99695	*
Granite Mountain	99790	*	Keewalik	99750	*
Grayling	99590	907-461-8001	Kenai	99611	**
Guard Island	99950	*	Kenny Cove	99612	*
Gulkana	99695	**	Ketchikan	99901	**
Gull Cove	99850	*	Kiana	99749	**
Gustavus	99826	**	King Cove	99612	**
			King Island	99790	*
Haines	99827	**	King Salmon	99613	**
Halibut Cove	99603	907-235-8000	Kipnuk	99614	907-598-8001
Hawk Inlet	99828	*	Kitoi Bay	99697	*
Haycock	99790	*	Kivalina	99750	**
Healy Fork	99743	**	Klawock	99925	**
Hogatza	99744	*	Kobuk	99751	907-948-8001
Hollis	99950	*	Kodiak	99615	**
Holy Cross	99602	907-481-8001	Koliganek	99695	907-596-8001
Homer	99603	**	Kokrines	99790	*
Hood Bay	99850	*	Kongiganak	99559	907-696-8001
Hoonah	99829	**	Kotlik	99620	907-839-8001

Place	Zip	Number	Place	Zip	Number
Kotzebue	99752	**	Naknek	99633	**
Koyuk	99753	907-965-8001	Napakiak	99634	907-543-2062
Koyukuk	99754	907-927-8001	Napaskiak	99559	907-543-2063
Kwethluk	99621	907-543-2033	Nellie Jean	99695	*
Kwigillingok	99622	907-769-8001	Nelson Lagoon	99695	907-989-8001
			Nenana	99760	**
Lake Minchumina	99623	907-939-0000	New Stuyahok	99636	907-693-8001
Larsen Bay	99624	907-857-8001	Newhalen	99606	*
Latouche	99695	*	Newtok	99559	907-369-8001
Lazy Bay	99627	*	Nightmute	99690	907-587-8001
Lemeasurier Isle	99850	*	Nikolai	99695	907-524-3741
Levelock	99625	907-246-3420	Nikolski	99638	**
Lignite	99700	*	Ninilchik	99639	**
Lincoln Rock	99950	*	Noatak	99761	**
Little Diomede	99790	907-443-2945	Nome	99762	**
Little Port Walter	99850	*	Nondalton	99640	907-571-1270
Livengood	99790	Via Fairbanks	Noorvik	99763	**
Loring	99950	*	North East Cape	99790	*
Lower Kalskag	99626	907-675-4316	North Pole	99705	Via Fairbanks
			Northway	99764	**
McCarthy	99695	*	Noyes Island	99950	*
McCord	99695	*	Nuiqsut	99723	907-493-8001
McGrath	99627	*	Nulato	99765	907-898-8001
McKinley Park	99755	**	Nunapitchuk	99641	907-543-2064
Main Bay	99695	*	Nunivak Island	99695	*
Manley Hot	99756	**	Nushagak	99695	*
Springs			Nyas	99642	*
Manokotak	99628	907-842-5978			
Marguerite Bay	99950	*	Oceanic	99695	*
Marshall	99695	907-639-8001	Old Crow	99790	*
Mary Island	99950	*	Old Harbor	99643	907-286-8001
May Creek	99695	*	Olga Bay	99697	*
Meade River	99790	*	Olsen Island	99695	*
Medfra	99629	*	Ophir	99695	*
Mekoryuk	99630	907-627-8001	Oscarville	99695	907-543-2066
Mentasta Lake	99695	907-883-4401	Ouzinkie	99644	907-486-5800
Meyers Chuck	99903	Call LD Op.			
Middleton Isle	99695	*	Palmer	99645	**
Miller House	99730	*	Patterson Bay	99850	*
Minto	99753	907-798-8001	Pauloff Harbor	99646	*
Montana	99695	*	Paxson	99737	**
Moose Pass	99631	*	Peak Island	99695	*
Moser Bay	99697	*	Pedro Bay	99647	907-793-8001
Moses Point	99759	*	Pelican	99832	*
Mount Edgecumbe	99835		Perry Island	99695	*
Mountain Village	99632	907-365-8001	Perryville	99648	907-877-8001
Murphy Dome	99790		Pile Bay	99695	*

Pillar Bay	99850	*
Pilot Point	99649	907-797-8001
Pilot Station	99650	907-429-8001
Pitkas Point	99649	907-398-8001
Platinum	99651	*
Pleasant Camp	99850	*
Point Baker	99927	907-559-8001
Point Hope	99766	907-852-2100
Point Lay	99790	907-824-8001
Point Nowell	99695	*
Point Retreat	99850	*
Point Spencer	99790	*
Poorman	99700	*
Pope Vannoy Lodge	99695	*
Porcupine Creek	99790	*
Portage Creek	99695	907-842-5966
Portage Junction	99652	*
Port Alexander	99834	907-568-8001
Port Alsworth	99653	907-781-8001
Port Althorp	99850	*
Port Ashton	99654	*
Port Bailey	99697	*
Port Chilkoot	99850	*
Port Clarence	99790	*
Port Graham	99695	907-433-8001
Port Heiden	99695	*
Portlock	99695	*
Port Moller	99695	*
Port Oceanic	99695	*
Port Protection	99950	907-489-8001
Port San Juan	99695	*
Port Vita	99697	*
Port Wakefield	99697	*
Port Walter	99850	*
Port Williams	99697	*
Quinhagak	99655	907-523-8001
Rampart	99767	907-358-8001
Ratz Harbor	99950	*
Red Devil	99656	907-447-8001
Red Mountain	99695	*
Rodman Bay	99850	*
Ruby	99768	907-689-8001
Ruby Creek	99790	*
Russian Mission	99657	907-759-8001

Saginaw Bay	99850	
St. George Island	99695	907-859-8001
(Pribilofs)		
St. Lawrence Island	99790	*
St. Mary's	99658	**
St. Michael	99659	907-996-8001
St. Paul Island	99660	907-546-8001
(Pribilofs)		
Sanak	99695	*
Sand Point	99661	*
San Juan	99697	*
Savok Bay	99850	
Savoonga	99769	907-399-8001
Sawyers Landing	99850	*
Scammon Bay	99662	907-422-8001
Scotch Cap	99695	*
Scotty Creek	99790	*
Selawik	99770	**
Seldovia	99663	**
Sentinel Island	99850	*
Seward	99664	**
Shageluk	99665	907-431-8001
Shaktoolik	99771	907-975-8001
Shearwater Bay	99697	*
Sheldon Point	99666	907-323-8001
Shemya	99697	*
Sheskalik	99790	*
Shishmaref	99772	*
Shungnak	99773	**
Sitka	99835	**
Sitkinak	99697	*
Skagway	99840	**
Skwentna	99667	*
Slam	99695	*
Sleetmute	99668	907-449-8001
Snug Harbor	99695	*
Soldotna	99669	**
Soloman	99790	*
Sourdough	99695	*
South Naknek	99670	907-246-3460
Squaw Harbor	99695	907-383-3322
Stebbins	99671	907-997-8001
Sterling	99672	**
Stevens Village	99774	907-478-8001
Stony River	99673	907-439-8001
Summit	99775	*

Sunset Cove	99850	*	Uganik	99697	*
Sunshine	99695	*	Ugaskik	99683	*
Suntrana	99790	*	Umiat	99790	*
Susitna	99695	*	Umnak	99695	*
Sutton	99674	*	Unalakleet	99684	*
			Unalaska	99685	*
Takotna	99675	907-524-3731	Unga	99695	*
Taku Harbor	99850	*	Ungalik	99695	*
Talkeetna	99676	**	Utopia	99790	*
Tanacross	99776	*	Uyak	99697	*
Tanana	99777	*			
Tatalina	99695	*	Valdez	99686	**
Tatitlek	99677	907-257-8001	Venetie	99781	907-849-8001
Tetlin	99779	907-883-2791	View Cove	99950	
Tevankof Bay	99850	*			
Tee Harbor	99850	*	Wainwright	99782	907-852-6355
Telida	99627	907-843-8001	Wales	99783	*
Teller	99778	*	Ward Cove	99928	*
Tenakee Springs	99841	907-736-8001	Washington Bay	99850	*
Terror Bay	99697	*	Wasilla	99687	**
The Sisters' Island	99850	*	Waterfall	99950	*
Thorne Bay	99950	*	West Point	99697	*
Tin City	99790	*	White Mountain	99784	907-625-8001
Todd	99850	*	Willow	99688	**
Togiak	99678	907-974-8001	Wiseman	99790	*
Tok	99780	**	Woodchopper	99790	*
Tokeen	99950	*	Wrangell	99929	**
Toksook Bay	99673	907-526-8001			
Tuluksak	99679	907-543-2089	Yakutat	99689	**
Tuntutuliak	99680	907-543-2101	Yankee Creek	99695	*
Tununak	99681	907-599-8001	Yentna	99695	*
Tuxekan Island	99950				
Tyonek	99682		Zasher Bay	99697	*

INDEX

Page numbers in italic refer to illustrations. Regional groupings of page numbers are abbreviated SC/SW (Southcentral/Southwest) and SE (Southeast).